T0313215

# Toward Deep Neural Networks

## WASD Neuronet Models, Algorithms, and Applications

# Chapman & Hall/CRC
# Artificial Intelligence and Robotics Series

*Series Editor: Roman Yampolskiy*

**Intelligent Autonomy of UAVs**
Advanced Missions and Future Use
*Yasmina Bestaoui Sebbane*

**Artificial Intelligence**
With an Introduction to Machine Learning, Second Edition
*Richard E. Neapolitan, Xia Jiang*

**Artificial Intelligence and the Two Singularities**
*Calum Chace*

**Behavior Trees in Robotics and AI**
An Introduction
*Michele Collendanchise, Petter Ögren*

**Artificial Intelligence Safety and Security**
*Roman V. Yampolskiy*

**Artificial Intelligence for Autonomous Networks**
*Mazin Gilbert*

**Virtual Humans**
*David Burden, Maggi Savin-Baden*

**Toward Deep Neural Networks: WASD Neuronet Models, Algorithms, and Applications**
*Yunong Zhang, Dechao Chen, Chengxu Ye*

*For more information about this series please visit:*
*https://www.crcpress.com/Chapman--HallCRC-Artificial-Intelligence-and-Robotics-Series/book-series/ARTILRO*

# Toward Deep Neural Networks

## WASD Neuronet Models, Algorithms, and Applications

Yunong Zhang
Dechao Chen
Chengxu Ye

CRC Press
Taylor & Francis Group
Boca Raton London New York

CRC Press is an imprint of the
Taylor & Francis Group, an **informa** business

CRC Press
Taylor & Francis Group
6000 Broken Sound Parkway NW, Suite 300
Boca Raton, FL 33487-2742

© 2019 by Taylor & Francis Group, LLC
CRC Press is an imprint of Taylor & Francis Group, an Informa business

No claim to original U.S. Government works

Printed on acid-free paper

International Standard Book Number-13: 978-1-138-38703-4 (Hardback)

---

**Library of Congress Cataloging-in-Publication Data**

---

Names: Zhang, Yunong, author. | Chen, Dechao, author. | Ye, Chengxu, author.
Title: Toward deep neural networks : WASD neuronet models, algorithms, and applications / Yunong Zhang, Dechao Chen, Chengxu Ye.
Description: Boca Raton, Florida : CRC Press, [2019] | Series: Chapman & Hall/CRC artificial intelligence and robotics series | Includes bibliographical references and index.
Identifiers: LCCN 2018050905| ISBN 9781138387034 (hardback : acid-free paper) | ISBN 9780429426445 (ebook)
Subjects: LCSH: Neural networks (Computer science)
Classification: LCC QA76.87 .Z47537 2019 | DDC 006.3/2--dc23
LC record available at https://lccn.loc.gov/2018050905

---

**Visit the Taylor & Francis Web site at**
**http://www.taylorandfrancis.com**

**and the CRC Press Web site at**
**http://www.crcpress.com**

To our parents and
ancestors, as always

# Contents

# IV   General Multi-Input Neuronet      105

# 9  Multi-Input Euler-Polynomial WASD Neuronet    107

# 10  Multi-Input Bernoulli-Polynomial WASD Neuronet    125

# 11  Multi-Input Hermite-Polynomial WASD Neuronet    137

# *Preface*

Due to the remarkable features such as parallel-processing, distributed storage, self-adaptive and self-learning abilities, artificial neuronets (AN) (or, say, artificial neural networks) have been widely investigated and applied in many scientific, engineering and practical fields. It is widely known that feed-forward neuronets are universal approximators. Among many feed-forward neuronet models, the feed-forward neuronet based on the error back-propagation (BP) training algorithm or its variants is one of the most popular and important, involving many theoretical analyses and real-world applications. Note that the BP-type neuronets proposed in the mid-1980s (or even earlier, in 1974) are a kind of multilayer feed-forward neuronets. Up to now, the BP-type neuronets and the corresponding training algorithms are still involved widely in many theoretical and practical areas.

BP algorithms are essentially gradient-based iterative methods, which adjust the AN weights to bring the input/output behavior into a desired mapping by taking a gradient-based descent direction. As researchers (including us) realize and experience quite frequently, the inherent weaknesses of BP-type neuronets are still there. Specifically, BP-type neuronets appear to have the following weaknesses: (i) possibility of being trapped into some local minima; (ii) difficulty in choosing appropriate learning rates; and (iii) inability to design the optimal or smallest neuronet structure in a deterministic way. Because of the above inherent weaknesses, many improved BP-type algorithms have been proposed and investigated. Generally, there are two general types of improvements. On one hand, the BP-type algorithms could be improved on the basis of the standard gradient-descent method. On the other hand, numerical optimization techniques could be employed for the training of neuronet model. It is worth pointing out that many researchers usually focus on the learning-algorithm itself to improve the performance of BP-type neuronets. However, almost all of the improved BP-type algorithms have not overcome the above inherent weaknesses.

Note that, during the construction of a neuronet model for the function approximation or any other applications, three important problems should be settled: (i) the selection of the activation function; (ii) the determination of the number of hidden-layer neurons; and (iii) the calculation of connecting weights between two different layers. Since the late 1990s, the authors have focused on solving the above problem of the conventional AN with single hidden layer mainly, which is the basis of and also a work toward deep neural networks. Based on the 20-year research experience on the topic of neuronets, as reported here in this book, we are now resolving the above inherent weaknesses of the BP-type neuronets while improving the neuronet performance, by means of using various kinds of activation functions (especially the linearly independent or orthogonal activation functions). In addition, different from other algorithmic improvements on the training procedure, our way of the problem solving exploits some elegant structure design, parameter setting, and pseudoinverse-based techniques. These finally lead to our proposed weights-and-structure-determination (WASD) algorithm for the feed-forward neuronets, which perform in a more efficient, accurate and deterministic way. Based on the comprehensive and systematic research of conventional AN, this book also aims to open a new door toward further research and applications of deep neural networks with multiple hidden layers, as the difficult problem of WASD has now been solved truly, systematically and methodologically. The in-depth research of the deep neural networks based on the WASD algorithm would be an interesting and open topic for readers, researchers and engineers in the future.

In this book, focusing on the neuronet models, algorithms and applications, we design, construct, develop, analyze, simulate and compare various WASD neuronet models, such as single-input WASD neuronet models, two-input WASD neuronet models, three-input WASD neuronet models, and general multi-input WASD neuronet models for function data approximations and many real-world applications (especially the population prediction). The main contributions lie in the following facts.

- As the fundamental knowledge, many linearly independent or orthogonal activation functions are presented and used to develop the pseudoinverse-based weights-direct-determination (WDD) subalgorithm for neuronets.

- As the promotive knowledge, by systematically showing and utilizing the "U/V" plots about relationship between the error and the number of hidden-layer neurons, with the aid of subalgorithm of optimal structure automatic determination, the WASD algorithm is developed on the basis of the above WDD subalgorithm and the linearly independent or orthogonal activation functions.

- The complete mathematical foundations, such as Weierstrass approximation, Bernstein polynomial approximation, Taylor polynomial approximation, and multivariate function approximation, are based and presented, leading to the close integration of mathematics (i.e., function approximation theories) and computers (e.g., computer algorithms). Both mathematics (i.e., function approximation theories) and computers (e.g., computer algorithms) collectively achieve the new altitude while we develop and apply the WASD neuronet.

- The systematic and complete research of WASD neuronet from single-input models to general multi-input models, as well as the corresponding training (or, say, approximation or learning and checking) and testing details are summarized and presented for readers.

- Numerous numerical results of function data approximations and real-world applications (especially the population prediction with abundant population data collection and presentation) are illustrated to substantiate the excellent performance in terms of training (or, say, approximation or learning and checking), generalization (or, say, testing) and prediction of WASD neuronet.

The idea for this book on models, algorithms and applications of neuronets was conceived during classroom teaching as well as the research discussion in the laboratory and at international scientific meetings. Most of the materials of this book are derived from the authors' papers published in journals and proceedings of the international conferences. In fact, since the early 1980s, the field of neuronets has undergone phases of exponential growth, generating many new theoretical concepts and algorithms (including the authors' ones). At the same time, these theoretical results and algorithms have been applied successfully to many practical applications. Our first priority is thus to cover each central topic in enough details to make the material clear and coherent; in other words, each part (and even each chapter) is written in a relatively self-contained manner.

This book contains 25 chapters which are classified into the following 7 parts.

Part I: Single-Input-Single-Output Neuronet (Chapters 1 through 3);

Part II: Two-Input-Single-Output Neuronet (Chapters 4 through 6);

Part III: Three-Input-Single-Output Neuronet (Chapters 7 and 8);

Part IV: General Multi-Input Neuronet (Chapters 9 through 12);

Part V: Population Applications Using Chebyshev-Activation Neuronet (Chapters 13 through 18);

Part VI: Population Applications Using Power-Activation Neuronet (Chapters 19 through 22);

Part VII: Other Applications (Chapters 23 through 25).

Chapter 1 - In this chapter, a single-input feed-forward neuronet model is constructed, which adopts a three-layer structure with hidden-layer neurons activated by a group of Euler polynomials. By employing the WDD subalgorithm, which obtains the optimal weights of the neuronet directly (i.e., just in one step), a WASD algorithm is presented to further determine the optimal number of hidden-layer neurons of the constructed Euler-polynomial neuronet. Numerical studies including comparisons substantiate the efficacy and superiority of Euler-polynomial neuronet with the proposed WASD algorithm.

Chapter 2 - In this chapter, based on the polynomial interpolation and approximation theory, a special type of single-input feed-forward neuronet is constructed with hidden-layer neurons activated by Bernoulli polynomials. Differing from the conventional BP algorithms and gradient-based training methods, a WDD subalgorithm is presented for Bernoulli-polynomial neuronet to determine weights directly (just in one general step), without a lengthy iterative BP-training process. Moreover, by analyzing and discovering the relationship between the performance of Bernoulli-polynomial neuronet and its number of hidden-layer neurons, a WASD algorithm is further proposed, which could obtain the optimal number of hidden-layer neurons in the constructed Bernoulli-polynomial neuronet in the sense of achieving the highest learning-accuracy for a specific data problem or target function. Numerical studies further substantiate the efficacy of such a WASD algorithm for single-input Bernoulli-polynomial neuronet.

Chapter 3 - In this chapter, a single-input Laguerre-polynomial neuronet is constructed. Based on this special neuronet model, a WDD subalgorithm is derived accordingly, which could obtain the optimal weights of such a Laguerre-polynomial neuronet directly (or, say, just in one step). Furthermore, a WASD algorithm is developed for determining immediately the smallest number of hidden-layer neurons. Numerical studies substantiate the efficacy of such a Laguerre-polynomial neuronet with the WASD algorithm.

Chapter 4 - In this chapter, a two-input Legendre-polynomial neuronet based on the theory of the multivariate function approximation is constructed and investigated. In addition, based on the WDD subalgorithm, two WASD algorithms with different growing speeds are built up to determine the optimal weights and structure of the two-input Legendre-polynomial neuronet. Numerical studies further verify the efficacy of the two-input Legendre-polynomial neuronet equipped with the two aforementioned WASD algorithms.

Chapter 5 - In this chapter, a two-input feed-forward neuronet using Chebyshev orthogonal polynomials (or, say, Chebyshev polynomials) of Class 1 is constructed and investigated. In addition, with the WDD subalgorithm exploited to obtain the optimal weights from hidden layer to output layer directly (i.e., just in one step), a WASD algorithm is further presented to determine the optimal number of hidden-layer neurons of two-input Chebyshev-polynomial-of-Class-1 neuronet. Such a WASD algorithm includes a procedure of pruning the presented neuronet (after the net grows up). Numerical studies further substantiate the efficacy of Chebyshev-polynomial-of-Class-1 neuronet equipped with the so-called WASD algorithm.

Chapter 6 - In this chapter, based on the theory of polynomial interpolation and approximation, a two-input feed-forward neuronet activated by a group of Chebyshev orthogonal polynomials (or, say, Chebyshev polynomials) of Class 2 is constructed and investigated. To overcome the weaknesses of conventional BP neuronets, a WDD subalgorithm is exploited to obtain the optimal linking weights of the proposed neuronet directly. Furthermore, a structure-automatic-determination (SAD) subalgorithm is developed to determine the optimal number of hidden-layer neurons of Chebyshev-polynomial-of-Class-2 neuronet, and thus the WASD algorithm is built up. Numerical studies further substantiate the efficacy and superior abilities of Chebyshev-polynomial-of-Class-2 neuronet in approximation, denoising and prediction, with the aid of the WASD algorithm which obtains the optimal number of hidden-layer neurons.

Chapter 7 - In this chapter, based on the function approximation theory and the Weierstrass approximation theorem, a three-input Euler-polynomial neuronet is established to learn the four-dimensional data (i.e., data in the form of three inputs and single output). In order to achieve satisfactory performance and efficacy of the three-input Euler polynomial neuronet, a WASD algorithm, which contains the WDD subalgorithm, is built up for the established three-input Euler-polynomial neuronet. Numerical results further substantiate the superior performance of the three-input Euler-polynomial neuronet equipped with the WASD algorithm in terms of training, testing and prediction.

Chapter 8 - In this chapter, a three-input feed-forward power-activation neuronet is constructed and investigated. For the three-input power-activation neuronet, a WASD algorithm is presented to solve function data approximation (or, say, learning) and prediction problems. With the WDD subalgorithm exploited, the WASD algorithm can obtain the optimal weights of the three-input power-activation neuronet between hidden layer and output layer directly. Moreover, the WASD algorithm determines the optimal structure (i.e., the optimal number of hidden-layer neurons) of the three-input power-activation neuronet adaptively by growing and pruning hidden-layer neurons during the training process. Numerical results of illustrative examples highlight the efficacy of the three-input power-activation neuronet equipped with the so-called WASD algorithm.

Chapter 9 - In this chapter, a multi-input Euler-polynomial neuronet, in short, MIEPN (specifically, four-input Euler-polynomial neuronet, FIEPN) is established and investigated. In order to achieve satisfactory performance of the established MIEPN, a WASD algorithm with pruning-while-growing (PWG) and twice-pruning (TP) techniques is built up for the established MIEPN. By employing the WDD subalgorithm, the WASD algorithm not only determines the optimal connecting weights between hidden layer and output layer directly, but also obtains the optimal number of hidden-layer neurons. Specifically, a sub-optimal structure is obtained via the PWG technique, then the redundant hidden-layer neurons are further pruned via the TP technique. Consequently, the optimal structure of the MIEPN is obtained. To provide a reasonable choice in practice, several different MATLAB computing routines related to the WDD subalgorithm are studied. Comparative numerical results of the FIEPN using these different MATLAB computing routines and the standard multi-layer perceptron (MLP) neuronet further verify the superior performance and efficacy of the proposed MIEPN equipped with the WASD algorithm including PWG and TP techniques in terms of training, testing and prediction.

Chapter 10 - In this chapter, a multi-input Bernoulli-polynomial neuronet (MIBPN) is discussed on the basis of function approximation theory. The MIBPN is trained by a WASD algorithm with TP. The WASD algorithm can obtain the optimal weights and structure for the MIBPN, and overcome the weaknesses of conventional BP-type neuronets such as slow training speed and local minima. With the TP technique, the neurons of less importance in the MIBPN are pruned for less computational complexity. Furthermore, this MIBPN can be extended to a multiple-input-multiple-output Bernoulli-polynomial neuronet (MIMOBPN), which can be applied as an important tool for classification. Numerical results show that the MIBPN has outstanding performance in function data approximation (or, say, learning) and generalization (or, say, testing). Besides, experiment results based on the real-world classification data-sets substantiate the high accuracy and strong robustness of the MIMOBPN equipped with the WASD algorithm for classification. Finally, the TP aided WASD neuronet of Bernoulli-polynomial type in the forms of MIBPN and MIMOBPN is established, together with the effective extension to robust classification.

Chapter 11 - In this chapter, based on the theory of polynomial-interpolation and curve-fitting, a multi-input feed-forward neuronet activated by Hermite orthogonal polynomials (or, say, Hermite polynomials, HP) is proposed and investigated. Besides, the design makes the multi-input Hermite-polynomial neuronet (MIHPN) have no weakness of dimension explosion. To determine the optimal weights of the MIHPN, the WDD subalgorithm is presented. To obtain the optimal structure of the MIHPN, the so-called WASD algorithm is finally proposed, which aims at achieving the best approximation accuracy while obtaining the minimal number of hidden-layer neurons. Numerical results further substantiate the efficacy of the MIHPN model and WASD algorithm.

Chapter 12 - In this chapter, to solve complex problems such as multi-input function approximation by using neuronets and to overcome the inherent defects of traditional BP-type neuronets, a single hidden-layer multi-input feed-forward sine-activation neuronet (MISAN) is proposed and investigated. Then, a two-stage-WASD (i.e., TS-WASD) algorithm, which is based on the WDD subalgorithm and the approximation theory of using linearly independent functions, is developed to train the proposed MISAN. Such a TS-WASD algorithm can efficiently and automatically obtain the relatively optimal MISAN structure. Numerical results illustrate the validity and efficacy of the MISAN model and the TS-WASD algorithm. That is, the proposed MISAN model equipped with the TS-WASD algorithm has great performance of approximation on multi-input function data.

Chapter 13 - In this chapter, a WASD neuronet activated by Chebyshev polynomials of Class 1 for function data approximation and to exploring its capability of prediction is presented and investigated. The learning-testing method and the concept of global minimum point are introduced to improve the prediction performance and extend the application of the WASD neuronet. Applying such a model to Asian population prediction substantiates its excellent performance. With numerical studies showing the prediction performance and a final prediction based on historical data, this chapter presents a reasonable tendency of the Asian population.

Chapter 14 - In this chapter, a Chebyshev-activation WASD neuronet approach for the population prediction is presented and investigated. This neuronet algorithm is applied to predicting European population, with numerous numerical studies conducted as a research basis to guarantee the feasibility and validity of our approach. It is predicted with the most possibility that European population will decrease in the near future.

Chapter 15 - In this chapter, a three-layer feed-forward neuronet activated by a group of Chebyshev polynomials of Class 1 and equipped with a WASD algorithm (or, say, Chebyshev-activation neuronet with WASD algorithm) is constructed and investigated to learn the historical data and predict the population. With the neuronet well trained by over 1000-year historical data, we successfully predict that the future Oceanian population will keep a steady increasing trend in the coming 15 years.

Chapter 16 - In this chapter, based on the past 513-year population data, a feed-forward neuronet equipped with the WASD algorithm is constructed for the recovery and prediction of Northern American population data. Besides, the neuronet is activated by a group of Chebyshev polynomials of Class 1, which is named Chebyshev-activation neuronet in this chapter. Moreover, the optimal normalization factor is found and utilized to improve the neuronet's performance. Due to the marvelous learning and generalization abilities of the presented Chebyshev-activation neuronet, we recover the missing population data from 1500 AD to 1950 AD as well as draw up the Northern American population prediction for the next few decades.

Chapter 17 - In this chapter, based on the historical population data over 2000 years, a feed-forward neuronet equipped with the WASD algorithm aided by TP technique is constructed and investigated. Besides, by introducing the cubic spline and error evaluation methods, the neuronet shows great performance in the population prediction. Due to the marvelous learning and generalization abilities of the presented TP-aided WASD neuronet, we successfully draw up the population prediction for the Indian subcontinent.

Chapter 18 - In this chapter, a neuronet approach for world population prediction is presented and investigated. Note that the historical population data contain the general regularity of the population development, and are also the comprehensive reflection of the population development under the influence of all factors (e.g., natural environment, policy and economy). Thus, using the past 10000-year rough data, a three-layer feed-forward neuronet equipped with the WASD algorithm is constructed for the prediction of the world population in this chapter. Via various numerical studies, such a neuronet with WASD algorithm indicates that there are several possibilities of the change of the world population in the future. With the highest possibility, the trend of the world population in the next decade is to rise, peak in 2020, and then decline.

Chapter 19 - In this chapter, implicitly considering almost all factors that influence population development, a three-layer feed-forward power-activation neuronet equipped with the WASD algorithm for the estimation, correction and prediction of Russian population is presented and investigated. Many numerical tests are conducted via power-activation neuronet using past 2013-year Russian population data. We estimate the Russian population from 1000 AD to 1800 AD, correct it around 1897 AD, and further indicate several possibilities of Russian population in the future. With the most possibility, Russian population is predicted to decrease steadily in the next decade; while it is still possible that Russian population will (finally) increase.

Chapter 20 - In this chapter, two types of improved feed-forward neuronet are constructed and investigated for the Russian population prediction. More specifically, a type of three-layer power-activation neuronet equipped with the BP algorithm and a type of three-layer power-activation neuronet equipped with the WASD algorithm are built on the basis of 2013-year (from 1 AD to 2013 AD) historical population data for the Russian population prediction. By a lot of numerical studies, the future declining trend of Russian population in the next decade is predicted with the highest possibility. In addition, via the Russian population prediction, the comparisons on the performance between the WASD neuronet and BP neuronet are conducted and summarized.

Chapter 21 - In this chapter, a three-layer feed-forward neuronet approach equipped with a WASD algorithm is presented and investigated for the population prediction of China. Numerical studies further substantiate the feasibility of such an approach and indicate that there are three kinds of possibilities for the progress of Chinese population in the next decade. With the highest possibility, Chinese population will keep continual increase with a gentle growth rate.

Chapter 22 - In this chapter, an enhanced feed-forward neuronet, i.e., a three-layer feed-forward power-activation neuronet equipped with the WASD algorithm is presented and investigated to predict the Chinese population. Numerical studies show that the Chinese population will continue to increase at a low rate in the next decade. The authors also compare the WASD algorithm with the BP algorithm for the power-activation neuronet, with numerical results showing the excellent performance of the former.

Chapter 23 - In this chapter, the ten-year prediction for the public debt of the United States (termed also the United States public debt, USPD) via a three-layer feed-forward neuronet is presented and investigated. It is worth mentioning here that this research work used the USPD data as of October 2013, and our research group reported the main prediction results of the USPD as of November 2015. Specifically, using the calendar year data of the USPD, the Chebyshev-activation neuronet is trained, and then is applied to prediction. Via a series of numerical studies, we find that there are several possibilities of the change of the USPD in the future, which are classified into two categories in terms of prediction trend: the continuous-increase trend and the increase-peak-decline trend. In the most possible situation, the neuronet indicates that the total public debt outstanding (TPDO) of the United States is predicted to increase, and it will double in 2019 and double again in 2024.

Chapter 24 - In this chapter, a WASD algorithm is presented and investigated for a power-activation neuronet to solve monthly time series learning and prediction problems. Besides, a simple and effective data preprocessing approach is employed. Based on the WDD subalgorithm and the relationship between the structure and the performance of the power-activation neuronet, the WASD algorithm can determine the weights and the optimal structure (i.e., the optimal numbers of input-layer and hidden-layer neurons) of the power-activation neuronet. Numerical studies further substantiate the superiority of the power-activation neuronet equipped with the WASD algorithm to predict monthly time series.

Chapter 25 - In this chapter, by combining the WDD subalgorithm and Levenberg-Marquardt (LM) method, a WASD algorithm for a three-layer feed-forward neuronet is presented and investigated. Note that the PWG and TP techniques are developed and exploited in the WASD algorithm with the aim of achieving a neuronet with a simple and economical structure. In order to verify the WASD efficacy and to address the problem of chronic kidney disease (CKD) for clinical applications in China, numerical studies about estimating glomerular filtration rate (GFR) by the WASD neuronet and traditional GFR-estimation equations are conducted and compared. Numerical results show that the WASD training speed is fast and that the estimating accuracy via the WASD neuronet is around 20% higher than those via traditional GFR-estimation equations. The WASD efficacy is thus substantiated with a significant value in GFR estimation of CKD for clinical applications.

This book is written for graduate students as well as academic and industrial researchers studying the developing fields of neuronets, computer mathematics, computer science, artificial intelligence, numerical algorithms, optimization, simulation and modeling, deep learning and data mining. It provides a comprehensive view of the combined research of these fields, in addition to its accomplishments, potentials and perspectives. We do hope that this book will generate curiosity and also happiness to its readers for learning more in the fields and the research, and that it will provide new challenges to seek new theoretical tools and practical applications. It may promise to become a major inspiration for both studies and research in neuronet modeling, numerical algorithm design, prediction, and data mining. Without doubt, this book can be extended. Any comments or suggestions are welcomed. The authors can be contacted via e-mails: zhynong@mail.sysu.edu.cn, chdchao@sina.com, and ycx@qhnu.edu.cn. The web page of Yunong Zhang is http://sdcs.sysu.edu.cn/content/2477.

# *Authors*

**Yunong Zhang** received a B.S. degree from Huazhong University of Science and Technology, Wuhan, China, in 1996, an M.S. degree from South China University of Technology, Guangzhou, China, in 1999, and a Ph.D. degree from Chinese University of Hong Kong, Shatin, Hong Kong, China, in 2003. He is currently a professor at the School of Information Science and Technology, Sun Yat-sen University, Guangzhou, China. Before joining Sun Yat-sen University in 2006, Dr. Zhang had been with the National University of Singapore, University of Strathclyde, and the National University of Ireland at Maynooth, since 2003. His main research interests include neuronets, robotics, computation and optimization. He has been working on the research and application of neuronets for 20 years. He has now published a total of 536 scientific works of various types with the number of SCI citations being 2486 and the number of Google citations being 5322. These include 12 monographs, 136 SCI papers (with 71 SCI papers published in the last 5 years), 34 IEEE-Transactions or magazine papers, 10 single-authored works, and 393 first-authored works. Dr. Zhang was supported by the Program for New Century Excellent Talents in Universities in 2007, was presented the Best Paper Award of ISSCAA in 2008 and the Best Paper Award of ICAL in 2011, and was among the Highly Cited Scholars of China selected and published by Elsevier from 2014–2017. His web-page is now available at `http://sdcs.sysu.edu.cn/content/2477`.

**Dechao Chen** received a B.S. degree from Guangdong University of Technology, Guangzhou, China, in 2013. He is currently pursuing his Ph.D. degree in Communication and Information Systems at the School of Information Science and Technology, Sun Yat-sen University, Guangzhou, China, under the direction of Professor Yunong Zhang. His research interests include robotics, neuronets, and nonlinear dynamics systems.

**Chengxu Ye** received a B.S. degree from Shanxi Normal University, Xian, China, in 1991, an M.S. degree from Qinghai Normal University, Xining, China, in 2008, and a Ph.D. degree from Sun Yat-sen University, Guangzhou, China, in 2015. He is currently a professor at the School of Computer Science, Qinghai Normal University, Xining, China. His main research interests include machine learning, neuronets, computation and optimization. He has published over 30 scientific papers in journals and conferences.

# *Acknowledgments*

This book basically comprises the results of many original research papers of the authors' research group, in which many authors of these original papers have done a great deal of detailed and creative research work. Therefore, we are much obliged to our contributing authors for their high-quality work. During the work on this book, we have had the pleasure of discussing its various aspects and results with many contributors and students. We highly appreciate their contributions, which particularly allowed us to greatly improve the presentation and quality of this book. Especially valuable was help provided by Guofu Wu, Binbin Qiu, Fangzheng Lai, Penghao He, Liu He, Liangyu He, Jinjin Guo, Min Yang, Huanchang Huang, Wan Li, Deyang Zhang, Huihui Gong, Jinjin Wang, Yaqiong Ding, Jian Li, Huinan Xiao, Chumin Li, Maotai Zou, Xuyun Yang, Jiadi Wang, Nanhao Wang, Shuo Yang, Zhongxian Xue, and Yang Shi. We are grateful to them for their help and suggestions.

The continuous support of our research by the National Natural Science Foundation of China (with number 61473323), by the Foundation of Key Laboratory of Autonomous Systems and Networked Control, Ministry of Education, China (with number 2013A07), by the Natural Science Foundation of Qinghai (with number 2016-ZJ-739), by the Laboratory Open Fund of Sun Yat-sen University (with number 20160209), and also by the Students Innovation Training Program of Sun Yat-sen University (with number 201602118) is gratefully acknowledged. Besides, we would like to thank the editors sincerely for the time and efforts spent in handling this book, as well as the constructive comments and suggestions provided. We are very grateful to the nice people at CRC Press of Taylor & Francis for their strong support during the preparation and publishing of this book.

To all these wonderful people we owe a deep sense of gratitude especially now when the research projects and the book have been completed.

# Part I

# Single-Input-Single-Output Neuronet

# Chapter 1

## *Single-Input Euler-Polynomial WASD Neuronet*

To overcome the intrinsic weaknesses of conventional back-propagation (BP) neuronets, a feed-forward neuronet model is constructed in this chapter, which adopts a three-layer structure with hidden-layer neurons activated by a group of Euler polynomials. By employing the weights-direct-determination (WDD) subalgorithm, which obtains the optimal weights of the neuronet directly (i.e., just in one step), a weights-and-structure-determination (WASD) algorithm is presented to further determine the optimal number of hidden-layer neurons of the constructed Euler-polynomial neuronet. Numerical studies including comparisons substantiate the efficacy and superiority of Euler-polynomial neuronet with the proposed WASD algorithm.

## 1.1  Introduction

In view of remarkable features such as parallelism, distributed storage and adaptive self-learning, artificial neuronets (AN) have been widely applied to many science and engineering fields, such as control system design [1–4], deep learning [5–9], knowledge extraction [10, 11], and robot inverse-kinematics [2, 12]. Being one of the most important neuronet models, conventional BP neuronets have been involved widely in many theoretical and practical areas [13–16]. However, there exist some intrinsic weaknesses in these BP-type neuronets, such as relatively slow convergence, local-minima existence, and uncertainties about the optimal number of hidden-layer neurons. Besides, BP-type neuronets usually have a high computational complexity for obtaining the optimal connecting weights. Moreover, for the BP-type neuronets, it is still a bottleneck problem to determine the optimal structure of a neuronet model [17].

In order to overcome the weaknesses of BP-type neuronets, a weight training algorithm was proposed in [14]. Different from the neuronet training improvement mentioned in [14] and references therein, we mainly focus on the activation function and the structure improvements. Based on the

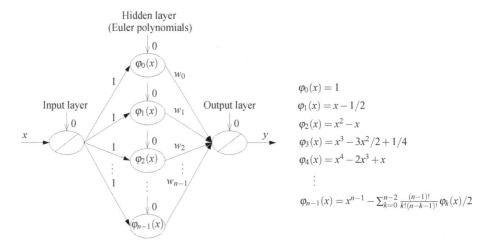

**FIGURE 1.1**: Model structure and activation functions of Euler-polynomial neuronet.

polynomial interpolation, approximation theory [18, 19], and our successful experience using linearly independent or orthogonal activation functions [20, 21], a single-input feed-forward neuronet is constructed elegantly in this chapter with hidden-layer neurons activated by a group of Euler polynomials. Then, a pseudoinverse-based WDD subalgorithm is employed for Euler-polynomial neuronet as well [20,21], which could determine "immediately" the optimal weights without lengthy BP iterative training.

Furthermore, determining the number of hidden-layer neurons is always viewed as an important and difficult task, since it may influence the overall performance of neuronets greatly. Generally speaking, fewer hidden neurons may hardly achieve a satisfactory performance, whereas too many hidden-layer neurons may lead to a higher complexity of software computation, circuit-implementation and even over-fitting phenomena [20, 22, 23]. According to the observed relation between the performance of Euler-polynomial neuronet and the number of its hidden-layer neurons, the structure automatic determination is also considered, and thus leads to the WASD algorithm. The proposed WASD algorithm can further generate the optimal number of hidden-layer neurons in a more deterministic manner, which adopts the WDD subalgorithm at its every trial. Numerical studies including comparisons substantiate that the constructed Euler-polynomial neuronet achieves much better performance with much shorter learning time by using the proposed WASD algorithm.

## 1.2   Neuronet Model and Theoretical Basis

In this section, we first construct the single-input-single-output (SISO) Euler-polynomial neuronet model with a three-layer structure. As shown in Fig. 1.1, input and output layers have one neuron each activated by a linear activation function $h(x) = x$, while the hidden layer has $n$ neurons activated by a group of degree-increasing Euler polynomials $\varphi_j(x)$, with $j = 0, 1, 2, \cdots, n - 1$. To simplify the neuronet model and its computation (including possible circuit implementation), the connecting weights between input- and hidden-layer neurons are fixed to 1, and thresholds of the neuronet are all fixed to 0. Besides, the following definition [24] describes the recurrence expression of Euler polynomials.

**Definition 1** Euler polynomials can be defined as

$$\varphi_j(x) = x^j - \frac{1}{2} \sum_{k=0}^{j-1} \left( \frac{j!}{k!(j-k)!} \varphi_k(x) \right), \tag{1.1}$$

where $\varphi_j(x)$ denotes a Euler polynomial of degree $j$ (with $j = 1, 2, 3, \cdots, n, \cdots$). Note that the first few analytic expressions of Euler polynomials are given in Fig. 1.1, and the 5th to 25th analytic expressions are shown in the appendix (i.e., Appendix A) to the chapter.

After constructing the SISO Euler-polynomial neuronet model, we present the simple theoretical basis on the approximation ability of Euler-polynomial neuronet. Based on the polynomial interpolation and approximation theory [18, 19], we could construct a weighted combination of polynomial functions $\varphi_j(x)$ to interpolate/approximate the unknown target function $f(x)$. In addition, we could have the following definition and lemma, which guarantee the approximation ability of Euler-polynomial neuronet.

**Definition 2** Assume that $f(x), \varphi_j(x) \in C[a,b]$, $j = 0, 1, \cdots, n-1$ [i.e., target function $f(x)$ and the $j$th polynomial function $\varphi_j(x)$ of polynomial-function sequence $\{\varphi_j(x)\}_{j=0}^{n-1}$ are continuous over the closed interval $[a,b]$], and that $\{\varphi_j(x)\}_{j=0}^{n-1}$ is a set of linearly independent polynomial functions. For the given weighting function $\rho(x)$ on interval $[a,b]$, appropriate coefficients $w_0, w_1, \cdots, w_{n-1}$ can be chosen for the generalized polynomial $\varphi(x) = \sum_{j=0}^{n-1} w_j \varphi_j(x)$ so as to minimize $\int_a^b (f(x) - \varphi(x))^2 \rho(x) \, dx$. Then, polynomial $\varphi(x)$ is termed the least-square approximation of target function $f(x)$ with respect to $\rho(x)$ over interval $[a,b]$ [20, 21, 25].

**Lemma 1** *For $f(x) \in C[a,b]$, its least-square approximation function $\varphi(x)$, e.g., Euler polynomial in this chapter, could exist uniquely, of which the coefficients, $w_0, w_1, \cdots, w_{n-1}$, are solvable [20, 21].*

In the constructed Euler-polynomial neuronet model, the relation between neuronet model input $x$ and output $y$ could be exactly expressed as

$$y = \varphi(x) = w_0 \varphi_0(x) + w_1 \varphi_1(x) + \cdots + w_{n-1} \varphi_{n-1}(x), \tag{1.2}$$

which is exactly the least-squares approximation to $f(x)$ as described and guaranteed in Definition 2 and Lemma 1. The approximation ability of Euler-polynomial neuronet is thus assured.

---

## 1.3 WASD Algorithm

The above section has presented Euler-polynomial neuronet model and the corresponding theoretical basis. In this section, as for the constructed Euler-polynomial neuronet, by considering the WDD subalgorithm and also the structure automatic determination, the WASD algorithm is proposed to directly determine the optimal weights $\{w_0, w_1, \cdots, w_{n-1}\}$ that connect the hidden layer and the output layer, and further automatically determine the optimal number $n$ of hidden-layer neurons.

### 1.3.1 Weights direct determination

With the model structure described in Fig. 1.1, Euler-polynomial neuronet can be viewed as a special type of BP neuronets, which can still adopt BP algorithms for its iterative training. Then, we have the following lemmas [21] about the weights-updating formulas of Euler-polynomial neuronet. First, we present the scalar update (SU) subalgorithm as follows.

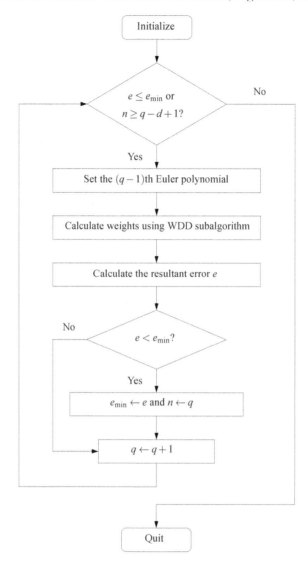

**FIGURE 1.2**: Flowchart of WASD algorithm for Euler-polynomial neuronet.

**Lemma 2** *Based on BP algorithms and negative-gradient methods, the weights update for Euler-polynomial neuronet (as shown in Fig. 1.1) can be designed as*

$$w_j(k+1) = w_j(k) - \eta \sum_{i=1}^{m} \left( \varphi_j(x_i) \left( \sum_{p=0}^{n-1} w_p(k) \varphi_p(x_i) - \gamma_i \right) \right), \tag{1.3}$$

*where $j = 0, 1, 2, \cdots, n-1$, iteration index $k = 0, 1, 2, \cdots$, learning rate $\eta > 0$ is small enough to guarantee the convergence of training procedure, and $(x_i, \gamma_i)|_{i=1}^{m}$ are the given training-sample pairs.*

Then, we present the vector update (VU) subalgorithm as follows.

**Lemma 3** *The scalar form of the weights-updating formula, i.e., (1.3), for Euler-polynomial neuronet, can be further reformulated in the following matrix-vector form:*

$$\mathbf{w}(k+1) = \mathbf{w}(k) - \eta \Psi^{\mathrm{T}} (\Psi \mathbf{w}(k) - \gamma), \tag{1.4}$$

*where superscript* $^{\mathrm{T}}$ *denotes the transpose of a matrix or vector, and weights vector* **w**, *desired-output vector* $\gamma$ *and input activation matrix* $\Psi$ *are defined respectively as*

$$
\mathbf{w} = \begin{bmatrix} w_0 \\ w_1 \\ \vdots \\ w_{n-1} \end{bmatrix} \in \mathbb{R}^n, \ \gamma = \begin{bmatrix} \gamma_1 \\ \gamma_2 \\ \vdots \\ \gamma_m \end{bmatrix} \in \mathbb{R}^m, \ \Psi = \begin{bmatrix} \varphi_0(x_1) & \varphi_1(x_1) & \cdots & \varphi_{n-1}(x_1) \\ \varphi_0(x_2) & \varphi_1(x_2) & \cdots & \varphi_{n-1}(x_2) \\ \vdots & \vdots & \ddots & \vdots \\ \varphi_0(x_m) & \varphi_1(x_m) & \cdots & \varphi_{n-1}(x_m) \end{bmatrix} \in \mathbb{R}^{m \times n}.
$$

It is worth pointing out here that Lemmas 2 and 3 are mathematically equivalent. As mentioned at the beginning of this chapter, the weights of Euler-polynomial neuronet can be determined without lengthy BP iterative training. Now, we show the following theoretical result [21] about the WDD subalgorithm for Euler-polynomial neuronet.

**Lemma 4** *With* **w**, $\Psi$, $\gamma$ *and other parameters defined the same as in Lemma 3, we can then determine the steady-state (optimal) weights of Euler-polynomial neuronet directly as*

$$
\mathbf{w} = (\Psi^{\mathrm{T}}\Psi)^{-1}\Psi^{\mathrm{T}}\gamma, \tag{1.5}
$$

*which could also be written as* $\mathbf{w} = \mathrm{pinv}(\Psi)\gamma$, *where* $\mathrm{pinv}(\Psi)$ *denotes the pseudoinverse of input activation matrix* $\Psi$ *and can be evaluated by calling MATLAB routine "*$\mathrm{pinv}(\cdot)$*" [18, 20, 21]. Based on the steady-state weights* **w** *in (1.5), Euler-polynomial neuronet can optimally approximate the unknown target function* $f(\cdot)$ *in the least-squares sense.*

### 1.3.2 Structure automatic determination

As perhaps we know, the number of hidden-layer neurons could affect greatly the performance of neuronets, but, up to now, there seemingly has been no deterministic theory to deal with this challenging issue. One of the reasons is that using conventional BP algorithms to iteratively update weights of neuronet may naturally introduce slow convergence, local-minima, and uncertain learning process, which generally hinder the exact finding of the optimal weights as well as the number of hidden-layer neurons in a neuronet. In this chapter, based on the above-presented WDD subalgorithm, we could firstly obtain the optimal weights of Euler-polynomial neuronet with respect to a given number of hidden-layer neurons; and then, by considering structure automatic determination, we can further find the optimal number of hidden-layer neurons in an automatically increasing and deterministically finding manner. Therefore, a new algorithm, called WASD algorithm, is thus proposed to determine both the optimal weights and the optimal number of hidden-layer neurons.

Before presenting this algorithm (of which the flowchart is shown in Fig. 1.2), we define the batch-processing error (BPE) function $e$ for Euler-polynomial neuronet as follows:

$$
e = \frac{1}{2} \sum_{i=1}^{m} \left( \gamma_i - \sum_{j=0}^{n-1} w_j \varphi_j(x_i) \right)^2. \tag{1.6}
$$

Our purpose is to select the number $n$ of hidden-layer neurons to minimize the above BPE. Besides, for the initialization of $e_{\min}$ shown in the flowchart, we set the initial value of $e_{\min}$ to be a very large value (e.g., $10^{10}$).

To observe and show the relationship between the BPE and the number of hidden-layer neurons, we have totally tested approximations of 22 target functions using the constructed Euler-polynomial neuronet, such as,

$$
f(x) = (1-x)^3 \exp(-x^2/2) + \cos^2(3x), \tag{1.7}
$$

$$
f(x) = \sin(8x)/\exp(x), \tag{1.8}
$$

$$
f(x) = \sin(6x)/\cos(x) - x. \tag{1.9}
$$

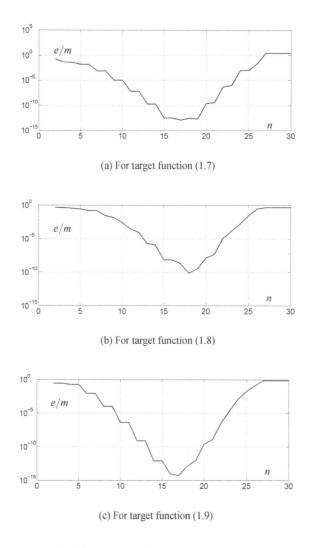

(a) For target function (1.7)

(b) For target function (1.8)

(c) For target function (1.9)

**FIGURE 1.3**: Average BPE of Euler-polynomial neuronet versus its number of hidden-layer neurons for target functions (1.7) through (1.9), respectively.

Specifically, Fig. 1.3 shows the average BPE (i.e., $e/m$) of the above three typical target functions (1.7) through (1.9) versus the number of hidden-layer neurons (i.e., $n$). We can see from the figure that the curves all look like the character "V". From the similar curves and others results, we could then design the WASD algorithm as follows (see Fig. 1.2 as well). To obtain the optimal number of hidden-layer neurons (i.e., the one with the minimal BPE), we increase the neuron number $q$ one by one (initially from $q = 2$) and test at $d$ test-points (e.g., $d = 4$). If the BPEs of the $q+1$, $q+2$, $\cdots$, $q+d-1$ hidden-layer neurons are all larger than that of $q$, we could say that $q$ is the optimal number of hidden-layer neurons (which is output as $n$) for Euler-polynomial neuronet.

Note that the WDD subalgorithm is applied mainly to computing the optimal weights (i.e., for a given $q$) in the WASD algorithm. Besides, the optimal number of hidden-layer neurons can be further decided rapidly and deterministically for Euler-polynomial neuronet. In the ensuing section, we present the numerical studies which verify and substantiate the efficacy and superior performance of the proposed WASD algorithm for Euler-polynomial neuronet.

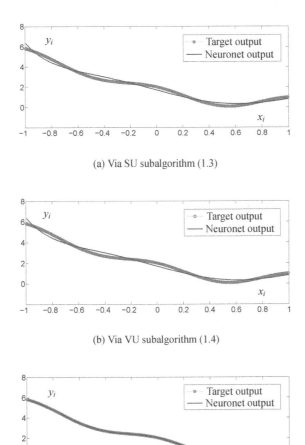

(a) Via SU subalgorithm (1.3)

(b) Via VU subalgorithm (1.4)

(c) Via WDD subalgorithm (1.5)

**FIGURE 1.4**: Training results of Euler-polynomial neuronet with three weight subalgorithms (1.3) through (1.5) for target function (1.7).

## 1.4 Numerical Studies

For the purpose of illustrating the efficacy of the constructed Euler-polynomial neuronet, we show the results by using three target functions; i.e., (1.7) through (1.9). The approximation results of other target functions is not presented in this chapter due to the results' similarity.

To compare the three subalgorithms presented in Section 3.3.1, we use the constructed Euler-polynomial neuronet to approximate target function (1.7) with SU (1.3), VU (1.4) and WDD (1.5) subalgorithms. In this comparison, the number of hidden-layer neurons is set as 12. We sample uniformly over interval $[-1.0, 1.0]$ with gap size 0.01 to generate the training data-set $\{(x_i, \gamma_i), i = 1, 2, \ldots, 201\}$ (i.e., $m = 201$). The corresponding results are shown in Table 1.1 and Fig. 1.4.

From Table 1.1, we can see that, for the constructed Euler-polynomial neuronet, the one-step WDD subalgorithm (1.5) is more efficient and effective than conventional BP iterative-training al-

**TABLE 1.1:**    Numerical results of Euler-polynomial neuronet with three weight subalgorithms (1.3) through (1.5) for target function (1.7).

| Subalgorithm | Step (k) | $t_{tra}$ (s) | $e_{tra}/m$ | $e_{tes}/m$ |
|---|---|---|---|---|
| SU subalgorithm (1.3) | $2 \times 10^5$ | 385 | $2.43 \times 10^{-2}$ | $2.39 \times 10^{-2}$ |
| VU subalgorithm (1.4) | $2 \times 10^5$ | 16.5 | $2.43 \times 10^{-2}$ | $2.39 \times 10^{-2}$ |
| WDD subalgorithm (1.5) | One step | 0.004 | $6.63 \times 10^{-8}$ | $6.92 \times 10^{-8}$ |

**TABLE 1.2:**    Numerical results of Euler-polynomial neuronet with WASD algorithm for target functions (1.7) through (1.9).

| Target function | $n_{opt}$ | $t_{run}$ (s) | $e_{opt}/m$ |
|---|---|---|---|
| Target function (1.7) | 17 | 0.064 | $1.32 \times 10^{-13}$ |
| Target function (1.8) | 18 | 0.075 | $7.12 \times 10^{-11}$ |
| Target function (1.9) | 17 | 0.063 | $5.61 \times 10^{-15}$ |

gorithms [i.e., here SU subalgorithm (1.3) and VU subalgorithm (1.4)]. The training time $t_{tra}$ corresponding to SU subalgorithm (1.3) and VU subalgorithm (1.4) are, respectively, 385 seconds and 16.5 seconds (both with 200,000 iterations). In comparison, the neuronet training time with WDD subalgorithm (1.5) is only 0.004 second. Moreover, the average training error $e_{tra}/m$ obtained by using one-step WDD subalgorithm (1.5) is just $6.63 \times 10^{-8}$; in contrast, those of SU subalgorithm (1.3) and VU subalgorithm (1.4) are both $2.43 \times 10^{-2}$. The similar results can also be found by the average testing error $e_{tes}/m$.

Besides, Fig. 1.4 shows the comparison between the target output and the neuronet output, where we can observe that, when WDD subalgorithm (1.5) is used, the neuronet output matches well with the target output. In contrast, by using SU subalgorithm (1.3) and VU subalgorithm (1.4) even with 200,000 iterations, the neuronet output still does not track the target output accurately. Thus, we summarize that the WDD subalgorithm achieves much better training performance than conventional BP iterative algorithms.

To verify the efficacy of the WASD algorithm for Euler-polynomial neuronet, we employ again the three target functions listed above [i.e., (1.7) through (1.9)]. From Fig. 1.3 and Table 1.2, we can see that the optimal number of hidden-layer neurons (i.e., $n_{opt}$), corresponding to the minimal BPE of target functions (1.7), (1.8) and (1.9), are respectively 17, 18 and 17. Besides, the run time $t_{run}$ for target function (1.7), (1.8) or (1.9) is respectively 0.064 second, 0.075 second or 0.063 second, being relatively small enough. The average BPE with the optimal number of hidden-layer neurons (i.e., $e_{opt}/m$) for target functions (1.7), (1.8) and (1.9), are respectively with the order $10^{-13}$, $10^{-11}$ and $10^{-15}$. In addition, Fig. 1.5 shows the output error of Euler-polynomial neuronet [i.e., $y(x_i) - \gamma_i$] synthesized with the optimal number of hidden-layer neurons. We can see that the errors are quite tiny (with the order of magnitude $10^{-7} \sim 10^{-5}$). This reveals the excellent approximation ability of Euler-polynomial neuronet trained with the proposed WASD algorithm.

## 1.5    Chapter Summary

In this chapter, to overcome the weaknesses of conventional BP neuronets, an SISO three-layer neuronet has been proposed, constructed and investigated, of which the hidden-layer neurons have been activated by Euler polynomials. Besides, a pseudoinverse-based WDD subalgorithm has been

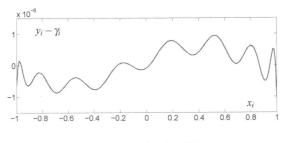

(a) For target function (1.7)

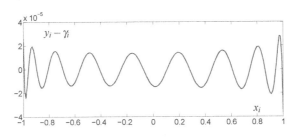

(b) For target function (1.8)

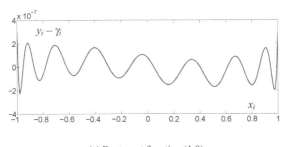

(c) For target function (1.9)

**FIGURE 1.5**: Output errors of Euler-polynomial neuronet with WASD algorithm for target functions (1.7) through (1.9).

employed as well for the constructed Euler-polynomial neuronet model by calculating the neuronet weights directly (without lengthy BP iterative training). Based on the WDD subalgorithm, a WASD algorithm has been further proposed for Euler-polynomial neuronet to find the optimal number of hidden-layer neurons in an automatic, effective and deterministic manner. Moreover, numerical studies have substantiated the efficacy and superiority of the proposed WASD algorithm for the constructed Euler-polynomial neuronet.

## Appendix A: The 5th to 25th Euler Polynomials

$$\varphi_5 = x^5 - \frac{5}{2}x^4 + \frac{5}{2}x^2 - \frac{1}{2},$$

$$\varphi_6 = x^6 - 3x^5 + 5x^3 - 3x,$$

$$\varphi_7 = x^7 - \frac{7}{2}x^6 + \frac{35}{4}x^4 - \frac{21}{2}x^2 + \frac{17}{8},$$

$$\varphi_8 = x^8 - 4x^7 + 14x^5 - 28x^3 + 17x,$$

$$\varphi_9 = x^9 - \frac{9}{2}x^8 + 21x^6 - 63x^4 + \frac{153}{2}x^2 - \frac{31}{2},$$

$$\varphi_{10} = x^{10} - 5x^9 + 30x^7 - 126x^5 + 255x^3 - 155x,$$

$$\varphi_{11} = x^{11} - \frac{11}{2}x^{10} + \frac{165}{4}x^8 - 231x^6 + \frac{2805}{4}x^4 - \frac{1705}{2}x^2 + \frac{691}{4},$$

$$\varphi_{12} = x^{12} - 6x^{11} + 55x^9 - 396x^7 + 1683x^5 - 3410x^3 + 2073x,$$

$$\varphi_{13} - x^{13} - \frac{13}{2}x^{12} + \frac{143}{2}x^{10} - \frac{1287}{2}x^8 + \frac{7293}{2}x^6 - \frac{22165}{2}x^4 + \frac{26949}{2}x^2 - \frac{5461}{2},$$

$$\varphi_{14} = x^{14} - 7x^{13} + 91x^{11} - 1001x^9 + 7293x^7 - 31031x^5 + 62881x^3 - 38227x,$$

$$\varphi_{15} = x^{15} - \frac{15}{2}x^{14} + \frac{455}{4}x^{12} - \frac{3003}{2}x^{10} + \frac{109395}{8}x^8 - \frac{155155}{2}x^6 + \frac{943215}{4}x^4 - \frac{573405}{2}x^2$$
$$+ \frac{929569}{16},$$

$$\varphi_{16} = x^{16} - 8x^{15} + 140x^{13} - 2184x^{11} + 24310x^9 - 177320x^7 + 754572x^5 - 1529080x^3$$
$$+ 929569x,$$

$$\varphi_{17} = x^{17} - \frac{17}{2}x^{16} + 170x^{14} - 3094x^{12} + 41327x^{10} - 376805x^8 + 2137954x^6 - 6498590x^4$$
$$+ \frac{15802673}{2}x^2 - \frac{3202291}{2},$$

$$\varphi_{18} = x^{18} - 9x^{17} + 204x^{15} - 4284x^{13} + 67626x^{11} - 753610x^9 + 5497596x^7 - 23394924x^5$$
$$+ 47408019x^3 - 28820619x,$$

$$\varphi_{19} = x^{19} - \frac{19}{2}x^{18} + \frac{969}{4}x^{16} - 5814x^{14} + \frac{214149}{2}x^{12} - 1431859x^{10} + \frac{26113581}{2}x^8 - 74083926x^6$$
$$+ \frac{900752361}{4}x^4 - \frac{547591761}{2}x^2 + \frac{221930581}{4},$$

$$\varphi_{20} = x^{20} - 10x^{19} + 285x^{17} - 7752x^{15} + 164730x^{13} - 2603380x^{11} + 29015090x^9 - 211668360x^7$$
$$+ 900752361x^5 - 1825305870x^3 + 1109652905x,$$

$$\varphi_{21} = x^{21} - \frac{21}{2}x^{20} + \frac{665}{2}x^{18} - \frac{20349}{2}x^{16} + 247095x^{14} - 4555915x^{12} + 60931689x^{10}$$
$$- 555629445x^8 + \frac{6305266527}{2}x^6 - \frac{19165711635}{2}x^4 + \frac{23302711005}{2}x^2 - \frac{4722116521}{2},$$

$$\varphi_{22} = x^{22} - 11x^{21} + 385x^{19} - 13167x^{17} + 362406x^{15} - 7710010x^{13} + 121863378x^{11}$$
$$- 1358205310x^9 + 9908275971x^7 - 42164565597x^5 + 85443273685x^3 - 51943281731x,$$

$$\varphi_{23} = x^{23} - \frac{23}{2}x^{22} + \frac{1771}{4}x^{20} - \frac{33649}{2}x^{18} + \frac{4167669}{8}x^{16} - 12666445x^{14} + \frac{467142949}{2}x^{12}$$
$$- 3123872213x^{10} + \frac{227890347333}{8}x^8 - \frac{323261669577}{2}x^6 + \frac{1965195294755}{4}x^4$$
$$- \frac{1194695479813}{2}x^2 + \frac{968383680827}{8},$$

$$\varphi_{24} = x^{24} - 12x^{23} + 506x^{21} - 21252x^{19} + 735471x^{17} - 20266312x^{15} + 431208876x^{13}$$
$$- 6815721192x^{11} + 75963449111x^{9} - 554162862132x^{7} + 2358234353706x^{5}$$
$$- 4778781919252x^{3} + 2905151042481x,$$

$$\varphi_{25} = x^{25} - \frac{25}{2}x^{24} + 575x^{22} - 26565x^{20} + \frac{2042975}{2}x^{18} - \frac{63332225}{2}x^{16} + 770015850x^{14}$$
$$- 14199419150x^{12} + \frac{379817245555}{2}x^{10} - \frac{3463517888325}{2}x^{8} + 9825976473775x^{6}$$
$$- 29867386995325x^{4} + \frac{72628776062025}{2}x^{2} - \frac{14717667114151}{2}.$$

# Chapter 2

## Single-Input Bernoulli-Polynomial WASD Neuronet

Conventional back-propagation (BP) neuronets have some inherent weaknesses such as slow convergence and local-minima existence. Based on the polynomial interpolation and approximation theory, a special type of feed-forward neuronet is constructed in this chapter with hidden-layer neurons activated by Bernoulli polynomials, which is different from the one activated by Euler polynomials in Chapter 1. Differing from the conventional BP algorithms and gradient-based training methods, a weights-direct-determination (WDD) subalgorithm is presented for Bernoulli-polynomial neuronet to determine weights directly (just in one general step), without a lengthy iterative BP-training process. Moreover, by analyzing and discovering the relationship between the performance of Bernoulli-polynomial neuronet and its number of hidden-layer neurons, a weights-and-structure-determination (WASD) algorithm is further proposed, which could obtain the optimal number of hidden-layer neurons in the constructed Bernoulli-polynomial neuronet in the sense of achieving the highest learning-accuracy for a specific data problem or target function. Numerical studies further substantiate the efficacy of such a WASD algorithm for single-input Bernoulli-polynomial neuronet.

## 2.1   Introduction

Artificial neuronets (AN) have become useful tools in dealing with various scientific and engineering problems such as the system design and control [1–4], deep learning [5–9], and robot inverse-kinematics [2, 12] due to the remarkable advantages such as parallelism, distributed storage and computation, adaptive-learning ability. Among the most important neuronet models, BP-type neuronets have been widely investigated and also applied to many practical fields [13, 22]. But the inherent weaknesses still exist in BP-type neuronets and the related algorithms (including those

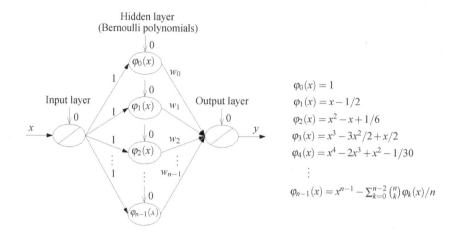

**FIGURE 2.1**: Model structure and activation functions of Bernoulli-polynomial neuronet.

improved variants), such as slow convergence of iterative training, local-minima existence of solution, and uncertainties in the optimal number of hidden-layer neurons [22].

Different from algorithmic improvements about the BP iterative-training process, by our successful experience [3, 20, 21], adopting linearly independent or orthogonal activation functions to construct the neuronet might be a much better choice. In Chapter 1, we have developed and investigated Euler-polynomial neuronet. In this chapter, based on the polynomial interpolation and approximation theory [18, 19], we further try enhancing the neuronet performance by constructing a single-input-single-output (SISO) neuronet, that is, the so-called Bernoulli-polynomial neuronet. This special neuronet has a three-layer structure as well, but with hidden-layer neurons activated by Bernoulli polynomials. More importantly, in order to avoid the usually lengthy iterative-training procedure (which is mostly based on gradient methods and BP algorithms), a pseudoinverse-based WDD subalgorithm is derived for the Bernoulli-polynomial neuronet, which can determine the theoretically optimal weights directly (or, say, just in one step).

Furthermore, as we may know, selecting the number of hidden-layer neurons is an important and difficult issue because it may affect the overall performance of neuronets very much. Specifically, fewer hidden neurons may not achieve a satisfactory performance, whereas too many hidden-layer neurons may lead to a higher complexity of circuit implementation, software computation and even over-fitting phenomena [20, 22]. By observing the relationship between the performance of Bernoulli-polynomial neuronet and the number of the hidden-layer neurons, a WASD algorithm is proposed further in this chapter for the constructed Bernoulli-polynomial neuronet. Specifically, it exploits the WDD subalgorithm at its every trial and generates finally the optimal number of hidden-layer neurons for Bernoulli-polynomial neuronet. Via the WASD algorithm, the highest accuracy of learning can be achieved by Bernoulli-polynomial neuronet for a specific data system or target function approximation (or say, function data approximation). Numerical results substantiate the efficacy and superiority of the WASD algorithm for Bernoulli-polynomial neuronet.

## 2.2 Neuronet Model and Theoretical Basis

In this section, we construct Bernoulli-polynomial neuronet model firstly, and then present some important theoretical basis to guarantee its approximation ability. Specifically, Fig. 2.1 shows the constructed model of Bernoulli-polynomial neuronet, which, in the hidden layer, has $n$ neurons activated by a group of degree-increasing Bernoulli polynomials $\varphi_j(x)$, with $j = 0, 1, \cdots, n-1$. Each input-layer or output-layer of Bernoulli-polynomial neuronet has one neuron activated by linear function. Moreover, the weights between input-layer and hidden-layer neurons are all fixed to be 1, whereas the weights between hidden-layer and output-layer neurons, denoted as $w_j$, are to be decided or adjusted. In addition, all neuronal thresholds are fixed to be 0. These settings could simplify the neuronet structure design, circuit implementation and computational complexity. More importantly, even so, the approximation ability of Bernoulli-polynomial neuronet can still be theoretically guaranteed.

About the constructed Bernoulli-polynomial neuronet in this chapter, people may wonder whether it works. Now we show the corresponding theoretical basis. As we may know [26–28], Bernoulli polynomials are quite important in various expansion and approximation formulas with many applications in combinatorics and number theory.

Firstly, as noticed, there are a variety of different expressions for Bernoulli polynomials. In this chapter, we present a simple recurrence relation of Bernoulli polynomials for the facility of such a neuronet construction. In [27], Bernoulli polynomials are defined via a matrix-determinant approach, and then, by simplifying it, the stable recurrence expression of Bernoulli polynomials can be shown as follows with $\varphi_0(x) = 1$:

$$\varphi_j(x) = x^j - \frac{1}{j+1} \sum_{k=0}^{j-1} \left( \binom{j+1}{k} \varphi_k(x) \right), \text{ with } \binom{j+1}{k} = \frac{(j+1)!}{k!(j+1-k)!}, \tag{2.1}$$

where $\varphi_j(x)$ denotes a Bernoulli polynomial of degree $j = 1, 2, 3, \cdots, n, \cdots$, with its first few analytic expressions given in Fig. 2.1 as well as in Appendix B to this chapter.

Similar to the fundamental idea appearing in our previous work [3, 20, 21], the final approximation mathematical essence of such a Bernoulli-polynomial neuronet construction can be viewed as a procedure of constructing a generalized polynomial function so as to interpolate or approximate an unknown target function using a given set of sample data. When approximating a target function $f(x)$, from Fig. 2.1, the relation between input- and output-neurons of Bernoulli-polynomial neuronet can be exactly expressed as

$$y = \varphi(x) = w_0 \varphi_0(x) + w_1 \varphi_1(x) + \cdots + w_{n-1} \varphi_{n-1}(x), \tag{2.2}$$

of which the learning and approximating abilities can be guaranteed by Definition 2 in Chapter 1 and the following lemma [20, 21, 25, 29].

**Lemma 5** *For $f(x) \in C[a,b]$, its least-square approximation function $\varphi(x)$, e.g., Bernoulli polynomial in this chapter, could exist uniquely, of which the coefficients (in other words, the weights of the neuronet model shown in Fig. 2.1), $w_0, w_1, \cdots, w_{n-1}$, are solvable.*

## 2.3 WASD Algorithm

The above section has presented Bernoulli-polynomial neuronet model and the corresponding theoretical basis. In this section, by considering the WDD subalgorithm and also the structure automatic determination, the WASD algorithm is proposed for the constructed Bernoulli-polynomial neuronet to directly determine the optimal weights $\{w_0, w_1, \cdots, w_{n-1}\}$ that connect the hidden layer and the output layer, and further automatically determine the optimal number $n$ of hidden-layer neurons.

### 2.3.1 Weights direct determination

From the above description of the Bernoulli-polynomial neuronet, it can be viewed as a special type of BP neuronets, which can still adopt BP algorithms as its iterative-training rule. However, if a BP algorithm is employed, it may take much time (or even infinite time) to converge to a solution under a user-specified accuracy of learning (e.g., $10^{-18}$ in the ensuing simulation-study of ours). As mentioned above, for Bernoulli-polynomial neuronet, its weights can be determined directly (i.e., via the so-called WDD subalgorithm), instead of a lengthy BP iterative-training procedure. Now we show it as follows.

By taking $\{(x_i, \gamma_i)|_{i=1}^m\}$ as the given data-set for training of the neuronet, we can define the batch-processing error (BPE) function $e$ for Bernoulli-polynomial neuronet as below:

$$e = \frac{1}{2} \sum_{i=1}^m \left( \gamma_i - \sum_{j=0}^{n-1} w_j \varphi_j(x_i) \right)^2. \tag{2.3}$$

Then we have the following lemma about the WDD subalgorithm for Bernoulli-polynomial neuronet [21, 30–37].

**Lemma 6** *Let superscript* $^\mathrm{T}$ *denote the transpose of a matrix or vector. As for Bernoulli-polynomial neuronet depicted in Fig. 2.1, let us define its weights vector* **w**, *target-output vector* $\gamma$, *and input-activation-matrix* $\Psi$, *respectively, as*

$$\mathbf{w} = \begin{bmatrix} w_0 \\ w_1 \\ \vdots \\ w_{n-1} \end{bmatrix} \in \mathbb{R}^n, \ \gamma = \begin{bmatrix} \gamma_1 \\ \gamma_2 \\ \vdots \\ \gamma_m \end{bmatrix} \in \mathbb{R}^m, \ \Psi = \begin{bmatrix} \varphi_0(x_1) & \varphi_1(x_1) & \dots & \varphi_{n-1}(x_1) \\ \varphi_0(x_2) & \varphi_1(x_2) & \dots & \varphi_{n-1}(x_2) \\ \vdots & \vdots & \ddots & \vdots \\ \varphi_0(x_m) & \varphi_1(x_m) & \dots & \varphi_{n-1}(x_m) \end{bmatrix} \in \mathbb{R}^{m \times n}.$$

*Then, with* $\mathrm{pinv}(\Psi)$ *denoting the pseudoinverse of a matrix* $\Psi$, *the steady-state (optimal) weights vector of the Bernoulli-polynomial neuronet can be determined directly as*

$$\mathbf{w} = \mathrm{pinv}(\Psi)\gamma = (\Psi^\mathrm{T}\Psi)^{-1}\Psi^\mathrm{T}\gamma, \tag{2.4}$$

*which is optimal in the sense of minimizing the BPE.*

### 2.3.2 Structure automatic determination

It might be well known that the number of hidden-layer neurons has an important influence on the performance of neuronets, but currently there is still no deterministic theory which handles this issue. As an attempt to develop a suitable algorithm for determining the optimal number of hidden-layer neurons in Bernoulli-polynomial neuronet, we firstly observe and analyze the relationship between the performance of Bernoulli-polynomial neuronet and the number of hidden-layer neurons via the approximation examples of a variety of target functions. For example, Fig. 2.2 shows the average BPE of Bernoulli-polynomial neuronet (specifically, $e/m$) for the following three tested

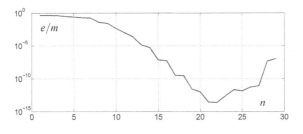

(a) For target function (2.5)

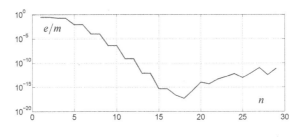

(b) For target function (2.6)

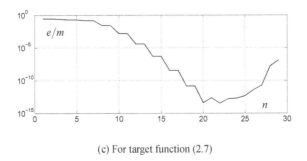

(c) For target function (2.7)

**FIGURE 2.2**: Average BPE of Bernoulli-polynomial neuronet versus its number of hidden-layer neurons for target functions (2.5) through (2.7), respectively.

target functions versus the number of hidden-layer neurons:

$$f(x) = \exp(x)\cos(3\pi x), \tag{2.5}$$

$$f(x) = \frac{\sin(6x)}{\cos(x)} - x, \tag{2.6}$$

$$f(x) = x\exp(x^2) + \cos(3\pi x), \tag{2.7}$$

which are out of the twelve target functions we have tested (but no other tests are presented in this chapter due to the similarity). From Fig. 2.2 and other testing results, we observe that the performance of Bernoulli-polynomial neuronet has a relatively consistent trend with respect to the number of hidden-layer neurons (which increases from 2 to 30), no matter what target function is tested. That is, at the beginning, the BPE defined in (2.3) would generally decrease over the increase of the number of hidden-layer neurons. In addition, the BPE-decreasing procedure will not terminate until it reaches the optimal number of hidden-layer neurons (at this point BPE is the smallest). After

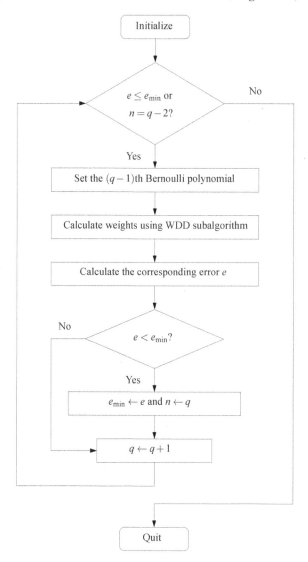

**FIGURE 2.3**: Flowchart of WASD algorithm for Bernoulli-polynomial neuronet.

that, as the number $n$ increases, the BPE will go up generally. So, we could search the optimal number of hidden-layer neurons by increasing $n$ one-by-one, in addition to using the aforementioned WDD subalgorithm. The WASD algorithm could be developed further and presented in Fig. 2.3.

In addition, it is worth mentioning that during the search process through increasing the number of hidden-layer neurons, the BPE error $e$ calculated at the current loop (with a larger value of the number of hidden-layer neurons, $q$) might become larger than (or equal to) that at the previous loop (e.g., with a smaller value of the number of hidden-layer neurons, $q-1$). The key point of the proposed WASD algorithm is to deal with such a situation. From our simulation results (e.g., Fig. 2.2), it is observed that, for (almost) all tested target functions, if $q-1$ is not the true optimal-number of hidden-layer neurons, the BPE error $e$ with $q+1$ hidden-neurons will become less than that with $q-1$ hidden neurons (although the BPE error $e$ with $q$ hidden neurons is larger than that with $q-1$ hidden neurons). Moreover, as from our simulative observation, if the errors $e$ with $q+1$ and $q$ hidden neurons are both larger than that with $q-1$ hidden neurons, we can say quite definitely

**TABLE 2.1:** Numerical results of Bernoulli-polynomial neuronet with WASD algorithm for target functions (2.5) through (2.7).

| Target function | $n_{opt}$ | $t_{run}$ (s) | $e_{tra}/m$ | $e_{tes}/m$ |
|---|---|---|---|---|
| Target function (2.5) | 23 | 0.062 | $2.44 \times 10^{-14}$ | $2.40 \times 10^{-14}$ |
| Target function (2.6) | 19 | 0.042 | $5.08 \times 10^{-18}$ | $5.02 \times 10^{-18}$ |
| Target function (2.7) | 23 | 0.060 | $3.62 \times 10^{-14}$ | $3.38 \times 10^{-14}$ |

that $q - 1$ is the optimal number $n$ of hidden-layer neurons of Bernoulli-polynomial neuronet for that specific approximation task. As $q$ starts from 2 and increases, such a WASD algorithm depicted in the algorithm part and Fig. 2.3 continues to search the optimal number of hidden-layer neurons until the above objective is achieved.

## 2.4 Numerical Studies

For the purpose of testing, verifying and illustrating the efficacy of the constructed Bernoulli-polynomial neuronet and the corresponding WASD algorithm, the mentioned three target functions, i.e., (2.5) through (2.7), in Section 3.3.2 are employed here for the simulation study. Let us take and sample uniformly over the interval $[-1.0, 1.0]$ with gap size 0.01 to generate the related data-sets $\{(x_i, \gamma_i), i = 1, 2, \cdots, 201\}$ (i.e., $m = 201$). Then, the constructed Bernoulli-polynomial neuronet is simulated with the WASD algorithm, and the numerical results are shown comparatively in Table 2.1, Figs. 2.4 and 2.5.

Moreover, it is worth pointing out that, with the optimal number of hidden-layer neurons as in Table 2.1 (e.g., in its last row), the Bernoulli-polynomial neuronet can achieve the smallest BPE error $e$ for that specific function-approximation task, which implies that its performance is deterministically the best. More importantly, by using the WASD algorithm (instead of using iterative BP-training algorithms based on the well-known gradient-descent method [4,9,13,21,22]), the constructed Bernoulli-polynomial neuronet can find the optimal number of hidden neurons, i.e., $n_{opt}$, and achieve the best performance in a very short run time $t_{run}$ (e.g., within 0.7 s; see the third column of Table 2.1). Besides, the average error of training, i.e., $e_{tra}/m$, and the average error of testing, i.e., $e_{tes}/m$, are both very tiny, which are shown in the rightmost two columns of Table 2.1 as well as in Fig. 2.5, so that we see little difference between the expected target output and the neuronet output. This might reveal the excellent approximation ability of Bernoulli-polynomial neuronet trained by the WASD algorithm [20–22]. Before ending this section, it is worth mentioning that, after training, we select 200 untrained points (with boundary points unconsidered [38]) to test the generalization ability of the Bernoulli-polynomial neuronet, and the results are excellent which are shown in the last column of Table 2.1.

## 2.5 Chapter Summary

To remedy the weaknesses of conventional BP neuronets, a type of feed-forward neuronet has been constructed by using the linearly independent Bernoulli polynomials to be the hidden-layer activation functions. Differing from using the conventional gradient-based methods [4,9,13,21,22] for BP iterative-training algorithms, we have presented a pseudoinverse-based WDD subalgorithm

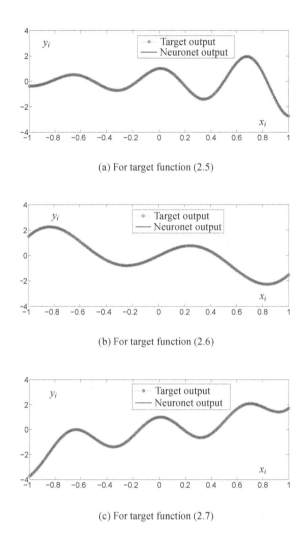

(a) For target function (2.5)

(b) For target function (2.6)

(c) For target function (2.7)

**FIGURE 2.4**: Approximation results of Bernoulli-polynomial neuronet with WASD algorithm for target functions (2.5) through (2.7).

[20,21], which could now calculate the neural-network weights directly (just in one step and with no more lengthy/time-consuming BP iterative training procedure). Moreover, based on the WDD sub-algorithm, a WASD algorithm has been further proposed for the constructed Bernoulli-polynomial neuronet, which could determine the optimal number of hidden-layer neurons much more effectively, rapidly and deterministically. Numerical results have substantiated the efficacy and superiority of the proposed WASD algorithm for Bernoulli-polynomial neuronet.

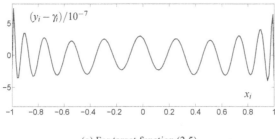

(a) For target function (2.5)

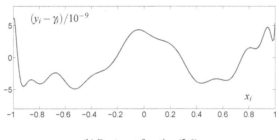

(b) For target function (2.6)

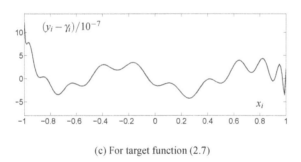

(c) For target function (2.7)

**FIGURE 2.5**: Approximation errors of Bernoulli-polynomial neuronet with WASD algorithm for target functions (2.5) through (2.7).

---

## Appendix B: The 5th to 25th Bernoulli Polynomials

$$\varphi_5(x) = x^5 - \frac{5}{2}x^4 + \frac{5}{3}x^3 - \frac{1}{6}x,$$

$$\varphi_6(x) = x^6 - 3x^5 + \frac{5}{2}x^4 - \frac{1}{2}x^2 + \frac{1}{42},$$

$$\varphi_7(x) = x^7 - \frac{7}{2}x^6 + \frac{7}{2}x^5 - \frac{7}{6}x^3 + \frac{1}{6}x,$$

$$\varphi_8(x) = x^8 - 4x^7 + \frac{14}{3}x^6 - \frac{7}{3}x^4 + \frac{2}{3}x^2 - \frac{1}{30},$$

$$\varphi_9(x) = x^9 - \frac{9}{2}x^8 + 6x^7 - \frac{21}{5}x^5 + 2x^3 - \frac{3}{10}x,$$

$$\varphi_{10}(x) = x^{10} - 5x^9 + \frac{15}{2}x^8 - 7x^6 + 5x^4 - \frac{3}{2}x^2 + \frac{5}{66},$$

$$\varphi_{11}(x) = x^{11} - \frac{11}{2}x^{10} + \frac{55}{6}x^9 - 11x^7 + 11x^5 - \frac{11}{2}x^3 + \frac{5}{6}x,$$

$$\varphi_{12}(x) = x^{12} - 6x^{11} + 11x^{10} - \frac{33}{2}x^8 + 22x^6 - \frac{33}{2}x^4 + 5x^2 - \frac{691}{2730},$$

$$\varphi_{13}(x) = x^{13} - \frac{13}{2}x^{12} + 13x^{11} - \frac{143}{6}x^9 + \frac{286}{7}x^7 - \frac{429}{10}x^5 + \frac{65}{3}x^3 - \frac{691}{210}x,$$

$$\varphi_{14}(x) = x^{14} - 7x^{13} + \frac{91}{6}x^{12} - \frac{1001}{30}x^{10} + \frac{143}{2}x^8 - \frac{1001}{10}x^6 + \frac{455}{6}x^4 - \frac{691}{30}x^2 + \frac{7}{6},$$

$$\varphi_{15}(x) = x^{15} - \frac{15}{2}x^{14} + \frac{35}{2}x^{13} - \frac{91}{2}x^{11} + \frac{715}{6}x^9 - \frac{429}{2}x^7 + \frac{455}{2}x^5 - \frac{691}{6}x^3 + \frac{35}{2}x,$$

$$\varphi_{16}(x) = x^{16} - 8x^{15} + 20x^{14} - \frac{182}{3}x^{12} + \frac{572}{3}x^{10} - 429x^8 + \frac{1820}{3}x^6 - \frac{1382}{3}x^4 + 140x^2$$
$$- \frac{3617}{510},$$

$$\varphi_{17}(x) = x^{17} - \frac{17}{2}x^{16} + \frac{68}{3}x^{15} - \frac{238}{3}x^{13} + \frac{884}{3}x^{11} - \frac{2431}{3}x^9 + \frac{4420}{3}x^7 - \frac{23494}{15}x^5$$
$$+ \frac{2380}{3}x^3 - \frac{3617}{30}x,$$

$$\varphi_{18}(x) = x^{18} - 9x^{17} + \frac{51}{2}x^{16} - 102x^{14} + 442x^{12} - \frac{7293}{5}x^{10} + 3315x^8 - \frac{23494}{5}x^6$$
$$+ 3570x^4 - \frac{10851}{10}x^2 + \frac{43867}{798},$$

$$\varphi_{19}(x) = x^{19} - \frac{19}{2}x^{18} + \frac{57}{2}x^{17} - \frac{646}{5}x^{15} + 646x^{13} - \frac{12597}{5}x^{11} + \frac{20995}{3}x^9 - \frac{446386}{35}x^7$$
$$+ 13566x^5 - \frac{68723}{10}x^3 + \frac{43867}{42}x,$$

$$\varphi_{20}(x) = x^{20} - 10x^{19} + \frac{95}{3}x^{18} - \frac{323}{2}x^{16} + \frac{6460}{7}x^{14} - 4199x^{12} + \frac{41990}{3}x^{10} - \frac{223193}{7}x^8$$
$$+ 45220x^6 - \frac{68723}{2}x^4 + \frac{219335}{21}x^2 - \frac{174611}{330}.$$

# Chapter 3

## Single-Input Laguerre-Polynomial WASD Neuronet

Determination of appropriate structure of a neuronet is an important issue for a given learning or training task since the neuronet performance depends much on it. To remedy the weakness of conventional back-propagation (BP) neuronets and corresponding learning algorithms, a Laguerre-polynomial neuronet is constructed in this chapter. Based on this special neuronet model, a weights-direct-determination (WDD) subalgorithm is derived accordingly, which could obtain the optimal weights of such a Laguerre-polynomial neuronet directly (or, say, just in one step). Furthermore, a weights-and-structure-determination (WASD) algorithm is developed for determining immediately the smallest number of hidden-layer neurons. Numerical studies substantiate the efficacy of such a Laguerre-polynomial neuronet with the WASD algorithm.

## 3.1 Introduction

Recently, artificial neuronets (AN) have been applied widely to many engineering and practical fields such as computational intelligence, pattern recognition, signal processing, and nonlinear control [1–4, 12, 20]. The conventional back-propagation (BP) algorithm is essentially a gradient-descent optimization strategy, which adjusts the weights to bring the input/output behavior into a desired mapping for a neuronet as of some application environment. However, BP-type neuronets have some inherent weaknesses [20, 39–44]. To resolve such weaknesses of BP-type neuronets, a Laguerre-polynomial neuronet is constructed in this chapter.

As discussed in the previous chapters, single-input-single-output (SISO) neuronets activated by a group of different kinds of polynomials, e.g., Euler polynomials in Chapter 1 or Bernoulli polynomials in Chapter 2, possess a different performance. By employing the weights-direct-determination (WDD) subalgorithm, which obtains the optimal weights of the neuronet directly (i.e., just in one step), a weights-and-structure-determination (WASD) algorithm is proposed to further determine the

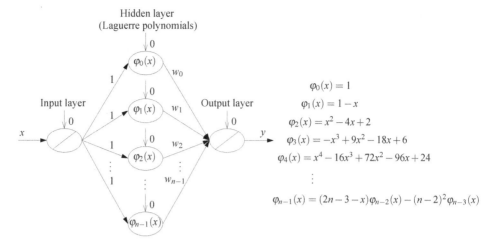

**FIGURE 3.1**: Model structure and activation functions of Laguerre-polynomial neuronet.

optimal number of hidden-layer neurons of the constructed Laguerre-polynomial neuronet. Numerical studies including comparisons substantiate the efficacy and superiority of Laguerre-polynomial neuronet with the proposed WASD algorithm.

## 3.2    Neuronet Model and Theoretical Basis

In this section, Laguerre-polynomial neuronet is constructed firstly with the corresponding theoretical basis about its approximation ability.

As shown in Fig. 3.1, Laguerre-polynomial neuronet consists of three layers. The input and output of the neuronet model are denoted as $x$ and $y$, respectively. The input and output layers each employ one neuron with a linear activation function, while the hidden layer has $n$ neurons activated by a group of order-increasing Laguerre orthogonal polynomials $\varphi_j(x)$, with $j = 0, 1, 2, \cdots, n-1$. Parameters $w_j$ denote the weights between the hidden-layer and output-layer neurons. Moreover, the weights between the input-layer and hidden-layer neurons are fixed to be 1, and all the neuronal thresholds are fixed to be 0, which would simplify the neuronet model and its possible circuit implementation. It is worth pointing out here that such a neuronet model can be viewed as a special BP neuronet and adopts the standard BP algorithm as its training rule.

After constructing Laguerre-polynomial neuronet (actually before that), we could present the corresponding theoretical basis on the approximation ability of the neuronet. By the polynomial interpolation and curve-fitting theory [25, 29], we could always construct a polynomial function $\varphi(x)$ (i.e., an underlying input-output function of Laguerre-polynomial neuronet) to approximate the unknown target function $f(x)$. For such an approximation, we could have the following definitions.

**Definition 3**    Define that $\varphi_j(x)$ is a polynomial of degree $j$, and that polynomial sequence $\{\varphi_j(x)\}_{j=0}^{n-1}$ is a set of $n$ orthogonal-polynomial functions with respect to some weighting function $v(x)$ over a finite or infinite interval $[a,b]$; i.e., for any $i, j \in \{0, 1, 2, \cdots, n-1\}$,

$$\begin{cases} \int_a^b \varphi_i(x)\varphi_j(x)v(x)\mathrm{d}x = 0, \text{ if } i \neq j, \\ \int_a^b \varphi_i(x)\varphi_j(x)v(x)\mathrm{d}x > 0, \text{ if } i = j. \end{cases} \tag{3.1}$$

Then, $\{\varphi_j(x)\}_{j=0}^{n-1}$ is termed as an orthogonal polynomial sequence with respect to weighting function $v(x)$ on the interval $[a,b]$.

**Definition 4** Laguerre polynomials could be defined by the following equation:

$$\varphi_{n-1}(x) = \exp(x) \frac{d^{n-1}(x^{n-1}\exp(-x))}{dx^{n-1}}, \ 0 \leq x < +\infty, \tag{3.2}$$

which is an orthogonal polynomial of degree $n-1$ with respect to weighting function $v(x) = \exp(-x)$ over interval $[0,+\infty)$, with its orthogonal relationship derived as below:

$$\begin{cases} \int_0^{+\infty} \varphi_i(x)\varphi_j(x)\exp(-x)dx = 0, \ \text{if } i \neq j, \\ \int_0^{+\infty} \varphi_i(x)\varphi_j(x)\exp(-x)dx = (i!)^2, \ \text{if } i = j. \end{cases} \tag{3.3}$$

Furthermore, the recurrence expression for Laguerre polynomials could be depicted as follows:

$$\varphi_{n-1}(x) = (2n-3-x)\varphi_{n-2}(x) - (n-2)^2\varphi_{n-3}(x), \ n = 3, 4, \cdots. \tag{3.4}$$

From the mathematical perspective of polynomial curve-fitting, the training of Laguerre-polynomial neuronet is essentially the establishment of the best functional approximation, and thus we would like to present the following theoretical basis about the approximation ability of Laguerre-polynomial neuronet [20, 25, 29].

**Lemma 7** *For $f(x) \in C[a,b]$, its least-square approximation function $\varphi(x)$, e.g., Laguerre polynomial in this chapter, could exist uniquely, of which the coefficients, $w_0, w_1, \cdots, w_{n-1}$, are solvable.*

When approximating the unknown target function $f(x)$, the relation between the input and output of Laguerre-polynomial neuronet could become exactly

$$y = \varphi(x) = w_0\varphi_0(x) + w_1\varphi_1(x) + \cdots + w_{n-1}\varphi_{n-1}(x), \tag{3.5}$$

of which the approximation ability is guaranteed by Definition 2 in Chapter 1, Definitions 3 and 4 as well as Lemma 7 in this chapter.

---

## 3.3 WASD Algorithm

The above section has presented Laguerre-polynomial neuronet model and the corresponding theoretical basis. In this section, as for the constructed Laguerre-polynomial neuronet, by considering the WDD subalgorithm, the WASD algorithm is presented to directly determine the optimal weights $\{w_0, w_1, \cdots, w_{n-1}\}$ that connect the hidden layer and the output layer, and further determine rapidly the optimal number $n$ of hidden-layer neurons.

### 3.3.1 Weights direct determination

As discussed above, weights between the hidden-layer and output-layer neurons could be generated so as to approximate effectively the unknown target function by learning (or to say, training with) the given data samples. More importantly, such weights between the hidden-layer and output-layer neurons of the neuronet could be determined directly by using the WDD subalgorithm, which generates the steady-state optimal weights just in one step without the lengthy BP iterative training.

The WDD subalgorithm could thus remove some inherent weaknesses of conventional BP algorithms, e.g., slow convergence.

Let us take $\{(x_i, \gamma_i)|_{i=1}^{m}\}$ as the training data-set, and define the batch-processing error (BPE) function $e$ as

$$e = \frac{1}{2} \sum_{i=1}^{m} \left( \gamma_i - \sum_{j=0}^{n-1} w_j \varphi_j(x_i) \right)^2.$$
(3.6)

Then we have the following results about the WDD subalgorithm [20, 45–50].

**Lemma 8** *The steady-state weights of Laguerre-polynomial neuronet can be obtained directly as follows:*

$$\mathbf{w} = (\Psi^{\mathrm{T}}\Psi)^{-1}\Psi^{\mathrm{T}}\gamma,$$
(3.7)

*where the weights vector* $\mathbf{w}$, *the target-output vector* $\gamma$, *and the input information matrix* $\Psi$ *are defined respectively as*

$$\mathbf{w} = \begin{bmatrix} w_0 \\ w_1 \\ \vdots \\ w_{n-1} \end{bmatrix} \in \mathbb{R}^n, \ \gamma = \begin{bmatrix} \gamma_1 \\ \gamma_2 \\ \vdots \\ \gamma_m \end{bmatrix} \in \mathbb{R}^m, \ \Psi = \begin{bmatrix} \varphi_0(x_1) & \varphi_1(x_1) & \cdots & \varphi_{n-1}(x_1) \\ \varphi_0(x_2) & \varphi_1(x_2) & \cdots & \varphi_{n-1}(x_2) \\ \vdots & \vdots & \ddots & \vdots \\ \varphi_0(x_m) & \varphi_1(x_m) & \cdots & \varphi_{n-1}(x_m) \end{bmatrix} \in \mathbb{R}^{m \times n}.$$

*In addition, Equation (3.7) can be rewritten as* $\mathbf{w} = \mathrm{pinv}(\Psi)\gamma$, *with* $\mathrm{pinv}(\Psi)$ *denoting the pseudoinverse of input information matrix* $\Psi$, *equaling* $(\Psi^{\mathrm{T}}\Psi)^{-1}\Psi^{\mathrm{T}}$ *here.*

### 3.3.2 Structure automatic determination

Based on the aforementioned WDD subalgorithm, a WASD algorithm could be developed further, which determines rapidly the optimal number of hidden-layer neurons for the constructed Laguerre-polynomial neuronet. The WASD algorithm could be designed and stated as following steps.

*Step 1:* Obtain training data-set $\{(x_i, \gamma_i)|_{i=1}^{m}\}$, with $x_i$ and $\gamma_i$ corresponding to the $i$th input- and output-values of target function $f(x)$, respectively. Note that $\gamma_i$ is also termed as expected, desired or target output.

*Step 2:* Construct Laguerre-polynomial neuronet. Initialize the number of hidden-layer neurons to be $n = 1$ and limit the maximal number of hidden-layer neurons to be $n_{\max}$ (e.g., 1000). Specify the target precision in the sense of BPE as $e_{\mathrm{tar}}$ (e.g., $10^{-5}$).

*Step 3:* If $n > n_{\max}$, then terminate the algorithm with a notice about the inability failure. Otherwise, compute the weights $\mathbf{w}$ by using Equation (3.7) and calculate the actual training BPE [defined by Equation (3.6)] at the present stage (i.e., with $n$ hidden-layer neurons).

*Step 4:* If the actual training BPE is greater than target BPE, i.e., $e > e_{\mathrm{tar}}$, then update $n = n + 1$ and go back to *Step 3* to continue this algorithm. Otherwise, terminate the algorithm by supplying the smallest number $n$ of hidden-layer neurons, the corresponding weights $\mathbf{w}$ and the actual training BPE.

In the above WASD algorithm, the WDD subalgorithm is applied to computing the weights of Laguerre-polynomial neuronet. Therefore, the optimal number of hidden-layer neurons can be decided rapidly and deterministically for Laguerre-polynomial neuronet. In the ensuing section, we would like to present numerical results which substantiate the efficacy and superior performance of the presented WASD algorithm for Laguerre-polynomial neuronet.

**TABLE 3.1:** Numerical results of Laguerre-polynomial neuronet with WASD algorithm.

| Target precision | $e_{tra}$ | $n_{opt}$ | $t_{run}$ (s) | $e_{tes}$ |
|---|---|---|---|---|
| $10^{-4}$ | $3.519 \times 10^5$ | 4 | 0.01326 | $3.361 \times 10^{-5}$ |
| $10^{-5}$ | $7.463 \times 10^7$ | 5 | 0.01337 | $6.986 \times 10^{-7}$ |
| $10^{-6}$ | $7.463 \times 10^7$ | 5 | 0.01339 | $6.986 \times 10^{-7}$ |
| $10^{-7}$ | $5.109 \times 10^8$ | 6 | 0.01379 | $4.722 \times 10^{-8}$ |
| $10^{-8}$ | $6.321 \times 10^9$ | 7 | 0.01425 | $5.828 \times 10^{-9}$ |

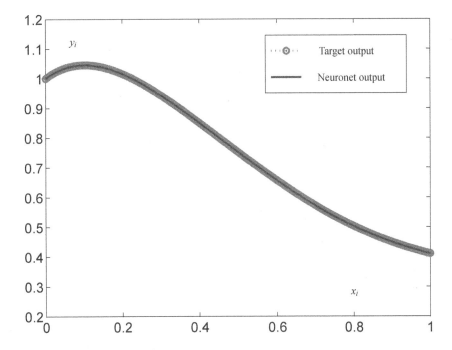

**FIGURE 3.2**: Training result of Laguerre-polynomial neuronet with WASD algorithm under target precision being $10^{-8}$.

## 3.4  Numerical Studies

For illustrative purposes, we choose the following target function as example:

$$f(x) = \frac{\cos^4 x}{(x+1)} + \frac{(x-1)}{(2x+1)} + \exp(-x).$$

Assume that we have the training data-set $\{(x_i, \gamma_i), i = 1, 2, \cdots, 201\}$ by sampling uniformly over interval $[0, 1]$ with step-size $x_{i+1} - x_i = 0.005$. Then, the constructed Laguerre-polynomial neuronet is simulated and compared. The detailed results are shown in Table 3.1 together with Figs. 3.2 and 3.3.

From Table 3.1, it is evident that, in the sense of some prescribed precision, the optimal (or, say, smallest) number of hidden-layer neurons can be determined immediately for Laguerre-polynomial

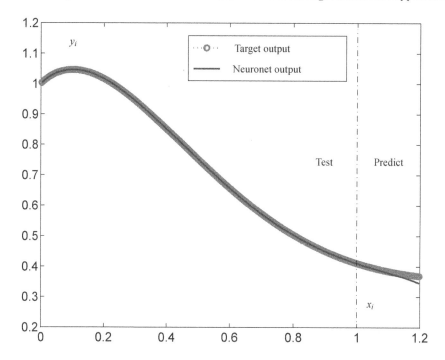

**FIGURE 3.3**: Testing and prediction results of Laguerre-polynomial neuronet with WASD algorithm under target precision being $10^{-8}$.

neuronet by using the WASD algorithm. To count the average run time, we have conducted the simulation for 1000 times per target precision. As can be seen from the fourth column of the table, it takes only 0.01425 second (run time $t_{run}$) to obtain the optimal number $n_{opt}$ of hidden-layer neurons even when the target precision is $10^{-8}$. Moreover, the training BPE $e_{tra}$ is only $6.321 \times 10^{-9}$, which reveals the excellent approximation ability of the constructed Laguerre-polynomial neuronet. This point is shown and substantiated further in Fig. 3.2. It is worth pointing out that, as for the fifth column of Table 3.1 about the testing BPE $e_{tes}$, we have selected totally $200 \times 5 = 1000$ untrained points $(x_i, \gamma_i)$ to test Laguerre-polynomial neuronet. The small (and tiny) testing errors show that this Laguerre-polynomial neuronet possesses a very good generalization ability. Besides, we could apply the trained Laguerre-polynomial neuronet for predictive purposes, e.g., over the untrained interval $[1, 1.2]$. The result is shown in Fig. 3.3, where the interval $[0, 1]$ corresponds to the testing part about the untrained points as mentioned in the preceding paragraph and the fifth column of Table 3.1. From the figure, we can see that Laguerre-polynomial neuronet could have a relatively good prediction ability over the extending neighborhood of training interval.

## 3.5    Chapter Summary

To remedy the weaknesses of conventional BP neuronets and their algorithms, a Laguerre-polynomial neuronet has been constructed based on the polynomial curve-fitting theory in this chapter. Starting from BP-type weights-updating formulas, we have derived and presented a WDD subalgorithm for calculating the optimal weights directly (or to say, just in one step). Moreover, based on the WDD subalgorithm, we have also presented a WASD algorithm to decide the optimal number of hidden-layer neurons efficiently and effectively. The longstanding difficulty of neuronet structure design might have thus been alleviated (and possibly removed) by the WASD algorithm. Moreover, numerical results have substantiated the efficacy of the constructed Laguerre-polynomial neuronet with the WASD algorithm.

# Part II

# Two-Input-Single-Output Neuronet

# Chapter 4

## *Two-Input Legendre-Polynomial WASD Neuronet*

In order to remedy the weaknesses of conventional back-propagation (BP) neuronets, a two-input Legendre-polynomial neuronet based on the theory of the multivariate function approximation is constructed and investigated in this chapter. In addition, based on the weights-direct-determination (WDD) subalgorithm, two weights-and-structure-determination (WASD) algorithms with different growing speeds are built up to determine the optimal weights and structure of the two-input Legendre-polynomial neuronet. Numerical studies further verify the efficacy of the two-input Legendre-polynomial neuronet equipped with the two aforementioned WASD algorithms.

## 4.1 Introduction

Recently, due to the remarkable features such as parallelism, distributed storage and adaptive self-learning capability, artificial neuronets (AN) have been applied widely to many science and engineering fields including control system design [51, 52], signal processing [2, 53], robot inverse kinematics [54] and pattern recognition [9, 55]. Besides, the back-propagation (BP) neuronet proposed by Rumelhart and McClelland in 1986 [56] is one of the most important models [57]. However, there exist intrinsic weaknesses in BP-type neuronets, such as relatively slow convergence, local-minima existence and uncertainties about the optimal number of hidden-layer neurons [21, 51].

To remedy such weaknesses of BP-type neuronets, it would be much better to use linearly independent or orthogonal activation functions (e.g., Legendre orthogonal polynomials used in this chapter) than to make some algorithmic improvements in the BP-training procedure. This can be concluded from the authors' successful experiences [51, 58, 59]. Note that previous works [58, 59] mainly focus on single-input-single-output (SISO) neuronets which may not meet directly the actual need that most practical systems have two inputs [60]. It is thus worth further investigating two-input neuronets. Based on the theory of the multivariate function approximation [61, 62], a two-input Legendre-polynomial neuronet is constructed and investigated in this chapter.

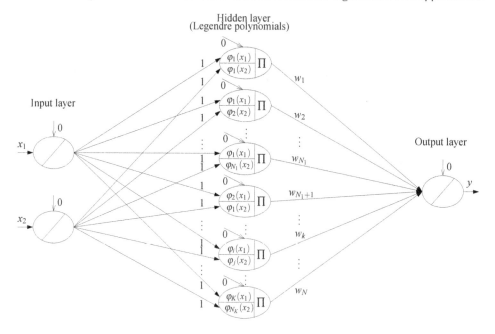

**FIGURE 4.1**: Model structure of two-input Legendre-polynomial neuronet.

Generally speaking, the weights of a neuronet between hidden-layer neurons and output-layer neurons can be obtained by either the conventional BP algorithm or the pseudoinverse-based WDD subalgorithm [58, 59]. It is worth pointing out that the latter can obtain the weights directly (i.e., just in one step), which avoids the lengthy and oscillating BP iterative-training process and has been proved to be very effective and efficient [28, 58]. Thus, the WDD subalgorithm is exploited to obtain the weights of the constructed two-input Legendre-polynomial neuronet. From previous works [28, 59], we know that the number of the hidden-layer neurons brings about a great influence on the performance of the neuronet. That is, fewer hidden-layer neurons might not achieve the desired learning performance, while too many neurons would cause not only structural and computational complexities, but also over-fitting phenomena on the input-output relationship [28]. Therefore, in this chapter, to obtain the optimal number of hidden-layer neurons (as well as the optimal weights) of the constructed two-input Legendre-polynomial neuronet, two WASD algorithms of growing type are designed on the basis of the WDD subalgorithm. Numerical results further substantiate the efficacy of the two-input Legendre-polynomial neuronet equipped with either of such two WASD algorithms.

---

## 4.2    Theoretical Basis

Before constructing the two-input Legendre-polynomial neuronet, the related theoretical basis is presented as follows [51, 63].

**Definition 5**  For the variable $x \in [-1, 1]$, the $(i+2)$th Legendre orthogonal polynomial can be defined as

$$\varphi_{i+2}(x) = \frac{2i+1}{i+1} x \varphi_{i+1}(x) - \frac{i}{i+1} \varphi_i(x), \text{ with } \varphi_1(x) = 1 \text{ and } \varphi_2(x) = x,$$

where $\varphi_i(x)$ also denotes the Legendre orthogonal polynomial of degree $i$, with $i = 1,2,3,\cdots$.

Then, based on the theory of the multivariate function approximation [61, 62], we have the following proposition.

**Proposition 1** *For two continuous independent variables $x_1$ and $x_2$, let $f(x_1,x_2)$ denote a given continuous function. Then, there exist polynomials $f_i(x_1)$ and $f_j(x_2)$ (with $i = 1,2,3,\cdots$ and $j = 1,2,3,\cdots$) to formulate $f(x_1,x_2)$, i.e.,*

$$f(x_1,x_2) = \sum_{i=1}^{\infty}\sum_{j=1}^{\infty} f_i(x_1)f_j(x_2). \tag{4.1}$$

According to the above theoretical basis, the weighted Legendre orthogonal polynomials can be used to formulate $f(x_1,x_2)$. That is, let $f_i(x_1) = w_i\varphi_i(x_1)$ and $f_j(x_2) = w_j\varphi_j(x_2)$, where $w_i$ and $w_j$ denote the weights for $\varphi_i$ and $\varphi_j$, respectively. Then (4.1) can be reformulated as

$$f(x_1,x_2) = \sum_{i=1}^{\infty}\sum_{j=1}^{\infty} w_i\varphi_i(x_1)w_j\varphi_j(x_2) = \sum_{i=1}^{\infty}\sum_{j=1}^{\infty} w_{ij}\varphi_i(x_1)\varphi_j(x_2),$$

where $w_{ij} = w_iw_j$ (with $i = 1,2,3,\cdots$ and $j = 1,2,3,\cdots$) denotes the weight for $\varphi_i(x_1)\varphi_j(x_2)$. Thus, the target function $f(x_1,x_2)$ can be approximated via a finite number of basis functions $\{\varphi_i(x_1)\varphi_j(x_2)\}$ with the corresponding optimal weights $\{w_{ij}\}$, i.e.,

$$f(x_1,x_2) \approx \sum_{i=1}^{K}\sum_{j=1}^{N_i} w_{ij}\varphi_i(x_1)\varphi_j(x_2).$$

Note that the basis functions $\{\varphi_i(x_1)\varphi_j(x_2)\}$ can be sequenced in different orders [64]. This implies that $N_i$ (i.e., the maximum of $j$ corresponding to a specific value of $i$) can be different for different $i$, with $i = 1,2,3,\cdots,K$. Therefore, the target function $f(x_1,x_2)$ can be approximated via the following form:

$$f(x_1,x_2) \approx \sum_{i=1}^{K}\varphi_i(x_1)\left(\sum_{j=1}^{N_i} w_{ij}\varphi_j(x_2)\right) = \sum_{k=1}^{N} w_k\psi_k(x_1,x_2),$$

where $N = \sum_{i=1}^{K} N_i$ denotes the total number of basis functions used to approximate $f(x_1,x_2)$. In addition, $\{w_k = w_{ij}$, with $k = 1,2,3,\cdots,N\}$ denotes the set of weights for $\{\psi_k(x_1,x_2)\}$, and $\psi_k(x_1,x_2) = \psi_k([x_1,x_2]^{\mathrm{T}}) = \varphi_i(x_1)\varphi_j(x_2)$ with superscript $^{\mathrm{T}}$ denoting transpose. Besides, with $k = \sum_{d=1}^{i} N_d - N_i + j$, we detail $\{\psi_k(x_1,x_2)\}$ below:

$$\begin{cases} \psi_1(x_1,x_2) = \varphi_1(x_1)\varphi_1(x_2), \\ \psi_2(x_1,x_2) = \varphi_1(x_1)\varphi_2(x_2), \\ \quad\vdots \\ \psi_{N_1}(x_1,x_2) = \varphi_1(x_1)\varphi_{N_1}(x_2), \\ \psi_{N_1+1}(x_1,x_2) = \varphi_2(x_1)\varphi_1(x_2), \\ \quad\vdots \\ \psi_{N_1+N_2}(x_1,x_2) = \varphi_2(x_1)\varphi_{N_2}(x_2), \\ \quad\vdots \\ \psi_k(x_1,x_2) = \varphi_i(x_1)\varphi_j(x_2), \\ \quad\vdots \\ \psi_N(x_1,x_2) = \varphi_K(x_1)\varphi_{N_K}(x_2). \end{cases} \tag{4.2}$$

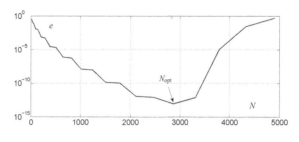

(a) For target function (4.5)

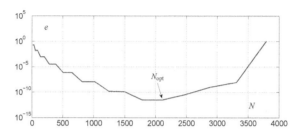

(b) For target function (4.6)

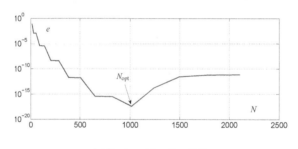

(c) For target function (4.7)

**FIGURE 4.2**: Relationship between MSE $e$ and number $N$ of hidden-layer neurons with Limitation I for target functions (4.5) through (4.7), respectively.

As mentioned above, the basis functions used to approximate the target function $f(x_1, x_2)$ can be generated in a given order. For better understanding, two typical orders are presented, which can be expressed as the following limitations via a given positive integer $q$ larger than 1 (i.e., $q > 1$):

• Limitation I. $K = q$, and $N_i = q$ with $i = 1, 2, \cdots, K$;

• Limitation II. $K = q - 1$, and $N_i = q - i$ with $i = 1, 2, 3, \cdots, K$.

Note that the total number of basis functions $N$ can be determined by $N = q^2$ corresponding to Limitation I or $N = q(q-1)/2$ corresponding to Limitation II. It is worth noting that these two limitations are further investigated in the ensuing sections.

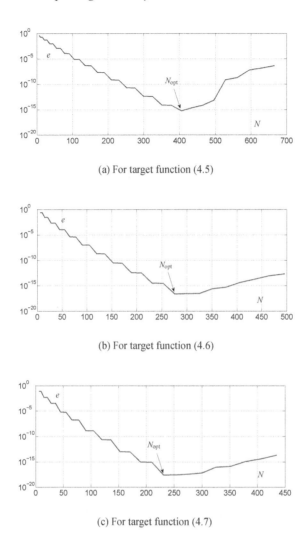

(a) For target function (4.5)

(b) For target function (4.6)

(c) For target function (4.7)

**FIGURE 4.3**: Relationship between MSE $e$ and number $N$ of hidden-layer neurons with Limitation II for target functions (4.5) through (4.7), respectively.

## 4.3 Neuronet Model and WASD Algorithms

According to the above theoretical basis and analysis, a two-input Legendre-polynomial neuronet is constructed in this section. Then, based on the WDD subalgorithm, two WASD algorithms are presented to further improve the performance of the two-input Legendre-polynomial neuronet.

### 4.3.1 Two-input Legendre-polynomial neuronet model

The model of the two-input Legendre-polynomial neuronet presented in this chapter is illustrated in Fig. 4.1. As seen from the figure, the two-input Legendre-polynomial neuronet consists of three layers. The neurons of the input layer and output layer are activated by the same kind of linear

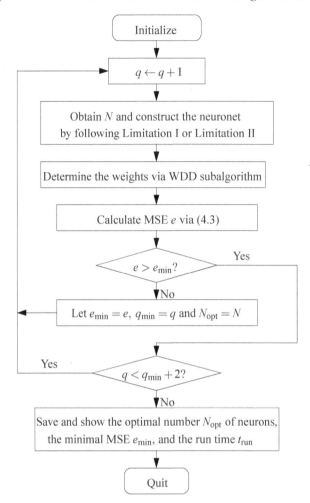

**FIGURE 4.4**: Flowchart of two WASD algorithms with different limitations for two-input Legendre-polynomial neuronet.

functions. Besides, the hidden layer has $N$ neurons (with $N = \sum_{i=1}^{K} N_i$), which are activated by a group of basis functions depicted in (4.2). In addition, $\{w_k\}$ (with $k = 1, 2, \cdots, N$) denotes the set of weights between the hidden-layer and output-layer neurons. Moreover, to simplify the model and computational complexities, the weights between the input-layer and hidden-layer neurons are all 1, and all neuronal thresholds are 0.

### 4.3.2    Two WASD algorithms

For the model of the two-input Legendre-polynomial neuronet shown in Fig. 4.1, the optimal weights between hidden-layer and output-layer neurons can be obtained directly (i.e., just in one step) via the so-called WDD subalgorithm [21] with the given training data. It is detailed as follows.

Let us take $\{(\mathbf{x}_m, \gamma_m)|_{m=1}^{M}\}$ as the training data-set, where $\mathbf{x}_m \in \mathbb{R}^2$ denotes the $m$th input vector $[x_{1m}, x_{2m}]^{\mathrm{T}}$, $\gamma_m$ denotes the desired output corresponding to $\mathbf{x}_m$, and $M$ denotes the total number of the training data-set. Then, the mean square error (MSE) is defined as

$$e = \frac{1}{M} \sum_{m=1}^{M} \left( \gamma_m - \sum_{k=1}^{N} w_k \psi_k(\mathbf{x}_m) \right)^2. \tag{4.3}$$

Thus, we have the following important theoretical result about the WDD subalgorithm [21].

For the two-input Legendre-polynomial neuronet with a known $N$, the optimal linking weights from hidden-layer to output-layer neurons can be obtained directly as

$$\mathbf{w} = (\Psi^{\mathrm{T}} \Psi)^{-1} \Psi^{\mathrm{T}} \gamma, \tag{4.4}$$

where the vector of weights $\mathbf{w}$, the vector of desired outputs $\gamma$, and the input-activation matrix $\Psi$ are defined, respectively, as

$$\mathbf{w} = \begin{bmatrix} w_1 \\ w_2 \\ \vdots \\ w_N \end{bmatrix} \in \mathbb{R}^N, \ \gamma = \begin{bmatrix} \gamma_1 \\ \gamma_2 \\ \vdots \\ \gamma_M \end{bmatrix} \in \mathbb{R}^M, \ \Psi = \begin{bmatrix} \psi_1(\mathbf{x}_1) & \psi_2(\mathbf{x}_1) & \dots & \psi_N(\mathbf{x}_1) \\ \psi_1(\mathbf{x}_2) & \psi_2(\mathbf{x}_2) & \dots & \psi_N(\mathbf{x}_2) \\ \vdots & \vdots & \ddots & \vdots \\ \psi_1(\mathbf{x}_M) & \psi_2(\mathbf{x}_M) & \dots & \psi_N(\mathbf{x}_M) \end{bmatrix} \in \mathbb{R}^{M \times N}.$$

As $(\Psi^{\mathrm{T}} \Psi)^{-1} \Psi^{\mathrm{T}}$ is the pseudoinverse of $\Psi$, (4.4) can be rewritten as $\mathbf{w} = \mathrm{pinv}(\Psi)\gamma$, where $\mathrm{pinv}(\Psi)$ denotes the pseudoinverse of $\Psi$ and can be evaluated via MATLAB routine "pinv" [51].

In light of the previous works [28,51,59], the number of hidden-layer neurons can affect greatly the performance of the neuronet. Thus, to obtain the optimal number of hidden-layer neurons (as well as the final optimal weights) of the two-input Legendre-polynomial neuronet, two WASD algorithms of growing type are comparatively developed and investigated in this subsection.

Before presenting such WASD algorithms, a variety of target functions have been tested to investigate the relationship between the MSE (4.3) and the number of hidden-layer neurons, such as the following three target functions:

$$f(x_1, x_2) = 10 \sin(x_1) \exp\left(-(2x_1)^2 - (2x_2)^2\right), \tag{4.5}$$

$$f(x_1, x_2) = 4 \exp\left(-x_1^2 - (2x_2)^2\right) + 10, \tag{4.6}$$

$$f(x_1, x_2) = \sin(\pi x_1 x_2) + 20. \tag{4.7}$$

Figs. 4.2 and 4.3 show the so-called "U/V" plots of the above three target functions (4.5) through (4.7) with Limitation I and Limitation II, respectively, which indicate the relationship between the MSE (i.e., $e$ with the data number $M = 1156$) and the number (i.e., $N$) of hidden-layer neurons of the two-input Legendre-polynomial neuronet. As seen from Figs. 4.2 and 4.3, there is a minimal of MSE corresponding to the optimal number $N_{\mathrm{opt}}$ of of hidden-layer neurons for each target function. Note that such a phenomenon (i.e., the existence of the minimal of $e$) appears for many other target functions (with related results omitted here due to similarity). Therefore, two WASD algorithms with different growing speeds are finally developed to determine the optimal number of hidden-layer neurons (or to say, the optimal model-structure) of the two-input Legendre-polynomial neuronet by searching the minimal MSE. For better understanding, the flowchart of the WASD algorithms is shown in Fig. 4.4. Note that the only difference between the two WASD algorithms developed in this chapter is the limitation exploited in the algorithms. That is, the limitation of WASD algorithms can be chosen as Limitation I or Limitation II, which will lead to different growing speeds of the number of hidden-layer neurons. Besides, the procedure is detailed as below.

a) The procedure has the following variables:

• $e$ denotes the MSE of the current neuronet;

• $e_{\min}$ denotes the minimal MSE found;

**TABLE 4.1:**    Approximation and testing results of two-input Legendre-polynomial neuronet with Limitation I for target functions (4.5) through (4.7).

| Target function | $N_{\text{opt}}$ | $e_{\text{app}}$ | $e_{\text{tes}}$ | $t_{\text{run}}$ (s) |
|---|---|---|---|---|
| Target function (4.5) | 2869 | $9.240 \times 10^{-14}$ | $6.606 \times 10^{-13}$ | 326.935 |
| Target function (4.6) | 2108 | $2.934 \times 10^{-12}$ | $6.726 \times 10^{-12}$ | 211.585 |
| Target function (4.7) | 1014 | $4.194 \times 10^{-18}$ | $2.403 \times 10^{-18}$ | 73.346 |

**TABLE 4.2:**    Approximation and testing results of two-input Legendre-polynomial neuronet with Limitation II for target functions (4.5) through (4.7).

| Target function | $N_{\text{opt}}$ | $e_{\text{app}}$ | $e_{\text{tes}}$ | $t_{\text{run}}$ (s) |
|---|---|---|---|---|
| Target function (4.5) | 406 | $5.937 \times 10^{-16}$ | $9.928 \times 10^{-16}$ | 13.731 |
| Target function (4.6) | 276 | $2.454 \times 10^{-17}$ | $8.715 \times 10^{-16}$ | 5.309 |
| Target function (4.7) | 231 | $2.645 \times 10^{-18}$ | $2.926 \times 10^{-18}$ | 3.570 |

- $q$ denotes the current positive integer used to construct the neuronet with Limitation I or Limitation II;
- $q_{\text{min}}$ denotes the positive integer corresponding to $e_{\text{min}}$;
- $N$ denotes the current number of hidden-layer neurons;
- $N_{\text{opt}}$ denotes the optimal number of hidden-layer neurons.

b) The procedure has the following steps:

*Step 1:* Obtain the set of training data pairs $\{(\mathbf{x}_m, \gamma_m)|_{m=1}^M\}$. Initialize the structure of the two-input Legendre-polynomial neuronet with $q = 2$, and set $q_{\text{min}} = 2$. Besides, $e_{\text{min}}$ is set initially large enough (e.g., 10).

*Step 2:* Let $q \leftarrow q + 1$. If Limitation I is chosen for the algorithm, then $N = q^2$; otherwise (if Limitation II is chosen for the algorithm), $N = q(q-1)/2$. Then construct the two-input Legendre-polynomial neuronet.

*Step 3:* Calculate the weights between hidden-layer and output-layer neurons via WDD (4.4) and the MSE $e$ via (4.3).

*Step 4:* If $e > e_{\text{min}}$, proceed to *Step 5*; otherwise, let $e_{\text{min}} = e$, $q_{\text{min}} = q$ and $N_{\text{opt}} = N$, and proceed to *Step 2*.

*Step 5:* If $q < q_{\text{min}} + 2$, then proceed to *Step 2*; otherwise, proceed to *Step 6*.

*Step 6:* Output and save the optimal number of hidden-layer neurons $N_{\text{opt}}$, the minimal MSE $e_{\text{min}}$ and the run time $t_{\text{run}}$. Then terminate the procedure.

## 4.4    Numerical Studies

In this section, numerical studies are performed to verify the efficacy of the two-input Legendre-polynomial neuronet equipped with one of the aforementioned two WASD algorithms. Note that, due to the similarity of results, the numerical results are shown only for the aforementioned target functions (4.5) through (4.7).

Tables 4.1 and 4.2 show the numerical-study results of the two-input Legendre-polynomial neuronet equipped with the WASD algorithms. For each target function, we sample uniformly over region $[-1,1]^2$ with gap size 0.06 to generate the training data-set $\{(\mathbf{x}_m, \gamma_m)|_{m=1}^{1156}\}$

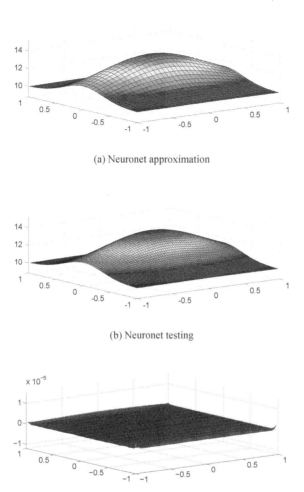

(a) Neuronet approximation

(b) Neuronet testing

(c) Relative error of testing

**FIGURE 4.5**: Approximation and testing results of two-input Legendre-polynomial neuronet with Limitation I for target function (4.6).

(i.e., $M = 1156$), which is used for approximation (or, say, learning). In addition, for testing, the data-set $\{(\mathbf{x}_m, \gamma_m)|_{m=1}^{4761}\}$ is generated by sampling uniformly over region $[-1, 1]^2$ with gap size 0.029. As shown in Tables 4.1 and 4.2, the optimal number $N_{\text{opt}}$ of hidden-layer neurons (corresponding to the minimal MSE $e_{\min}$) for each target function is determined successfully via the WASD algorithms. Besides, $e_{\text{app}}$ and $e_{\text{tes}}$ shown in Tables 4.1 and 4.2 denote the approximation MSE and testing MSE, respectively. From Tables 4.1 and 4.2, we see that the two-input Legendre-polynomial neuronet equipped with either of the two algorithms can approximate accurately the target functions with tiny $e_{\text{app}}$ (i.e., of order $10^{-12} \sim 10^{-18}$). Moreover, as shown in Tables 4.1 and 4.2, the two-input Legendre-polynomial neuronet can achieve superior performance on testing. These results substantiate the abilities of approximation and generalization of the two-input Legendre-polynomial neuronet. Note that, for the above three target functions (4.5) through (4.7), the WASD algorithm with Limitation II takes little time to determine the corresponding optimal numbers of hidden-layer neurons, which shows the efficacy. For better understanding, Figs. 4.5 and 4.6 illustrate the numerical results of the two-input Legendre-polynomial neuronet working on target function (4.6) with the

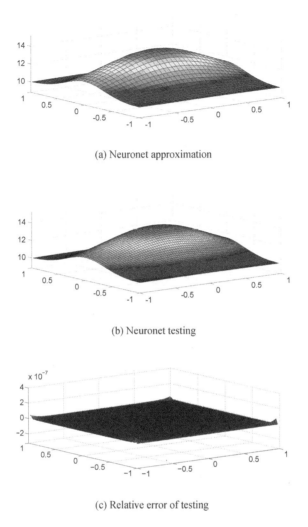

(a) Neuronet approximation

(b) Neuronet testing

(c) Relative error of testing

**FIGURE 4.6**: Approximation and testing results of two-input Legendre-polynomial neuronet with Limitation II for target function (4.6).

numerical results on (4.5) and (4.7) omitted due to the similarity, which intuitively and visually show the well performance of the two-input Legendre-polynomial neuronet equipped with either of the two WASD algorithms in terms of approximation (i.e., learning) and testing (i.e., generalization).

For further investigation, we sample the target function (4.7) over region $[-0.9, 0.9]^2$ with gap size 0.06 to generate the training data-set $\{(\mathbf{x}_m, \gamma_m)|_{m=1}^{961}\}$ (i.e., $M = 961$). Based on such a data-set, the two-input Legendre-polynomial neuronet is used to predict the target function (4.7) over region $\{[-1, 1]^2 \sim [-0.9, 0.9]^2\}$, and the corresponding numerical results are illustrated in Figs. 4.7 and 4.8. As seen from the Figs. 4.7 and 4.8, the two-input Legendre-polynomial neuronet equipped with either of the two WASD algorithms can achieve excellent performance in terms of prediction and testing, which substantiates the excellent abilities of the two-input Legendre-polynomial neuronet.

In summary, we can conclude from Tables 4.1 and 4.2 as well as Figs. 4.5 through 4.8 that, with superior approximation, generalization and prediction performance, less run time, and simpler

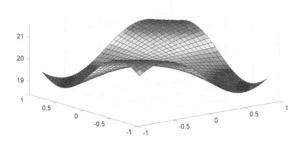

(a) Neuronet approximation

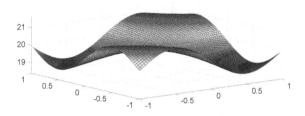

(b) Neuronet prediction and testing

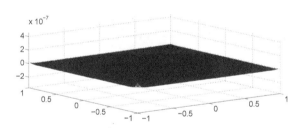

(c) Relative error of prediction and testing

**FIGURE 4.7**: Approximation, prediction and testing results of two-input Legendre-polynomial neuronet with Limitation I for target function (4.7).

structure of the two-input Legendre-polynomial neuronet, the WASD algorithm with Limitation II is much better than the one with Limitation I (though both algorithms work excellently).

## 4.5  Chapter Summary

In this chapter, a two-input Legendre-polynomial neuronet has been presented and investigated, which has solidly laid a basis for further research on multi-input neuronets. In addition, two WASD algorithms of growing type have been developed to determine the optimal number of hidden-layer

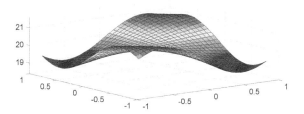

(a) Neuronet approximation

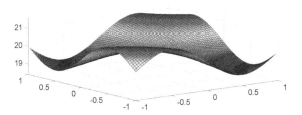

(b) Neuronet prediction and testing

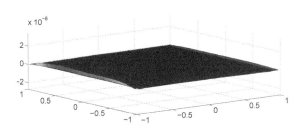

(c) Relative error of prediction and testing

**FIGURE 4.8**: Approximation, prediction and testing results of two-input Legendre-polynomial neuronet with Limitation II for target function (4.7).

neurons and simultaneously obtain the weights between the hidden-layer and output-layer neurons directly. Numerical-study results have further substantiated the efficacy of the two-input Legendre-polynomial neuronet equipped with the two WASD algorithms on approximation, generalization and prediction.

# Chapter 5

## *Two-Input Chebyshev-Polynomial-of-Class-1 WASD Neuronet*

A two-input feed-forward neuronet using Chebyshev orthogonal polynomials (or, say, Chebyshev polynomials) of Class 1 is constructed and investigated in this chapter. In addition, with the weights-direct-determination (WDD) subalgorithm exploited to obtain the optimal weights from hidden layer to output layer directly (i.e., just in one step), an algorithm called weights-and-structure-determination (WASD) algorithm is further presented to determine the optimal number of hidden-layer neurons of two-input Chebyshev-polynomial-of-Class-1 neuronet. Such a WASD algorithm includes a procedure of pruning the presented neuronet (after the net grows up). Numerical studies further substantiate the efficacy of Chebyshev-polynomial-of-Class-1 neuronet equipped with the so-called WASD algorithm.

---

## 5.1  Introduction

Recently, the back-propagation (BP) neuronet proposed firstly by Rumelhart and McClelland in 1986 [56] has become one of the most widely applied neuronet models [21, 65]. However, BP-type neuronets have some inherent weaknesses, e.g., slow convergence and uncertainties about the optimal number of hidden-layer neurons [65]. Different from algorithmic improvements about the BP iterative-training procedure, we have focused on activation-function and neuronet-structure improvement to achieve better efficacy, which has been substantiated in the previous works [65, 66]. Note that the neuronets investigated in [66] are the single-input-single-output (SISO) neuronets. In view of the fact that most practical systems have multiple inputs (e.g., two inputs) [67], it is worth further investigating the neuronet with multiple inputs.

Unlike the SISO model structure presented in previous chapters, based on the theories of probability [68], polynomial interpolation and approximation [21, 69], a new type of two-input feed-forward neuronet using Chebyshev polynomials of Class 1 is constructed and investigated in this chapter. In addition, with the purpose of avoiding lengthy BP iterative-training procedure and improving the efficacy of Chebyshev-polynomial-of-Class-1 neuronet, a WASD algorithm, which is based on the WDD subalgorithm [66], is designed and detailed. According to [66], the performance of neuronets relates closely to the number of hidden-layer neurons, and thus it is specially important to determine the optimal number of hidden-layer neurons. In light of the above analysis, the WASD algorithm presented in this chapter is elegantly designed to determine the optimal number of hidden-layer neurons of Chebyshev-polynomial-of-Class-1 neuronet such that superior performances on approximation, testing and prediction are achieved. Numerical studies further substantiate the efficacy of Chebyshev-polynomial-of-Class-1 neuronet equipped with the WASD algorithm.

## 5.2   Theoretical Basis

In this section, the theoretical basis is presented for constructing Chebyshev-polynomial-of-Class-1 neuronet. Note that the theoretical basis presented in this chapter is mainly based on the probability theory [68]. The theoretical analysis based on the polynomial interpolation and approximation theory can also be found in other chapters. To lay a basis for further discussion, a proposition is given firstly as follows [68].

**Proposition 2** *For two continuous independent variables $x_1$ and $x_2$, the joint probability density function $f(x_1,x_2)$ is formulated as*

$$f(x_1,x_2) = f_1(x_1)f_2(x_2),$$

*where $f_1(x_1)$ denotes the marginal probability density function on $x_1$ and $f_2(x_2)$ denotes the marginal probability density function on $x_2$.*

Note that the joint probability density function and the marginal probability density functions in Proposition 2 can be much generalized as the inspiring basis of this Chebyshev-polynomial-of-Class-1 neuronet research, which differ from the traditional/standard definitions appearing in the probability theory [68]. That is, (1) those functions can be positive, zero, negative or even indefinite; and (2) integral values of those functions can be positive, zero, negative or even indefinite as well.

**Lemma 9** *For the variable $x \in [-1,1]$, Chebyshev polynomials of Class 1 can be defined as below [66]:*

$$\varphi_{i+2}(x) = 2x\varphi_{i+1}(x) - \varphi_i(x), \text{with } \varphi_0(x) = 1 \text{ and } \varphi_1(x) = x,$$

*where $\varphi_i(x)$ denotes the Chebyshev polynomial of Class 1 of degree $i$ (with $i = 0,1,2,\cdots$).*

Note that Chebyshev polynomials of Class 1 differ much from Chebyshev polynomials of Class 2, since Chebyshev polynomial of Class 1 of degree 1 equals $x$ while Chebyshev polynomial of Class 2 of degree 1 equals $2x$, which leads to a huge discrepancy between Chebyshev polynomial of Class 1 and Chebyshev polynomial of Class 2 of degree $i$ with $i = 2,3,4,\cdots$. In light of the theories of polynomial interpolation and approximation [21, 69], an unknown target function $f(x)$ can be approximated by its least-square approximation function as

$$f(x) \approx \sum_{i=0}^{N-1} w_i\varphi_i(x), \tag{5.1}$$

where $w_i$ is the weight for $\varphi_i(x)$ and $N$ is the total number of Chebyshev polynomials of Class 1 used to approximate the target function. Based on Proposition 2 and Lemma 9, we have the following proposition on the approximation of target functions with two continuous independent variables.

**Proposition 3** *For a target function $f(x_1, x_2)$ with two continuous independent variables $x_1$ and $x_2$, it can be best estimated by approximating simultaneously the functions $f_1(x_1)$ and $f_2(x_2)$ via Chebyshev polynomials of Class 1.*

According to Proposition 3 and Equation (5.1), we have

$$f(x_1, x_2) = f_1(x_1) f_2(x_2) \approx \left( \sum_{i=0}^{N_1-1} w_i \varphi_i(x_1) \right) \left( \sum_{j=0}^{N_2-1} w_j \varphi_j(x_2) \right) = \sum_{i=0}^{N_1-1} \sum_{j=0}^{N_2-1} w_{ij} \varphi_i(x_1) \varphi_j(x_2).$$

Note that the resultant weight $w_{ij} = w_i w_j$ denotes the weight for $\varphi_i(x_1) \varphi_j(x_2)$. Thus, the unknown target function $f(x_1, x_2)$ can be best estimated by its least-square approximation function which is obtained via the optimal weights $\{w_{ij}\}$ corresponding to basis functions $\{\varphi_i(x_1) \varphi_j(x_2)\}$.

In light of the graded lexicographic order [65] and the above analysis, basis functions $\{\varphi_i(x_1) \varphi_j(x_2)\}$ with graded lexicographic order can be used to best estimate the target function $f(x_1, x_2)$. In detail, let $\tau$ be the total degree of $\varphi_i(x_1)$ and $\varphi_j(x_2)$, i.e., $\tau = i + j$. Then, a maximal value of $\tau$ defined as $\zeta$ is given to obtain the corresponding basis functions used to approximate the target function. In other words, $\tau$ is constrained by $\zeta$ (i.e., $\tau = 0, 1, \cdots, \zeta$). Thus, the least-square approximation function of $f(x_1, x_2)$ is reformulated as

$$f(x_1, x_2) \approx \sum_{k=1}^{N} w_k \psi_k(x_1, x_2),$$

where integer $N = N_1 N_2 = (\zeta + 1)(\zeta + 2)/2$ denotes the total number of basis functions. In addition, $w_k = w_{ij}$ denotes the weight for $\psi_k(x_1, x_2)$, and $\psi_k(x_1, x_2) = \psi_k([x_1, x_2]^\mathrm{T}) = \varphi_i(x_1) \varphi_j(x_2)$ with $k = (i + j)(i + j + 1)/2 + i + 1$. Besides,

$$\begin{cases} \psi_1(x_1, x_2) = \varphi_0(x_1) \varphi_0(x_2), \\ \psi_2(x_1, x_2) = \varphi_0(x_1) \varphi_1(x_2), \\ \psi_3(x_1, x_2) = \varphi_1(x_1) \varphi_0(x_2), \\ \quad \vdots \\ \psi_{\tau(\tau+1)/2+1}(x_1, x_2) = \varphi_0(x_1) \varphi_\tau(x_2), \\ \psi_{\tau(\tau+1)/2+2}(x_1, x_2) = \varphi_1(x_1) \varphi_{\tau-1}(x_2), \\ \quad \vdots \\ \psi_{\tau(\tau+1)/2+\tau+1}(x_1, x_2) = \varphi_\tau(x_1) \varphi_0(x_2), \\ \quad \vdots \\ \psi_N(x_1, x_2) = \varphi_\zeta(x_1) \varphi_0(x_2). \end{cases}$$

## 5.3 Neuronet Model and WASD Algorithm

In this section, the model of Chebyshev-polynomial-of-Class-1 neuronet is constructed, and then the WASD algorithm is developed to guarantee and improve the performance.

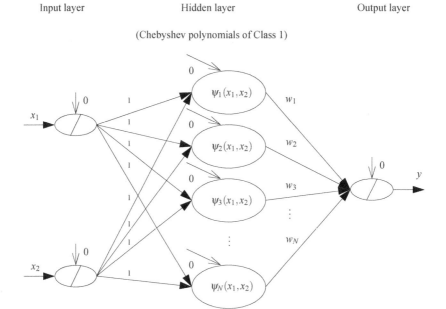

Input layer        Hidden layer        Output layer

(Chebyshev polynomials of Class 1)

**FIGURE 5.1**: Model structure of two-input Chebyshev-activation (specifically, Chebyshev-polynomial-of-Class-1) neuronet.

### 5.3.1    Two-input Chebyshev-polynomial-of-Class-1 neuronet model

On the above-presented theoretical basis, the model of Chebyshev-polynomial-of-Class-1 neuronet is constructed with its structure shown in Fig. 5.1. As seen from Fig. 5.1, the model of Chebyshev-polynomial-of-Class-1 neuronet adopts a conventional three-layer structure, including the input layer, the hidden layer and the output layer. Besides, the input layer includes two inputs $x_1$ and $x_2$, and the output layer includes single output $y$. In order to simplify the proposed model and computational complexity, the connecting weights between the input-layer and hidden-layer neurons are fixed to be 1. In addition, all neuronal thresholds are fixed to be 0.

### 5.3.2    WASD algorithm

To guarantee and improve the performance of Chebyshev-polynomial-of-Class-1 neuronet, the WASD algorithm is developed in this subsection, which obtains the optimal weights from the hidden layer to the output layer directly and determines the optimal number of hidden-layer neurons.

For unknown target function $f(x_1, x_2)$ with $x_1, x_2 \in [-1, 1]$, we have the data of sample pairs $\{(\mathbf{x}_m, \gamma_m), m = 1, 2, \cdots, M\}$ for training, where $M$ denotes the total number of the sample pairs, $\mathbf{x}_m$ denotes $[x_{1m}, x_{2m}]^{\mathrm{T}}$ and $\gamma_m$ denotes the $m$th desired output. Then, the half average square error (HASE) for Chebyshev-polynomial-of-Class-1 neuronet is defined as

$$\bar{e} = \frac{1}{2M} \sum_{m=1}^{M} \left( \gamma_m - \sum_{k=1}^{N} w_k \psi_k(\mathbf{x}_m) \right)^2. \tag{5.2}$$

Besides, the weights vector $\mathbf{w}$, the desired-output vector $\gamma$ and the input-activation matrix $\Psi$ are

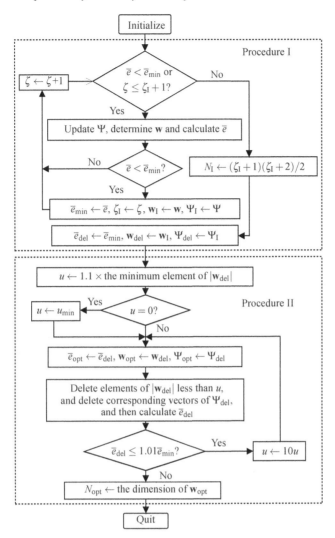

**FIGURE 5.2**: Flowchart of pruning-included WASD algorithm for Chebyshev-polynomial-of-Class-1 neuronet.

defined respectively as

$$\mathbf{w} = \begin{bmatrix} w_1 \\ w_2 \\ \vdots \\ w_N \end{bmatrix} \in \mathbb{R}^N, \ \gamma = \begin{bmatrix} \gamma_1 \\ \gamma_2 \\ \vdots \\ \gamma_M \end{bmatrix} \in \mathbb{R}^M, \Psi = \begin{bmatrix} \psi_1(\mathbf{x}_1) & \psi_2(\mathbf{x}_1) & \dots & \psi_N(\mathbf{x}_1) \\ \psi_1(\mathbf{x}_2) & \psi_2(\mathbf{x}_2) & \dots & \psi_N(\mathbf{x}_2) \\ \vdots & \vdots & \ddots & \vdots \\ \psi_1(\mathbf{x}_M) & \psi_2(\mathbf{x}_M) & \dots & \psi_N(\mathbf{x}_M) \end{bmatrix} \in \mathbb{R}^{M \times N}.$$

Thus, the optimal weights of Chebyshev-polynomial-of-Class-1 neuronet (for a known $N$) is obtained directly via the following WDD subalgorithm [66]:

$$\mathbf{w} = (\Psi^{\mathrm{T}}\Psi)^{-1}\Psi^{\mathrm{T}}\gamma. \tag{5.3}$$

Note that (5.3) can also be rewritten as $\mathbf{w} = \mathrm{pinv}(\Psi)\gamma$, where $\mathrm{pinv}(\Psi)$ denotes the pseudoinverse of $\Psi$ and can be evaluated via MATLAB routine "pinv" [70].

In light of the previous works [66], the performance of neuronets relates closely to the number of

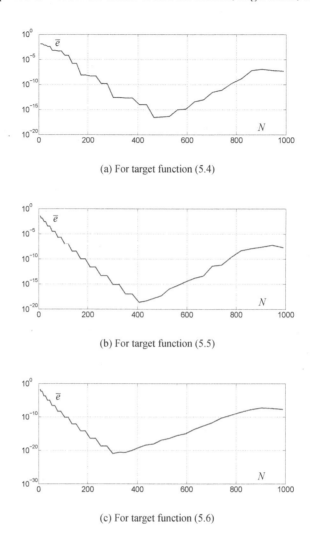

(a) For target function (5.4)

(b) For target function (5.5)

(c) For target function (5.6)

**FIGURE 5.3**: HASE of Chebyshev-polynomial-of-Class-1 neuronet versus its number of hidden-layer neurons for target functions (5.4) through (5.6), respectively.

hidden-layer neurons, which is also true in the case of Chebyshev-polynomial-of-Class-1 neuronet. Therefore, the main purpose of the WASD algorithm based on the above-presented WDD subalgorithm is to determine the optimal number of hidden-layer neurons of Chebyshev-polynomial-of-Class-1 neuronet. For better understanding, the flowchart of such a pruning-included WASD algorithm is shown in Fig. 5.2, which consists of two major procedures (i.e., Procedures I and II). It is worth pointing out that $u_{\min}$ shown in Procedure II of Fig. 5.2 equals $2^{-52}$ [70] and is used to avoid the situation of $u$ being zero. In addition, notations $\bar{e}_{\mathrm{del}}$, $\mathbf{w}_{\mathrm{I}}$, $\mathbf{w}_{\mathrm{del}}$, $\Psi_{\mathrm{I}}$ and $\Psi_{\mathrm{del}}$ are the procedure variables during Procedure I of the pruning-included WASD algorithm.

Actually before and after proposing the WASD flowchart, the relationship is fully investigated between the performance [i.e., the HASE (5.2)] of Chebyshev-polynomial-of-Class-1 neuronet and the number of hidden-layer neurons via a variety of target functions, such as the typical ones:

$$f(x_1, x_2) = \frac{x_2 \cos\left(\sqrt{100x_1^2 + 100x_2^2 + 1}\right)}{\exp(-2x_1^2 - 2x_2^2) + 2} + 20, \tag{5.4}$$

$$f(x_1, x_2) = 4x_1 \exp(-4x_1^2 - 4x_2^2) + x_2^2 + 20, \tag{5.5}$$

$$f(x_1, x_2) = \frac{x_2 \sin(\pi x_1 x_2)}{\exp(x_1^2)} + 20. \tag{5.6}$$

The corresponding numerical results are given in Figs. 5.3 through 5.6. Note that, in the numerical studies, the set of sample pairs $\{(x_m, \gamma_m), m = 1, 2, \cdots, 2116\}$ (i.e., $M = 2116$) is generated by sampling uniformly over region $[-0.9, 0.9]^2$ with gap size 0.04. As seen from Fig. 5.3 which illustrates the relationship between the HASE (i.e., $\bar{e}$) of the above three target functions and the number of hidden-layer neurons (i.e., $N$), all curves look like the character "U" or "V". That is, the so-called "U/V" plots. In view of similar characteristics of many other target functions, Procedure I of the WASD algorithm is thus designed to obtain the number of hidden-layer neurons of the grown Chebyshev-polynomial-of-Class-1 neuronet with the minimal HASE [i.e., $\bar{e}_{\min}$ corresponding to $N_1 = (\zeta_1 + 1)(\zeta_1 + 2)/2$]. For better understanding, Fig. 5.4 shows the numerical results which substantiate the efficacy of Procedure I of the WASD algorithm. Besides, Fig. 5.5 shows the magnitude distribution of $|w_k|$ (with $k = 1, 2, \cdots, N_1$). As seen from Fig. 5.5, many weights are tiny, which implies that their corresponding hidden-layer neurons almost have no important influence on the performance, and thus the structure of Chebyshev-polynomial-of-Class-1 neuronet can be pruned appropriately (by deleting the very much less important hidden-layer neurons). In view of the similar characteristics of many other target functions, Procedure II of the WASD algorithm is developed to successfully obtain the optimal number of hidden-layer neurons (i.e., $N_{\text{opt}}$) of Chebyshev-polynomial-of-Class-1 neuronet, with the efficacy of Procedure II substantiated in Fig. 5.6.

## 5.4 Numerical Studies

To substantiate the efficacy of Chebyshev-polynomial-of-Class-1 neuronet equipped with the WASD algorithm (i.e., in terms of approximation, testing and prediction), numerical studies about a variety of target functions are performed. Note that numerical results (i.e., Figs. 5.4 through 5.10 as well as Tables 5.1 and 5.2) based on three target functions (5.4) through (5.6) are shown and analyzed in this section.

For numerical verification, the set of sample pairs $\{(x_m, \gamma_m), m = 1, 2, \cdots, 2116\}$ is used for approximation, which is the same as the one given in Subsection 5.3.2 (i.e., $M = 2116$). In addition, the set of sample pairs $\{(x_m, \gamma_m), m = 1, 2, \cdots, 3721\}$ (i.e., $M = 3721$) for testing is generated by sampling uniformly over region $[-0.9, 0.9]^2$ with new gap size 0.03. Furthermore, the set of sample pairs $\{(x_m, \gamma_m), m = 1, 2, \cdots, 1920\}$ (i.e., $M = 1920$) for prediction is generated by sampling uniformly over region $\{[-1.0, 1.0]^2 \sim [-0.9, 0.9]^2\}$ with new gap size 0.02.

Tables 5.1 and 5.2 show the numerical results of Chebyshev-polynomial-of-Class-1 neuronet equipped with the WASD algorithm. As shown in Table 5.1, the number $N_1$ of hidden-layer neurons of the grown Chebyshev-polynomial-of-Class-1 neuronet with the minimum HASE for each target function is determined via Procedure I of the WASD algorithm, which can also be seen from Fig. 5.4 with $N_1$ marked with asterisk. In addition, as seen from Table 5.2, the optimal number of hidden-layer neurons of the pruned Chebyshev-polynomial-of-Class-1 neuronet for each target function (i.e., $N_{\text{opt}}$) is determined via Procedure II of the WASD algorithm. Comparing Tables 5.1 and 5.2,

**TABLE 5.1:** Numerical results of Chebyshev-polynomial-of-Class-1 neuronet via Procedure I of WASD algorithm for target functions (5.4) through (5.6).

| Target function | $N_{\mathrm{I}}$ | $\bar{e}_{\mathrm{app}}$ | $\bar{e}_{\mathrm{pre}}$ | $\bar{e}_{\mathrm{tes}}$ | $t_{\mathrm{tes}}$ (s) |
|---|---|---|---|---|---|
| Target function (5.4) | 465 | $2.85 \times 10^{-17}$ | $5.25 \times 10^{-6}$ | $5.81 \times 10^{-17}$ | 6.08 |
| Target function (5.5) | 406 | $2.31 \times 10^{-19}$ | $9.56 \times 10^{-10}$ | $2.63 \times 10^{-19}$ | 4.69 |
| Target function (5.6) | 300 | $1.11 \times 10^{-21}$ | $1.03 \times 10^{-15}$ | $2.63 \times 10^{-19}$ | 2.57 |

**TABLE 5.2:** Numerical results of Chebyshev-polynomial-of-Class-1 neuronet via Procedure II of WASD algorithm for target functions (5.4) through (5.6).

| Target function | $N_{\mathrm{opt}}$ | $\bar{e}_{\mathrm{app}}$ | $\bar{e}_{\mathrm{pre}}$ | $\bar{e}_{\mathrm{tes}}$ | $t_{\mathrm{tes}}$ (s) |
|---|---|---|---|---|---|
| Target function (5.4) | 147 | $2.86 \times 10^{-17}$ | $5.25 \times 10^{-6}$ | $5.81 \times 10^{-17}$ | 0.65 |
| Target function (5.5) | 177 | $2.31 \times 10^{-19}$ | $9.56 \times 10^{-10}$ | $2.63 \times 10^{-19}$ | 0.94 |
| Target function (5.6) | 71 | $1.05 \times 10^{-21}$ | $1.03 \times 10^{-15}$ | $1.17 \times 10^{-21}$ | 0.17 |

we see that more than 56.40% of the hidden-layer neurons have been deleted via Procedure II of the WASD algorithm while the corresponding $\bar{e}$ of approximation, prediction and testing (i.e., $\bar{e}_{\mathrm{app}}$, $\bar{e}_{\mathrm{pre}}$ and $\bar{e}_{\mathrm{tes}}$) increase by less than 0.36%. In addition, Chebyshev-polynomial-of-Class-1 neuronet with $N_{\mathrm{opt}}$ has much shorter testing time, i.e., $t_{\mathrm{tes}}$, than the one with $N_{\mathrm{I}}$, which, together with the above analysis, show the effectiveness/necessity of Procedure II of the WASD algorithm. Thus, by exploiting the proposed WASD algorithm, the optimal number of hidden-layer neurons is automatically determined to achieve the best performance of Chebyshev-polynomial-of-Class-1 neuronet (without prescribing the precision parameter). Note that, for the above three target functions (5.4) through (5.6), it takes 33.73, 21.88 and 13.02 seconds, respectively, to determine the corresponding optimal numbers of hidden-layer neurons, which, in some context, shows the efficacy of the proposed WASD algorithm.

With the optimal number of hidden-layer neurons of Chebyshev-polynomial-of-Class-1 neuronet determined, $\bar{e}_{\mathrm{app}}$ and $\bar{e}_{\mathrm{tes}}$ illustrated in Table 5.2 are very tiny (i.e., of order $10^{-17} \sim 10^{-21}$). For better understanding, the corresponding graphical results are shown in Figs. 5.7 through 5.10, which substantiate well the superior performance of Chebyshev-polynomial-of-Class-1 neuronet equipped with the WASD algorithm on approximation and testing. In addition, for further investigation, the numerical results of Chebyshev-polynomial-of-Class-1 neuronet on prediction are given in Fig. 5.8(b) and Fig. 5.8(c) as well as Fig. 5.10(b) and Fig. 5.10(c). As seen from these subfigures as well as Table 5.2, $\bar{e}_{\mathrm{pre}}$ of Chebyshev-polynomial-of-Class-1 neuronet is tiny enough (i.e., of order $10^{-6} \sim 10^{-15}$), which substantiates the superior performance of Chebyshev-polynomial-of-Class-1 neuronet equipped with the WASD algorithm on prediction.

## 5.5   Chapter Summary

In this chapter, a new type of two-input feed-forward neuronet using Chebyshev polynomials of Class 1 has been proposed, constructed and investigated, which is the start and basis of the investigation on multi-input neuronets of learning type. In addition, the novel WASD algorithm has been proposed and developed to determine the optimal number of hidden-layer neurons and its corresponding optimal weights for Chebyshev-polynomial-of-Class-1 neuronet. Numerical studies have further substantiated the success and efficacy of Chebyshev-polynomial-of-Class-1 neuronet equipped with the WASD algorithm.

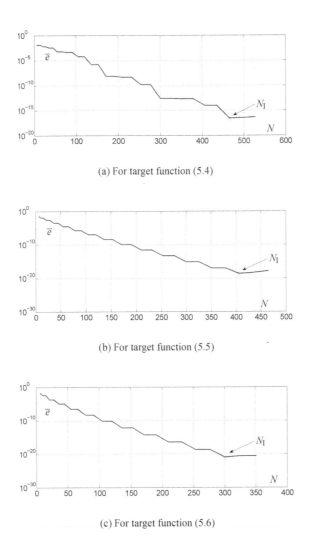

(a) For target function (5.4)

(b) For target function (5.5)

(c) For target function (5.6)

**FIGURE 5.4**: Number of hidden-layer neurons of Chebyshev-polynomial-of-Class-1 neuronet with minimum HASE by Procedure I of WASD algorithm for target functions (5.4) through (5.6), respectively.

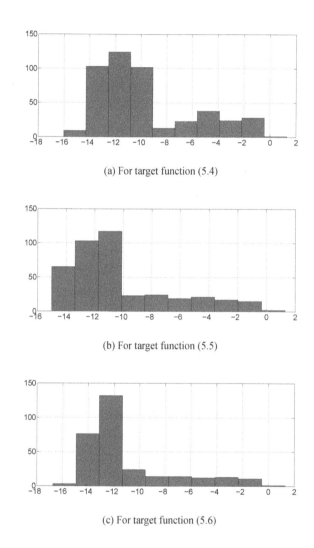

(a) For target function (5.4)

(b) For target function (5.5)

(c) For target function (5.6)

**FIGURE 5.5**: Histogram of $\log_{10}|w_k|$ with $k = 1, 2, \cdots, N_I$ for Chebyshev-polynomial-of-Class-1 neuronet growing up.

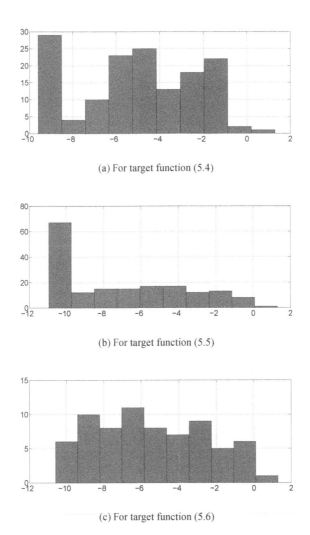

(a) For target function (5.4)

(b) For target function (5.5)

(c) For target function (5.6)

**FIGURE 5.6**: Histogram of $\log_{10}|w_k|$ with $k = 1, 2, \cdots, N_{\text{opt}}$ for Chebyshev-polynomial-of-Class-1 neuronet being pruned finally.

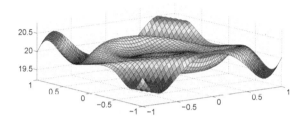

(a) Target function (5.4)

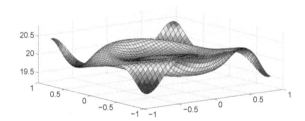

(b) Neuronet approximation

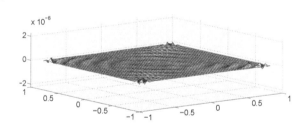

(c) Relative error of approximation

**FIGURE 5.7**: Approximation results of Chebyshev-polynomial-of-Class-1 neuronet with optimal number of hidden-layer neurons for target function (5.4).

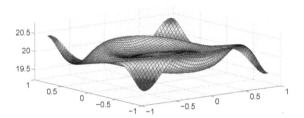

(a) Testing result of neuronet

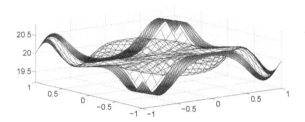

(b) Prediction result of neuronet

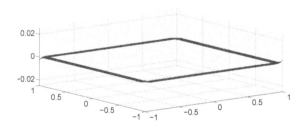

(c) Relative error of prediction

**FIGURE 5.8**: Testing and prediction results of Chebyshev-polynomial-of-Class-1 neuronet with optimal number of hidden-layer neurons for target function (5.4).

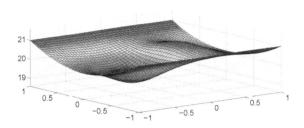

(a) Target function (5.5)

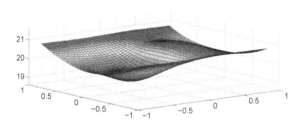

(b) Neuronet approximation

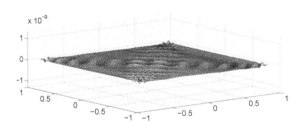

(c) Relative error of approximation

**FIGURE 5.9**: Approximation results of Chebyshev-polynomial-of-Class-1 neuronet with optimal number of hidden-layer neurons for target function (5.5).

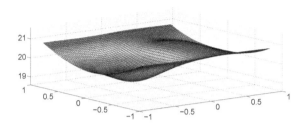

(a) Testing result of neuronet

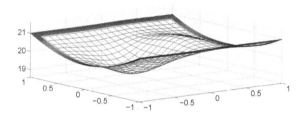

(b) Prediction result of neuronet

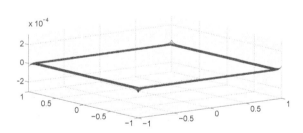

(c) Relative error of prediction

**FIGURE 5.10**: Testing and prediction results of Chebyshev-polynomial-of-Class-1 neuronet with optimal number of hidden-layer neurons for target function (5.5).

# Chapter 6

## *Two-Input Chebyshev-Polynomial-of-Class-2 WASD Neuronet*

Based on the theory of polynomial interpolation and approximation, a two-input feed-forward neuronet activated by a group of Chebyshev orthogonal polynomials (or, say, Chebyshev polynomials) of Class 2 is constructed and investigated in this chapter. To overcome the weaknesses of conventional back-propagation (BP) neuronets, a weights-direct-determination (WDD) subalgorithm is exploited to obtain the optimal linking weights of the proposed neuronet directly. Furthermore, a structure-automatic-determination (SAD) subalgorithm is developed to determine the optimal number of hidden-layer neurons of Chebyshev-polynomial-of-Class-2 neuronet, and thus the weights-and-structure-determination (WASD) algorithm is built up. Numerical studies further substantiate the efficacy and superior abilities of Chebyshev-polynomial-of-Class-2 neuronet in approximation, denoising and prediction, with the aid of the WASD algorithm which obtains the optimal number of hidden-layer neurons.

## 6.1   Introduction

With outstanding features such as parallelism, distributed storage and adaptive self-learning ability, artificial neuronets (AN) have been widely investigated and sharply developed in many science and engineering fields, such as control system design [1–3, 71], image processing [9], and robot inverse kinematics [12, 71]. However, back-propagation (BP) neuronets have some inherent weaknesses, such as, relatively slow convergence, local-minima existence, and uncertainties about the optimal number of hidden-layer neurons [17, 72].

Different from algorithmic improvements in the BP training procedure, using linearly independent or orthogonal activation functions (e.g., Chebyshev polynomials of Class 2 in this chapter) to remedy the weaknesses of BP-type neuronets can be a better way, which is reflected in our successful experience [17, 20, 21, 28, 72, 73]. Besides, as our previous success was mainly of single-input-single-output (SISO) AN, it is worth further investigating AN with two inputs, in view of the fact that some of practical systems have two inputs [60]. Thus, with the aims of overcoming the weaknesses of BP-type neuronets and investigating AN with two inputs, based on the probability theory [68] and the theories of polynomial interpolation and approximation [19, 74], a new feed-forward two-input neuronet activated by a group of Chebyshev polynomials of Class 2 is constructed in this chapter.

In order to avoid the usually lengthy iterative-training procedure and improve the efficacy of Chebyshev-polynomial-of-Class-2 neuronet, a WASD algorithm is designed for such a neuronet. In particular, the so-called WASD algorithm is developed based on the SAD subalgorithm exploited in our previous works [17, 20, 21, 28]. Being one part of the WASD algorithm, the WDD subalgorithm, which has been proved very effective and efficient on improving the performance of neuronets [17, 20, 21, 28, 72], can determine the optimal weights connecting hidden-layer and output-layer neurons directly (or to say, just in one step). Since the performance of neuronet is greatly affected by the number of the hidden-layer neurons, it is very important and meaningful to determine the optimal number of hidden-layer neurons efficiently. Specifically speaking, fewer hidden-layer neurons may not achieve the desired performance, while too many hidden-layer neurons bring about more structural and computational complexities (in addition to structural risk related to over-fitting phenomena) and cost too much time in obtaining the expected results [17, 23, 28, 72].

In view of the advantages of the WDD subalgorithm and SAD subalgorithm, we present in this chapter a WASD algorithm to obtain efficiently the optimal number of hidden-layer neurons of the two-input Chebyshev-polynomial-of-Class-2 neuronet. Numerical studies further substantiate the efficacy and superior performance of Chebyshev-polynomial-of-Class-2 neuronet equipped with the WASD algorithm in approximation, denoising and prediction.

## 6.2    Theoretical Basis

To lay a basis for further discussion, the theoretical basis is presented in this section, which guarantees the approximation ability of Chebyshev-polynomial-of-Class-2 neuronet. In addition, a proposition is given so as to obtain the actual activation functions with two variables for the hidden-layer neurons in Chebyshev-polynomial-of-Class-2 neuronet.

**Lemma 10** *Chebyshev polynomials of Class 2 can be defined as below [72, 73]:*

$$\varphi_{i+2}(x) = 2x\varphi_{i+1}(x) - \varphi_i(x), \text{with } \varphi_1(x) = 1 \text{ and } \varphi_2(x) = 2x,$$

*where $\varphi_i(x)$ denotes the Chebyshev polynomial of Class 2 of degree $i$ (with $i = 1, 2, 3, \cdots$).*

Evidently, in approximating target function $f(x)$ with a single variable $x$ as an input argument, based on the theory of polynomial interpolation and approximation, the target function $f(x)$ can be approximated as follows:

$$f(x) \approx \sum_{i=1}^{N} w_i \varphi_i(x),$$

where $w_i$ is the weight for $\varphi_i(x)$, and $N$ is the total number of Chebyshev polynomials of Class 2 used to approximate the target function. Thus, based on Proposition 2 of Chapter 5 and Lemma 10, we have the following proposition on the approximation of the target function with two continuous independent variables.

**Proposition 4** *For a target function $f(x_1, x_2)$ with two continuous independent variables $x_1$ and $x_2$, it can be best estimated by approximating simultaneously the functions $f_1(x_1)$ and $f_2(x_2)$ via Chebyshev polynomials of Class 2.*

**Proof.** According to Proposition 2 of Chapter 5 and Lemma 10, the target function $f(x_1, x_2)$ can be reformulated as

$$f(x_1, x_2) = f_1(x_1) f_2(x_2) \approx \left( \sum_{i=1}^{N_1} w_i \varphi_i(x_1) \right) \left( \sum_{j=1}^{N_2} w_j \varphi_j(x_2) \right) = \sum_{i=1}^{N_1} \sum_{j=1}^{N_2} w_{ij} \varphi_i(x_1) \varphi_j(x_2)$$

$$= \sum_{k=1}^{N} w_k \psi_k(x_1, x_2),$$

where $N = N_1 N_2$ denotes the total number of Chebyshev polynomials of Class 2 used to approximate $f(x_1, x_2)$, the resultant weight $w_k = w_{ij} = w_i w_j$ (with $i = 1, 2, \cdots, N_1$ and $j = 1, 2, \cdots, N_2$) denotes the weight for $\psi_k(x_1, x_2)$, and $\psi_k([x_1, x_2]^{\mathrm{T}}) = \psi_k(x_1, x_2) = \varphi_i(x_1) \varphi_j(x_2)$ with superscript $^{\mathrm{T}}$ denoting transpose. Besides, $k = (i-1)N_2 + j$ and

$$\begin{cases} \psi_1(x_1, x_2) = \varphi_1(x_1) \varphi_1(x_2), \\ \psi_2(x_1, x_2) = \varphi_1(x_1) \varphi_2(x_2), \\ \quad \vdots \\ \psi_{N_2}(x_1, x_2) = \varphi_1(x_1) \varphi_{N_2}(x_2), \\ \psi_{N_2+1}(x_1, x_2) = \varphi_2(x_1) \varphi_1(x_2), \\ \quad \vdots \end{cases}$$

Therefore, the target function $f(x_1, x_2)$ can be best estimated by obtaining the optimal weights $\{w_k\}$ for basis functions $\{\psi_k(x_1, x_2)\}$ (with $k = 1, 2, \cdots, N$).

---

## 6.3 Neuronet Model and WASD Algorithm

In this section, the model structure of feed-forward two-input neuronet activated by a group of Chebyshev polynomials of Class 2 is constructed and investigated. Then, the WASD algorithm is developed accordingly to further improve the performance of Chebyshev-polynomial-of-Class-2 neuronet.

### 6.3.1 Two-input Chebyshev-polynomial-of-Class-2 neuronet model

According to Proposition 4, we construct a new type of two-input feed-forward neuronet activated by Chebyshev polynomials of Class 2, which is different from the one presented in Chapter 5. The corresponding model structure of Chebyshev-polynomial-of-Class-2 neuronet is shown in Fig. 6.1. The neuronet model has two inputs $x_1$ and $x_2$ and single output $y$. To simplify the neuronet model and its computation, as in Fig. 6.1, the connecting weights from input layer to hidden layer are all fixed to 1, and all neuronal thresholds are fixed to 0.

### 6.3.2 WASD algorithm

For the neuronet shown in Fig. 6.1, the conventional BP algorithm can be exploited to determine the linking weights $\{w_k\}$. However, the BP algorithm has clear weaknesses; e.g., it may take

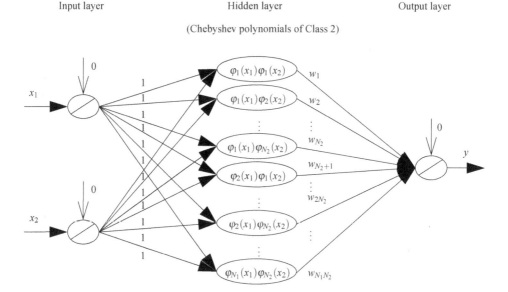

**FIGURE 6.1**: Model structure of two-input Chebyshev-activation (specifically, Chebyshev-polynomial-of-Class-2) neuronet.

much time to converge to a result and it cannot find the optimal number of hidden-layer neurons. Actually, from our previous works [17,20,21,28], the weights can be determined directly by using a pseudoinverse-based algorithm, i.e., the so-called WDD subalgorithm.

Specifically, to present the WASD algorithm (including the WDD subalgorithm) more clearly, we give $(\mathbf{x}_m, \gamma_m)|_{m=1}^M$ as the sample pairs for training, where $\mathbf{x}_m \in \mathbb{R}^2$ denotes the $m$th input vector $[x_{m1}, x_{m2}]^T$, and $\gamma_m$ denotes the $m$th desired output (or to say, target output). Then, the batch-processing error (BPE) function is defined as

$$e = \frac{1}{2} \sum_{m=1}^M \left( \gamma_m - \sum_{k=1}^N w_k \psi_k(\mathbf{x}_m) \right)^2 \tag{6.1}$$

where $N$ denotes the total number of the hidden-layer neurons, and $\psi_k(\cdot)$ denotes the activation function of the $k$th hidden-layer neuron of Chebyshev-polynomial-of-Class-2 neuronet. It is worth mentioning that, if the optimal linking weights are determined, the BPE function (6.1) achieves its minimal value.

From our previous works [17,20,21,28], the optimal linking weights can be determined directly by using the following WDD subalgorithm:

$$\mathbf{w} = (\mathbf{\Psi}^T \mathbf{\Psi})^{-1} \mathbf{\Psi}^T \gamma$$

where $\mathbf{w}$ is the vector of the linking weights, $\gamma$ is the vector of the desired outputs, and $\mathbf{\Psi}$ is the input-activation matrix, which are defined respectively as

$$\mathbf{w} = \begin{bmatrix} w_1 \\ w_2 \\ \vdots \\ w_N \end{bmatrix} \in \mathbb{R}^N, \quad \gamma = \begin{bmatrix} \gamma_1 \\ \gamma_2 \\ \vdots \\ \gamma_M \end{bmatrix} \in \mathbb{R}^M, \quad \mathbf{\Psi} = \begin{bmatrix} \psi_1(\mathbf{x}_1) & \psi_2(\mathbf{x}_1) & \dots & \psi_N(\mathbf{x}_1) \\ \psi_1(\mathbf{x}_2) & \psi_2(\mathbf{x}_2) & \dots & \psi_N(\mathbf{x}_2) \\ \vdots & \vdots & \ddots & \vdots \\ \psi_1(\mathbf{x}_M) & \psi_2(\mathbf{x}_M) & \dots & \psi_N(\mathbf{x}_M) \end{bmatrix} \in \mathbb{R}^{M \times N}.$$

It is worth pointing out that $\mathbf{w}$ can also be written as $\mathbf{w} = \text{pinv}(\mathbf{\Psi})\gamma$, where $\text{pinv}(\mathbf{\Psi})$ denotes the

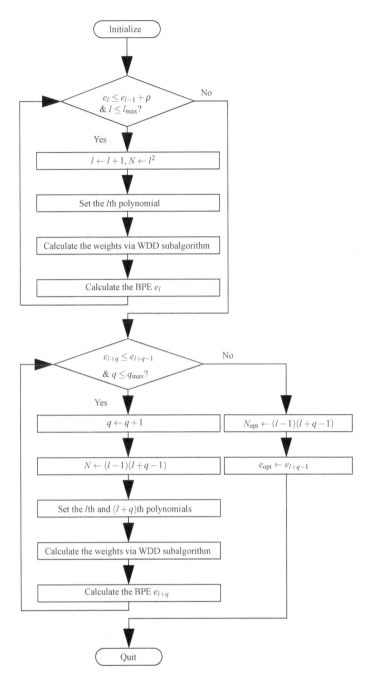

**FIGURE 6.2**: Flowchart of WASD algorithm for Chebyshev-polynomial-of-Class-2 neuronet.

pseudoinverse of input-activation matrix $\Psi$ and can be evaluated directly via MATLAB or others' routine "pinv" [18, 70].

Moreover, as investigated previously [17, 28], the number of hidden-layer neurons can affect greatly the performance of neuronets in the case of SISO neuronets, which is true also in the case of the two-input Chebyshev-polynomial-of-Class-2 neuronet. In this chapter, the relationship between the performance of the two-input Chebyshev-polynomial-of-Class-2 neuronet and the number of

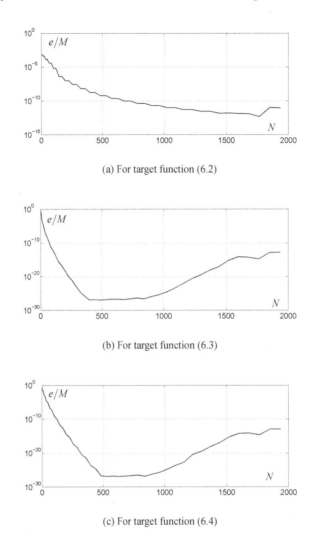

(a) For target function (6.2)

(b) For target function (6.3)

(c) For target function (6.4)

**FIGURE 6.3**: Average BPE of Chebyshev-polynomial-of-Class-2 neuronet versus its number of hidden-layer neurons for target functions (6.2) through (6.4), respectively.

hidden-layer neurons is investigated and analyzed via the BPE function (6.1), and thus the WASD algorithm is developed for determining the optimal number of hidden-layer neurons, $N_{\text{opt}}$. Before presenting such a WASD algorithm (of which the flowchart is shown in Fig. 6.2), a variety of target functions have been tested to investigate the relationship between the BPE function (6.1) and the number of hidden-layer neurons, such as the following three target functions:

$$f(x_1, x_2) = \frac{50x_1x_2 \sin(\sqrt{10x_1^2 + 10x_2^2})}{x_1^2 + x_2^2} + 20, \qquad (6.2)$$

$$f(x_1, x_2) = (2 + x_2)\exp(-\sin(x_1x_2)), \qquad (6.3)$$

$$f(x_1, x_2) = (1 - x_1)^3 \sin(x_2)\exp(-x_1^2 - x_2^2) + 1. \qquad (6.4)$$

**TABLE 6.1:** Numerical results of Chebyshev-polynomial-of-Class-2 neuronet via WDD subalgorithm with $N = 400$ for target functions (6.2) through (6.4).

| Target | $t_{run}$ (s) | $e_{app}/M$ | $e_{tes}/M$ | $\varepsilon_{app}$ | $\varepsilon_{tes}$ | $e_{den}/M$ |
|--------|------|-----|-----|-----|-----|-----|
| (6.2) | 2.46 | $6.62 \times 10^{-10}$ | $1.04 \times 10^{-4}$ | $1.41 \times 10^{-5}$ | $1.80 \times 10^{-3}$ | $6.21 \times 10^{-6}$ |
| (6.3) | 2.80 | $7.17 \times 10^{-25}$ | $7.82 \times 10^{-25}$ | $3.84 \times 10^{-12}$ | $3.75 \times 10^{-12}$ | $1.00 \times 10^{-2}$ |
| (6.4) | 2.43 | $2.22 \times 10^{-25}$ | $2.46 \times 10^{-25}$ | $4.69 \times 10^{-10}$ | $2.59 \times 10^{-10}$ | $2.00 \times 10^{-3}$ |

Specifically, Fig. 6.3 illustrates the average BPE (i.e., $e/M$ with $M$ being set as 2116) of the above three target functions versus the number of hidden-layer neurons (i.e., $N$). As seen from the figure, the curves all look like the character "V" or "U". From the similar curves and also from other testing results, we can then design the WASD algorithm shown in Fig. 6.2 and briefed as the following. That is, to obtain the optimal number of hidden-layer neurons with the minimal value of BPE, we increase the searching number $l$ (with the maximal $l$ being $l_{max}$) one-by-one to obtain the number of hidden-layer neurons, $N = l^2$. In addition, $q = 0, 1, 2, \cdots, q_{max}$, where, according to the experience of numerical studies of this chapter, we choose $q_{max} = 3$ together with $\rho = 0.1e_l$. By following the flowchart of the WASD algorithm, the minimal value of the BPE (i.e., $e_{opt}$) and the optimal number of hidden-layer neurons (i.e., $N_{opt}$) are obtained finally. Therefore, the optimal structure and performance of Chebyshev-polynomial-of-Class-2 neuronet can be achieved by exploiting the presented WASD algorithm.

## 6.4 Numerical Studies

In this section, numerical results are presented to substantiate the efficacy and superior abilities of the presented Chebyshev-polynomial-of-Class-2 neuronet in terms of approximation (or, say, learning), testing (or, say, generalization), denoising and prediction, with the aid of the WASD algorithm which obtains the optimal number of hidden-layer neurons of Chebyshev-polynomial-of-Class-2 neuronet. Note that, due to space limitation and results similarity, the numerical results are shown only for the aforementioned three target functions, i.e., (6.2) through (6.4), respectively.

Firstly, to verify the abilities of Chebyshev-polynomial-of-Class-2 neuronet in terms of approximation, testing, denoising and prediction, the number of the hidden-layer neurons is set to be 400 as an example. We sample uniformly over region $[-0.9, 0.9]^2$ with gap size 0.04 to generate a square matrix called the input matrix of the training data-set $\{(\mathbf{x}_m, \gamma_m), m = 1, 2, \cdots, 2116\}$ (i.e., $M = 2116$). Besides, we choose the intervals $[-1, -0.9]$ and $[0.9, 1]$ as the unlearned intervals to test the prediction ability of Chebyshev-polynomial-of-Class-2 neuronet. The corresponding numerical results are shown in Table 6.1 and Figs. 6.4 through 6.7. As seen from Table 6.1, the run time $t_{run}$ of WDD subalgorithm (or, say, the computing time of WDD subalgorithm) is very short, and the average BPEs of approximation and testing are quite small. These substantiate well the efficacy and superior approximation ability of Chebyshev-polynomial-of-Class-2 neuronet. Note that $\varepsilon_{app}$ and $\varepsilon_{tes}$ represent the maximal relative error of approximation and testing, respectively. In addition, the average BPE of denoising, i.e., $e_{den}/M$, shown in Table 6.1 is small, which substantiates the denoising ability of Chebyshev-polynomial-of-Class-2 neuronet. For better understanding, Figs. 6.4 through 6.7 illustrate the numerical results of Chebyshev-polynomial-of-Class-2 neuronet working on target functions (6.2) and (6.4) [with the numerical results on (6.3) omitted due to results similarity], which intuitively and visually show the good performance of Chebyshev-polynomial-of-Class-2 neuronet (in terms of approximation and denoising). Note that approximation and denoising could be two contradicting abilities, as a "super" neuronet like Chebyshev-polynomial-of-Class-2 neuronet could

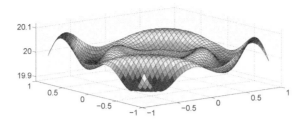

(a) Target function (6.2)

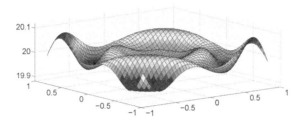

(b) Neuronet approximation

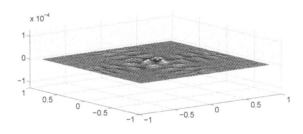

(c) Relative error of approximation

**FIGURE 6.4**: Approximation results of Chebyshev-polynomial-of-Class-2 neuronet with $N = 400$ for target function (6.2).

even learn well the noisy data or the noise; see Fig. 6.3 and Table 6.1, where the approximation errors are even of order $10^{-10} \sim 10^{-30}$. Furthermore, with the aim of verifying the prediction ability of the well-trained Chebyshev-polynomial-of-Class-2 neuronet, Fig. 6.7(a) illustrates the graphical results about target function (6.4). Comparing Fig. 6.7(a) with Fig. 6.6(a) (and also comparing the related numerical results on other target functions), we have the observation that Chebyshev-polynomial-of-Class-2 neuronet has relatively good or even very good prediction performance.

Secondly, for further investigation, Fig. 6.8 illustrates the results about the searching process of the optimal number of hidden-layer neurons by exploiting the presented WASD algorithm for Chebyshev-polynomial-of-Class-2 neuronet. As seen from the figure, which is compared with Fig. 6.3, the optimal number $N_{\text{opt}}$ of hidden-layer neurons of Chebyshev-polynomial-of-Class-2 neuronet is obtained efficiently and accurately via the WASD algorithm. In addition, the numerical results shown in Table 6.2 substantiate the effectiveness, efficiency and accuracy of Chebyshev-polynomial-of-Class-2 neuronet equipped with the WASD algorithm.

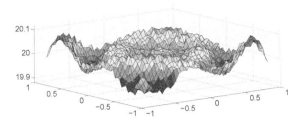

(a) Target function with random noise

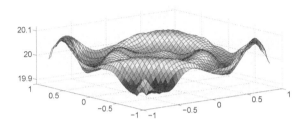

(b) Neuronet denoising

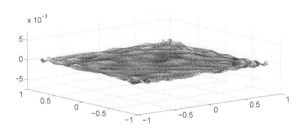

(c) Relative error of denoising

**FIGURE 6.5**: Denoising results of Chebyshev-polynomial-of-Class-2 neuronet with $N = 400$ for target function (6.2).

In summary, the above numerical results (i.e., Tables 6.1 and 6.2 as well as Figs. 6.4 through 6.8) all substantiate the efficacy and superior performance of the proposed Chebyshev-polynomial-of-Class-2 neuronet equipped with the WASD algorithm (including the proposed Chebyshev-polynomial-of-Class-2 neuronet equipped with the WDD subalgorithm as a special case).

## 6.5   Chapter Summary

To remedy the weaknesses of conventional BP-type neuronets and to lay a solid basis for future solution of two-input neuronets, the two-input feed-forward neuronet activated by a group of Chebyshev polynomials of Class 2 has been constructed and investigated in this chapter. In addition,

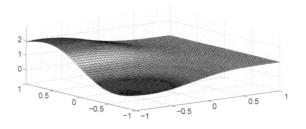

(a) Target function (6.4)

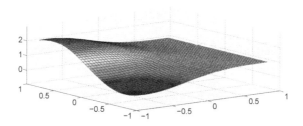

(b) Neuronet approximation

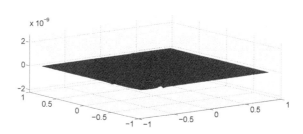

(c) Relative error of approximation

**FIGURE 6.6**: Approximation results of Chebyshev-polynomial-of-Class-2 neuronet with $N = 400$ for target function (6.4).

the WASD algorithm has been developed to obtain the optimal number of hidden-layer neurons and simultaneously determine the optimal linking weights of Chebyshev-polynomial-of-Class-2 neuronet directly. Numerical results have further substantiated the efficacy and accuracy of the proposed Chebyshev-polynomial-of-Class-2 neuronet equipped with the WASD algorithm.

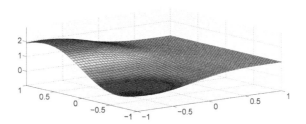

(a) Prediction result of neuronet

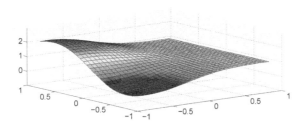

(b) Testing result of neuronet

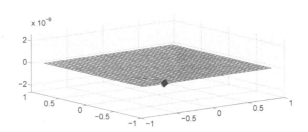

(c) Relative error of testing

**FIGURE 6.7**: Prediction and testing results of Chebyshev-polynomial-of-Class-2 neuronet with $N = 400$ for target function (6.4).

**TABLE 6.2:** Numerical results of Chebyshev-polynomial-of-Class-2 neuronet via WASD algorithm for target functions (6.2) through (6.4).

| Target | $N_{opt}$ | $t_{run}$ (s) | $e_{opt}/M$ |
|--------|-----------|---------------|-------------|
| (6.2) | 1806 | 1259.7 | $2.58 \times 10^{-13}$ |
| (6.3) | 440 | 32.90 | $3.89 \times 10^{-28}$ |
| (6.4) | 600 | 89.95 | $3.73 \times 10^{-28}$ |

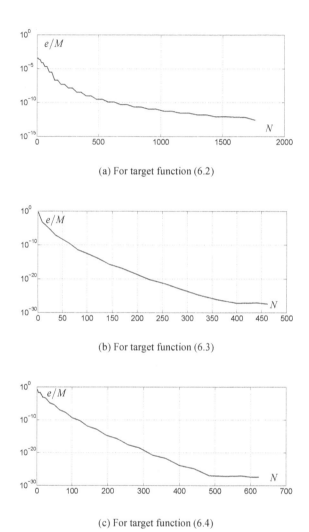

(a) For target function (6.2)

(b) For target function (6.3)

(c) For target function (6.4)

**FIGURE 6.8**: Searching process of Chebyshev-polynomial-of-Class-2 neuronet with WASD algorithm to obtain optimal number of hidden-layer neurons for target functions (6.2) through (6.4), respectively.

# Part III

# Three-Input-Single-Output Neuronet

# Chapter 7

## *Three-Input Euler-Polynomial WASD Neuronet*

Based on the function approximation theory and the Weierstrass approximation theorem, a three-input Euler-polynomial neuronet is established in this chapter to learn the four-dimensional data (i.e., data in the form of three inputs and single output). In order to achieve satisfactory performance and efficacy of the three-input Euler polynomial neuronet, a weights-and-structure-determination (WASD) algorithm, which contains the weights-direct-determination (WDD) subalgorithm, is built up for the established three-input Euler-polynomial neuronet. Numerical results further substantiate the superior performance of the three-input Euler-polynomial neuronet equipped with the WASD algorithm in terms of training, testing and prediction.

## 7.1 Introduction

Multi-input artificial neuronets (AN) are simplified systems, which emulate the organization structures, signal processing methods and system functions of biological neuronets [28, 73, 75]. Owing to the outstanding characteristics such as parallel processing, distributed storage, self-organization, self-adaptation, self-learning and high fault tolerance [75], the multi-input AN has been widely applied in the fields of data mining [76], information and communication engineering [77], pattern recognition [21, 55, 78], and other science and engineering fields [17]. The neuronet based on back-propagation (BP) algorithms is one of the most widely applied and maturely studied multi-input AN models [75, 79]. However, conventional BP algorithms also have some inherent shortages, such as the existence of local minima, the slow speed of training (or, say, learning), and the difficulty (or, say, high computational complexity) in determining the optimal weights and structure of the multi-input neuronet [17, 21, 79].

In order to overcome the above weaknesses of multi-input BP-type neuronets and improve the performance of neuronets, the authors have focused on the usage of different activation functions and the determination of the optimal neuronet structure, with the effectiveness of this approach substantiated in the previous works [20,21,28,75,78]. It is worth mentioning that the single-input-single-output (SISO) neuronet activated by a group of Euler polynomials has been investigated in Chapter 1, and the efficacy and superiority of the proposed neuronet has also been substantiated [17]. In view of the fact that the multi-input (especially, three-input) systems are also frequently encountered systems, it is worth further investigating the three-input neuronets. According to the function approximation theory and the Weierstrass approximation theorem [80–82], a three-input Euler-polynomial neuronet with hidden-layer neurons activated by a group of products of Euler polynomials is established and investigated in this chapter.

As we know, the number of hidden-layer neurons can also influence greatly the overall performance of multi-input neuronets. Specifically speaking, with too few hidden-layer neurons, the neuronet may fail to achieve the expected learning accuracy, while excess hidden-layer neurons may result in over-fitting phenomenon and higher computational complexity [17,28,75]. In light of the above analysis, it is meaningful and important to obtain the optimal number of hidden-layer neurons (or, say, the optimal structure) for the three-input neuronet. For this reason, a WASD algorithm is built up for the established three-input Euler-polynomial neuronet. More specifically, the WASD algorithm exploits the WDD subalgorithm to determine the optimal weights between hidden-layer and output-layer neurons directly (i.e., just in one step) on one hand [17,21,73,75]; and, on the other hand, it can obtain the optimal structure of the three-input Euler-polynomial neuronet during the training process. Numerical results further substantiate that the three-input Euler-polynomial neuronet equipped with the WASD algorithm has superior performance in terms of function data training, testing and prediction.

## 7.2    Theoretical Basis

Theoretically, the AN can approximate any continuous target function with any degree of accuracy [83]. For better understanding, the detailed descriptions of related essential definition and theorems are given in this section. Moreover, based on the presented theorems and the authors' previous successful experience [17,20,21,28,75,78], a proposition is put forward to lay a basis for establishing the three-input Euler-polynomial neuronet. Note that the definition of Euler polynomials has been presented in Definition 1 of Chapter 1. Besides, the following theorem is the so-called Weierstrass approximation theorem [80–82,84,85].

**Theorem 1** *Let $g(x)$ be a continuous real-valued function defined on $[a,b]$, then, for any $\varepsilon > 0$, there must be a polynomial $h(x)$ such that, for all $x \in [a,b]$,*

$$|g(x) - h(x)| < \varepsilon.$$

It means that any continuous function defined on a closed and bounded interval can be uniformly approximated by polynomial with any degree of accuracy.

**Theorem 2** *For a continuous real-valued function $f(x_1, x_2, \cdots, x_k)$ with $k$ variables, which is defined over $S_k = \{(x_1, x_2, \cdots, x_k) \in \mathbb{R}^k | 0 \leq x_q \leq 1, q = 1, 2, \cdots, k\}$, Weierstrass polynomial (i.e., Bernstein polynomial) can be constructed as*

$$B_{n_1 n_2 \cdots n_k}^f(x_1, x_2, \cdots, x_k) = \sum_{v_1=0}^{n_1} \cdots \sum_{v_k=0}^{n_k} f\left(\frac{v_1}{n_1}, \cdots, \frac{v_k}{n_k}\right) p_{n_1 v_1}(x_1) \cdots p_{n_k v_k}(x_k), \quad (7.1)$$

*where*

$$p_{n_q v_q}(x_q) = C_{n_q}^{v_q} x_q^{v_q} (1 - x_q)^{n_q - v_q} \quad (with\ q = 1, 2, \cdots, k),$$

Input layer      Hidden layer      Output layer

(Euler polynomials)

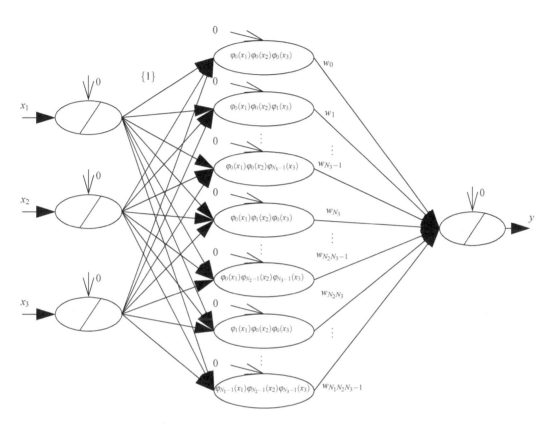

**FIGURE 7.1**: Model structure of three-input Euler-polynomial neuronet.

*and $C_{n_q}^{v_q}$ denotes a binomial coefficient; and then*

$$\lim_{n_1,n_2,\cdots,n_k \to \infty} B_{n_1 n_2 \cdots n_k}^f(x_1,x_2,\cdots,x_k) = f(x_1,x_2,\cdots,x_k).$$

That is to say, $f(x_1,x_2,\cdots,x_k)$ can be uniformly approximated by $B_{n_1 n_2 \cdots n_k}^f(x_1,x_2,\cdots,x_k)$ over $S_k$. It is worth pointing out that Theorem 2 was investigated and proved in [80, 86].

**Proposition 5** *According to Theorems 1 and 2, $\{p_{n_q v_q}(x_q),\ v_q = 0,1,\cdots,n_q,\ q = 1,2,\cdots,k\}$ can be replaced with k groups of Euler polynomials to learn the data of $f(x_1,x_2,\cdots,x_k)$. That is, for the given values of q and $v_q$, let the $v_q$th degree of the qth group of Euler polynomials [i.e., $\varphi_{v_q}(x_q)$] replace $p_{n_q v_q}(x_q)$, where $x_q \in [a,b]$ (with $a,b \in \mathbb{R}$ and $a \le b$).*

Without loss of generality, the continuous real-valued target function of three variables $f(x_1,x_2,x_3)$ (e.g., with $a = -1.6$, $b = 1.6$ and $n_q = N_q - 1$, $q = 1,2,3$) is investigated in this chapter. According to the above proposition, we have

$$f(x_1,x_2,x_3) \approx \sum_{v_1=0}^{N_1-1}\sum_{v_2=0}^{N_2-1}\sum_{v_3=0}^{N_3-1} w_{v_1 v_2 v_3}\varphi_{v_1}(x_1)\varphi_{v_2}(x_2)\varphi_{v_3}(x_3) = \sum_{l=0}^{N-1} w_l \psi_l(x_1,x_2,x_3),$$

where $w_{v_1 v_2 v_3}$ corresponds to $f(v_1/n_1,v_2/n_2,v_3/n_3)$ in (7.1), $N_1$, $N_2$ and $N_3$ denote the numbers of Euler polynomials used to replace $\{p_{n_1 v_1}(x_1),\ v_1 = 0,1,\cdots,n_1\}$, $\{p_{n_2 v_2}(x_2),\ v_2 = 0,1,\cdots,n_2\}$

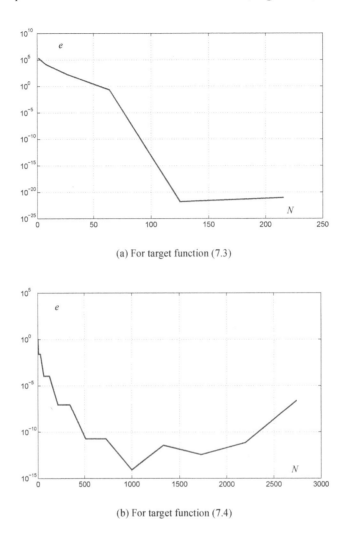

(a) For target function (7.3)

(b) For target function (7.4)

**FIGURE 7.2**: Training MSE of three-input Euler-polynomial neuronet versus its number of hidden-layer neurons for target functions (7.3) and (7.4), respectively.

and $\{p_{n_3 v_3}(x_3),\ v_3 = 0, 1, \cdots, n_3\}$, respectively, and $N = N_1 N_2 N_3$ denotes the total number of products of Euler polynomials used to learn the data of $f(x_1, x_2, x_3)$. Besides, the weight $w_l = w_{v_1 v_2 v_3}$ denotes the weight for $\psi_l(x_1, x_2, x_3)$, and $\psi_l(x_1, x_2, x_3) = \varphi_{v_1}(x_1) \varphi_{v_2}(x_2) \varphi_{v_3}(x_3)$, in which,

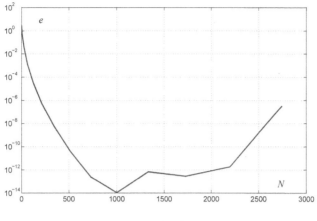

(a) For target function (7.5)

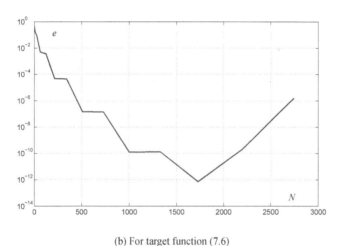

(b) For target function (7.6)

**FIGURE 7.3**: Training MSE of three-input Euler-polynomial neuronet versus its number of hidden-layer neurons for target functions (7.5) and (7.6), respectively.

$l = v_1 N_2 N_3 + v_2 N_3 + v_3$. Then, $\{\psi_l(x_1, x_2, x_3)\}$ can be expressed as below:

$$
\begin{cases}
\psi_0(x_1, x_2, x_3) = \varphi_0(x_1)\varphi_0(x_2)\varphi_0(x_3), \\
\psi_1(x_1, x_2, x_3) = \varphi_0(x_1)\varphi_0(x_2)\varphi_1(x_3), \\
\quad\vdots \\
\psi_{N_3-1}(x_1, x_2, x_3) = \varphi_0(x_1)\varphi_0(x_2)\varphi_{N_3-1}(x_3), \\
\psi_{N_3}(x_1, x_2, x_3) = \varphi_0(x_1)\varphi_1(x_2)\varphi_0(x_3), \\
\quad\vdots \\
\psi_{N_2 N_3-1}(x_1, x_2, x_3) = \varphi_0(x_1)\varphi_{N_2-1}(x_2)\varphi_{N_3-1}(x_3), \\
\psi_{N_2 N_3}(x_1, x_2, x_3) = \varphi_1(x_1)\varphi_0(x_2)\varphi_0(x_3), \\
\quad\vdots \\
\psi_{N_1 N_2 N_3-1}(x_1, x_2, x_3) = \varphi_{N_1-1}(x_1)\varphi_{N_2-1}(x_2)\varphi_{N_3-1}(x_3).
\end{cases}
$$

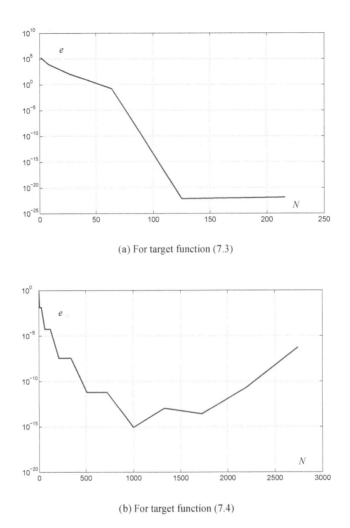

(a) For target function (7.3)

(b) For target function (7.4)

**FIGURE 7.4**: Testing MSE of three-input Euler-polynomial neuronet versus its number of hidden-layer neurons for target functions (7.3) and (7.4), respectively.

Therefore, the target function $f(x_1, x_2, x_3)$ can be uniformly approximated by obtaining the optimal weights $\{w_l\}$ for basis functions $\{\psi_l(x_1, x_2, x_3) = \psi_l(\mathbf{x})\}$ and obtaining the proper number of basis functions (where $\mathbf{x}$ denotes the vector of inputs $[x_1, x_2, x_3]^{\mathrm{T}}$, and superscript $^{\mathrm{T}}$ denotes transpose).

## 7.3    Neuronet Model and WASD Algorithm

In this section, the model of the three-input Euler-polynomial neuronet is established. Furthermore, a WASD algorithm is applied to the established neuronet model so as to obtain the optimal performance (i.e., training, testing and prediction performance) of the neuronet.

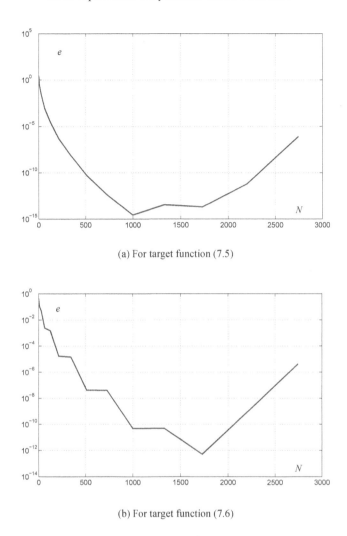

(a) For target function (7.5)

(b) For target function (7.6)

**FIGURE 7.5**: Testing MSE of three-input Euler-polynomial neuronet versus its number of hidden-layer neurons for target functions (7.5) and (7.6), respectively.

### 7.3.1  Three-input Euler-polynomial neuronet model

Based on the aforementioned theoretical basis, the three-input Euler-polynomial neuronet is established. As shown in Fig. 7.1, the three-input Euler-polynomial neuronet adopts a three-layer structure (i.e., the input layer, the hidden layer and the output layer). Each neuron in the input layer is connected to all neurons in the hidden layer and all neurons in the hidden layer are connected to the neuron in the output layer. The input layer contain three inputs $x_1$, $x_2$ and $x_3$. In addition, the activation functions of hidden-layer neurons are a group of products of Euler polynomials $\{\varphi_{v_1}(x_1)\varphi_{v_2}(x_2)\varphi_{v_3}(x_3)\}$ (i.e., $\{\psi_l(x_1,x_2,x_3)\}$), the linking weights between hidden layer and output layer are $\{w_l\}$ and the output of the three-input Euler-polynomial neuronet is $y$. Besides, for the purpose of simplifying the established neuronet and reducing the computational complexity, the linking weights between input layer and hidden layer are set to be 1, and all neuronal thresholds are set to be 0.

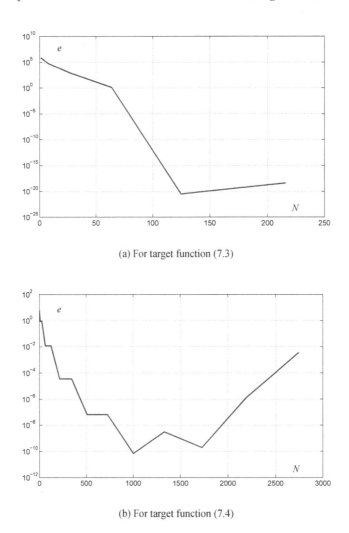

(a) For target function (7.3)

(b) For target function (7.4)

**FIGURE 7.6**: Prediction MSE of three-input Euler-polynomial neuronet versus its number of hidden-layer neurons for target functions (7.3) and (7.4), respectively.

### 7.3.2 WASD algorithm

In order to obtain the optimal number of hidden-layer neurons and the optimal linking weights between hidden layer and output layer of the three-input Euler-polynomial neuronet, a WASD algorithm containing the WDD subalgorithm is presented as follows in details.

Let $M$ be the total number of training samples, then the training-sample set can be expressed as $\{(\mathbf{x}_m, \gamma_m)|\mathbf{x}_m \in \mathbb{R}^3, \gamma_m \in \mathbb{R}, m = 0, 1, \cdots, M-1\}$, where $\mathbf{x}_m = [x_{m1}, x_{m2}, x_{m3}]^{\mathrm{T}}$ denotes the $m$th input vector, and $\gamma_m$ denotes the corresponding desired output. For evaluating the performance of the three-input Euler-polynomial neuronet, the mean square error (MSE) function is defined as

$$e = \frac{1}{M}\sum_{m=0}^{M-1}\left(\sum_{l=0}^{N-1} w_l \psi_l(\mathbf{x}_m) - \gamma_m\right)^2,$$

where $N$ denotes the total number of the hidden-layer neurons in Fig. 7.1, and $\psi_l(\cdot)$ denotes the activation function of the $l$th hidden-layer neuron of the three-input Euler-polynomial neuronet. It is

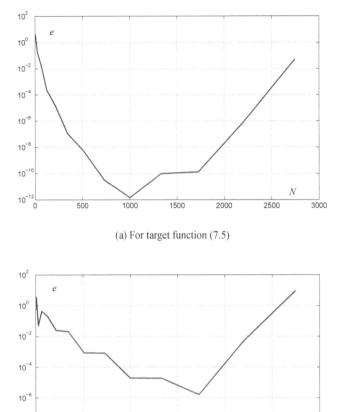

(a) For target function (7.5)

(b) For target function (7.6)

**FIGURE 7.7**: Prediction MSE of three-input Euler-polynomial neuronet versus its number of hidden-layer neurons for target functions (7.5) and (7.6), respectively.

worth mentioning that, for a given value of $N$, the MSE can be minimized by finding the optimal linking weights (i.e., the optimal $\{w_l\}$).

Suppose the number of hidden-layer neurons is $N$, and let $\Psi$, $\mathbf{w}$, and $\gamma$ denote, respectively, the input-activation matrix, the vector of the linking weights between hidden layer and output layer, and the vector of the desired output:

$$\Psi = \begin{bmatrix} \psi_0(\mathbf{x}_0) & \psi_1(\mathbf{x}_0) & \cdots & \psi_{N-1}(\mathbf{x}_0) \\ \psi_0(\mathbf{x}_1) & \psi_1(\mathbf{x}_1) & \cdots & \psi_{N-1}(\mathbf{x}_1) \\ \vdots & \vdots & \ddots & \vdots \\ \psi_0(\mathbf{x}_{M-1}) & \psi_1(\mathbf{x}_{M-1}) & \cdots & \psi_{N-1}(\mathbf{x}_{M-1}) \end{bmatrix} \in \mathbb{R}^{M \times N},$$

$$\mathbf{w} = [w_0, w_1, \cdots, w_{N-1}]^{\mathrm{T}} \in \mathbb{R}^N, \ \gamma = [\gamma_0, \gamma_1, \cdots, \gamma_{M-1}]^{\mathrm{T}} \in \mathbb{R}^M.$$

Then the optimal linking weights of the three-input Euler-polynomial neuronet can be directly determined by the so-called WDD subalgorithm [17,20,21,28], which can be expressed as the following

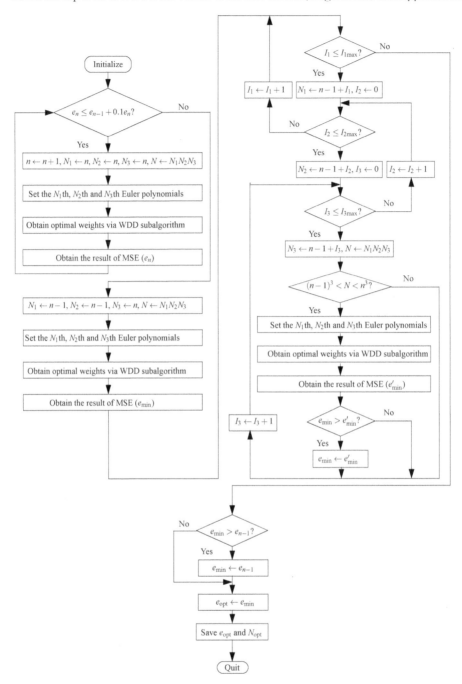

**FIGURE 7.8**: Flowchart of WASD algorithm for three-input Euler-polynomial neuronet.

computation formula:

$$\mathbf{w} = (\mathbf{\Psi}^{\mathrm{T}}\mathbf{\Psi})^{-1}\mathbf{\Psi}^{\mathrm{T}}\gamma. \tag{7.2}$$

It is worth mentioning that (7.2) can also be written as $\mathbf{w} = \mathrm{pinv}(\mathbf{\Psi})\gamma$, where $\mathrm{pinv}(\mathbf{\Psi})$ denotes the pseudoinverse of $\mathbf{\Psi}$ [equal to $(\mathbf{\Psi}^{\mathrm{T}}\mathbf{\Psi})^{-1}\mathbf{\Psi}^{\mathrm{T}}$ in usual situations] and works robustly even for the situation of $\mathbf{\Psi}$ being rank deficient [87].

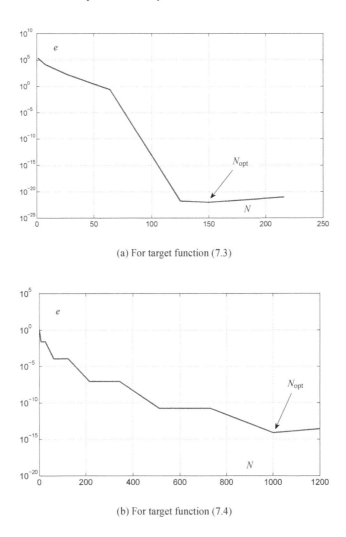

(a) For target function (7.3)

(b) For target function (7.4)

**FIGURE 7.9**: Searching process of three-input Euler-polynomial neuronet with WASD algorithm to obtain optimal number of hidden-layer neurons for target functions (7.3) and (7.4), respectively.

Furthermore, as mentioned above, the number of hidden-layer neurons can influence greatly the performance of the neuronet, and it is meaningful and important to obtain the optimal number of hidden-layer neurons. Moreover, the optimal number of hidden-layer neurons can be obtained by minimizing the values of the MSE function by considering different numbers of hidden-layer neurons. In order to illustrate the existence of the optimal number of hidden-layer neurons (i.e., $N_{\text{opt}}$) of the three-input Euler-polynomial neuronet, plenty of target functions have been tested to investigate the relationship between the MSE and the number of hidden-layer neurons, such as the

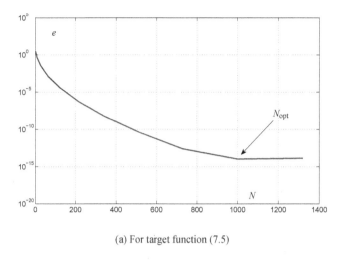

(a) For target function (7.5)

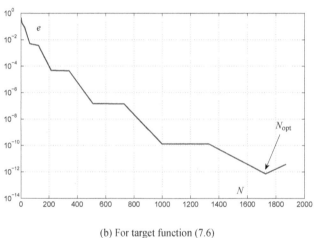

(b) For target function (7.6)

**FIGURE 7.10**: Searching process of three-input Euler-polynomial neuronet with WASD algorithm to obtain optimal number of hidden-layer neurons for target functions (7.5) and (7.6), respectively.

following four target functions:

$$f(x_1, x_2, x_3) = (x_1 + 5)^4 + x_1^3 + x_2^2 + x_3 + 30, \tag{7.3}$$

$$f(x_1, x_2, x_3) = \ln|(x_1 + x_2 + 10)| + \sin(x_2 x_3) + 20, \tag{7.4}$$

$$f(x_1, x_2, x_3) = \cos(x_2)\exp(x_1) - 2\sin(x_3) + 20, \tag{7.5}$$

$$f(x_1, x_2, x_3) = \frac{x_1 x_3 - x_2^2 + x_3^3}{10 - x_1^2} + \sin(x_1 x_2 + x_1 x_3) + 30. \tag{7.6}$$

Figs. 7.2 through 7.7 present, respectively, the relationship between the MSE (i.e., $e$) and the number of hidden-layer neurons (i.e., $N$) about four target functions (7.3) through (7.6), as for training (with the total number of training samples, $M = 4096$), testing (with the total number of testing samples, $M = 3375$) and prediction (with the total number of prediction samples, $M = 1000$). Note that all the curves shown in Figs. 7.2 through 7.7 have shapes roughly like the letter "U" or "V", thus called "U/V" plots. Additionally, each of the "U/V" plots has its own minimum point. Based on the

**TABLE 7.1:** Numerical results of three-input Euler-polynomial neuronet for target functions (7.3) through (7.6).

| Target function | $N_{opt}$ | $N_1$ | $N_2$ | $N_3$ | $e_{tra}$ | $e_{tes}$ | $e_{pre}$ |
|---|---|---|---|---|---|---|---|
| (7.3) | 150 | 5 | 6 | 5 | $9.95 \times 10^{-23}$ | $6.68 \times 10^{-23}$ | $1.54 \times 10^{-20}$ |
| (7.4) | 1000 | 10 | 10 | 10 | $8.14 \times 10^{-15}$ | $8.33 \times 10^{-16}$ | $6.84 \times 10^{-11}$ |
| (7.5) | 1000 | 10 | 10 | 10 | $1.07 \times 10^{-14}$ | $2.72 \times 10^{-15}$ | $1.43 \times 10^{-12}$ |
| (7.6) | 1728 | 12 | 12 | 12 | $7.32 \times 10^{-13}$ | $5.23 \times 10^{-13}$ | $1.69 \times 10^{-6}$ |

**TABLE 7.2:** Training outputs of three-input Euler-polynomial neuronet with $N_{opt} = 1000$ found by WASD algorithm for target function (7.5).

| $x_1$ | $x_2$ | $x_3$ | $\gamma$ | $y$ |
|---|---|---|---|---|
| $-1.50$ | $-1.50$ | $-1.50$ | 22.010773576344675 | 22.010774912579347 |
| 0.90 | 0.10 | $-1.50$ | 24.442305313740064 | 24.442305277013823 |
| 0.30 | $-1.50$ | $-1.30$ | 22.022601605528813 | 22.022601728443256 |
| $-0.50$ | 0.10 | $-1.10$ | 22.385915252905768 | 22.385915230950985 |
| $\vdots$ | $\vdots$ | $\vdots$ | $\vdots$ | $\vdots$ |
| 1.30 | 0.10 | $-0.90$ | 25.217619287176895 | 25.217619243130677 |
| 0.70 | $-1.50$ | $-0.70$ | 21.430882605852602 | 21.430882600129681 |
| $-0.70$ | $-1.50$ | $-0.30$ | 20.626167468102189 | 20.626167493865818 |
| $-1.50$ | 0.10 | $-0.10$ | 20.421682272040496 | 20.421682250937138 |
| $\vdots$ | $\vdots$ | $\vdots$ | $\vdots$ | $\vdots$ |
| 0.30 | 0.10 | 0.10 | 21.143448302781696 | 21.143448273846953 |
| $-0.30$ | $-1.50$ | 0.30 | 19.461362994552793 | 19.461362972860286 |
| $-1.10$ | 0.10 | 0.50 | 19.372357037571792 | 19.372357005551564 |
| 1.10 | 0.10 | 1.30 | 21.062041336179039 | 21.062041267038989 |
| $\vdots$ | $\vdots$ | $\vdots$ | $\vdots$ | $\vdots$ |

similar characteristics of other testing target functions (which are not shown in this chapter due to similarity), the WASD algorithm is thus designed to determine $N_{opt}$ by obtaining the minimal value of $e$ (i.e., $e_{opt}$) of the "U/V" plots.

More specifically, the flowchart of the WASD algorithm for the three-input Euler-polynomial neuronet is shown in Fig. 7.8 and briefed as the following. Firstly, in order to acquire the minimal value of $e$, let $n$ grow one-by-one with $N = N_1 N_2 N_3 = n^3$. Secondly, $N_{opt}$ is further obtained by calculating and minimizing the MSE of the three-input Euler-polynomial neuronet with different structures. It means that the values of $N_1$, $N_2$ and $N_3$ are not completely the same, with inequality $(n-1)^3 < N = N_1 N_2 N_3 < n^3$ satisfied. In detail, three parameters (i.e., $I_1$, $I_2$ and $I_3$) are used to investigate different structures, where $I_1 = 0, 1, \cdots, I_{1max}$, $I_2 = 0, 1, \cdots, I_{2max}$ and $I_3 = 0, 1, \cdots, I_{3max}$ ($I_{1max}$, $I_{2max}$ and $I_{3max}$ are set to be 2 in this chapter). Finally, by following the flowchart of the WASD algorithm, the $N_{opt}$ and $e_{opt}$ can be obtained: the optimal structure and weights of the three-input Euler-polynomial neuronet can be determined, and the best performance of the three-input Euler-polynomial neuronet can be guaranteed.

**TABLE 7.3:**   Testing outputs of three-input Euler-polynomial neuronet with $N_{opt} = 1000$ found by WASD algorithm for target function (7.5).

| $x_1$ | $x_2$ | $x_3$ | $\gamma$ | $y$ |
|---|---|---|---|---|
| $-1.35$ | $-1.35$ | $-1.35$ | 22.008222066298512 | 22.008222998232910 |
| 0.81 | 0.09 | $-1.35$ | 24.190256818543240 | 24.190256789003566 |
| 0.27 | $-1.35$ | $-1.17$ | 22.128392170037017 | 22.128392126443043 |
| $-0.45$ | 0.09 | $-0.99$ | 22.307099457454132 | 22.307099426755396 |
| $\vdots$ | $\vdots$ | $\vdots$ | $\vdots$ | $\vdots$ |
| $-0.99$ | $-1.35$ | $-0.81$ | 21.529952128842019 | 21.529952195202871 |
| 1.17 | 0.09 | $-0.81$ | 24.657526722827271 | 24.657526637362750 |
| 0.63 | $-1.35$ | $-0.63$ | 21.589498788500070 | 21.589498697796575 |
| $-0.09$ | 0.09 | $-0.45$ | 21.780163329978233 | 21.780163332580315 |
| $\vdots$ | $\vdots$ | $\vdots$ | $\vdots$ | $\vdots$ |
| 0.99 | $-1.35$ | $-0.09$ | 20.769155444375823 | 20.769155334876260 |
| 0.45 | $-1.35$ | 1.35 | 18.392024140418531 | 18.392024060058706 |
| 0.99 | 0.09 | 1.17 | 20.838841132440070 | 20.838841091333723 |
| 1.35 | $-1.35$ | 0.45 | 19.974870917963599 | 19.974870755027119 |
| $\vdots$ | $\vdots$ | $\vdots$ | $\vdots$ | $\vdots$ |

## 7.4   Numerical Studies

In this section, numerical results are presented to verify and substantiate the performance and efficacy of the three-input Euler-polynomial neuronet equipped with the WASD algorithm in terms of training (or, say, learning), testing and prediction. Note that, due to the similarity of results, only typical numerical results of training, testing and prediction about four target functions (7.3) through (7.6) are presented and analyzed in this chapter.

To verify the performance of the constructed three-input Euler-polynomial neuronet and WASD algorithm, we sample uniformly over the region $[-1.5, 1.5]^3$ with gap size 0.20 to generate a training sample set $\{(\mathbf{x}_m, \gamma_m), m = 1, 2, \cdots, 4096\}$ (i.e., $M = 4096$). Besides, the region $[-1.35, 1.35]^3$ with gap size 0.18 is used for testing, while the untrained regions $[-1.60, -1.50]^3$ and $[1.50, 1.60]^3$ (i.e., $x_1, x_2, x_3 \in [-1.60, -1.50] \bigcup [1.50, 1.60]$) with gap size 0.02 is used for prediction.

For better understanding, the searching process of $N_{opt}$ about four target functions (7.3) through (7.6) by exploiting the WASD algorithm for the three-input Euler-polynomial neuronet is visually presented in Figs. 7.9 and 7.10. With the determined optimal structures (i.e., $N_{opt} = N_1 N_2 N_3$) of the three-input Euler-polynomial neuronet about four target functions (7.3) through (7.6), the corresponding minimal values of MSE (specifically, $e_{tra}$, $e_{tes}$ and $e_{pre}$) are listed in Table 7.1. Note that $e_{tra}$, $e_{tes}$ and $e_{pre}$ denote, respectively, the values of MSE function of the three-input Euler-polynomial neuronet in terms of training, testing and prediction. The efficacy and accuracy of the three-input Euler-polynomial neuronet equipped with the WASD algorithm is substantiated by the tiny values of $e_{tra}$, $e_{tes}$ and $e_{pre}$ with their orders of magnitude being $10^{-6} \sim 10^{-23}$.

In order to further substantiate the performance of the three-input Euler-polynomial neuronet equipped with the WASD algorithm, numerical results (with $N_{opt} = 1000$) about target function (7.5) are listed in Tables 7.2 through 7.4 (some other results are omitted due to the similarity). Compared with the desired outputs (i.e., $\gamma$) of target function (7.5), the output results (i.e., $y$) of training, testing and prediction substantiate clearly the accuracy of the three-input Euler-polynomial neuronet equipped with the WASD algorithm. The above numerical results all substantiate the superior

**TABLE 7.4:** Prediction outputs of three-input Euler-polynomial neuronet with $N_{\text{opt}} = 1000$ found by WASD algorithm for target function (7.5).

| $x_1$ | $x_2$ | $x_3$ | $\gamma$ | $y$ |
|---|---|---|---|---|
| −1.60 | −1.60 | −1.60 | 21.993251924203271 | 21.993248141165925 |
| −1.54 | −1.52 | −1.60 | 22.010032296087459 | 22.010032370569537 |
| 1.50 | 1.54 | −1.60 | 22.137144951712660 | 22.137145758078333 |
| 1.58 | −1.60 | −1.60 | 21.857384815601012 | 21.857386405975468 |
| ⋮ | ⋮ | ⋮ | ⋮ | ⋮ |
| −1.58 | −1.52 | 1.50 | 18.015468306312389 | 18.015468774585752 |
| −1.52 | 1.54 | 1.50 | 18.011744484909830 | 18.011744492244365 |
| 1.54 | −1.60 | 1.50 | 17.868806219147800 | 17.868809176208373 |
| −1.52 | 1.54 | 1.60 | 18.007587252034927 | 18.007587110480316 |
| ⋮ | ⋮ | ⋮ | ⋮ | ⋮ |
| 1.50 | 1.54 | −1.50 | 22.132987718837761 | 22.132988379701299 |
| 1.58 | −1.60 | −1.50 | 21.853227582726110 | 21.853229584666902 |
| 1.54 | −1.60 | 1.60 | 17.864648986272897 | 17.864651788387718 |
| 1.60 | −1.52 | 1.60 | 18.252340464124970 | 18.252340591381795 |
| ⋮ | ⋮ | ⋮ | ⋮ | ⋮ |

efficacy and performance of the three-input Euler-polynomial neuronet equipped with the WASD algorithm.

## 7.5 Chapter Summary

In this chapter, a three-input Euler-polynomial neuronet has been established and investigated to learn the four-dimensional data. Moreover, a so-called WASD algorithm has been developed to determine the optimal weights and structure of the established three-input Euler-polynomial neuronet. The numerical results have substantiated the efficacy, accuracy and superior performance of the three-input Euler-polynomial neuronet equipped with the WASD algorithm in terms of training, testing and prediction.

# Chapter 8

## *Three-Input Power-Activation WASD Neuronet*

In this chapter, a three-input feed-forward power-activation neuronet is constructed and investigated. For the three-input power-activation neuronet, a weights-and-structure-determination (WASD) algorithm is presented to solve function data approximation (or, say, learning) and prediction problems. With the weights-direct-determination (WDD) subalgorithm exploited, the WASD algorithm can obtain the optimal weights of the three-input power-activation neuronet between hidden layer and output layer directly. Moreover, the WASD algorithm determines the optimal structure (i.e., the optimal number of hidden-layer neurons) of the three-input power-activation neuronet adaptively by growing and pruning hidden-layer neurons during the training process. Numerical results of illustrative examples highlight the efficacy of the three-input power-activation neuronet equipped with the so-called WASD algorithm.

## 8.1   Introduction

Numerous engineering applications such as nonlinear system identification and control [88], classification [89] and forecast [90] are difficult tasks because most system models are not perfectly known. Instead, input and output data of many systems can be observed easily. Therefore, function data approximation (or say, learning) becomes one of the most important tasks, which refers to learning sample data to functions and models (e.g., approximators) [91]. Neuronet was proved to be a universal approximator by various researchers [92–95]. Theoretically, a three-layer feed-forward neuronet can approximate any nonlinear continuous function with an arbitrary accuracy [96–98].

In this chapter, with the three-layer structure adopted, a new type of three-input feed-forward power-activation neuronet is constructed and investigated for function data approximation. In light

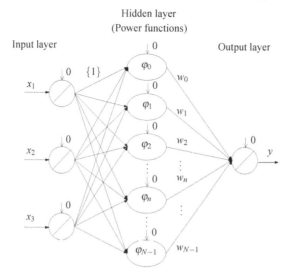

**FIGURE 8.1**: Model structure of three-input power-activation neuronet.

of the previous works [28, 96, 99], the number of hidden-layer neurons influences greatly the over-all performance of neuronets. Specifically speaking, the neuronet with too few hidden-layer neurons may fail to achieve the expected learning accuracy, while excess hidden-layer neurons may result in over-fitting phenomenon, poor generalization ability and high computational complexity [28, 99, 100]. Therefore, it is especially important and meaningful to determine the optimal structure of the neuronet. For this reason, a novel WASD algorithm is presented for the three-input power-activation neuronet in this chapter. More specifically, (1) the WASD algorithm exploits the WDD subalgorithm [21, 99] to determine the optimal weights between hidden-layer and output-layer neurons of the three-input power-activation neuronet directly; (2) the WASD algorithm grows and prunes hidden-layer neurons during the training process to obtain the optimal structure (i.e., the optimal number of hidden-layer neurons) of the three-input power-activation neuronet. Numerical results further substantiate that the proposed three-input power-activation neuronet equipped with the above WASD algorithm has superior performances in terms of function data approximation (or, say, learning), testing (or, say, generalization) and prediction.

## 8.2    Theoretical Basis and Analysis

In this section, the detailed descriptions of related theoretical basis and analysis are presented for constructing the three-input power-activation neuronet. Firstly, the theorem of Taylor polynomial approximation [18] is given as follows.

**Theorem 3** *Suppose that a target function $f$ has the $(K+1)$th-order continuous derivative on interval $[a, b]$, and $K$ is a nonnegative integer, then for $x \in [a, b]$,*

$$f(x) = P_K(x) + R_K(x),$$

*where $R_K(x)$ is the error term and $P_K(x)$ is a polynomial that can be used to approximate $f(x)$. That* *is, with a fixed value $c \in [a,b]$, $f(x)$ can be approximated as*

$$f(x) \approx P_K(x) = \sum_{i=0}^{K} \frac{f^{(i)}(c)}{i!}(x-c)^i,$$

*where $i!$ denotes the factorial of $i$ and $f^{(i)}(c)$ denotes the value of the $i$th-order derivative of $f(x)$ at the point $c$.*

Note that $P_K(x)$ is the so-called $K$-order Taylor series of function $f(x)$. In the special case with $c = 0$, $P_K(x)$ is also called the Maclaurin series [101].

**Proposition 6** *The theorem of Taylor polynomial approximation can be generalized to functions with more than one variable [96, 101, 102]. For a target function $f(x_1, \cdots, x_g)$ with g variables, which has the $(K+1)$th-order continuous partial derivatives in a neighborhood of the origin $(0, \cdots, 0)$, the $K$-order Taylor series $P_K(x_1, \cdots, x_g)$ about the origin is*

$$P_K(x_1, \cdots, x_g) = \sum_{i=0}^{K} \sum_{i_1 + \cdots + i_g = i} \frac{x_1^{i_1} \cdots x_g^{i_g}}{i_1! \cdots i_g!} \left( \frac{\partial^{i_1 + \cdots + i_g} f(0, \cdots, 0)}{\partial x_1^{i_1} \cdots \partial x_g^{i_g}} \right),$$

*where $i_1, \cdots, i_g$ are nonnegative integers.*

In this chapter, a continuous real target function $f(x_1, x_2, x_3)$ with three variables is investigated. Note that the target function $f(x_1, x_2, x_3)$ has the $(K+1)$th-order continuous partial derivatives in a neighborhood of the origin $(0,0,0)$. According to the above theoretical result, the $K$-order Taylor series $P_K(x_1, x_2, x_3)$ of $f(x_1, x_2, x_3)$ about the origin $(0,0,0)$ is

$$P_K(x_1, x_2, x_3) = \sum_{i=0}^{K} \sum_{i_1 + i_2 + i_3 = i} \frac{x_1^{i_1} x_2^{i_2} x_3^{i_3}}{i_1! i_2! i_3!} \left( \frac{\partial^{i_1 + i_2 + i_3} f(0,0,0)}{\partial x_1^{i_1} \partial x_2^{i_2} \partial x_3^{i_3}} \right),$$

which can be used to approximate $f(x_1, x_2, x_3)$, i.e.,

$$f(x_1, x_2, x_3) \approx P_K(x_1, x_2, x_3).$$

In addition, $P_K(x_1, x_2, x_3)$ can be rewritten in the form of $K$-order power series, then we have

$$\begin{aligned}
f(x_1, x_2, x_3) \approx & w_{000} x_1^0 x_2^0 x_3^0 + w_{100} x_1^1 x_2^0 x_3^0 + w_{010} x_1^0 x_2^1 x_3^0 + \\
& w_{001} x_1^0 x_2^0 x_3^1 + w_{200} x_1^2 x_2^0 x_3^0 + w_{110} x_1^1 x_2^1 x_3^0 + \\
& w_{101} x_1^1 x_2^0 x_3^1 + w_{020} x_1^0 x_2^2 x_3^0 + w_{011} x_1^0 x_2^1 x_3^1 + \\
& w_{002} x_1^0 x_2^0 x_3^2 + \cdots + w_{i_1 i_2 i_3} x_1^{i_1} x_2^{i_2} x_3^{i_3} + \cdots + \\
& w_{K00} x_1^K x_2^0 x_3^0 + \cdots + w_{00K} x_1^0 x_2^0 x_3^K,
\end{aligned}$$

where the weight for $x_1^{i_1} x_2^{i_2} x_3^{i_3}$ can be expressed as

$$w_{i_1 i_2 i_3} = \frac{1}{i_1! i_2! i_3!} \left( \frac{\partial^{i_1 + i_2 + i_3} f(0,0,0)}{\partial x_1^{i_1} \partial x_2^{i_2} \partial x_3^{i_3}} \right).$$

Thus, an unknown target function $f(x_1, x_2, x_3)$ can be best estimated via the optimal weights $\{w_{i_1 i_2 i_3}\}$ corresponding to basis functions $\{x_1^{i_1} x_2^{i_2} x_3^{i_3}\}$.

In this chapter, the basis functions $\{x_1^{i_1} x_2^{i_2} x_3^{i_3}\}$ are sequenced by a method detailed as below, which is similar to the graded lexicographic order [103] to some extent.

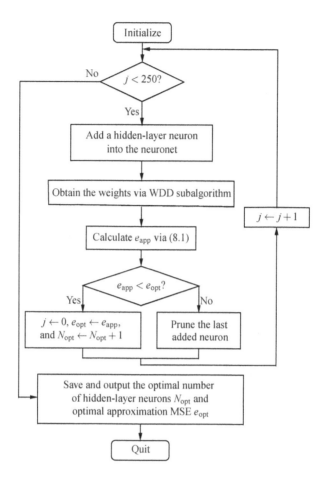

**FIGURE 8.2**: Flowchart of WASD algorithm for three-input power-activation neuronet.

Let $\varphi_n = \varphi_n(x_1, x_2, x_3) = x_1^{i_1} x_2^{i_2} x_3^{i_3}$ and $\varphi_{n'} = \varphi_{n'}(x_1, x_2, x_3) = x_1^{i_1'} x_2^{i_2'} x_3^{i_3'}$ be two different basis functions sequenced by the new method, where $n$ and $n'$ are two different nonnegative integers. Then, we say that $n > n'$ if either of the following two conditions is satisfied, that is,

*Condition 1:* $(i_1 + i_2 + i_3) > (i_1' + i_2' + i_3')$;

*Condition 2:* $(i_1 + i_2 + i_3) = (i_1' + i_2' + i_3')$ and the first nonzero element of the difference $(i_1 - i_1', i_2 - i_2', i_3 - i_3')$ is negative.

For better understanding, the basis functions $\{\varphi_n | n = 0, 1, \cdots, 9\}$ sequenced by the method are listed below:

$$\begin{aligned}
&\varphi_0 = x_1^0 x_2^0 x_3^0, \quad \varphi_1 = x_1^1 x_2^0 x_3^0, \quad \varphi_2 = x_1^0 x_2^1 x_3^0, \quad \varphi_3 = x_1^0 x_2^0 x_3^1, \\
&\varphi_4 = x_1^2 x_2^0 x_3^0, \quad \varphi_5 = x_1^1 x_2^1 x_3^0, \quad \varphi_6 = x_1^1 x_2^0 x_3^1, \quad \varphi_7 = x_1^0 x_2^2 x_3^0, \\
&\varphi_8 = x_1^0 x_2^1 x_3^1, \quad \varphi_9 = x_1^0 x_2^0 x_3^2.
\end{aligned}$$

In light of the above theoretical analysis, the unknown target function $f(x_1, x_2, x_3)$ can be approximated by an approximator $\varphi = \varphi(x_1, x_2, x_3)$, i.e., $y = \sum_{n=0}^{N-1} w_n \varphi_n$, where $N$ denotes the number of basis functions used to approximate $f(x_1, x_2, x_3)$ and $\{w_n | n = 0, 1, \cdots, N-1\}$ denote the corresponding weights for the basis functions $\{\varphi_n | n = 0, 1, \cdots, N-1\}$.

## 8.3 Neuronet Model and WASD Algorithm

In this section, the model of the three-input power-activation neuronet is constructed, and then the WASD algorithm is developed to achieve the superior performance of the three-input power-activation neuronet.

### 8.3.1 Three-input power-activation neuronet model

According to the theoretical basis and analysis in Section 8.2, the three-input power-activation neuronet is proposed with its structure shown in Fig. 8.1. As seen from Fig. 8.1, a conventional three-layer structure, which includes the input layer, hidden layer and output layer, is applied in the three-input power-activation neuronet. The input-layer and output-layer neurons are activated by simple linear identical functions. In addition, the hidden layer has $N$ neurons, which are activated by a group of basis functions $\{\varphi_n | n = 0, 1, \cdots, N-1\}$. The weights linking the input-layer and hidden-layer neurons are set to be 1, and $\{w_n | n = 0, 1, \cdots, N-1\}$ shown in Fig. 8.1 denote the weights linking the hidden-layer and output-layer neurons which should be determined. In order to simplify the computational complexity, all neuronal thresholds are 0.

### 8.3.2 WASD algorithm

In order to achieve the superior performance of the proposed three-input power-activation neuronet model, the WASD algorithm is presented in this subsection. The WASD algorithm can obtain the optimal weights from hidden layer to output layer directly by utilizing the so-called WDD subalgorithm. Moreover, the WASD algorithm can determine the optimal structure (i.e., the optimal number of hidden-layer neurons) of the three-input power-activation neuronet adaptively by growing and pruning hidden-layer neurons during the training process.

For the purpose of illustration, a set of sample data is given as $\{(\mathbf{x}_m, \gamma_m) | \mathbf{x}_m \in \mathbb{R}^3, \gamma_m \in \mathbb{R}, m = 1, 2, \cdots, M\}$, where $\mathbf{x}_m = [x_{1m}, x_{2m}, x_{3m}]^{\mathrm{T}}$, with superscript $^{\mathrm{T}}$ denoting the transpose of a vector or a matrix, denotes the $m$th sample input vector, and $\gamma_m$ denotes the $m$th sample output (or, say, the desired output). Note that $M$ is the total number of samples. Then, the mean square error (MSE) for the three-input power-activation neuronet is defined as

$$e = \frac{1}{M} \sum_{m=1}^{M} \left( \gamma_m - \sum_{n=0}^{N-1} w_n \varphi_n(\mathbf{x}_m) \right)^2, \tag{8.1}$$

where $\varphi_n(\mathbf{x}_m) = \varphi_n([x_{1m}, x_{2m}, x_{3m}]^{\mathrm{T}}) = \varphi_n(x_{1m}, x_{2m}, x_{3m})$. It is worth mentioning that $e$ is an important argument for measuring the performances of the three-input power-activation neuronet in function data approximation, testing and prediction. Besides, the weight vector $\mathbf{w}$, the desired-output vector $\gamma$ and the input-activation matrix $\Psi$ are defined, respectively, as

$$\mathbf{w} = \begin{bmatrix} w_0 \\ w_1 \\ \vdots \\ w_{N-1} \end{bmatrix}^{\mathrm{T}} \in \mathbb{R}^N, \quad \gamma = \begin{bmatrix} \gamma_1 \\ \gamma_2 \\ \vdots \\ \gamma_M \end{bmatrix}^{\mathrm{T}} \in \mathbb{R}^M, \quad \Psi = \begin{bmatrix} \varphi_0(\mathbf{x}_1) & \varphi_1(\mathbf{x}_1) & \cdots & \varphi_{N-1}(\mathbf{x}_1) \\ \varphi_0(\mathbf{x}_2) & \varphi_1(\mathbf{x}_2) & \cdots & \varphi_{N-1}(\mathbf{x}_2) \\ \vdots & \vdots & \ddots & \vdots \\ \varphi_0(\mathbf{x}_M) & \varphi_1(\mathbf{x}_M) & \cdots & \varphi_{N-1}(\mathbf{x}_M) \end{bmatrix} \in \mathbb{R}^{M \times N}.$$

Then, the optimal weights can be determined directly via the following so-called WDD subalgorithm [21, 28, 99]:

$$\mathbf{w} = (\Psi^{\mathrm{T}} \Psi)^{-1} \Psi^{\mathrm{T}} \gamma. \tag{8.2}$$

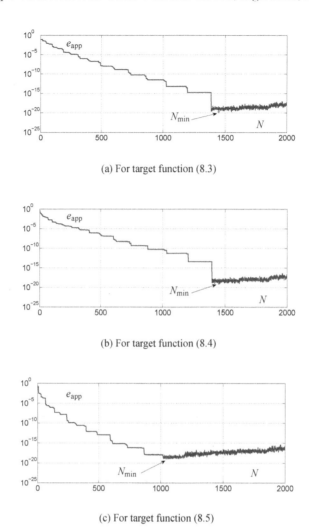

(a) For target function (8.3)

(b) For target function (8.4)

(c) For target function (8.5)

**FIGURE 8.3**: Relationship between approximation MSE $e_{app}$ and number $N$ of hidden-layer neurons.

The WDD subalgorithm (8.2) can be rewritten as $\mathbf{w} = \text{pinv}(\Psi)\gamma$, where $\text{pinv}(\Psi)$ denotes the pseudoinverse of $\Psi$. Moreover, $\text{pinv}(\Psi)$ can be done by calling MATLAB routine "pinv" [96].

In light of previous works [28, 99], the number of hidden-layer neurons influences greatly the overall performance of neuronets as well as the three-input power-activation neuronet. Thus, it is important and meaningful to determine the optimal structure of the three-input power-activation neuronet. For this reason, a WASD algorithm is designed in this chapter to determine the optimal structure of the three-input power-activation neuronet, which grows and prunes hidden-layer neurons according to the changes of the approximation MSE (i.e., $e_{app}$) during the training process. For better understanding, the flowchart of the WASD algorithm is shown in Fig. 8.2. It is worth pointing out that $j$ shown in Fig. 8.2 denotes a counter and is initially set to be zero. Without loss of generality, the maximal value of the counter is set as 250 in the flowchart of the WASD algorithm. In addition, $e_{opt}$ shown in Fig. 8.2 is initially set to be large enough.

Actually before presenting the WASD algorithm, we have fully investigated the relationship between $e_{app}$ (i.e., the approximation ability) and the number $N$ of hidden-layer neurons of the

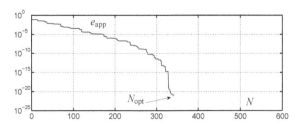

(a) For target function (8.3)

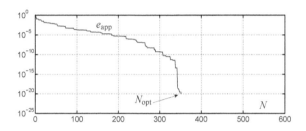

(b) For target function (8.4)

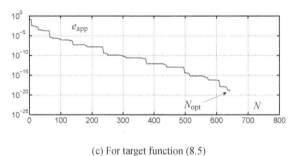

(c) For target function (8.5)

**FIGURE 8.4**: Finding optimal number $N_{opt}$ of hidden-layer neurons for three-input power-activation neuronet via WASD algorithm.

three-input power-activation neuronet via a variety of target functions. The following three target functions are chosen for the purpose of better illustration:

$$f(x_1,x_2,x_3) = 10x_2x_3\sin(x_1)\exp(-2x_1^2 - 2x_2^2) + 5, \tag{8.3}$$

$$f(x_1,x_2,x_3) = x_2\exp(x_1\sin(\pi x_1 x_3)) + x_1 x_3^2 + 10, \tag{8.4}$$

$$f(x_1,x_2,x_3) = \frac{0.05x_3\exp(x_2)\sin(x_1)}{10 - x_2^2} + \sin(x_1x_2 + x_1x_3) + 30. \tag{8.5}$$

The numerical results of target functions (8.3) through (8.5) are shown in Fig. 8.3 which illustrate clearly the relationship between $e_{app}$ and the number (i.e., $N$) of hidden-layer neurons. As seen from Fig. 8.3, all curves decline like the shape of a ladder before the particular point $(N_{min}, e_{min})$, and, after the particular point $(N_{min}, e_{min})$, the curves show an increasing trend with oscillation, where $N_{min}$ denotes the number of hidden-layer neurons with the minimal approximation MSE $e_{min}$. It is worth mentioning that such characteristics can be found in the training process of many other target functions. It means that there exists a structure of the three-input power-activation neuronet with the best performance in approximation, i.e., the particular point $(N_{\min}, e_{\min})$, for most of target functions. Besides, we can obtain this particular point $(N_{\min}, e_{\min})$ easily via the following pure-growing (PG) type algorithm: (1) record the point with the minimal $e_{\text{app}}$ found by far as the number of hidden-layer neurons increases one by one; (2) when $e_{\text{app}}$ begins to increase, look forward 250 points (or, say, 250 neurons) to make sure that $(N_{\min}, e_{\min})$ is found.

Unfortunately, the structure of the three-input power-activation neuronet determined via the above-mentioned PG type algorithm is fat, since the number of hidden-layer neurons is pretty large, which may lead to a very high computational complexity. To propose a more effective algorithm for the determination of the number of hidden-layer neurons, numerical results on a variety of target functions are further investigated. As seen from Fig. 8.3, the increase of the hidden-layer neurons $N$ may not result in the corresponding decrease in the $e_{\text{app}}$ before the particular point $(N_{\min}, e_{\min})$, which implies that some hidden-layer neurons are redundant for function data approximation. In view of the similar characteristics of many other target functions, the WASD algorithm is developed to prune the redundant hidden-layer neurons (while growing) during the training process. As mentioned above, the MSE is an important argument for measuring the performance of the three-input power-activation neuronet. Thus, such a WASD algorithm of pruning-while-growing (PWG) type is designed to determine the optimal number of hidden-layer neurons by growing and pruning the hidden-layer neurons according to the changes of the approximation MSE (i.e., $e_{\text{app}}$). Specifically speaking, if the newly added hidden-layer neuron makes the three-input power-activation neuronet achieve better performance in approximation (or, say, makes the approximation MSE decrease), reserve the new hidden-layer neuron; otherwise, prune this newly added hidden-layer neuron. In this way, the WASD algorithm can determine the optimal structure (i.e., the optimal number of hidden-layer neurons $N_{\text{opt}}$) of the three-input power-activation neuronet with its efficacy substantiated in Fig. 8.4.

## 8.4   Numerical Studies

In this section, numerical studies are performed to substantiate the efficacy of the three-input power-activation neuronet equipped with the WASD algorithm in terms of function data approximation, testing and prediction. In consideration of similarity of results, numerical results are shown only for the aforementioned target functions (8.3) through (8.5).

### 8.4.1   Approximation

To verify the superior approximation ability of the three-input power-activation neuronet equipped with the WASD algorithm, numerical results about function data approximation are presented and analyzed.

For each target function, we sample uniformly over the region $[-1, 0.8]^3$ with gap size 0.2 to generate a set of sample data $\{(\mathbf{x}_m, \gamma_m) | \mathbf{x}_m \in \mathbb{R}^3, \gamma_m \in \mathbb{R}, m = 1, 2, \cdots, 1000\}$ (i.e., the number of samples $M = 1000$) for training. Via numerical studies on target function (8.3) through (8.5), the approximation performance between three-input power-activation neuronet with PWG-type WASD algorithm and PG algorithm is provided in Table 8.1. As shown in the table, the optimal number of hidden-layer neurons determined via the WASD algorithm for each target function (i.e., $N_{\text{opt}}$) is less than 650, while the number of hidden-layer neurons determined via the PG algorithm for each target function (i.e., $N_{\min}$) is more than 1000. Moreover, the approximation MSE corresponding to $N_{\text{opt}}$ (i.e., $e_{\text{opt}}$) is smaller than that corresponding to $N_{\min}$ (i.e., $e_{\min}$) for each target function. In other

**TABLE 8.1:** Approximation results of three-input power-activation neuronet with PWG-type WASD algorithm and PG algorithm.

| Target function | Via PWG-type WASD algorithm | | Via PG algorithm | |
|---|---|---|---|---|
| | $N_{opt}$ | $e_{opt}$ | $N_{min}$ | $e_{min}$ |
| (8.3) | 340 | $1.2717 \times 10^{-21}$ | 1447 | $1.9324 \times 10^{-20}$ |
| (8.4) | 351 | $1.8979 \times 10^{-20}$ | 1447 | $7.3417 \times 10^{-20}$ |
| (8.5) | 640 | $1.3804 \times 10^{-19}$ | 1048 | $1.2433 \times 10^{-18}$ |

**TABLE 8.2:** Testing results of three-input power-activation neuronet with PWG-type WASD algorithm and PG algorithm.

| Target function | Via PWG-type WASD algorithm | | Via PG algorithm | |
|---|---|---|---|---|
| | $t_{tes}$ (s) | $e_{tes}$ | $t_{tes}$ (s) | $e_{tes}$ |
| (8.3) | 2.24 | $1.6471 \times 10^{-6}$ | 32.03 | $2.4867 \times 10^{-5}$ |
| (8.4) | 2.29 | $2.0294 \times 10^{-7}$ | 32.54 | $9.0050 \times 10^{-7}$ |
| (8.5) | 7.30 | $1.0279 \times 10^{-12}$ | 17.21 | $1.2193 \times 10^{-10}$ |

words, the three-input power-activation neuronet with WASD algorithm achieves better performance on approximation with simpler structure (or to say, fewer hidden-layer neurons) compared with the neuronet with PG algorithm. Together with the above analysis, numerical results have verified the efficacy of the three-input power-activation neuronet with WASD algorithm on function data approximation.

### 8.4.2 Testing and prediction

To further substantiate the superiority of the three-input power-activation neuronet with WASD algorithm on testing (or, say, generalization), a set of sample data with 1331 samples is generated by sampling uniformly over region $[-0.85, 0.75]^3$ with gap size 0.15. The numerical results on testing are shown in Table 8.2. From the table, we can see that the three-input power-activation neuronet with WASD algorithm achieves superior performance in terms of testing MSE (i.e., $e_{tes}$) being very small (i.e., of order $10^{-6} \sim 10^{-12}$), which also substantiates the good generalization ability of the three-input power-activation neuronet with WASD algorithm. Besides, Table 8.2 shows that the three-input power-activation neuronet with has smaller testing MSE and much shorter testing time (i.e., $t_{tes}$) than the neuronet with PG algorithm for each target function, which further substantiates the better efficacy and the less computational complexity of the three-input power-activation neuronet with WASD algorithm on testing.

Following the above numerical results about the generalization ability, we further investigate the prediction ability of the three-input power-activation neuronet with WASD algorithm. To perform numerical studies about prediction, some samples are selected beyond region $[-1, 0.8]^3$. Due to space limitation, prediction results of the three-input power-activation neuronet with WASD algorithm are shown only for target function (8.5), which are given in Table 8.3. From the table, we can easily find that the output of the three-input power-activation neuronet with WASD algorithm (i.e., $y_{pre}$) is approximately equal to the desired output (i.e., $\gamma_{pre}$) for each sample. Note that, for the selected samples shown in Table 8.3, the MSE of prediction $e_{pre}$ is less than $10^{-4}$, which further substantiates the efficacy of the proposed three-input power-activation neuronet with WASD algorithm on prediction.

**TABLE 8.3:**    Prediction results of three-input power-activation neuronet with WASD algorithm for target function (8.5).

| $x_1$ | $x_2$ | $x_3$ | $y_{pre}$ | $\gamma_{pre}$ |
|---|---|---|---|---|
| 0.85 | 0.85 | 0.85 | 31.00010686784 | 31.00015019266 |
| 0.85 | 0.90 | 0.90 | 31.00805437999 | 31.00821618498 |
| 0.90 | 0.90 | 0.95 | 31.00508232559 | 31.00552443671 |
| 0.90 | 0.95 | 0.95 | 31.00040031355 | 31.00090214440 |
| 0.95 | 0.95 | 1.00 | 30.97094431295 | 30.97214275323 |
| −1.05 | 0.85 | 0.85 | 29.01362877198 | 29.01355709640 |
| −1.05 | −1.05 | 0.85 | 30.20708959075 | 30.20700998407 |
| −1.10 | 0.90 | −0.85 | 29.95519878420 | 29.95516490634 |
| 0.90 | −1.05 | −1.10 | 29.06335040214 | 29.06389783763 |
| 1.00 | −1.10 | 0.90 | 29.80251202694 | 29.80276463520 |
| −1.05 | −1.05 | −1.05 | 30.80756705825 | 30.80733487673 |
| −1.10 | −1.05 | −1.10 | 30.70376596239 | 30.70278082275 |
| −1.15 | −1.15 | −1.10 | 30.52928221080 | 30.52800377075 |
| −1.20 | −1.15 | −1.15 | 30.37803454799 | 30.37435458838 |
| −1.20 | −1.20 | −1.20 | 30.26924215768 | 30.26058704670 |

**TABLE 8.4:**    Numerical results of three-input power-activation neuronet with WASD algorithm under further simplification.

| Target function | $N_{sim}$ | $e_{app}$ | $e_{tes}$ | $t_{tes}$ (s) |
|---|---|---|---|---|
| (8.3) | 79 | $2.1513 \times 10^{-23}$ | $1.6471 \times 10^{-6}$ | 0.17 |
| (8.4) | 101 | $6.4547 \times 10^{-21}$ | $2.0294 \times 10^{-7}$ | 0.26 |
| (8.5) | 635 | $1.8787 \times 10^{-19}$ | $1.0279 \times 10^{-12}$ | 7.18 |

In summary, we can conclude from Tables 8.2 and 8.3 that the proposed three-input power-activation neuronet with WASD algorithm achieves good performances in terms of testing and prediction.

### 8.4.3    Further simplification

As mentioned above, the WASD algorithm is designed to prune redundant hidden-layer neurons during the training process in order to determine the structure of the three-input power-activation neuronet. Besides, the above numerical results have substantiated that the three-input power-activation neuronet with the PWG-type WASD algorithm has better performances and a simpler structure than the neuronet with PG algorithm which does not include a pruning process. As an extension and exploration, we further prune the redundant hidden-layer neurons of the three-input power-activation neuronet with WASD algorithm in expectation for even better performances and an even simpler structure, i.e., the further simplification of the three-input power-activation neuronet with WASD algorithm. Specifically speaking, first of all, for a determined structure of the three-input power-activation neuronet with WASD algorithm (i.e., $N_{opt}$), the influence factor $\delta_l$ of the $l$th hidden-layer neuron to the neuronet output is defined as

$$\delta_l = \frac{|\text{sum}(w_l \mathbf{o}_l)|}{\sum_{n=0}^{N_{opt}-1} |\text{sum}(w_n \mathbf{o}_n)|},$$

where $\mathbf{o}_l = [\varphi_l(\mathbf{x}_1), \varphi_l(\mathbf{x}_2), \cdots, \varphi_l(\mathbf{x}_M)]^\mathsf{T}$ denotes the output vector of the $l$th hidden-layer neuron, and $\mathrm{sum}(w_l\mathbf{o}_l)$ denotes the summation of the elements of the weighted output vector $w_l\mathbf{o}_l$; so do $\mathbf{o}_n$ and $\mathrm{sum}(w_n\mathbf{o}_n)$; and $|\cdot|$ denotes the absolute value of a scalar argument. Then, the three-input power-activation neuronet with a further simpler structure can be obtained by pruning hidden-layer neurons, of which the influence factors are small enough (e.g., less than $10^{-12}$). Moreover, the corresponding numerical results are given in Table 8.4, where $N_{\mathrm{sim}}$ denotes the number of hidden-layer neurons with simplification structure of the neuronet. Comparing Table 8.1 and Table 8.4, we see that more than 70% of the hidden-layer neurons have been deleted for target functions (8.3) and (8.4), and 5 hidden-layer neurons have been deleted for target function (8.5). In addition, the three-input power-activation neuronet has better approximation performance for target functions (8.3) and (8.4), which is illustrated via Table 8.1 and Table 8.4. Moreover, with the structure being further simpler, the three-input power-activation neuronet has shorter testing time and barely changed generalization performance for target functions (8.3) through (8.5), which is illustrated via Table 8.2 and Table 8.4.

## 8.5 Chapter Summary

In order to explore the abilities of multi-input neuronets, a new type of feed-forward three-input power-activation neuronet has been presented, constructed and investigated in this chapter. Then, the relationship between the number of hidden-layer neurons and the approximation performance of the three-input power-activation neuronet has been fully investigated on the basis of the WDD subalgorithm. In light of the above investigation, a novel WASD algorithm of PWG type (i.e., the PWG-type WASD algorithm) has been proposed to determine the optimal weights and the optimal number of hidden-layer neurons for the three-input power-activation neuronet. Numerical results have further substantiated the superiority of the three-input power-activation neuronet equipped with the PWG-type WASD algorithm in terms of approximation, testing and prediction. Finally, a further simplification has been done on the three-input power-activation neuronet with WASD algorithm in expectation for even better performances and an even simpler structure. Numerical results and comparisons have shown the advantages of the further simplification on the three-input power-activation neuronet with WASD algorithm, i.e., the resultant final three-input power-activation neuronet.

# Part IV

# General Multi-Input Neuronet

# Chapter 9

## *Multi-Input Euler-Polynomial WASD Neuronet*

Differing from the conventional back-propagation (BP) neuronets, a multi-input Euler-polynomial neuronet, in short, MIEPN (specifically, four-input Euler-polynomial neuronet, FIEPN) is established and investigated in this chapter. In order to achieve satisfactory performance of the established MIEPN, a weights-and-structure-determination (WASD) algorithm with pruning-while-growing (PWG) and twice-pruning (TP) techniques is built up for the established MIEPN. By employing the weights-direct-determination (WDD) subalgorithm, the WASD algorithm not only determines the optimal connecting weights between hidden layer and output layer directly, but also obtains the optimal number of hidden-layer neurons. Specifically, a sub-optimal structure is obtained via the PWG technique, then the redundant hidden-layer neurons are further pruned via the TP technique. Consequently, the optimal structure of the MIEPN is obtained. To provide a reasonable choice in practice, several different MATLAB computing routines related to the WDD subalgorithm are studied. Comparative numerical results of the FIEPN using these different MATLAB computing routines and the standard multi-layer perceptron (MLP) neuronet further verify the superior performance and efficacy of the proposed MIEPN equipped with the WASD algorithm including PWG and TP techniques in terms of training, testing and prediction.

## 9.1 Introduction

With the rapid development of information technology, artificial intelligence and digital electronic technology, many meaningful theoretical investigation results, as well as software and hardware implementations of an artificial neuronet, especially the neuronets based on back-propagation (BP) algorithms, have been proposed and developed [104–112]. As we know, it is meaningful and important to obtain the optimal connecting weights and the optimal number of hidden-layer neurons (i.e., the optimal structure) of the neuronets, especially the general multi-input neuronets, which can largely reduce the computational complexity and facilitate the realization of hardware, and improve the performance of the neuronets [104]. However, BP-type algorithms usually have a high computational complexity for obtaining the optimal connecting weights [104]. Moreover, for the general multi-input BP-type neuronets, it is still a bottleneck problem to determine the optimal neuronet structure [17, 21, 105].

Since multi-input systems are the most frequently encountered systems, based on the authors' previous experience [17,21,99], a novel MIEPN [specifically, FIEPN] is established and investigated in this chapter, which is different from the BP-type neuronets. Moreover, a WASD algorithm with PWG and TP techniques is built up for the established FIEPN.

With the WDD subalgorithm employed, both the optimal connecting weights between hidden layer and output layer and the optimal number of hidden-layer neurons can be determined and obtained by the WASD algorithm. Specifically, the optimal connecting weights are determined directly by the WDD subalgorithm. In addition, a sub optimal structure is obtained via the PWG technique, then the redundant hidden-layer neurons are further pruned via the TP technique. Consequently, the optimal structure of the FIEPN is obtained. It is worth pointing out that the realizations of the so-called PWG and TP techniques are based on a lexicographic ordering method, which is employed to number the hidden-layer neurons. Numerical results substantiate the superior performance of the proposed FIEPN equipped with the WASD algorithm in terms of training, testing and prediction.

The remainder of this chapter is organized into six sections. Section 9.2 presents the related theoretical basis and analysis of the FIEPN. Section 9.3 describes the details of the neuronet, including the structure and the related parameters. Meanwhile, the lexicographic ordering method is developed in Section 9.3. The WDD subalgorithm and its theoretical analysis and related MATLAB computing routines are discussed and analyzed in Section 9.4. The WASD algorithm with PWG and TP techniques is presented and illustrated in Section 9.5. In Section 9.6, comparative numerical results of the FIEPN using different MATLAB computing routines and the standard MLP neuronet are presented to verify the performance and efficacy of the proposed MIEPN equipped with the WASD algorithm for function (data) training, testing and prediction in the form of four inputs and single output. Finally, conclusions are drawn in Section 9.7. Before ending this section, the main contributions of this chapter are summarized as follows.

- A novel multi-input (specifically, four-input) Euler-polynomial neuronet with its hidden-layer neurons activated by a group of generalized Euler-polynomials is established and investigated, which is different from the conventional BP neuronets.

- Rigorous theoretical analyses on the normal equation and WDD subalgorithm are presented. In addition, four MATLAB computing routines used for realizing the WDD subalgorithm are studied, analyzed and compared. Eventually, according to the theoretical analysis and numerical results, a reasonable MATLAB computing routine is preferably suggested.

- A lexicographic ordering method is employed to number the neurons. Then, in order to make the FIEPN achieve the superior performance, a WASD algorithm with PWG and TP techniques is proposed and developed.

- Numerical studies are performed and analyzed, which substantiate the efficacy of the FIEPN equipped with the WASD algorithm including PWG and TP techniques for function (data) training, testing and prediction.

## 9.2 Theoretical Basis and Analysis

For better understanding, the detailed descriptions of related essential theoretical basis and analysis are given in this section. Moreover, based on the presented theoretical basis and the authors' previous successful works [17,21,99], two propositions are proposed to lay a basis for establishing the MIEPN model.

Firstly, according to Definition 1 of Chapter 1, all the Euler-polynomials can be derived from the recursive formula (1.3); for example, the first three polynomials are expressed as $\varphi_1(x) = 1$, $\varphi_2(x) = x - 1/2\varphi_1(x) = x - 1/2$ and $\varphi_3(x) = x^2 - 1/2(\varphi_1(x) + 2\varphi_2(x)) = x^2 - x$. Then, we have the following theorem [80, 113, 114].

**Theorem 4** *Let $g(x)$ be a continuous function defined on $[a,b]$, then, for any $\varepsilon > 0$, there must be a polynomial $p(x)$ such that, for all $x \in [a,b]$,*

$$|g(x) - p(x)| < \varepsilon.$$

That is to say, any continuous function defined on a closed and bounded interval can be uniformly approximated by a polynomial with an arbitrary accuracy.

**Definition 6**   Let $f(x_1, x_2, \cdots, x_k)$ be a function of $k$ variables, the polynomial

$$B^f_{n_1 n_2 \cdots n_k}(x_1, x_2, \cdots, x_k) = \sum_{v_1=0}^{n_1} \cdots \sum_{v_k=0}^{n_k} f\left(\frac{v_1}{n_1}, \cdots, \frac{v_k}{n_k}\right) \prod_{q=1}^{k} C_{n_q}^{v_q} x_q^{v_q} (1 - x_q)^{n_q - v_q} \tag{9.1}$$

are called multivariate Bernstein polynomial of $f(x_1, x_2, \cdots, x_k)$, where $C_{n_q}^{v_q}$ denotes a binomial coefficient with $n_q = n_1, n_2, \cdots, n_k$ and $v_q = 0, 1, \cdots, n_q$ [80].

Besides, we have the following theorem about the uniform convergence [80, 113, 114].

**Theorem 5** *Let $f(x_1, x_2, \cdots, x_k)$ be a continuous function, which is defined over $S_k = \{(x_1, x_2, \cdots, x_k) \in \mathbb{R}^k | 0 \le x_q \le 1, \ q = 1, 2, \cdots, k\}$. Then the multivariate Bernstein polynomials $B^f_{n_1 n_2 \cdots n_k}(x_1, x_2, \cdots, x_k)$ converge uniformly to $f(x_1, x_2, \cdots, x_k)$ for $n_1, n_2 \cdots, n_k \to \infty$, of which the expression can be expressed as*

$$\lim_{n_1, n_2, \cdots, n_k \to \infty} B^f_{n_1 n_2 \cdots n_k}(x_1, x_2, \cdots, x_k) = f(x_1, x_2, \cdots, x_k).$$

It is worth pointing out that Definition 6 and Theorem 5 present an approach to construct the polynomial used to approximate the multivariate continuous function. Specifically, with a form of products of polynomials [i.e., $\prod_{q=1}^{k} C_{n_q}^{v_q} x_q^{v_q} (1 - x_q)^{n_q - v_q}$] adopted, the above Bernstein polynomial (9.1) can be constructed.

Similar to the above form of products of Bernstein polynomials, the following proposition of Euler-polynomial can be extended.

**Proposition 7** *With a form of products of Euler-polynomials employed, we can construct a generalized Euler-polynomial*

$$\psi_n(\mathbf{x}) = \psi_n(x_1, x_2, \cdots, x_k) = \varphi_{n_1}(x_1) \varphi_{n_2}(x_2) \cdots \varphi_{n_k}(x_k),$$

*where $n = 1, 2, \cdots, N$, with $n_1, n_2, \cdots, n_k$, $k$ and $N$ being positive integers.*

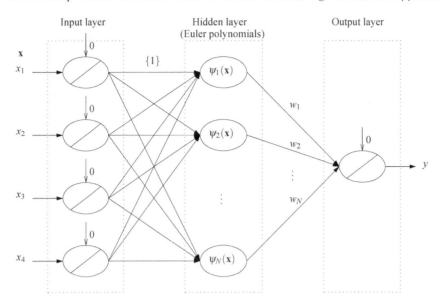

**FIGURE 9.1**: Model structure of multi-input (specifically, four-input) Euler-polynomial neuronet.

In consideration of the fact that the numerical studies in this chapter are based on four-input function approximation, it is necessary to introduce some theoretical foundation on function approximation. Given a set of data points $\{(x_m, \gamma_m)|x_m \in \mathbb{R}, \gamma_m \in \mathbb{R}, m = 1, 2, \cdots, M\}$, where $M$ denotes the total number of data points, $x_m$ denotes the $m$th input and $\gamma_m$ denotes the corresponding target output. The unknown functional relationship between $\gamma$ and $x$ can be denoted as $\gamma = f(x)$ [i.e., $\gamma_m = f(x_m)$], then a linear combination $S(x) = \sum_{n=1}^{N} w_n \varphi_n(x)$ can approximate $f(x)$ [or, say, $S(x)$ can be used to approximate the data points] in a least-square sense by minimizing

$$\sum_{m=1}^{M} (S(x_m) - \gamma_m)^2 = \sum_{m=1}^{M} \left( \sum_{n=1}^{N} w_n \varphi_n(x_m) - \gamma_m \right)^2,$$

where $\{\varphi_n(x)\}_{n=1}^{N}$ are a group of linearly independent polynomials (e.g., Euler polynomials in this chapter), $w_n \in \mathbb{R}$ is the $n$th weight coefficient, and $N \in \mathbb{R}$ is the number of the polynomials.

The above function (data) approximation problem can be generalized to a multi-input function (data) approximation problem as the following proposition.

**Proposition 8** *For a given set of data points $\{(\mathbf{x}_m, \gamma_m)|\mathbf{x}_m \in \mathbb{R}^k, \gamma_m \in \mathbb{R}, m = 1, 2, \cdots, M\}$, where $k$ and $M$ are positive integers, $\mathbf{x}_m = [x_{m1}, x_{m2}, \cdots, x_{mk}]^{\mathrm{T}}$ denotes the $m$th input vector (with the superscript $^{\mathrm{T}}$ denoting the transpose of a vector or a matrix), and $\gamma_m$ denotes the corresponding target output. Then, an unknown function with $k$ variables $f(\mathbf{x}) = f(x_1, x_2, \cdots, x_k)$ can be approximated by the linear combination $\sum_{n=1}^{N} w_n \psi_n(\mathbf{x})$ of the basis functions $\{\psi_n(\mathbf{x}) = \psi_n(x_1, x_2, \cdots, x_k) = \varphi_{n_1}(x_1)\varphi_{n_2}(x_2)\cdots\varphi_{n_k}(x_k)\}_{n=1}^{N}$ where $x_k \in [a, b]$ (with $a \leq b \in \mathbb{R}$). That is to say, $f(\mathbf{x}) \approx \sum_{n=1}^{N} w_n \psi_n(\mathbf{x}) = \sum_{n=1}^{N} w_n \psi_n(x_1, x_2, \cdots, x_k)$.*

Without loss of generality, a four-input function (data) approximation problem (i.e., $k = 4$) is investigated in this chapter, and the continuous unknown target function of four variables is $f(x_1, x_2, x_3, x_4)$ (e.g., $x_1, x_2, x_3, x_4 \in [a, b]$ with $a = -1$ and $b = 1$). According to the above propositions, for the $m$th group of data points, we have

$$f(x_{m1}, x_{m2}, x_{m3}, x_{m4}) \approx \sum_{n=1}^{N} w_n \psi_n(\mathbf{x}_m) = \sum_{n=1}^{N} w_n \psi_n(x_{m1}, x_{m2}, x_{m3}, x_{m4}).$$

**TABLE 9.1:** Neurons numbered and ordered by lexicographic ordering method.

| $o$ | $s$ | $n_1$ | $n_2$ | $n_3$ | $n_4$ | $o$ | $s$ | $n_1$ | $n_2$ | $n_3$ | $n_4$ |
|---|---|---|---|---|---|---|---|---|---|---|---|
| 1 | 4 | 1 | 1 | 1 | 1 | 1023 | 18 | 13 | 1 | 2 | 2 |
| 2 | 5 | 2 | 1 | 1 | 1 | 1024 | 18 | 13 | 1 | 1 | 3 |
| 3 | 5 | 1 | 2 | 1 | 1 | 1025 | 18 | 12 | 4 | 1 | 1 |
| 4 | 5 | 1 | 1 | 2 | 1 | 1026 | 18 | 12 | 3 | 2 | 1 |
| 5 | 5 | 1 | 1 | 1 | 2 | 1027 | 18 | 12 | 2 | 3 | 1 |
| ⋮ | ⋮ | ⋮ | ⋮ | ⋮ | ⋮ | ⋮ | ⋮ | ⋮ | ⋮ | ⋮ | ⋮ |
| 1015 | 17 | 1 | 1 | 1 | 14 | 3304 | 24 | 1 | 1 | 8 | 14 |
| 1016 | 18 | 15 | 1 | 1 | 1 | 3305 | 24 | 1 | 1 | 7 | 15 |
| 1017 | 18 | 14 | 2 | 1 | 1 | 3306 | 24 | 1 | 1 | 6 | 16 |
| 1018 | 18 | 14 | 1 | 2 | 1 | 3307 | 24 | 1 | 1 | 5 | 17 |
| 1019 | 18 | 14 | 1 | 1 | 2 | 3308 | 24 | 1 | 1 | 4 | 18 |
| 1020 | 18 | 13 | 3 | 1 | 1 | 3309 | 24 | 1 | 1 | 3 | 19 |
| 1021 | 18 | 13 | 2 | 2 | 1 | 3310 | 24 | 1 | 1 | 2 | 20 |
| 1022 | 18 | 13 | 1 | 3 | 1 | 3311 | 24 | 1 | 1 | 1 | 21 |

Therefore, the data of target function $f(x_1, x_2, x_3, x_4)$ can be fitted well by determining the optimal weights $\{w_n\}_{n=1}^N$ for the basis functions $\{\psi_n(\mathbf{x})\}_{n=1}^N$ and obtaining the proper number of the basis functions.

## 9.3 MIEPN Model

Based on the aforementioned theoretical basis and analysis, a novel FIEPN model is established in this section. Besides, a lexicographic ordering method is briefly developed and discussed.

Fig. 9.1 presents the FIEPN model, which has four inputs (i.e., $x_1$, $x_2$, $x_3$ and $x_4$) and single output (i.e., $y$). As shown in Fig. 9.1, the FIEPN model adopts a conventional structure of three layers (including input layer, hidden layer and output layer). To simplify the neuronet model and its computation, all the connecting weights between input layer and hidden layer are set to be 1 and all the thresholds of neurons are fixed to 0. The connecting weights between hidden layer and output layer are $\{w_n\}_{n=1}^N$, which can be determined directly by the WDD subalgorithm. Besides, the hidden-layer neurons are activated by the basis functions $\{\psi_n(\mathbf{x}) = \psi_n(x_1, x_2, x_3, x_4) = \varphi_{n_1}(x_1)\varphi_{n_2}(x_2)\varphi_{n_3}(x_3)\varphi_{n_4}(x_4)\}_{n=1}^N$, where $n$ denotes the $n$th hidden-layer neuron of the proposed FIEPN, and $n_j$ corresponds to Euler-polynomial $\varphi_{n_j}(x_j)$ with $j = 1, 2, 3, 4$. Besides, the neurons of the input and output layers are activated by the linear function $h(x) = x$.

In addition, a lexicographic ordering method, which is the foundation of the realization of the WASD algorithm with PWG and TP techniques, is necessary to be briefly introduced here. In consideration of the fact that the activation functions of the hidden-layer neurons are the basis functions $\{\psi_n(\mathbf{x}) = \psi_n(x_1, x_2, x_3, x_4) = \varphi_{n_1}(x_1)\varphi_{n_2}(x_2)\varphi_{n_3}(x_3)\varphi_{n_4}(x_4)\}_{n=1}^N$, the neurons are numbered via a lexicographic ordering method for growing and pruning the neurons one-by-one. As shown in Table 9.1, the neurons are numbered and ordered according to the sum of $n_1$, $n_2$, $n_3$ and $n_4$ (i.e., $s$), and detailed information about a part of all the numbered neurons' relevant values are shown in a lexicographic order. Based on the authors' previous successful experience [17, 21, 99], 3311 neurons (the maximal value of $s$ is 24) are numbered and ordered because the total number of hidden-layer neurons is generally less than 2000. Then, the number of currently found optimal hidden-layer neurons can be obtained during the training process by calculating the formula $n_{cur} = o - d$, where $o$ denotes the order of existing neurons in Table 9.1, and $d$ denotes the number of deleted neurons during training process. Especially, since the above mentioned $s$ denotes the sum of indices $n_1$, $n_2$, $n_3$ and $n_4$, $o$ cannot be replaced by $s$ in the formula. For better understanding, an explanatory example is given as follows. For the first three neurons in Table 9.1 with $o = 3$, if the third neuron is redundant and deleted from the three neurons (i.e., $d = 1$), then the number of currently found optimal neurons is $n_{cur} = o - d = 3 - 1 = 2$ rather than $n_{cur} = s - d = 5 - 1 = 4$.

---

## 9.4    WDD Subalgorithm

In order to determine the optimal connecting weights between the hidden layer and output layer of the FIEPN, a WDD subalgorithm is introduced, discussed and analyzed in detail as follows.

Suppose that a large set of data points (e.g., the total number of the data points is 38416) is collected and recorded, then, for training the FIEPN, $M$ (e.g., $M = 6000$) samples are randomly selected from the large set of data points to generate a set of training data points. Thus the training-sample set can be defined as $\{(\mathbf{x}_m, \gamma_m) | \mathbf{x}_m \in \mathbb{R}^4, \gamma_m \in \mathbb{R}, m = 1, 2, \cdots, M\}$, where $\mathbf{x}_m = [x_{m1}, x_{m2}, x_{m3}, x_{m4}]^T$ denotes the $m$th input vector, and $\gamma_m$ denotes the corresponding target output. In order to monitor and evaluate the performance of the FIEPN model, the mean square error (MSE) performance function is defined as

$$e = \frac{1}{M} \sum_{m=1}^{M} \left( \sum_{n=1}^{N} w_n \psi_n(x_m) - \gamma_m \right)^2, \tag{9.2}$$

where $N$ denotes the total number of the hidden-layer neurons in Fig. 9.1, and $\psi_n(\cdot)$ denotes the activation function of the $n$th hidden-layer neuron of the FIEPN model. It is worth pointing out that, for a given value of $N$, the value of the MSE can be minimized by determining the optimal connecting weights between hidden layer and output layer in Fig. 9.1.

Suppose that the number of hidden-layer neurons is $N$. Let $\Psi$, $\mathbf{w}$, and $\gamma$ denote, respectively, the input-activation matrix, the connecting-weight vector between hidden layer and output layer, and the target output vector as follows:

$$\Psi = \begin{bmatrix} \psi_1(\mathbf{x}_1) & \psi_2(\mathbf{x}_1) & \cdots & \psi_N(\mathbf{x}_1) \\ \psi_1(\mathbf{x}_2) & \psi_2(\mathbf{x}_2) & \cdots & \psi_N(\mathbf{x}_2) \\ \vdots & \vdots & \ddots & \vdots \\ \psi_1(\mathbf{x}_M) & \psi_2(\mathbf{x}_M) & \cdots & \psi_N(\mathbf{x}_M) \end{bmatrix} \in \mathbb{R}^{M \times N},$$

$$\mathbf{w} = [w_1, w_2, \cdots, w_N]^T \in \mathbb{R}^N, \ \gamma = [\gamma_1, \gamma_2, \cdots, \gamma_M]^T \in \mathbb{R}^M.$$

By taking the partial derivative of $e$ with respect to $\mathbf{w}$, setting it to be zero, and reformulating the resultant equation, then we have

$$\Psi^T \Psi \mathbf{w} = \Psi^T \gamma. \tag{9.3}$$

It is worth mentioning that a detailed derivation of (9.3) is presented in Appendix C to this chapter for the sake of completeness. The above equation is the so-called normal equation and $\Psi^T \Psi$ is a normal matrix. Note that (9.3) can also be derived from the conventional BP iterative equations and the detailed derivation process, explanation and illustration can be found in the authors' previous works [21, 99]. In addition, the existence of the normal equation's solution can be ensured by the fact that the equality $\text{rank}(\Psi^T \Psi) = \text{rank}([\Psi^T \Psi, \Psi^T \gamma])$ holds true, or to say, the normal equation is theoretically solvable, where rank$(\cdot)$ denotes the rank of a matrix. For better understanding, a theorem on the same solution of two different homogeneous linear equations is provided, then a theorem and the detailed proof on the solution of the normal Equation (9.3) are presented in Appendix D to this chapter.

Generally speaking, the input-activation matrix $\Psi$ has full column rank and the square matrix $\Psi^T\Psi$ is a nonsingular matrix owning to the linear independence of the activation functions. Based on the authors' previous successful experience [17, 21, 99], the optimal connecting weights of the FIEPN [i.e., the least-square solution of (9.3)] can be directly determined by the so-called WDD subalgorithm, which can be expressed as the following computation formula:

$$\mathbf{w} = (\Psi^T\Psi)^{-1}\Psi^T\gamma = \text{pinv}(\Psi)\gamma = \Psi^\dagger\gamma, \tag{9.4}$$

where $\text{pinv}(\Psi)$ and $\Psi^\dagger$ both denote the pseudoinverse of $\Psi$.

Notice that (9.3) has one solution, at least, and that (9.4) is the least-square solution of the equation. Moreover, let

$$A = \Psi^T\Psi = \begin{bmatrix} \psi_1(\mathbf{x}_1) & \psi_1(\mathbf{x}_2) & \cdots & \psi_1(\mathbf{x}_M) \\ \psi_2(\mathbf{x}_1) & \psi_2(\mathbf{x}_2) & \cdots & \psi_2(\mathbf{x}_M) \\ \vdots & \vdots & \ddots & \vdots \\ \psi_N(\mathbf{x}_1) & \psi_N(\mathbf{x}_2) & \cdots & \psi_N(\mathbf{x}_M) \end{bmatrix} \begin{bmatrix} \psi_1(\mathbf{x}_1) & \psi_2(\mathbf{x}_1) & \cdots & \psi_N(\mathbf{x}_1) \\ \psi_1(\mathbf{x}_2) & \psi_2(\mathbf{x}_2) & \cdots & \psi_N(\mathbf{x}_2) \\ \vdots & \vdots & \ddots & \vdots \\ \psi_1(\mathbf{x}_M) & \psi_2(\mathbf{x}_M) & \cdots & \psi_N(\mathbf{x}_M) \end{bmatrix}$$

$$= \begin{bmatrix} \sum_{m=1}^{M}\psi_1^2(\mathbf{x}_m) & \sum_{m=1}^{M}\psi_1(\mathbf{x}_m)\psi_2(\mathbf{x}_m) & \cdots & \sum_{m=1}^{M}\psi_1(\mathbf{x}_m)\psi_N(\mathbf{x}_m) \\ \sum_{m=1}^{M}\psi_2(\mathbf{x}_m)\psi_1(\mathbf{x}_m) & \sum_{m=1}^{M}\psi_2^2(\mathbf{x}_m) & \cdots & \sum_{m=1}^{M}\psi_1(\mathbf{x}_m)\psi_N(\mathbf{x}_m) \\ \vdots & \vdots & \ddots & \vdots \\ \sum_{m=1}^{M}\psi_N(\mathbf{x}_m)\psi_1(\mathbf{x}_m) & \sum_{m=1}^{M}\psi_N(\mathbf{x}_m)\psi_2(\mathbf{x}_m) & \cdots & \sum_{m=1}^{M}\psi_N^2(\mathbf{x}_m) \end{bmatrix}$$

$$= \sum_{m=1}^{M} \begin{bmatrix} \psi_1^2(\mathbf{x}_m) & \psi_1(\mathbf{x}_m)\psi_2(\mathbf{x}_m) & \cdots & \psi_1(\mathbf{x}_m)\psi_N(\mathbf{x}_m) \\ \psi_2(\mathbf{x}_m)\psi_1(\mathbf{x}_m) & \psi_2^2(\mathbf{x}_m) & \cdots & \psi_1(\mathbf{x}_m)\psi_N(\mathbf{x}_m) \\ \vdots & \vdots & \ddots & \vdots \\ \psi_N(\mathbf{x}_m)\psi_1(\mathbf{x}_m) & \psi_N(\mathbf{x}_m)\psi_2(\mathbf{x}_m) & \cdots & \psi_N^2(\mathbf{x}_m) \end{bmatrix}$$

and

$$\mathbf{b} = \Psi^T\gamma = \begin{bmatrix} \psi_1(\mathbf{x}_1) & \psi_1(\mathbf{x}_2) & \cdots & \psi_1(\mathbf{x}_M) \\ \psi_2(\mathbf{x}_1) & \psi_2(\mathbf{x}_2) & \cdots & \psi_2(\mathbf{x}_M) \\ \vdots & \vdots & \ddots & \vdots \\ \psi_N(\mathbf{x}_1) & \psi_N(\mathbf{x}_2) & \cdots & \psi_N(\mathbf{x}_M) \end{bmatrix} \begin{bmatrix} \gamma_1 \\ \gamma_2 \\ \vdots \\ \gamma_M \end{bmatrix}$$

$$= \begin{bmatrix} \sum_{m=1}^{M}\psi_1(\mathbf{x}_m)\gamma_m \\ \sum_{m=1}^{M}\psi_2(\mathbf{x}_m)\gamma_m \\ \vdots \\ \sum_{m=1}^{M}\psi_N(\mathbf{x}_m)\gamma_m \end{bmatrix} = \sum_{m=1}^{M} \begin{bmatrix} \psi_1(\mathbf{x}_m)\gamma_m \\ \psi_2(\mathbf{x}_m)\gamma_m \\ \vdots \\ \psi_N(\mathbf{x}_m)\gamma_m \end{bmatrix},$$

then, (9.3) can be reformulated and simplified as

$$A\mathbf{w} = \mathbf{b}, \tag{9.5}$$

where $A$ is a real-valued symmetric matrix and all the eigenvalues of $A$ are real. Theoretically, (9.3) and (9.5) have the same solution, and the latter is much more convenient to be solved owning to the symmetry and the relatively low dimension of the normal matrix $A$.

**Remark 1** To the best of the authors' knowledge, the solution of (9.3) and (9.5) can be obtained by any of the following four MATLAB computing routines:

(1) pinv($\Psi$) $* \gamma$ (where MATLAB uses "pinv" to calculate the pseudoinverse of a matrix, and "$*$" denotes matrix multiplication);

(2) $A\backslash\mathbf{b}$ (where MATLAB uses "$\backslash$" to execute the matrix left division operation);

(3) inv($A$) $*\mathbf{b}$ (where MATLAB uses "inv" to calculate the inverse of a matrix);

(4) pinv($A$) $*\mathbf{b}$.

By executing these computing routines, the optimal connecting weights $\{w_n\}_{n=1}^N$ can be directly determined. It is worth pointing out that each of the four computing routines only obtains the approximate solution of $\mathbf{w}$. However, the running time and accuracy of approximation results are quite different by using different computing routines in the specific MATLAB computing environment (i.e., MATLAB R2008a environment). In order to select an appropriate computing routine for the proposed FIEPN, it is important and meaningful to discuss about the differences among the above four MATLAB routines, and such a comparative study is for the first time made for the FIEPN to obtain the optimal connecting weights.

**Remark 2** Theoretically, the routine pinv($\Psi$) is usually much more time-consuming and complex than pinv($A$) in view of $\Psi \in \mathbb{R}^{M \times N}$ and $A = \Psi^{\mathrm{T}}\Psi \in \mathbb{R}^{N \times N}$ with $M > N$ satisfied (meaning that $A$ has the relatively low dimension). In addition, the routine pinv($\Psi$) usually needs more memory than pinv($A$) because the routine pinv($\cdot$) is based on singular value decomposition (SVD) [87, 115, 116]. Specifically speaking, the input-activation matrix $\Psi \in \mathbb{R}^{M \times N}$ can be factored as

$$\Psi = U\Gamma V^{\mathrm{T}} = U \begin{bmatrix} H & 0 \\ 0 & 0 \end{bmatrix} V^{\mathrm{T}},$$

where $U \in \mathbb{R}^{M \times M}$ is an orthogonal matrix whose columns are the eigenvectors of $\Psi\Psi^{\mathrm{T}}$, $V \in \mathbb{R}^{N \times N}$ is an orthogonal matrix whose columns are the eigenvectors of $\Psi^{\mathrm{T}}\Psi$, and $\Gamma \in \mathbb{R}^{M \times N}$, $H = \mathrm{diag}(\sigma_1, \sigma_2, \cdots, \sigma_r) \in \mathbb{R}^{r \times r}$ is zero everywhere except for entries on the main diagonal, where $r = \mathrm{rank}(\Psi)$ and $\sigma_1 \geq \sigma_2 \geq \cdots \geq \sigma_r > 0$. Notice that $A \in \mathbb{R}^{N \times N}$ can also be factored as the matrix multiplication of three $N \times N$ matrices (including two orthogonal matrices and one diagonal matrix) by using this SVD method. Since $M > N$ is generally satisfied in the studied problem, the routine pinv($\Psi$) needs more memory of computer than pinv($A$). In this sense, it is meaningful to realize the dimensionality reduction by (9.5) and exploiting the routine pinv($A$) in MATLAB, which can be seen from the ensuing numerical studies and results in this chapter.

---

## 9.5   WASD Algorithm with PWG and TP Techniques

According to the authors' previous work [17], the performance of the neuronet can be influenced greatly by the number of hidden-layer neurons, and it is meaningful and important to obtain the optimal number of hidden-layer neurons. Besides, the optimal number of hidden-layer neurons can be obtained by minimizing the values of the MSE by considering different numbers of hidden-layer neurons. In order to investigate and illustrate the relationship between the MSE (denoted as $e$) and the number of hidden-layer neurons (denoted as $N$), plenty of target functions are tested and investigated, such as the following function (only one example is presented due to results' similarity):

$$f(x_1, x_2, x_3, x_4) = (x_1 + x_3)^2 + x_2^4 + x_4^3 + 10.$$

As shown in Fig. 9.2, the value of $e$ decreases dramatically in the beginning with the number of

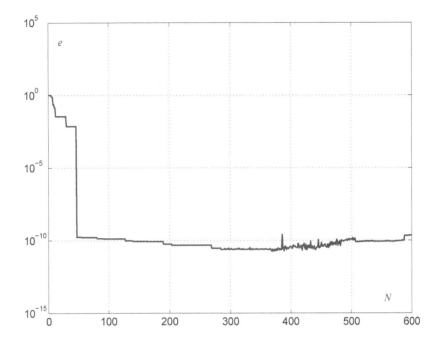

**FIGURE 9.2**: MSE $e$ of FIEPN versus its number $N$ of hidden-layer neurons.

neurons increasing. In its following period of interval, i.e., $N \in [50, 600]$, the value of $e$ generally keeps relatively flat, except for sometimes oscillating slightly (with the magnitude order being about $10^{-10}$). This flat trend means that many of these neurons are redundant. Especially, within the oscillating interval, the number of neurons is difficult to determine. For simplifying the structure and obtaining a better performance, it is necessary to prune these redundant neurons. Based on the authors' previous successful experience [17, 21, 99], a WASD algorithm with PWG and TP techniques is proposed to fulfill this task and obtain the optimal number of hidden-layer neurons (i.e., $N_{opt}$).

For comparison and illustration, the above target function is also fitted by employing the WASD algorithm with PWG and TP techniques. It is worth pointing out that such a WASD algorithm with PWG and TP techniques has a superior performance on the function approximation problem solving (i.e., with the maximal magnitude order of error being $10^{-24}$), which can be seen from the ensuing numerical results in this chapter.

More specifically, the WASD algorithm with PWG and TP techniques can be briefly described as follows. Firstly, in order to acquire the minimal value of $e$ (i.e., $e_{min}$), let $o$ grow one-by-one with $n_{cur} = o - d$ and $N_{sub} = n_{cur}$ with subscripts "cur" and "sub" corresponding to words "current" and "sub-optimal", respectively. Meanwhile, the value of $e_{min}$ is updated by obtaining the smaller value from the current value of $e$ and the last stored $e_{min}$. Besides, if $e > e_{min}$, then prune the last added neuron (the $o$th neuron in the lexicographic table). In addition, forward-looking counter $c$ calculates the number of the neurons which are pruned continuously. Note that, in the neuronet, if $c_{max}$ is set too small, the satisfactory accuracy may not be achieved; while, if $c_{max}$ is set too large, it would be time-consuming. Thus, in the numerical studies, $c_{max}$ is set to be 25 according to the authors' experience. By this way, the FIEPN with a sub optimal structure can be established. Secondly, in order to further prune the possible redundant neurons of the FIEPN, the ergodic index $\kappa$ is designed to help the TP technique search for the redundant neurons. Then, with the redundant neurons being further pruned, the optimal structure of the FIEPN is obtained. Finally, by following the WASD algorithm with PWG and TP techniques, the $N_{opt}$ and $e_{min}$ can be obtained, i.e., the optimal structure and

---

**Algorithm 1** WASD algorithm with PWG technique

---

**Require:** order $o$ of existing neurons, number $d$ of deleted neurons, forward-looking counter $c$, number $n_{cur}$ of currently found optimal neurons, input vector $\mathbf{x}_m$ and target output $\gamma_m$ with $m = 1, 2, \cdots, M$

Initialize the parameters $o \leftarrow 1$, $d \leftarrow 0$, $n_{cur} \leftarrow 1$, $N_{opt} \leftarrow 1$, $e_{min} \leftarrow 10$ (or better "inf"), and $c \leftarrow 0$

**Repeat**

    Obtain the values of $n_1$, $n_2$, $n_3$ and $n_4$ from Table 9.1

    Set the $n_1$th, $n_2$th, $n_3$th and $n_4$th Euler polynomials $\varphi_{n_1}(x_{m1})$, $\varphi_{n_2}(x_{m2})$, $\varphi_{n_3}(x_{m3})$ and $\varphi_{n_4}(x_{m4})$

    Calculate the values of $\psi_{n_{cur}}(\mathbf{x}_m) = \varphi_{n_1}(x_{m1})\varphi_{n_2}(x_{m2})\varphi_{n_3}(x_{m3})\varphi_{n_4}(x_{m4})$

    Obtain the input-activation matrix $\Psi$

    Determine the optimal weights via the WDD subalgorithm

    Obtain the MSE result (i.e., $e$)

    **If** $e_{min} > e$ **then**

        $e_{min} \leftarrow e$

        $c \leftarrow 0$

    **else**

        $c \leftarrow c + 1$

        $d \leftarrow d + 1$

    **end if**

    $n_{cur} \leftarrow o - d$

    $N_{sub} \leftarrow n_{cur}$

    $o \leftarrow o + 1$

**until** $(o > 3311)$ or $(c > c_{max})$

**Return** actual output $y$, sub optimal number $N_{sub}$ of hidden-layer neurons, and current minimal MSE value $e_{min}$

---

weights of the FIEPN are determined, and the performance of the FIEPN is guaranteed. For better understanding, the WASD algorithm with PWG and TP techniques is presented via algorithms 1 and 2. In summary, the PWG technique is employed to establish a FIEPN with a sub optimal structure containing possible redundant neurons which influence the performance of the neuronet. Then, the TP technique is exploited to delete these redundant neurons and determine the final optimal structure of the FIEPN.

---

## 9.6    Numerical Studies

In this section, numerical studies are performed to substantiate the performance and efficacy of the proposed FIEPN equipped with the WASD algorithm including PWG and TP techniques in terms of four-input function (data) training, testing and prediction. Note that the studies are carried out in MATLAB R2008a environment operated on a personal computer with Pentium E5300 2.6-GHz CPU, 2-GB DDR3 memory and Windows 7 Professional operating system.

To substantiate the efficacy of the FIEPN equipped with the WASD algorithm including PWG and TP techniques, the data training, testing and prediction studies of various target functions are performed. In this chapter, only some typical numerical results of training, testing and prediction are presented and analyzed due to space limitation and results' similarity. Simply put, the data are uniformly sampled over the region $[-1, 1]^4$ with the gap size 0.15 (i.e., $x_1$, $x_2$, $x_3$ and $x_4 \in [-1, 1]$ are uniformly sampled with the gap size 0.15). Since the total number of uniformly sampled data is

**TABLE 9.2:** Training, testing and prediction results of FIEPN equipped with WASD algorithm including only PWG technique by using MATLAB computing routine $\mathbf{w} = \text{pinv}(\Psi) * \gamma$ for target functions (9.6) through (9.9).

| Target | $t_{\text{run}}$ (s) | $N_{\text{sub}}$ | $e_{\text{tra}}$ | $e_{\text{tes}}$ | $e_{\text{pre}}$ |
|--------|--------|-------|--------|--------|--------|
| (9.6) | 20.4412 | 56 | $1.8396 \times 10^{-27}$ | $1.8051 \times 10^{-27}$ | $2.6041 \times 10^{-26}$ |
| (9.7) | 2875.6493 | 562 | $9.2321 \times 10^{-17}$ | $1.3395 \times 10^{-16}$ | $1.2956 \times 10^{-10}$ |
| (9.8) | 3477.5176 | 594 | $1.4979 \times 10^{-18}$ | $1.8789 \times 10^{-18}$ | $5.6315 \times 10^{-13}$ |
| (9.9) | 3346.5370 | 526 | $3.5239 \times 10^{-19}$ | $4.0602 \times 10^{-19}$ | $2.4977 \times 10^{-11}$ |

---

**Algorithm 2** WASD algorithm with TP technique

---

**Require:** number $N_{\text{sub}}$ of hidden-layer neurons, minimal MSE value $e_{\text{min}}$ obtained from Algorithm 1, and ergodic index $\kappa$
Initialize the parameter $\kappa \leftarrow 1$
**Repeat**
    Delete the $\kappa$th neuron
    Obtain the input-activation matrix $\Psi$
    Determine the optimal weights via the WDD method
    Obtain the result of MSE (i.e., $e$)
    **If** $e_{\text{min}} > e$ **then**
        $e_{\text{min}} \leftarrow e$
        $N_{\text{opt}} \leftarrow N_{\text{sub}} - 1$
    **else**
        Restore the $\kappa$th neuron
    **end if**
    $\kappa \leftarrow \kappa + 1$
**until** $\kappa > N_{\text{sub}}$
**Return** actual output $y$, optimal number $N_{\text{opt}}$ of hidden-layer neurons, and minimal MSE value $e_{\text{min}}$

---

too large (38416 points), 6000 points of which are selected randomly for training. In addition, the target function is used to generate the corresponding target output, and thus a set of training data points $\{(\mathbf{x}_m, \gamma_m) | \mathbf{x}_m \in \mathbb{R}^4, \gamma_m \in \mathbb{R}, m = 1, 2, \cdots, 6000\}$ is obtained. In the same way, 3604 testing data points can also be selected from the remaining data points. Besides, with $x_1$, $x_2$, $x_3$ and $x_4$ $\in [-1.2, -1] \bigcup [1, 1.2]$ uniformly sampled with the gap size 0.05, and then randomly selected from the uniformly sampled data, the data for prediction are acquired (where the number of data points for prediction is 2500). As mentioned before, plenty of functions are investigated and tested to verify the performance of FIEPN equipped with the WASD algorithm. Due to the similarity, four target functions are presented as follows:

$$f(x_1, x_2, x_3, x_4) = (x_1 + x_3)^2 + x_2^4 + x_4^3 + 10, \tag{9.6}$$

$$f(x_1, x_2, x_3, x_4) = x_3 \exp(x_1 + x_2) + x_4^3 + 20, \tag{9.7}$$

$$f(x_1, x_2, x_3, x_4) = (x_1 + x_2)^2 + \ln(x_3^2 + x_4^3 + 15), \tag{9.8}$$

$$f(x_1, x_2, x_3, x_4) = (x_1 + x_2)^2 + \sqrt{x_3 + x_4^4 + 30}. \tag{9.9}$$

For illustrating the effectiveness of the proposed FIEPN equipped with the WASD algorithm, the above four target functions depicted in (9.6) through (9.9) are tested respectively. For comparisons, four different MATLAB computing routines related to the WDD subalgorithm are investigated. The corresponding average results of 10 trials (runs) for each function approximation case are shown

**TABLE 9.3:**    Training, testing and prediction results of FIEPN equipped with WASD algorithm including both PWG and TP techniques by using MATLAB computing routine $\mathbf{w} = \text{pinv}(\Psi) * \gamma$ for target functions (9.6) through (9.9).

| Target | Pruned neurons | $N_{\text{opt}}$ | $e_{\text{tra}}$ | $e_{\text{tes}}$ | $e_{\text{pre}}$ |
|---|---|---|---|---|---|
| (9.6) | 0 | 56 | $1.8396 \times 10^{-27}$ | $1.8051 \times 10^{-27}$ | $2.6041 \times 10^{-26}$ |
| (9.7) | 1 | 561 | $9.2283 \times 10^{-17}$ | $1.3366 \times 10^{-16}$ | $1.2962 \times 10^{-10}$ |
| (9.8) | 3 | 591 | $1.4921 \times 10^{-18}$ | $1.8652 \times 10^{-18}$ | $5.6250 \times 10^{-13}$ |
| (9.9) | 2 | 524 | $3.5143 \times 10^{-19}$ | $4.0342 \times 10^{-19}$ | $2.4969 \times 10^{-11}$ |

**TABLE 9.4:**    Training, testing and prediction results of FIEPN equipped with WASD algorithm including only PWG technique by using MATLAB computing routine $\mathbf{w} = A \backslash \mathbf{b}$ for target functions (9.6) through (9.9).

| Target | $t_{\text{run}}$ (s) | $N_{\text{sub}}$ | $e_{\text{tra}}$ | $e_{\text{tes}}$ | $e_{\text{pre}}$ |
|---|---|---|---|---|---|
| (9.6) | 10.4385 | 55 | $3.8219 \times 10^{-25}$ | $3.6430 \times 10^{-25}$ | $2.4436 \times 10^{-23}$ |
| (9.7) | 1283.0102 | 578 | $5.2168 \times 10^{-18}$ | $7.7962 \times 10^{-18}$ | $1.2731 \times 10^{-11}$ |
| (9.8) | 994.0273 | 545 | $2.0939 \times 10^{-18}$ | $2.6863 \times 10^{-18}$ | $1.8452 \times 10^{-12}$ |
| (9.9) | 589.0621 | 480 | $2.9107 \times 10^{-18}$ | $3.0983 \times 10^{-18}$ | $2.6449 \times 10^{-11}$ |

in Tables 9.2 through 9.9. Specifically, the optimal structure of the FIEPN (i.e., $N_{\text{opt}}$) and the corresponding minimal MSE values (i.e., $e_{\text{tra}}$, $e_{\text{tes}}$ and $e_{\text{pre}}$) are listed in Tables 9.2 through 9.9. Note that $e_{\text{tra}}$, $e_{\text{tes}}$ and $e_{\text{pre}}$ denote, respectively, the MSE values of the FIEPN in terms of training, testing and prediction. The efficacy and accuracy of the proposed FIEPN equipped with the WASD algorithm are substantiated by the tiny values of $e_{\text{tra}}$, $e_{\text{tes}}$ and $e_{\text{pre}}$ with their magnitude orders being $10^{-12} \sim 10^{-27}$, $10^{-12} \sim 10^{-27}$ and $10^{-7} \sim 10^{-25}$, respectively. It is easy to find that all the results of target function (9.6) are smaller than the results presented in Fig. 9.2 (i.e., around the magnitude order $10^{-10}$), and many redundant neurons are pruned by employing the proposed WASD algorithm with the PWG and TP Techniques. From Tables 9.2 through 9.9, we can see that all the four MATLAB computing routines have their own advantages and disadvantages, which are listed as follows. Firstly, about the numerical accuracy, all the error results of these computing routines are tiny enough, i.e., maximal values of $e_{\text{tra}}$, $e_{\text{tes}}$ and $e_{\text{pre}}$ are less than $10^{-12}$, $10^{-12}$ and $10^{-7}$, respectively. Secondly, in terms of the running time, the last two computing routines are more efficient. Thirdly, in view of the singulary, robustness, and accuracy of the results, the fourth computing routine is the best, i.e., $\mathbf{w} = \text{pinv}(A) * \mathbf{b}$. The reasons are analyzed as the following remark.

**Remark 3** In MATLAB, the normal matrix $A$ may become close to the singular situation during the computation, which results in the computing routines $\mathbf{w} = A \backslash \mathbf{b}$ and $\mathbf{w} = \text{inv}(A) * \mathbf{b}$ facing a warning such as "Matrix is close to singular or badly scaled. Results may be inaccurate". To the best knowledge of the authors, the fourth computing routine $\text{pinv}(\cdot)$ can work robustly even for the situation of $\Psi$ being rank deficient (i.e., the singular situation that follows). Based on these reasons, it is reasonable to employ the computing routine $\mathbf{w} = \text{pinv}(A) * \mathbf{b}$ to realize the WDD subalgorithm in practice.

In order to further substantiate the performance of the proposed FIEPN equipped with the WASD algorithm including PWG and TP techniques, some numerical outputs of target function (9.9) are listed in Tables 9.10 through 9.12. Note that these numerical outputs are obtained by using the computing routine $\mathbf{w} = \text{pinv}(A) * \mathbf{b}$ to realize the WDD subalgorithm. Compared with the target outputs (i.e., $\gamma$) of target function (9.9), all the actual FIEPN outputs (i.e., $y$) of training, testing and prediction illustrate well the accuracy of the FIEPN equipped with the WASD algorithm including PWG and TP techniques.

**TABLE 9.5:** Training, testing and prediction results of FIEPN equipped with WASD algorithm including both PWG and TP techniques by using MATLAB computing routine $\mathbf{w} = A \backslash \mathbf{b}$ for target functions (9.6) through (9.9).

| Target | Pruned neurons | $N_{\text{opt}}$ | $e_{\text{tra}}$ | $e_{\text{tes}}$ | $e_{\text{pre}}$ |
|--------|---------------|--------|--------|--------|--------|
| (9.6) | 7 | 48 | $8.7204 \times 10^{-26}$ | $8.7141 \times 10^{-26}$ | $5.1908 \times 10^{-24}$ |
| (9.7) | 21 | 557 | $2.4011 \times 10^{-18}$ | $3.2862 \times 10^{-18}$ | $7.6591 \times 10^{-12}$ |
| (9.8) | 18 | 527 | $1.9168 \times 10^{-18}$ | $2.4281 \times 10^{-18}$ | $1.4103 \times 10^{-12}$ |
| (9.9) | 0 | 480 | $2.9107 \times 10^{-18}$ | $3.0983 \times 10^{-18}$ | $2.6449 \times 10^{-11}$ |

**TABLE 9.6:** Training, testing and prediction results of FIEPN equipped with WASD algorithm including only PWG technique by using MATLAB computing routine $\mathbf{w} = \text{inv}(A) * \mathbf{b}$ for target functions (9.6) through (9.9).

| Target | $t_{\text{run}}$ (s) | $N_{\text{sub}}$ | $e_{\text{tra}}$ | $e_{\text{tes}}$ | $e_{\text{pre}}$ |
|--------|--------|--------|--------|--------|--------|
| (9.6) | 11.6215 | 57 | $4.1097 \times 10^{-24}$ | $4.1079 \times 10^{-24}$ | $2.6572 \times 10^{-23}$ |
| (9.7) | 300.4413 | 305 | $1.7103 \times 10^{-12}$ | $2.0022 \times 10^{-12}$ | $1.5144 \times 10^{-7}$ |
| (9.8) | 230.4753 | 256 | $4.3946 \times 10^{-14}$ | $4.6034 \times 10^{-14}$ | $2.8764 \times 10^{-10}$ |
| (9.9) | 224.0810 | 254 | $1.0337 \times 10^{-14}$ | $1.1340 \times 10^{-14}$ | $3.6556 \times 10^{-10}$ |

**TABLE 9.7:** Training, testing and prediction results of FIEPN equipped with WASD algorithm including both PWG and TP techniques by using MATLAB computing routine $\mathbf{w} = \text{inv}(A) * \mathbf{b}$ for target functions (9.6) through (9.9).

| Target | Pruned neurons | $N_{\text{opt}}$ | $e_{\text{tra}}$ | $e_{\text{tes}}$ | $e_{\text{pre}}$ |
|--------|---------------|--------|--------|--------|--------|
| (9.6) | 1 | 56 | $2.9938 \times 10^{-24}$ | $3.0316 \times 10^{-24}$ | $6.3676 \times 10^{-23}$ |
| (9.7) | 3 | 302 | $1.7019 \times 10^{-12}$ | $1.9787 \times 10^{-12}$ | $1.5072 \times 10^{-7}$ |
| (9.8) | 3 | 253 | $4.3919 \times 10^{-14}$ | $4.5999 \times 10^{-14}$ | $2.8806 \times 10^{-10}$ |
| (9.9) | 3 | 251 | $9.0721 \times 10^{-15}$ | $9.9964 \times 10^{-15}$ | $3.5947 \times 10^{-10}$ |

**TABLE 9.8:** Training, testing and prediction results of FIEPN equipped with WASD algorithm including only PWG technique by using MATLAB computing routine $\mathbf{w} = \text{pinv}(A) * \mathbf{b}$ for target functions (9.6) through (9.9).

| Target | $t_{\text{run}}$ (s) | $N_{\text{sub}}$ | $e_{\text{tra}}$ | $e_{\text{tes}}$ | $e_{\text{pre}}$ |
|--------|--------|--------|--------|--------|--------|
| (9.6) | 12.5455 | 58 | $3.1071 \times 10^{-24}$ | $3.1369 \times 10^{-24}$ | $7.4574 \times 10^{-23}$ |
| (9.7) | 365.9305 | 307 | $1.7208 \times 10^{-12}$ | $2.0151 \times 10^{-12}$ | $1.4278 \times 10^{-7}$ |
| (9.8) | 241.66533 | 275 | $4.3740 \times 10^{-14}$ | $4.6588 \times 10^{-14}$ | $2.8485 \times 10^{-10}$ |
| (9.9) | 203.0970 | 267 | $7.5506 \times 10^{-15}$ | $8.3082 \times 10^{-15}$ | $4.0114 \times 10^{-10}$ |

**TABLE 9.9:**  Training, testing and prediction results of FIEPN equipped with WASD algorithm including both PWG and TP techniques by using MATLAB computing routine $\mathbf{w} = \text{pinv}(A) * \mathbf{b}$ for target functions (9.6) through (9.9).

| Target | Pruned neurons | $N_{\text{opt}}$ | $e_{\text{tra}}$ | $e_{\text{tes}}$ | $e_{\text{pre}}$ |
|--------|----------------|------------------|------------------|------------------|------------------|
| (9.6)  | 0              | 58               | $3.1071 \times 10^{-24}$ | $3.1369 \times 10^{-24}$ | $7.4574 \times 10^{-23}$ |
| (9.7)  | 2              | 305              | $1.7034 \times 10^{-12}$ | $1.9902 \times 10^{-12}$ | $1.4288 \times 10^{-7}$ |
| (9.8)  | 1              | 274              | $4.3714 \times 10^{-14}$ | $4.6705 \times 10^{-14}$ | $2.8432 \times 10^{-10}$ |
| (9.9)  | 3              | 264              | $7.2782 \times 10^{-15}$ | $8.1199 \times 10^{-15}$ | $3.9358 \times 10^{-10}$ |

**TABLE 9.10:**  Training-type outputs of FIEPN equipped with WASD algorithm including both PWG and TP techniques by using MATLAB computing routine $\mathbf{w} = \text{pinv}(A) * \mathbf{b}$ for target function (9.9).

| $x_1$ | $x_2$ | $x_3$ | $x_4$ | $\gamma$ | $y$ |
|-------|-------|-------|-------|----------|-----|
| 0.65  | −0.25 | −0.25 | −0.10 | 5.614365224295124 | 5.614368404717769 |
| 0.65  | −0.40 | 0.05  | −0.40 | 5.546622536924208 | 5.546619537877386 |
| −0.85 | −0.55 | 0.95  | 0.80  | 7.559964285600400 | 7.559963938819673 |
| −0.70 | 0.20  | −0.85 | 0.35  | 5.650463521772923 | 5.650459640963481 |
| −0.55 | 0.95  | −1.00 | 0.35  | 5.546557922272813 | 5.546553653164967 |
| $\vdots$ | $\vdots$ | $\vdots$ | $\vdots$ | $\vdots$ | $\vdots$ |
| −0.40 | −1.00 | −0.25 | 0.05  | 7.414356630254388 | 7.414359197619043 |
| −0.70 | −0.55 | 0.50  | −0.55 | 7.093458890644551 | 7.093459265025412 |
| −0.85 | 0.20  | −0.85 | −0.55 | 5.830041608716478 | 5.830042086664571 |
| 0.05  | −0.70 | −0.10 | −0.55 | 5.898950150416782 | 5.898950801906203 |
| 0.95  | −0.10 | 0.50  | 0.50  | 6.250836096873996 | 6.250836566044499 |
| $\vdots$ | $\vdots$ | $\vdots$ | $\vdots$ | $\vdots$ | $\vdots$ |
| 0.80  | 0.95  | 0.95  | 0.35  | 8.627120943963750 | 8.627117694459917 |
| −0.55 | 0.20  | 0.65  | 0.65  | 5.674842411091016 | 5.674846525389731 |
| −0.70 | −0.25 | −0.85 | −0.70 | 6.323763690321658 | 6.323768057333683 |
| −0.85 | −0.85 | 0.50  | 0.35  | 8.414038943562943 | 8.414035490152752 |
| −0.40 | 0.50  | −1.00 | −0.40 | 5.397541183137258 | 5.397537541393289 |
| $\vdots$ | $\vdots$ | $\vdots$ | $\vdots$ | $\vdots$ | $\vdots$ |

For better comparison, a second set of studies with function approximations are organized to compare the performance of the proposed FIEPN with the standard MLP neuronet initialized with Widrow's method and trained with Levenberg-Marquardt (LM) method (i.e., the MLP-W-LM). Note that the resultant MLP-W-LM is carried out by using the neuronet toolbox in MATLAB R2008a environment.

Specifically, the MLP-W-LM is a four-input single-output feed-forward neuronet with a single hidden layer activated by tan-sigmoidal function $\text{tansig}(x) = 2/(1 + \exp(-2x)) - 1$. Without loss of generality, the input-layer and output-layer neurons are activated by a simple linear function, the connecting weights between the hidden-layer and output-layer neurons are the parameters to be tuned, and the neuronal thresholds of the input and output layers are fixed to be 0. The connecting weights between the input-layer and hidden-layer neurons and the neuronal thresholds of the hidden layer are the parameters also to be tuned (different from the FIEPN). The MSE is important for measuring the performance of neuronets. With illustrative examples, we investigate the relationship between the performance of the MLP-W-LM and the number of its hidden-layer neurons. In view of the fact that the performance of the MLP-W-LM is affected by the randomly chosen initial

**TABLE 9.11:** Testing-type outputs of FIEPN equipped with WASD algorithm including both PWG and TP techniques by using MATLAB computing routine $\mathbf{w} = \mathrm{pinv}(A) * \mathbf{b}$ for target function (9.9).

| $x_1$ | $x_2$ | $x_3$ | $x_4$ | $\gamma$ | $y$ |
|---|---|---|---|---|---|
| $-1.00$ | $-1.00$ | $-0.85$ | $0.35$ | 9.400463521772924 | 9.400463375725598 |
| $-1.00$ | $-0.40$ | $0.95$ | $0.95$ | 7.596000909332787 | 7.596000840621019 |
| $-1.00$ | $0.50$ | $-0.70$ | $0.35$ | 5.664333407724352 | 5.664333268544830 |
| $-0.85$ | $-0.85$ | $-0.10$ | $0.20$ | 8.358235547230933 | 8.358235533652652 |
| $-0.85$ | $-0.10$ | $0.65$ | $-0.40$ | 6.441055768429167 | 6.441055904422289 |
| $\vdots$ | $\vdots$ | $\vdots$ | $\vdots$ | $\vdots$ | $\vdots$ |
| $-0.70$ | $-0.70$ | $0.65$ | $0.50$ | 7.501885960573349 | 7.501885985988775 |
| $-0.70$ | $0.20$ | $0.65$ | $-0.40$ | 5.788555768429167 | 5.788555898571794 |
| $-0.55$ | $-1.00$ | $-0.70$ | $0.80$ | 7.853151337225672 | 7.853151236822366 |
| $-0.40$ | $-0.10$ | $0.65$ | $0.05$ | 5.786244778728628 | 5.786244695371899 |
| $-0.25$ | $-0.55$ | $0.80$ | $0.20$ | 6.189918918326645 | 6.189918953111843 |
| $\vdots$ | $\vdots$ | $\vdots$ | $\vdots$ | $\vdots$ | $\vdots$ |
| $0.05$ | $-0.55$ | $-0.70$ | $0.50$ | 5.668717560456533 | 5.668717575468671 |
| $0.20$ | $-0.85$ | $-0.85$ | $-0.40$ | 5.823944251309088 | 5.823944077371336 |
| $0.35$ | $-0.55$ | $0.20$ | $-0.55$ | 5.543772002000083 | 5.543772022878508 |
| $0.80$ | $0.05$ | $-0.10$ | $-0.70$ | 6.212500000000000 | 6.212499973420534 |
| $0.95$ | $0.95$ | $0.65$ | $0.65$ | 9.162342411091016 | 9.162342233203839 |
| $\vdots$ | $\vdots$ | $\vdots$ | $\vdots$ | $\vdots$ | $\vdots$ |

parameters (e.g., the weights and biases), studies of each target function approximation are conducted to obtain the average results illustrated via MSE and running time for 10 trials. Tables 9.13 through 9.16 show the training, testing and prediction results of four target functions (9.6) through (9.9) via the MLP-W-LM with 1000 iterations.

Tables 9.13 through 9.16 show that, as the number of hidden-layer neurons (i.e., $N$) increases, the running time also increases, which is extremely long. That is to say, with the specific number of hidden-layer neurons, the MLP-W-LM is more time-consuming than the proposed FIEPN. In addition, the MLP-W-LM cannot achieve lower MSE values (i.e., $e_{\mathrm{tra}}$, $e_{\mathrm{tes}}$ and $e_{\mathrm{pre}}$) with their magnitude orders being, respectively, $10^{-7} \sim 10^{-9}$, $10^{-7} \sim 10^{-9}$ and $10^{-2} \sim 10^{-5}$, which are much larger than those related to the FIEPN equipped with the WASD algorithm. The above comparative studies illustrate that the FIEPN has better approximation performance in terms of running time and accuracy than the MLP-W-LM.

In summary, all the above numerical results substantiate the efficacy and superior performance of the proposed FIEPN equipped with the WASD algorithm including PWG and TP techniques.

## 9.7 Chapter Summary

In this chapter, a novel multi-input (specifically, four-input) Euler-polynomial neuronet has been established and investigated to learn the five-dimensional data. Moreover, based on the WDD subalgorithm, a so-called WASD algorithm with PWG and TP techniques has been developed to determine the optimal weights and structure of the established FIEPN. In addition, four MATLAB

**TABLE 9.12:**   Prediction-type outputs of FIEPN equipped with WASD algorithm including both PWG and TP techniques by using MATLAB computing routine $\mathbf{w} = \text{pinv}(A) * \mathbf{b}$ for target function (9.9).

| $x_1$ | $x_2$ | $x_3$ | $x_4$ | $\gamma$ | $y$ |
|---|---|---|---|---|---|
| 1.15 | −1.15 | −1.00 | 1.05 | 5.496863310106956 | 5.496864879678905 |
| −1.15 | 1.05 | −1.10 | −1.15 | 5.546154464066190 | 5.546151325491925 |
| −1.0 | −1.10 | −1.05 | −1.20 | 9.979883302188656 | 9.979872778882021 |
| 1.00 | 1.15 | −1.10 | −1.00 | 10.090589245796926 | 10.090589691644684 |
| 1.00 | 1.00 | 1.20 | −1.10 | 9.715251525523614 | 9.715243268660711 |
| $\vdots$ | $\vdots$ | $\vdots$ | $\vdots$ | $\vdots$ | $\vdots$ |
| 1.20 | 1.15 | 1.10 | 1.20 | 11.282152767311583 | 11.282089563568819 |
| 1.05 | −1.05 | −1.15 | 1.15 | 5.531636850878770 | 5.531640062483269 |
| 1.10 | 1.15 | 1.00 | 1.20 | 10.813465136392326 | 10.813404620799680 |
| 1.00 | −1.20 | −1.00 | −1.20 | 5.614369919551447 | 5.614358911896336 |
| −1.15 | 1.20 | −1.00 | −1.00 | 5.479725575051662 | 5.479725572925054 |
| $\vdots$ | $\vdots$ | $\vdots$ | $\vdots$ | $\vdots$ | $\vdots$ |
| 1.10 | −1.00 | 1.05 | 1.05 | 5.690273430918621 | 5.690266899381265 |
| 1.20 | 1.15 | 1.00 | −1.15 | 11.245174746130516 | 11.245154993934802 |
| −1.20 | 1.00 | −1.00 | −1.00 | 5.517225575051661 | 5.517225310532932 |
| −1.15 | −1.20 | −1.05 | −1.10 | 11.037398004496545 | 11.037397383766857 |
| 1.15 | −1.15 | 1.15 | 1.10 | 5.710875589609706 | 5.710859039869366 |
| $\vdots$ | $\vdots$ | $\vdots$ | $\vdots$ | $\vdots$ | $\vdots$ |

**TABLE 9.13:**   Training, testing and prediction results of FIEPN via MLP-W-LM with 1000 iterations for target function (9.6).

| $N$ | $t_{\text{run}}$ (s) | $e_{\text{tra}}$ | $e_{\text{tes}}$ | $e_{\text{pre}}$ |
|---|---|---|---|---|
| 50 | 488.8578 | $1.4966 \times 10^{-7}$ | $1.5431 \times 10^{-7}$ | $2.0747 \times 10^{-2}$ |
| 100 | 1219.5327 | $7.9014 \times 10^{-8}$ | $8.4184 \times 10^{-8}$ | $8.9728 \times 10^{-3}$ |
| 150 | 2324.6128 | $7.0727 \times 10^{-8}$ | $7.7092 \times 10^{-8}$ | $7.3446 \times 10^{-3}$ |
| 200 | 3301.2133 | $6.6959 \times 10^{-8}$ | $7.6687 \times 10^{-8}$ | $7.3253 \times 10^{-3}$ |

computing routines related to the WDD subalgorithm are studied and tested. Finally, numerical results have substantiated the efficacy, accuracy and superior performance of the proposed FIEPN equipped with the WASD algorithm including PWG and TP techniques in terms of training, testing and prediction. By comparing all the numerical results, a reasonable choice of four MATLAB computing routines is given.

## Appendix C: Detailed Derivation of Normal Equation

In this appendix, a detailed derivation of (9.3) is presented for the sake of completeness. By following (9.2), we have

$$e = \frac{1}{M}\|\Psi\mathbf{w} - \gamma\|^2 = \frac{1}{M}(\Psi\mathbf{w} - \gamma)^{\text{T}}(\Psi\mathbf{w} - \gamma)$$

**TABLE 9.14:** Training, testing and prediction results of FIEPN via MLP-W-LM with 1000 iterations for target function (9.7).

| $N$ | $t_{run}$ (s) | $e_{tra}$ | $e_{tes}$ | $e_{pre}$ |
|-----|-----------|-----------|-----------|-----------|
| 50 | 607.4943 | $1.1059 \times 10^{-7}$ | $1.1619 \times 10^{-7}$ | $4.9186 \times 10^{-2}$ |
| 100 | 1642.3637 | $9.2760 \times 10^{-8}$ | $1.0145 \times 10^{-7}$ | $6.6694 \times 10^{-2}$ |
| 150 | 2233.6452 | $7.7284 \times 10^{-8}$ | $8.8812 \times 10^{-8}$ | $1.9049 \times 10^{-2}$ |
| 200 | 4181.2442 | $7.8906 \times 10^{-8}$ | $9.3004 \times 10^{-8}$ | $3.0398 \times 10^{-2}$ |

**TABLE 9.15:** Training, testing and prediction results of FIEPN via MLP-W-LM with 1000 iterations for target function (9.8).

| $N$ | $t_{run}$ (s) | $e_{tra}$ | $e_{tes}$ | $e_{pre}$ |
|-----|-----------|-----------|-----------|-----------|
| 50 | 521.4820 | $8.8139 \times 10^{-9}$ | $9.3505 \times 10^{-9}$ | $6.4986 \times 10^{-5}$ |
| 100 | 1283.5389 | $6.3755 \times 10^{-9}$ | $7.1677 \times 10^{-9}$ | $6.4448 \times 10^{-5}$ |
| 150 | 2333.1368 | $7.5312 \times 10^{-9}$ | $8.6811 \times 10^{-9}$ | $4.6300 \times 10^{-4}$ |
| 200 | 3467.0867 | $8.5838 \times 10^{-9}$ | $1.2453 \times 10^{-8}$ | $7.8632 \times 10^{-4}$ |

$$= \frac{1}{M}(\mathbf{w}^T \Psi^T \Psi \mathbf{w} - \mathbf{w}^T \Psi^T \gamma - \gamma^T \Psi \mathbf{w} + \gamma^T \gamma)$$

$$= \frac{1}{M}(\mathbf{w}^T \Psi^T \Psi \mathbf{w} - 2\mathbf{w}^T \Psi^T \gamma + \gamma^T \gamma),$$

where $\| \cdot \|$ denotes the two-norm of a vector. The optimal performance of the FIEPN can be acquired by minimizing the value of $e$. According to the related mathematical theory [117], the following equation can be obtained by taking the partial derivative of $e$ with respect to $\mathbf{w}$ and setting it to be zero

$$\frac{\partial e}{\partial \mathbf{w}} = \frac{1}{M}(\Psi^T \Psi \mathbf{w} + \Psi^T \Psi \mathbf{w} - 2\Psi^T \gamma) = \frac{2}{M}\Psi^T(\Psi \mathbf{w} - \gamma) = 0,$$

which is equivalent to

$$\Psi^T(\Psi \mathbf{w} - \gamma) = 0.$$

Thus it transforms the problem of determining the optimal $\mathbf{w}$ into the solution of a nonhomogeneous linear equation, which can be reformulated as

$$\Psi^T \Psi \mathbf{w} = \Psi^T \gamma. \tag{9.10}$$

Note that (9.10) is exactly the same as (9.3). Thus the derivation is complete.

## Appendix D: Supplemental Theorems

In this appendix, a theorem on the same solutions of two different homogeneous linear equations is provided, and then a theorem and its detailed proof on the solution existence of the normal Equation (9.3) are presented.

**Theorem 6** *Suppose the matrices $F \in \mathbb{R}^{M \times N}$ and $G \in \mathbb{R}^{T \times N}$. Then the sufficient and necessary condition of the proposition that homogeneous linear equations*

$$\begin{cases} F\mathbf{z} = 0, \\ G\mathbf{z} = 0, \end{cases}$$

**TABLE 9.16:**    Training, testing and prediction results of FIEPN via MLP-W-LM with 1000 iterations for target function (9.9).

| $N$ | $t_{run}$ (s) | $e_{tra}$ | $e_{tes}$ | $e_{pre}$ |
|-----|-----------|-----------|-----------|-----------|
| 50  | 629.8234  | $8.0588 \times 10^{-9}$ | $8.3272 \times 10^{-9}$ | $1.0518 \times 10^{-3}$ |
| 100 | 1332.1383 | $4.2466 \times 10^{-9}$ | $4.6462 \times 10^{-9}$ | $2.8048 \times 10^{-4}$ |
| 150 | 2294.7359 | $3.8905 \times 10^{-9}$ | $4.3303 \times 10^{-9}$ | $2.1991 \times 10^{-4}$ |
| 200 | 3491.0450 | $5.3304 \times 10^{-9}$ | $6.2275 \times 10^{-9}$ | $1.0456 \times 10^{-3}$ |

*and*

$$F\mathbf{z} = 0$$

*have the same solutions is that there must exist a matrix $P \in \mathbb{R}^{T \times M}$ with $G = PF$ satisfied, where $\mathbf{z} \in \mathbb{R}^N$ is the unknown vector to be obtained, and M, N and T are positive integers [118].*

**Theorem 7** *The relationship* $\mathrm{rank}(\Psi^T \Psi) = \mathrm{rank}([\Psi^T\Psi, \Psi^T\gamma])$ *is always satisfied, and thus the solution of normal Equation (9.3) must always exist.*

**Proof.** Considering two homogeneous linear equations $\Psi\mathbf{z} = 0$ and $\Psi^T\Psi\mathbf{z} = 0$. According to the above theorem (i.e., Theorem 6), it is obvious that

$$\begin{cases} \Psi\mathbf{z} = 0, \\ \Psi^T\Psi\mathbf{z} = 0, \end{cases} \tag{9.11}$$

and

$$\Psi\mathbf{z} = 0, \tag{9.12}$$

have the same solutions. Suppose that

$$\begin{cases} \Psi\mathbf{z} = 0, \\ \Psi^T\Psi\mathbf{z} = 0, \end{cases} \tag{9.13}$$

and

$$\Psi^T\Psi\mathbf{z} = 0, \tag{9.14}$$

have the same solutions. According to the assumption and Theorem 6, there must exist a matrix $Q$ with $\Psi = Q\Psi^T\Psi$ satisfied. It can also be reformulated as $\Psi^T\Psi Q^T = \Psi^T$. According to the matrix theory [116], the rank relationship $\mathrm{rank}(\Psi^T) \leq \mathrm{rank}([\Psi^T\Psi, \Psi^T]) = \mathrm{rank}(\Psi^T[\Psi, I]) \leq \mathrm{rank}(\Psi^T)$ is satisfied, which means $\mathrm{rank}([\Psi^T\Psi, \Psi^T]) = \mathrm{rank}(\Psi^T)$, and thus the assumption is true and $Q$ must exist. Since (9.11) and (9.12) have the same solutions, and (9.13) and (9.14) have the same solutions, it is easy to conclude that (9.12) and (9.14) have the same solutions. That is to say, $\Psi\mathbf{z} = 0$ and $\Psi^T\Psi\mathbf{z} = 0$ have the same solutions, and $\mathrm{rank}(\Psi) = \mathrm{rank}(\Psi^T) = \mathrm{rank}(\Psi^T\Psi)$. As for (9.3), with the relationship $\mathrm{rank}(\Psi^T) = \mathrm{rank}(\Psi^T\Psi) \leq \mathrm{rank}([\Psi^T\Psi, \Psi^T\gamma]) = \mathrm{rank}(\Psi^T[\Psi, \gamma]) \leq \mathrm{rank}(\Psi^T) = \mathrm{rank}(\Psi^T\Psi)$ satisfied, which is equivalent to $\mathrm{rank}(\Psi^T\Psi) = \mathrm{rank}([\Psi^T\Psi, \Psi^T\gamma])$, the solution existence of the normal equation can be ensured. Thus the proof is complete.    □

# Chapter 10

## Multi-Input Bernoulli-Polynomial WASD Neuronet

This chapter proposes a multi-input Bernoulli-polynomial neuronet (MIBPN) on the basis of function approximation theory. The MIBPN is trained by a weights-and-structure-determination (WASD) algorithm with twice-pruning (TP). The WASD algorithm can obtain the optimal weights and structure for the MIBPN, and overcome the weaknesses of conventional back-propagation (BP) neuronets such as slow training speed and local minima. With the TP technique, the neurons of less importance in the MIBPN are pruned for less computational complexity. Furthermore, this MIBPN can be extended to a multiple-input-multiple-output Bernoulli-polynomial neuronet (MIMOBPN), which can be applied as an important tool for classification. Numerical results show that the MIBPN has outstanding performance in function data approximation (or, say, learning) and generalization (or, say, testing). Besides, experiment results based on the real-world classification data-sets substantiate the high accuracy and strong robustness of the MIMOBPN equipped with the WASD algorithm for classification. Finally, the TP aided WASD neuronet of Bernoulli-polynomial type in the forms of MIBPN and MIMOBPN is established, together with the effective extension to robust classification.

## 10.1 Introduction

Traditionally, it has been proved that a three-layer feed-forward neuronet, which is trained by error BP algorithm and thus named BP neuronet, can approximate any nonlinear continuous function with arbitrary accuracy as a universal approximator [119]. However, inherent problems like slow training speed and local minima always exist in the BP neuronets (including the multi-input BP neuronets). Besides, to determine the optimal size of the neuronet is a hard task. It is known that neuronet structure influences the neuronet performance significantly. As a consequence, this chapter intends to overcome the problems existing in the conventional multi-input BP neuronets and to determine the optimal neuronet structure for better practical applications.

Different from the way of algorithmic improvement, we focus on the direct enhancement on neuronet structure and activation functions. Previously, we have investigated several neuronets activated by some orthogonal polynomials including Chebyshev polynomials and Legendre polynomials [66]. This chapter, however, focuses on the non-orthogonal polynomials so as to extend the investigation. Therefore, as an important role in analytic theory of numbers and numerical analysis, Bernoulli polynomials are chosen as the fundamental elements of multi-input neuronet activation-functions in this chapter. In view of the fact that most systems have multiple inputs, it is essential to further explore the multi-input situation, and consequently a MIBPN is constructed. Without loss of generality and for the convenience of interpretation, we specifically focus on a four-input Bernoulli-polynomial neuronet (FIBPN) in this chapter. Note that the construction of other Bernoulli neuronets with different numbers of inputs is similar to that of the FIBPN. With the aid of the weights-direct-determination (WDD) subalgorithm (which avoids lengthy iterations and determines optimal weights directly), we propose the WASD algorithm with the TP technique for the FIBPN to obtain the optimal neuronet structure. Specifically, the structure of the FIBPN grows dynamically by adding the hidden-layer neuron that diminishes the training error or pruning the one that increases the training error. As the second pruning, to seek a simpler and more efficient neuronet structure, neurons with fewer contributions are pruned after the FIBPN acquires a grown structure and obtains steady performance. Numerical studies substantiate that the proposed FIBPN equipped with the TP-aided WASD algorithm has superior performance in terms of function data approximation and generalization.

Moreover, the MIBPN is then applied to solving classification problems in this chapter. As we know, classification is one of the commonest tasks in human activity. For example, classification can be applied in medical diagnosis [120], bankruptcy prediction [121] and handwritten character recognition [122]. For the MIBPN applied to classification, its inputs denote the attributes of the instances; and its outputs denote the categories of the instances. In view of the numbers of attributes and categories, it is necessary to extend the MIBPN to a MIMOBPN. The MIMOBPN is also trained by the TP-aided WASD algorithm, and the optimal weights and structure of the MIMOBPN are thus determined. Experiment results based on the real-world classification data-sets substantiate that the MIMOBPN can handle the classification problems successfully. Furthermore, even when noise exists, the MIMOBPN keeps the high accuracy for classification, displaying its strong robustness.

The rest of this chapter is organized into the following five sections. In Section 10.2, the model of FIBPN is presented and the theoretical basis is analysed. Section 10.3 presents the WASD algorithm. Section 10.4 illustrates three target functions and their approximation results. In Section 10.5, MIBPN and MIMOBPN are established with extension to robust classification. Section 10.6 concludes this chapter with final remarks.

## 10.2    Neuronet Model and Theoretical Basis

This section constructs a novel MIBPN (specifically, the FIBPN) together with the related theoretical basis.

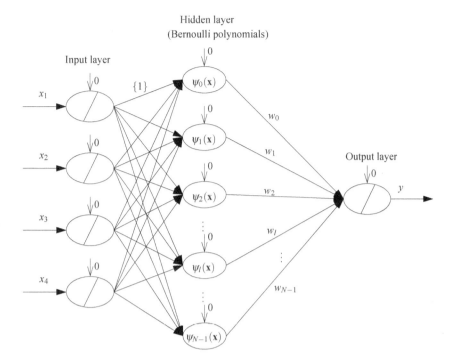

**FIGURE 10.1**: Model structure of FIBPN.

### 10.2.1  FIBPN model

The FIBPN consists of three layers, i.e., an input layer with four neurons, a hidden layer with $n$ neurons and an output layer with one neuron. The neurons in input and output layers are activated by simple linear function $h(x) = x$, whereas the activation function in each hidden-layer neuron is the product of four Bernoulli polynomials. To simplify the circuit implementation and the computational complexity, all neuronal thresholds in the FIBPN are set to be 0, and the weights between input and hidden layers are set to be 1. Figure 10.1 shows the model structure of the constructed FIBPN. As the cardinal factor for the performance of the FIBPN, the weights between hidden and output layers are to be decided in the next section by the WASD algorithm.

### 10.2.2  Theoretical basis

While the related theoretical basis for the Bernoulli-polynomial type neuronet is mentioned in the authors' previous work [123], the FIBPN constructed in this chapter is mainly based on the Weierstrass approximation theorem and the theory of multivariate function approximation.

Following the recurrence expression of Bernoulli polynomial [28], we can acquire a proposition [123] for the activation function of the FIBPN. That is, without loss of generality, we focus on the function approximation of four variables; and, according to the proposition in [123], the target function

$$f(x_1, x_2, x_3, x_4) \approx \sum_{l=0}^{N-1} w_l \psi_l(x_1, x_2, x_3, x_4)$$

$$= \sum_{v_1=0}^{N_1-1} \sum_{v_2=0}^{N_2-1} \sum_{v_3=0}^{N_3-1} \sum_{v_4=0}^{N_4-1} w_{v_1, v_2, v_3, v_4} \varphi_{v_1}(x_1) \varphi_{v_2}(x_2) \varphi_{v_3}(x_3) \varphi_{v_4}(x_4),$$

where $N_1$, $N_2$, $N_3$ and $N_4$, respectively, denote the numbers of Bernoulli polynomials of $x_1$, $x_2$, $x_3$ and $x_4$, with $N = N_1N_2N_3N_4$ being the total number of products of Bernoulli polynomials. Besides, in neuronet terminology, $w_l = w_{v_1,v_2,v_3,v_4}$ denotes the weight for the activation function $\psi_l(x_1,x_2,x_3,x_4) = \varphi_{v_1}(x_1)\varphi_{v_2}(x_2)\varphi_{v_3}(x_3)\varphi_{v_4}(x_4)$.

In order to obtain a more agreeable structure of the FIBPN and to develop the TP-aided WASD algorithm better, we sort the activation functions (or termed, basis functions) $\{\psi_l(x_1,x_2,x_3,x_4)\}$ according to the graded lexicographic order [124] as follows. Let $\psi_l(x_1,x_2,x_3,x_4) = \varphi_{v_1}(x_1)\varphi_{v_2}(x_2)\varphi_{v_3}(x_3)\varphi_{v_4}(x_4)$ be a basis function sequenced by the graded lexicographic order and let $\psi_{l'}(x_1,x_2,x_3,x_4) = \varphi_{v'_1}(x_1)\varphi_{v'_2}(x_2)\varphi_{v'_3}(x_3)\varphi_{v'_4}(x_4)$ be a different one. So, $l > l'$ and $\psi_l(x_1,x_2,x_3,x_4)$ is sorted behind $\psi_{l'}(x_1,x_2,x_3,x_4)$ if either of the following two conditions can be satisfied.

*Condition 1:* $(v_1 + v_2 + v_3 + v_4) > (v'_1 + v'_2 + v'_3 + v'_4)$.

*Condition 2:* $(v_1 + v_2 + v_3 + v_4) = (v'_1 + v'_2 + v'_3 + v'_4)$, but the first nonzero element of the difference $(v_1 - v'_1, v_2 - v'_2, v_3 - v'_3, v_4 - v'_4)$ is positive.

For better understanding, the first 15 basis functions (or termed, activation functions) $\psi_l(x_1,x_2,x_3,x_4)$ sorted by the graded lexicographic order are shown below.

$$
\begin{cases}
\psi_0(x_1,x_2,x_3,x_4) = \varphi_0(x_1)\varphi_0(x_2)\varphi_0(x_3)\varphi_0(x_4), \\
\psi_1(x_1,x_2,x_3,x_4) = \varphi_0(x_1)\varphi_0(x_2)\varphi_0(x_3)\varphi_1(x_4), \\
\psi_2(x_1,x_2,x_3,x_4) = \varphi_0(x_1)\varphi_0(x_2)\varphi_1(x_3)\varphi_0(x_4), \\
\psi_3(x_1,x_2,x_3,x_4) = \varphi_0(x_1)\varphi_1(x_2)\varphi_0(x_3)\varphi_0(x_4), \\
\psi_4(x_1,x_2,x_3,x_4) = \varphi_1(x_1)\varphi_0(x_2)\varphi_0(x_3)\varphi_0(x_4), \\
\psi_5(x_1,x_2,x_3,x_4) = \varphi_0(x_1)\varphi_0(x_2)\varphi_0(x_3)\varphi_2(x_4), \\
\psi_6(x_1,x_2,x_3,x_4) = \varphi_0(x_1)\varphi_0(x_2)\varphi_1(x_3)\varphi_1(x_4), \\
\psi_7(x_1,x_2,x_3,x_4) = \varphi_0(x_1)\varphi_0(x_2)\varphi_2(x_3)\varphi_0(x_4), \\
\psi_8(x_1,x_2,x_3,x_4) = \varphi_0(x_1)\varphi_1(x_2)\varphi_0(x_3)\varphi_1(x_4), \\
\psi_9(x_1,x_2,x_3,x_4) = \varphi_0(x_1)\varphi_1(x_2)\varphi_1(x_3)\varphi_0(x_4), \\
\psi_{10}(x_1,x_2,x_3,x_4) = \varphi_0(x_1)\varphi_2(x_2)\varphi_0(x_3)\varphi_0(x_4), \\
\psi_{11}(x_1,x_2,x_3,x_4) = \varphi_1(x_1)\varphi_0(x_2)\varphi_0(x_3)\varphi_1(x_4), \\
\psi_{12}(x_1,x_2,x_3,x_4) = \varphi_1(x_1)\varphi_0(x_2)\varphi_1(x_3)\varphi_0(x_4), \\
\psi_{13}(x_1,x_2,x_3,x_4) = \varphi_1(x_1)\varphi_1(x_2)\varphi_0(x_3)\varphi_0(x_4), \\
\psi_{14}(x_1,x_2,x_3,x_4) = \varphi_2(x_1)\varphi_0(x_2)\varphi_0(x_3)\varphi_0(x_4).
\end{cases}
$$

As a result, the target function $f(x_1,x_2,x_3,x_4)$ can be effectively approximated by the polynomial constructed above, provided that we obtain the optimal weights $\{w_l\}$ corresponding to the activation functions $\{\psi_l(\mathbf{x})\}$ between the hidden layer and the output layer as well as the most appropriate number of the hidden neurons. Here, input vector $\mathbf{x} = [x_1,x_2,x_3,x_4]^{\mathrm{T}}$, and superscript $^{\mathrm{T}}$ denotes the transpose of a vector or a matrix. In other words, it is our task to determine not only the optimal weights between hidden and output layers, but also the optimal structure of the hidden layer in the FIBPN (or, say, the optimal structure of the FIBPN).

## 10.3    Weights and Structure Determination

In order to construct finally the FIBPN, two tasks need to be completed. One is to obtain the optimal structure of the hidden layer, including the specific activation function of each hidden neuron

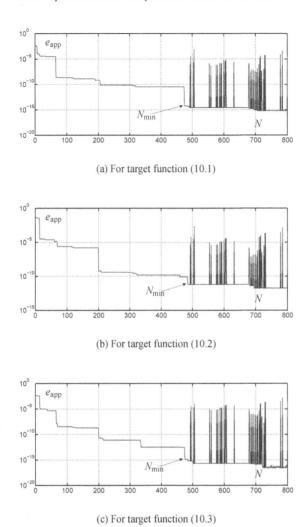

(a) For target function (10.1)

(b) For target function (10.2)

(c) For target function (10.3)

**FIGURE 10.2**: Approximation error of FIBPN versus its number of hidden-layer neurons without using PWG technique (i.e., only adding) for target functions (10.1) through (10.3), respectively.

and the optimal number of hidden neurons (i.e., $N_{opt}$). The other is to obtain the optimal weights between the hidden and output layers after the determination of the hidden-layer structure. Since the method of generating specific activation functions has been discussed in Subsection 10.2.2, in this section, we mainly explore and develop the TP-aided WASD algorithm (based on the WDD subalgorithm) to obtain the optimal number of hidden neurons and the optimal weights between the hidden and output layers.

In the authors' previous works [28, 123], the WDD subalgorithm has been proposed and investigated. Note that such a WDD subalgorithm can determine the optimal weights between the hidden and output layers directly, which avoids the lengthy and inefficient iterative computation. Based on this, the TP-aided WASD algorithm can be developed through the following two parts. One is to generate a basic framework of the FIBPN through the pruning-while-growing (PWG) technique; and the other is to prune the less important neurons of the hidden layer via pruning-after-grown (PAG) technique so as to determine the final structure of the FIBPN.

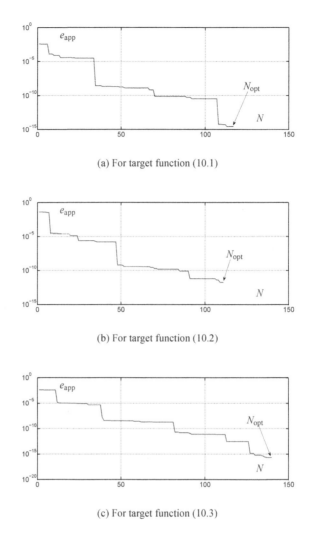

(a) For target function (10.1)

(b) For target function (10.2)

(c) For target function (10.3)

**FIGURE 10.3**: Approximation error of FIBPN versus its number of hidden-layer neurons with PWG technique used (i.e., adding and pruning) for target functions (10.1) through (10.3), respectively.

### 10.3.1   Pruning-while-growing technique

As we know, the neuronet performance cannot be satisfactory if the number of the hidden neurons is insufficient or exceeds an appropriate value [28]. In other words, there exists an optimal number of hidden neurons. Consequently, we construct the FIBPN with the beginning of only one hidden neuron, and add new neurons one-by-one to the FIBPN. However, different from adding neurons simply, when a new neuron is added via the WASD algorithm, the approximation error (i.e., $e_{app}$) is calculated in the form of MSE (mean square error). More importantly, if the training error increases (i.e., $e_{app}$ is larger than the minimum MSE $e_{min}$), the last-added neuron will be pruned to ensure that all hidden neurons can enhance the learning performance of the FIBPN. This is the so-called first pruning. Finally, the neuronet would acquire steady performance (i.e., the approximation error converges to a stable value) after a number of useful neurons are added while a number of harmful neurons are pruned in a continuous manner. Thus, this PWG part finishes.

**TABLE 10.1:** Performance of FIBPN with grown structure for target functions (10.1) through (10.3).

| Target function | $N_{hid}$ | $e_{app}$ | $e_{tes}$ |
|---|---|---|---|
| (10.1) | 117 | $2.8006 \times 10^{-15}$ | $1.6745 \times 10^{-15}$ |
| (10.2) | 111 | $1.7912 \times 10^{-12}$ | $5.8609 \times 10^{-13}$ |
| (10.3) | 140 | $2.0854 \times 10^{-16}$ | $1.2961 \times 10^{-16}$ |

### 10.3.2 Pruning-after-grown technique

After the FIBPN obtains a grown structure and achieves good approximation performance, its scale should be taken into consideration again for the less computational complexity. When the neuronet is not large enough and still growing, each hidden neuron plays a significant role. That is because the training MSE $e$ has not converged to a stable value yet and the FIBPN needs more neurons to promote its learning ability. However, once a grown structure with adequate neurons is acquired, some hidden neurons become not so necessary as before and can be pruned without a clear decrease in terms of the approximation performance. If some hidden neurons obtained through the PWG technique are pruned, the approximation error would raise to a slight extent. However, it is still worth pruning because the number of hidden neurons can diminish heavily and even halve. From this viewpoint, the PAG technique is necessarily presented.

Evidently, the weights between the hidden and output layers are the impact factors of the hidden neurons, indicating the importance of each hidden neuron and the extent of contribution they make to the neuronet output. Note that it is unreasonable and unlikely that each hidden neuron shares the same weight. According to the WDD subalgorithm, all weights between hidden and output layers in the FIBPN are optimal. Thus, they are generally distinct, and some weights may be too small so that they have little influence on neuronet output. As the second pruning, all hidden neurons obtained through the PWG technique are checked, and the neurons with the absolute values of their corresponding weights smaller than a particular value $w_{min}$ (in this chapter, $w_{min} = 10^{-6}$) will be pruned. Besides, the WDD subalgorithm has to be applied again to determine the optimal weights for the remaining neurons. Thus, this PAG part finishes.

## 10.4 Numerical Studies

Three target functions and their approximation results are substantiated in this section as follows.

$$f(x_1, x_2, x_3, x_4) = \exp(\cos(x_1 x_2)) + x_3 \sin(x_4) + 10, \tag{10.1}$$

$$f(x_1, x_2, x_3, x_4) = \sin(\pi x_1 x_2) + x_3 x_4 + 20, \tag{10.2}$$

$$f(x_1, x_2, x_3, x_4) = \exp(x_1 x_2) + \cos(\sin(x_3 x_4)) + 20. \tag{10.3}$$

For each target function above, we sample uniformly over the region $[-0.5, 0.5]^4$ with interval size 0.13 to generate a set of sample data $\{(\mathbf{x}_m, \gamma_m) | \mathbf{x}_m \in \mathbb{R}^4, \gamma_m \in \mathbb{R}, m = 1, 2, \cdots, 6561\}$ (i.e., the number of samples $M = 6561$) for training. The data for generalization is sampled uniformly over the region $[-0.5, 0.5]^4$ with interval size 0.18.

### 10.4.1 Comparative numerical results of PWG technique

Generally speaking, the number of hidden neurons would have its most appropriate value. Figure 10.2 verifies this point by illustrating the relation between the neuronet approximation error and the

**TABLE 10.2:** Performance of FIBPN with final structure for target functions (10.1) through (10.3).

| Target function | $N_{hid}$ | $e_{app}$ | $e_{tes}$ |
|:---:|:---:|:---:|:---:|
| (10.1) | 57 | $2.8006 \times 10^{-15}$ | $1.6743 \times 10^{-15}$ |
| (10.2) | 54 | $1.7912 \times 10^{-12}$ | $5.8608 \times 10^{-13}$ |
| (10.3) | 83 | $2.0882 \times 10^{-16}$ | $1.2945 \times 10^{-16}$ |

**TABLE 10.3:** Performance comparison of two FIBPN models with different structures for target functions (10.1) through (10.3).

| Target function | $d_{hid}$ | $i_{app}$ |
|:---:|:---:|:---:|
| (10.1) | 60 (51.28%) | $1.53 \times 10^{-20}$ (0.01%) |
| (10.2) | 57 (51.35%) | $6.40 \times 10^{-21}$ (0.00%) |
| (10.3) | 57 (40.71%) | $2.73 \times 10^{-19}$ (0.13%) |

number of hidden neurons. Note that, in Fig. 10.2, the neuronet structure (i.e., the number of hidden neurons) grows freely without using the PWG technique (i.e., only adding with no pruning); and that the experiment stops when the number of hidden neurons reaches a relatively large value (i.e., 800 in this chapter) so as not to be endless. We can see from the figure that the learning capability of such a FIBPN improves with the increase of hidden neurons. However, once the number of the hidden neurons exceeds the appropriate value (i.e., $N_{min}$), its approximation performance fluctuates violently. That is to say, it may lead to over-fitting. So, there exists indeed the most appropriate value for the number of hidden neurons, which ensures the best neuronet performance and avoids the over-fitting possibility.

On the other hand, Fig. 10.3 substantiates that the proposed PWG technique can successfully find out the most appropriate hidden-neuron number (i.e., $N_{opt}$) for the FIBPN. It is worth pointing out that not all added hidden neurons can diminish the approximation error and improve the neuronet performance. Consequently, as we can see from Fig. 10.3, those redundant neurons are pruned via the PWG technique but the FIBPN still achieves the excellent performance. That is, not only the hidden neurons of the FIBPN in Fig. 10.3 are much fewer (i.e., the neuronet structure is much simpler), but also the over-fitting possibility in Fig. 10.2 can be avoided. Specifically, each $N_{min}$ in Fig. 10.2 is larger than 400, but each $N_{opt}$ obtained through the PWG technique in Fig. 10.3 is smaller than 150. Furthermore, with a grown structure obtained through this technique (i.e., the first part of TP-aided WASD algorithm), the FIBPN can acquire almost the best performance in function data approximation and generalization. The detailed function data approximation and generalization performance is displayed in Table 10.1, where $N_{hid}$ denotes the number of hidden neurons, and $e_{tes}$ denotes the testing error of the neuronet. According to the table, all approximation errors for the three target functions are so small that they reach order $10^{-12}$ or even smaller to order $10^{-16}$. As for the generalization ability, each testing error is smaller than the corresponding approximation error. That is to say, based on the Weierstrass approximation theorem and the theory of multivariate function approximation, the FIBPN can be used as an excellent function data approximator. Therefore, the PWG technique not only can find an appropriate and optimal number of hidden neurons to ensure the neuronet performance in function data approximation and generalization, but also simplify the neuronet structure by pruning less important neurons during the growing process.

**TABLE 10.4:** Performance comparison of different neuronets using WASD, LM and BFGS algorithms for target functions (10.1) through (10.3).

|  |  | Using WASD | Using LM | Using BFGS |
|---|---|---|---|---|
| Target Function (10.1) | $e_{app}$ | $2.80 \times 10^{-15}$ | $6.28 \times 10^{-9}$ | $7.48 \times 10^{-6}$ |
|  | $e_{tes}$ | $1.67 \times 10^{-15}$ | $7.56 \times 10^{-8}$ | $7.15 \times 10^{-6}$ |
| Target Function (10.2) | $e_{app}$ | $1.79 \times 10^{-12}$ | $2.34 \times 10^{-8}$ | $1.24 \times 10^{-5}$ |
|  | $e_{tes}$ | $5.86 \times 10^{-13}$ | $1.83 \times 10^{-8}$ | $1.29 \times 10^{-5}$ |
| Target Function (10.3) | $e_{app}$ | $2.09 \times 10^{-16}$ | $3.55 \times 10^{-9}$ | $2.43 \times 10^{-4}$ |
|  | $e_{tes}$ | $1.29 \times 10^{-16}$ | $9.11 \times 10^{-7}$ | $2.81 \times 10^{-4}$ |

### 10.4.2 Comparative numerical results of PAG technique

As discussed in the above subsection, since we employ the PWG technique, the approximation error converges to a stable value and the FIBPN achieves excellent performance. In this subsection, the numerical results of the FIBPN using the PAG technique are presented. Specifically, Table 10.2 shows the hidden-neuron number and the neuronet performance of the FIBPN with the final structure determined by the PAG technique, and Table 10.3 substantiates the specific differences between the FIBPN with two different structures determined before and after the employment of the PAG technique.

As shown in Table 10.2, with a more simplified structure obtained through the PAG technique, the FIBPN achieves excellent performance as a function data approximator. In other words, the proposed method of pruning hidden neurons via the PAG technique is effective and efficient. Besides, the efficiency of the PAG technique can be substantiated by Table 10.3, where $d_{hid}$ and $i_{app}$ denote the decrease of hidden neurons and the increase of approximation error, respectively. That is, the approximation errors just increase by 0.13% at most and by 0.05% on average, whereas the neuronet scales diminish by 40.71% at least and by 47.78% on average. Especially, for the target function (10.2), the approximation error just increases by 0.0005%, but the neuronet scale diminishes by over 50%. These comparisons mean that it is advisable to prune a neuronet to a smaller size at the expense of a relative slight decline in approximation performance. Therefore, the neuronet can be more practical, economical, efficient and effective, especially in terms of hardware implementation and computation, if the PAG technique is applied.

### 10.4.3 Numerical comparison with conventional BP neuronets

In order to further substantiate the superior approximation performance of the TP-aided WASD neuronet FIBPN, we compare it with two conventional BP neuronets trained by the Levenberg-Marquardt (LM) method and the BFGS algorithm, respectively. The BP neuronets are constructed via the MATLAB toolbox, which are set to contain three layers, with both input layer and output layer activated by linear functions $h(x) = x$ and with the hidden layer activated by unipolar sigmoid functions. We use the TP-aided WASD neuronet FIBPN proposed in this chapter and the two BP neuronets to approximate the same target functions given above [i.e., target functions (10.1) through (10.3)]. The number of hidden neurons and the training time of the two BP neuronets are set to be the same as those of the proposed FIBPN for each target function so as to compare the two BP neuronets with the FIBPN under the same conditions. The numerical results are displayed in Table 10.4. As seen from the table, the FIBPN using WASD algorithm is much better than the conventional BP neuronets using LM and BFGS algorithms both in approximation and generalization. As a result, the FIBPN equipped with the TP-aided WASD algorithm can be applied as a superior function data approximator.

**TABLE 10.5:**    Features of three classification data-sets.

| Data-set | Attribute number | Category number | Size |
|---|---|---|---|
| Iris | 4 | 3 | 150 |
| Wine | 13 | 3 | 178 |
| Breast Cancer | 9 | 2 | 683 |

**TABLE 10.6:**    Testing accuracy rates of MIMOBPN and RBFN for classification of three different data-sets.

| Neuronet | Training percentage | Iris | | | Wine | | | Breast Cancer | | |
|---|---|---|---|---|---|---|---|---|---|---|
| | | Min | Max | Avg | Min | Max | Avg | Min | Max | Avg |
| MIMOBPN | 50% | 92% | 100% | 96% | 92% | 100% | 97% | 94% | 99% | 96% |
| MIMOBPN | 70% | 91% | 100% | 96% | 92% | 100% | 97% | 92% | 100% | 96% |
| RBFN | 50% | 88% | 99% | 94% | 75% | 97% | 87% | 94% | 97% | 96% |
| RBFN | 70% | 84% | 100% | 95% | 75% | 98% | 88% | 85% | 98% | 96% |

In addition, we test various target functions and data-sets, of which the numerical results all substantiate that the FIBPN equipped with the TP-aided WASD algorithm can be applied as a superior function data approximator in view of its effectiveness and efficiency on function data approximation and generalization.

## 10.5    Extension to Robust Classification

As one of the commonest tasks in human activity, classification can be used to tackle many problems in various areas including business, science, industry and medicine. Different from traditional statistical classification methods, neuronets provide an effective way to solve the practical problems and become a significant tool for classification. Consequently, it is necessary and full of practical meaning to extend the MIBPN (specifically, FIBPN) for classification. In this section, the extended neuronet model is discussed, and then the neuronet performance for classification is shown.

Neuronets can identify the category according to the attributes, so they can be employed to solve the classification problem. In this research, the input and output of the neuronet correspond to the attribute and the category, respectively. For the reason that there are multiple categories in practical applications, the MIBPN needs to be extended to a multiple-input-multiple-output Bernoulli-polynomial neuronet (i.e., MIMOBPN) for classification. For a certain classification problem of $\alpha$ attributes and $\beta$ categories, the MIMOBPN consists of $\beta$ sub-neuronets, which are similar to the FIBPN but with $\alpha$ inputs. Each sub-neuronet can be treated as an extended MIBPN which contains $\alpha$ inputs and one output. The activation functions in the hidden layer of such a sub-neuronet can also be obtained through the proposition in [123] as well as the formulation in Subsection 10.2.2; and the weights and structure of each sub-neuronet are also determined by the TP-aided WASD algorithm. After training, each sub-neuronet outputs a certain category. That is, if an instance of $\alpha$ attributes belongs to a certain category, then the corresponding sub-neuronet outputs 1, and the other sub-neuronets output 0. In this manner, the MIMOBPN solves the classification problem by dividing the whole classification problem into $\beta$ subproblems.

Numerical experiments are based on three typical real-world classification data-sets from the University of California Irvine (UCI) Machine Learning Repository. The features of the three data-sets are shown in Table 10.5. Each data-set is divided into two parts, one for training and the other for testing. For each data-set, we choose two different percentages of the data for training: one is

**TABLE 10.7:** Testing accuracy rates of MIMOBPN and RBFN based on 50% data for training with random noise.

| Neuronet | Noise amplitude | Iris | | | Wine | | | Breast Cancer | | |
|---|---|---|---|---|---|---|---|---|---|---|
| | | Min | Max | Avg | Min | Max | Avg | Min | Max | Avg |
| MIMOBPN | 5% | 91% | 100% | 95% | 92% | 100% | 97% | 94% | 98% | 96% |
| MIMOBPN | 10% | 91% | 99% | 96% | 91% | 100% | 97% | 93% | 98% | 96% |
| MIMOBPN | 20% | 85% | 99% | 93% | 91% | 100% | 97% | 94% | 98% | 96% |
| RBFN | 5% | 83% | 99% | 93% | 78% | 94% | 86% | 94% | 98% | 96% |
| RBFN | 10% | 75% | 99% | 91% | 75% | 97% | 86% | 94% | 98% | 96% |
| RBFN | 20% | 65% | 97% | 86% | 71% | 94% | 83% | 93% | 98% | 96% |

50% and the other is 70%. Thus, the corresponding percentages of the data for testing are 50% and 30%, respectively. In addition, 100 experiments are conducted for each percentage. That is, 100 pairs of training and testing data-sets for each percentage (i.e., 50% and 70%) are generated. Thus, 200 pairs of training and testing data-sets for each classification data-set are generated for numerical experiments. Note that both 50% and 70% of data are chosen randomly in each experiment. For further demonstrating the superiority of the proposed MIMOBPN, comparative numerical results between the radial-basis-function neuronet (RBFN) and the MIMOBPN for the same classification problems are shown in Tables 10.6 and 10.7.

Specifically, Table 10.6 shows the testing accuracy rates of the proposed MIMOBPN and the RBFN for classification of the three different data-sets. Note that "Min", "Max" and "Avg" in the tables respectively denote the minimal, maximal and average values of the testing accuracy rates. As we see from Table 10.6, the MIMOBPN solves the classification problems more successfully. For the three data-sets, no matter whether 50% or 70% of data are used for training, all of the average accuracy rates of the MIMOBPN exceed 95%, and sometimes the testing accuracy rates even reach 100%. Evidently, compared with the RBFN, the MIMOBPN can obtain higher accuracy. Besides, we test the robustness of the proposed TP-aided WASD neuronet MIMOBPN by adding random noise into the training data-set. In detail, 50% of the data are chosen as the training data-set, and then the random noise with different amplitudes of 5%, 10% and 20% are added to it. The corresponding testing accuracy rates of the MIMOBPN and the RBFN are shown in Table 10.7. According to the table, the MIMOBPN can maintain high testing accuracy rates with the average rates around 95% (though the noise is added). Comparing the "Avg" columns of Tables 10.6 and 10.7, we see that the decline caused by the noise is so small and it makes almost no clear effect. That is, the proposed TP-aided WASD neuronet MIMOBPN has strong robustness. Besides, other methods for classification problem solving will be investigated comparatively as a future research direction.

In summary, the numerical experiment results presented above have substantiated the high accuracy and strong robustness of the MIMOBPN for classification. It is also worth pointing out that the three real-world classification data-sets are from different areas including plant, chemistry and medicine. Accordingly, the MIMOBPN, as believed, can be used as a powerful classifier in practical applications.

## 10.6 Chapter Summary

In this chapter, we have proposed and studied a novel multi-input Bernoulli-polynomial neuronet, in short, MIBPN (e.g., four-input Bernoulli-polynomial neuronet, FIBPN). In order to determine the optimal neuronet structure, a corresponding TP-aided WASD algorithm has been proposed based on the previously presented WDD subalgorithm. In this WASD algorithm, not only the relation between the hidden-neuron number and the neuronet performance has been fully analyzed and investigated, but also the effect of each neuron has been taken into consideration. Therefore, the neuronet equipped with this WASD algorithm can obtain an optimal structure with a remarkable property that is to prune the neurons which make less contributions to the neuronet. Moreover, the MIBPN has been extended successfully to a multiple-input-multiple-output Bernoulli-polynomial neuronet (MIMOBPN) for classification which is usable for tackling many practical problems. Numerical experiment results have further substantiated the effectiveness and efficiency of the proposed TP-aided WASD neuronet in the forms of MIBPN and MIMOBPN in terms of function data approximation, generalization and classification.

# Chapter 11

## Multi-Input Hermite-Polynomial WASD Neuronet

Based on the theory of polynomial-interpolation and curve-fitting, a multi-input feed-forward neuronet activated by Hermite orthogonal polynomials (or, say, Hermite polynomials, HP) is proposed and investigated in this chapter. Besides, the design makes the multi-input Hermite-polynomial neuronet (MIHPN) have no weakness of dimension explosion. To determine the optimal weights of the MIHPN, the weights-direct-determination (WDD) subalgorithm is presented. To obtain the optimal structure of the MIHPN, the so-called weights-and-structure-determination (WASD) algorithm is finally proposed, which aims at achieving the best approximation accuracy while obtaining the minimal number of hidden-layer neurons. Numerical results further substantiate the efficacy of the MIHPN model and WASD algorithm.

## 11.1   Introduction

Note that artificial neuronets (AN) have been widely applied to many different engineering and scientific fields, such as control system design [125], pattern recognition [126] and robot [127]. Being one of the most important neuronet models, back-propagation (BP) neuronets (including the multi-input BP neuronet) have also been widely investigated in many theoretical and practical areas. However, the conventional BP algorithms have the following drawbacks [128]: (1) lengthy iterative training; (2) more chance to fall into local minima; (3) difficulty in choosing appropriate learning parameters; and (4) inability to determine the optimal number, i.e., $N_{opt}$, of hidden-layer neurons (or termed, hidden neurons). To solve such problems occurring in BP neuronets, many researchers presented improved algorithms [125, 128], such as conjugate gradient method, quasi-Newton method and Levenberg-Marquardt (LM) method. However, these improved algorithms still need an iterative training process which costs a considerable amount of time and introduces many uncertainties.

In addition to the computation of weights, the determination of structure is important for BP neuronets. The structure corresponds to the number of hidden-layer neurons [99]. The determination of the optimal neuronet structure is equivalent to the determination of the optimal number of hidden-layer neurons. In many cases, the number of hidden-layer neurons not only influences the computational complexity, but also the performance of neuronets; i.e., structural risk. Specifically, if there are fewer neurons, the training ability of the neuronet is worse in the form of largely increased training error [99]. On the other hand, if there are too many hidden-layer neurons, the structural complexity increases, which even leads to over-fitting phenomena. So, determining the number of hidden-layer neurons is always viewed as an important but very difficult task [99]. To overcome these difficulties in the determination of weights and structure, the authors have presented an effective algorithm in the previous study [125, 129]. However, that algorithm was mostly employed to deal with single-input BP-type neuronets. The disadvantage of BP neuronets and that single-input AN form may have restricted greatly the applications of neuronets in practice.

Therefore, in this chapter, a MIHPN is proposed and analyzed, in view of the fact that multi-input BP neuronets are more useful. It is worth pointing out that this MIHPN is greatly different from the Hermite interpolation neuronet in terms of neuronet structure and activation functions. Furthermore, the weights-and-structure-determination (WASD) algorithm is presented to obtain the optimal structure and weights of the MIHPN. Specifically, WASD algorithm, which is based on the WDD subalgorithm [130], can (1) determine directly the weights connecting the hidden layer and output layer and (2) obtain automatically the optimal structure of the MIHPN. These two aims are achieved by finding the smallest training error. Numerical results further substantiate the efficacy of the MIHPN and WASD algorithm.

## 11.2  MIHPN Model and WASD Algorithm

In this section, we firstly propose the MIHPN model by giving related important definition of Hermite polynomials (HP). Then, the WASD is presented to determine the optimal weights and structure of the MIHPN model.

### 11.2.1  MIHPN model

As shown in Fig. 11.1, the MIHPN model consists of three layers of neurons. The weights from input layer to hidden layer are randomly generated between 0 and 1 [45]. Besides, the thresholds of all neurons are set to be 0. The input-layer and output-layer neurons are activated by the linear function $g(x) = x$, while the hidden-layer neurons are activated by a group of HP [18, 19, 25].

**Definition 7**  The $j$th Hermite polynomial $\varphi_j(x)$ with $0 \leq x < +\infty$ satisfies the following recursive formula:

$$\varphi_j(x) = 2x\varphi_{j-1}(x) - 2(j-2)\varphi_{j-2}(x),$$

where   $\varphi_1(x) = 1$,  $\varphi_2(x) = 2x$,  $\varphi_3(x) = 4x^2 - 2$,  $\varphi_4(x) = 8x^3 - 12x$,  $\varphi_5(x) = 16x^4 - 48x^2 + 12$, $\varphi_6(x) = 32x^5 - 160x^3 + 120x$,  $\cdots$

The characteristic of HP guarantees that the MIHPN has the ability of approximation. For readers' convenience, the related definition and lemma about the approximation ability of HP are given in Appendix E to this chapter.

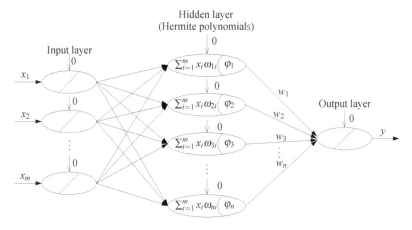

**FIGURE 11.1**: Model structure of MIHPN with input-to-hidden weights $\omega$ positively randomly generated.

### 11.2.2 WASD algorithm

The set of training samples can be denoted by $\{(\mathbf{x}_i, \gamma_i)\}_{i=1}^{N}$, where $\mathbf{x}_i = [x_{i1}, x_{i2}, \cdots, x_{im}]^{\mathrm{T}} \in \mathbb{R}^m$ and $\gamma_i \in \mathbb{R}$. The vector $\omega_j = [\omega_{j1}, \omega_{j2}, \cdots, \omega_{jm}]^{\mathrm{T}}$ denotes the positive vector of the randomly generated weights linking from the input-layer neurons to the $j$th neuron of the hidden layer. Besides, $w_i$ denotes the weight from the $i$th hidden-layer neuron to the output-layer neuron, which can be calculated directly by the WDD subalgorithm. Corresponding to the MIHPN, we define the following average error ($e$):

$$e = \frac{1}{N} \sum_{i=1}^{N} \left( \gamma_i - \sum_{j=1}^{n} w_j \varphi_j \left( \sum_{k=1}^{m} x_{ik} \omega_{jk} \right) \right)^2. \tag{11.1}$$

Besides, $\sum_{k=1}^{m} x_{ik} \omega_{jk}$ is substituted by $\chi_{ij}$ hereinafter. According to the authors' previous research, the weights of the MIHPN model can be directly determined through the following theorem [129].

**Theorem 8** *With the weights vector* $\mathbf{w} = [w_1, w_2, \cdots, w_n]^{\mathrm{T}} \in \mathbb{R}^n$ *and the target-outputs vector* $\gamma = [\gamma_1, \gamma_2, \cdots, \gamma_N]^{\mathrm{T}} \in \mathbb{R}^N$ *defined (note that superscript* $^{\mathrm{T}}$ *denotes the transpose operator), the hidden-to-output weights of the MIHPN depicted in Fig. 11.1 can be determined as*

$$\mathbf{w} = (\Psi^{\mathrm{T}} \Psi)^{-1} \Psi^{\mathrm{T}} \gamma = \mathrm{pinv}(\Psi) \gamma = \Psi^{\dagger} \gamma, \tag{11.2}$$

*where the input-activation matrix* $\Psi$ *is constructed as*

$$\Psi = \begin{bmatrix} \varphi_1(\chi_{11}) & \varphi_2(\chi_{12}) & \cdots & \varphi_N(\chi_{1N}) \\ \varphi_1(\chi_{21}) & \varphi_2(\chi_{22}) & \cdots & \varphi_N(\chi_{2N}) \\ \vdots & \vdots & \ddots & \vdots \\ \varphi_1(\chi_{M1}) & \varphi_2(\chi_{M2}) & \cdots & \varphi_N(\chi_{MN}) \end{bmatrix} \in \mathbb{R}^{M \times N}.$$

Besides, superscript $^{-1}$ denotes the inverse operator, while $\mathrm{pinv}(\cdot)$ and superscript $^{\dagger}$ denote the pseudoinverse operator.

As mentioned, the performance of BP-type neuronets varies with the number of hidden-layer neurons. If some hidden-layer neurons are actually redundant, they may cost extra computing time and even lead to over-fitting phenomena. In contrast, without enough neurons, BP-type neuronets cannot achieve good approximation results. So, to illustrate these characteristics, without loss of

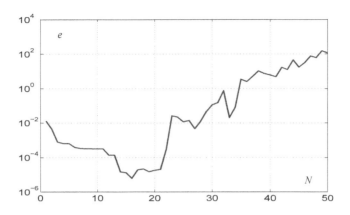

(a) For target function (11.3)

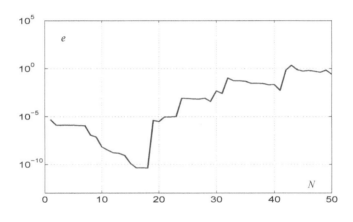

(b) For target function (11.4)

**FIGURE 11.2**: Average error of MIHPN versus its number of hidden-layer neurons for target functions (11.3) and (11.4), respectively.

generality, the following four target functions (as examples) apply to the proposed MIHPN model depicted in Fig. 11.1.

$$f(x_1,x_2) = \frac{(x_1 - 1.5)(x_2 + 1.5)}{5}\exp(-2(x_1 - 1.5)^2 - 2(x_2 - 1.5)^2) + 20, \qquad (11.3)$$

$$f(x_1,x_2) = \frac{x_1 x_2}{50x_1 + \exp(2x_2)} + 10, \qquad (11.4)$$

$$f(x_1,x_2) = \frac{5x_1 x_2}{x_1^2 + x_2^2} + 50, \qquad (11.5)$$

$$f(x_1,x_2) = \frac{\cos(2\pi x_1)\cos(2\pi x_2)}{(3 + 20\cos^2 2x_1 \cos^2 2x_2)} + 20. \qquad (11.6)$$

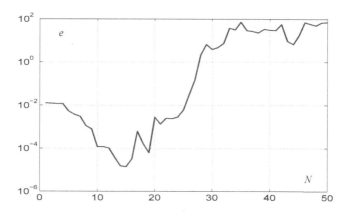

(a) For target function (11.5)

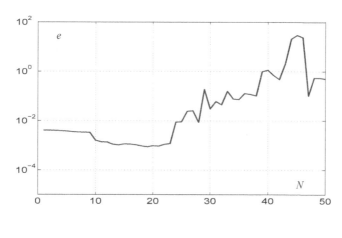

(b) For target function (11.6)

**FIGURE 11.3**: Average error of MIHPN versus its number of hidden-layer neurons for target functions (11.5) and (11.6), respectively.

The set of samples $\{(\mathbf{x}_i = [x_{i1}, x_{i2}]^T, \gamma_i)\}_{i=1}^M$ are thus generated from the region $[1.0, 2.0]^2$ with gap size 0.04 along the $x_1$ and $x_2$ axes, with $N = 676$.

The relation curves between the average error and the number of hidden-layer neurons are shown in Fig. 11.2 and Fig. 11.3. As seen from the figure, we can find that the $e$ fluctuates when the number of hidden-layer neurons increases. For different target functions, the optimal number, i.e., $N_{opt}$, of hidden-layer neurons is also distinct. So, it is obvious that determining an optimal, a suboptimal or a proper number of hidden-layer neurons is quite important. According to previous research [129, 130], we can always find a proper range about the number of hidden-layer neurons or even the optimal number of hidden-layer neurons. With the proper or optimal number of hidden-layer neurons, the smallest $e$ is obtained and the comprehensive abilities (including training, testing, denoising and predicting abilities) of the neuronet is superior.

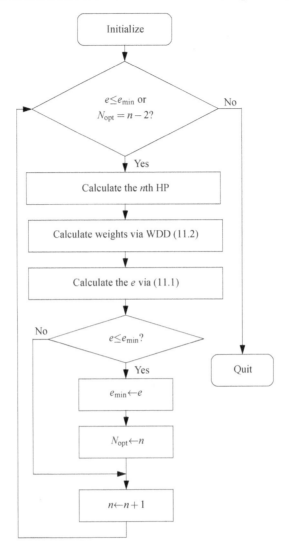

**FIGURE 11.4**: Flowchart of WASD algorithm for MIHPN.

A new algorithm called WASD is thus presented to determine the optimal number of hidden-layer neurons as well as the hidden-to-output weights, which guarantee the smallest training error (in terms of $e$) and a suitably minimal structure of the MIHPN model. The algorithmic procedure of the WASD algorithm is shown in Fig. 11.4 and detailed as below [130].

(a) The procedure has the following new variables:

- $e_{\min}$ denotes the minimal $e$ found;

- $n$ denotes the current number of hidden-layer neurons;

- $N_{\mathrm{opt}}$ denotes the optimal number of hidden-layer neurons that has been found.

(b) The procedure has the following steps.

*Step 1:* Input the set of training samples $\{([x_{i1}, x_{i2}]^{\mathrm{T}}, \gamma_i)\}_{i=1}^{M}$. Construct and initialize the MIHPN model, where the initial number of hidden-layer neurons is 1 (i.e., $N_{\mathrm{opt}} = n = 1$). Besides, $e$ and $e_{\min}$ are set initially the same (e.g., 10).

**TABLE 11.1:** Training and testing results of MIHPN with WASD algorithm.

| Target function | $N_{\text{opt}}$ | $t_{\text{run}}$ | $e_{\text{tra}}$ | $e_{\text{tes}}$ |
|---|---|---|---|---|
| (11.3) | 16 | 0.4431 | $1.9583 \times 10^{-5}$ | $9.1806 \times 10^{-6}$ |
| (11.4) | 17 | 0.2446 | $7.9230 \times 10^{-10}$ | $6.1956 \times 10^{-10}$ |
| (11.5) | 16 | 0.4452 | $8.8010 \times 10^{-6}$ | $3.6383 \times 10^{-6}$ |
| (11.6) | 18 | 0.5215 | $4.0106 \times 10^{-4}$ | $1.7795 \times 10^{-4}$ |

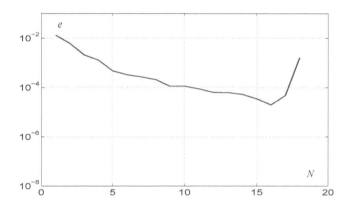

(a) For target function (11.3)

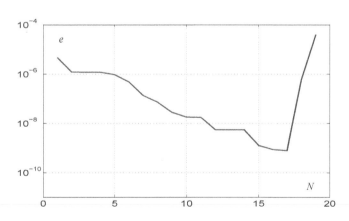

(b) For target function (11.4)

**FIGURE 11.5**: Average error of MIHPN during training process versus its number of hidden-layer neurons for target functions (11.3) and (11.4), respectively.

*Step 2:* Check the two conditions: $e \leq e_{\text{min}}$ and $e_{\text{min}} = n - 2$. If one condition is satisfied, proceed to *Step 3*; otherwise (i.e., both are unsatisfied), proceed to *Step 6* (i.e., the ending step of the procedure).

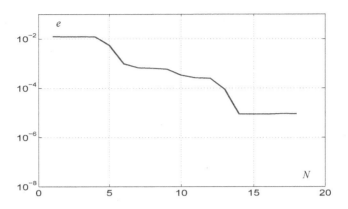

(a) For target function (11.5)

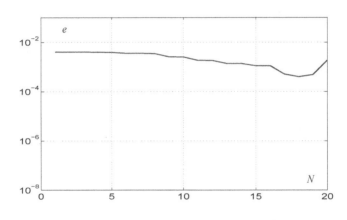

(b) For target function (11.6)

**FIGURE 11.6**: Average error of MIHPN during training process versus its number of hidden-layer neurons for target functions (11.5) and (11.6), respectively.

*Step 3:* Calculate the $n$th HP via Definition 7. Calculate the hidden-to-output weights $\mathbf{w}$ via the WDD subalgorithm (11.2) as well as the corresponding $e$ via (11.1).

*Step 4:* Check the condition: $e \leq e_{\min}$. If true, do $e_{\min} = e$ and $N_{\text{opt}} = n$; then proceed to *Step 5*. Otherwise, directly proceed to *Step 5* (i.e., with no execution of assignment statements).

*Step 5:* Let $n \leftarrow n + 1$, and then proceed to *Step 2*.

*Step 6:* Output the run time, the optimal number of hidden-layer neurons that has been finally found and stored in $N_{\text{opt}}$, the corresponding optimal hidden-to-output weights $\mathbf{w}$ and the corresponding smallest average error stored in $e_{\min}$. The procedure is now terminated.

**TABLE 11.2:** Denoising results of MIHPN with WASD algorithm.

| Target function | $e$ (50 dB noise) | $e$ (40 dB noise) |
|---|---|---|
| (11.3) | $9.1656 \times 10^{-6}$ | $1.3924 \times 10^{-5}$ |
| (11.4) | $1.1293 \times 10^{-7}$ | $1.7645 \times 10^{-6}$ |
| (11.5) | $2.4858 \times 10^{-5}$ | $5.5317 \times 10^{-5}$ |
| (11.6) | $5.5464 \times 10^{-4}$ | $6.0130 \times 10^{-4}$ |

## 11.3 Numerical Studies

In this section, we firstly conduct the numerical training and testing experiments to substantiate the efficacy of the MIHPN model equipped with the WASD algorithm. Then, the denoising ability of the MIHPN is studied.

### 11.3.1 Training and testing

During the verification of the approximation ability of the MIHPN, the same target functions, training samples and gap size are used. The WASD algorithm is employed. After that, we sample untrained points from the region $[1.005, 1.995]^2$ with new gap size 0.03 to test the generalization performance of the MIHPN. The training and testing results are presented in Table 11.1, Fig. 11.5, and Fig. 11.6.

Specifically, from Table 11.1, we see that the optimal numbers of hidden-layer neurons, corresponding to the smallest average errors of target functions (11.3), (11.4), (11.5) and (11.6), are automatically determined as 16, 17, 16 and 18, respectively. This procedure does not need an AN user to prescribe a precision parameter or any other parameters of training, which shows great convenience. Moreover, the run time, i.e., $t_{run}$, spent on training is quite short (less than 1 second), which substantiates the efficiency of the presented MIHPN model and WASD algorithm. In addition, the average errors of training are small (with order $10^{-4}$ to $10^{-10}$), which means that the MIHPN model equipped with the WASD algorithm has a good approximation ability (i.e., good learning ability). Comparing the average errors of training and testing, we further see that both of them have the same or similar order, which substantiates a good generalization ability of the presented MIHPN model equipped with the WASD algorithm.

As an example, Fig. 11.7 and Fig.11.8 show the training and testing results about target function (11.3), which intuitively and visually show the good performance (in terms of approximation and generalization) of the MIHPN model.

### 11.3.2 Denoising

To further check the abilities (e.g., the denoising ability) of the MIHPN model, we add 50 dB and 40 dB Gaussian white noise to the output of the four target functions. Then the WASD algorithm is adopted to determine the optimal structure and the hidden-to-output weights of the MIHPN model. The numerical results of denoising are presented in Table 11.2, while, as an illustrative example, Fig. 11.9 shows the denoising results about target function (11.3) with 40 dB noise added.

Specifically, comparing the average errors of training and testing in Table 11.1, we find that the average errors in Table 11.2 do not have much difference, no matter whether and how much the noise is added. From Fig. 11.9, we also see that the errors between the outputs of the MIHPN (i.e., the

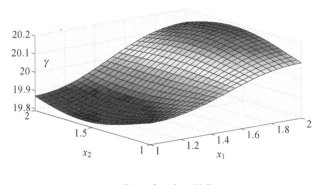

(a) Target function (11.3)

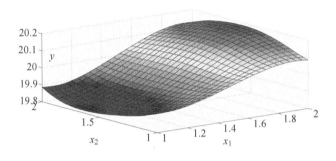

(b) Training results of MIHPN

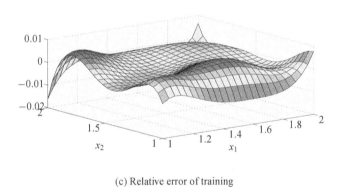

(c) Relative error of training

**FIGURE 11.7**: Training results of MIHPN equipped with WASD algorithm for target function (11.3).

denoised results) and the true target outputs are still quite small. Therefore, it can be concluded that the MIHPN model equipped with the WASD algorithm has a very good denoising performance.

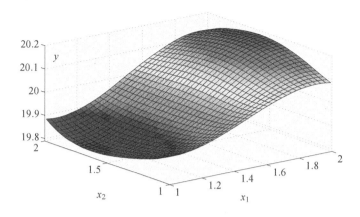

(a) Testing results of MIHPN

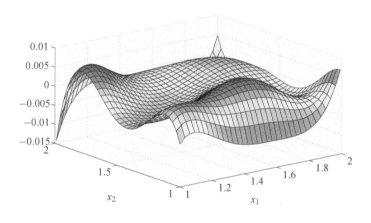

(b) Relative error of testing

**FIGURE 11.8**: Testing results of MIHPN after trained by WASD algorithm for target function (11.3).

## 11.4 Chapter Summary

In this chapter, a novel MIHPN model has been proposed and investigated. In order to improve the performance of the MIHPN model, the pseudoinverse-based WDD subalgorithm has been employed to directly determine the linking weights, which has overcome the weaknesses of conventional BP iterative-training algorithms. Furthermore, the WASD algorithm, based on the WDD subalgorithm, has been finally developed, which can quickly and automatically determine the optimal number of hidden-layer neurons (or, say, the optimal structure of the MIHPN model). The numerical-testing results have further substantiated that the MIHPN model equipped with the WASD algorithm has good training, generalization and denoising abilities.

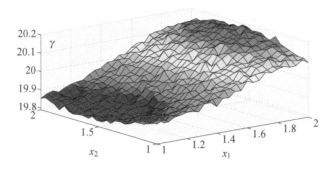

(a) Target function (11.3) with random noise

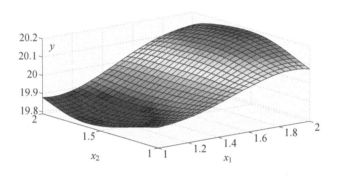

(b) Denoising results of MIHPN

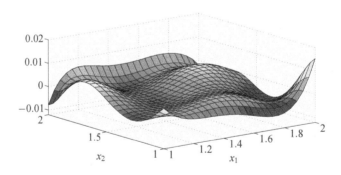

(c) Relative error of denoising

**FIGURE 11.9**: Denoising results of MIHPN after trained by WASD algorithm for target function (11.3) with 40 dB noise added.

## Appendix E: Related Definition and Lemma about Approximation Ability of HP

The following definition and theorem [17–19, 25, 129, 130] prove the approximation ability of the BP-type neuronets using HP as hidden-layer activation functions.

**Definition 8**    Given a target function (or, say, an objective function) $f(x)$ and a set of linearly independent functions $\{\varphi_j(x)\}_{j=1}^n$ being continuous on the interval $[a,b]$, the minimal value of $\int_a^b (f(x) - \varphi(x))^2 dx$ can be obtained by optimizing a group of coefficients $w_1, w_2, \cdots w_n$ of $\varphi(x) = \sum_{j=1}^n w_j \varphi_j(x)$. In this sense, approximating function $\varphi(x)$ is called the least-squares-approximation function for target function $f(x)$.

**Lemma 11**  *For target function $f(x) \in C[a,b]$, its least-squares-approximation function $\varphi(x)$ defined in Definition 8 exists uniquely, and the corresponding coefficients $w_1, w_2, \cdots w_n$ can be solved via the form of a system of linear equations.*

For the MIHPN model constructed in Fig. 11.1, the activation functions used in hidden-layer neurons are orthogonal functions. According to Definitions 7 and 8 as well as Theorem 8 and Lemma 11, when the MIHPN model is used to approximate target function $f(x)$, the relation between output and input can be thus given as $\varphi(x) = w_1\varphi_1(x) + w_2\varphi_2(x) + w_3\varphi_3(x) \cdots + w_n\varphi_n(x)$, which is exactly the least-squares-approximation function for $f(x)$. The extension to multi-input approximation seems feasible and straightforward, and the approximation ability of the proposed MIHPN model is thus generalized.

# Chapter 12

## *Multi-Input Sine-Activation WASD Neuronet*

To solve complex problems such as multi-input function approximation by using neuronets and to overcome the inherent defects of traditional back-propagation (BP) neuronets, a single hidden-layer multi-input feed-forward sine-activation neuronet (MISAN) is proposed and investigated in this chapter. Then, a two-stage weights-and-structure-determination (TS-WASD) algorithm, which is based on the weights-direct-determination (WDD) subalgorithm and the approximation theory of using linearly independent functions, is developed to train the proposed MISAN. Such a TS-WASD algorithm can efficiently and automatically obtain the relatively optimal MISAN structure. Numerical results illustrate the validity and efficacy of the MISAN model and the TS-WASD algorithm. That is, the proposed MISAN model equipped with the TS-WASD algorithm has great performance of approximation on multi-input function data.

## 12.1   Introduction

Function approximation, for its broad applications, has been regarded as the main researching field by many researchers ever since the early 19th century [131–133]. Given sets of input data and output data, researchers usually want to find out their relationship, better expressed in a mathematical function. However, it is by no means an easy job to find the very function for any researcher, especially when an output is the combined result of many inputs [131].

In recent decades, with the development of mathematical theory and computer technology, many algorithms have been proposed to solve function approximation problems, such as Fourier series approximation, Lagrange orthogonal polynomial approximation, and Chebyshev polynomial approximation [18]. Among such algorithms, neuronet is also a usual choice [134, 135]. Besides, it has been proved that, in a linear normed space $C[a,b]$, any target function $f(x_1, x_2, \cdots, x_k) \in C[a,b]$ can be best approximated via arbitrary linearly independent vectors $\{g_0, g_1, \cdots, g_k\}$ in $C[a,b]$ [136].

It is widely acknowledged that feed-forward neuronets are universal approximators [137–142]. It has been proved by [143] and [144] that any continuous function can be approximated on a compact set with uniform topology by a neuronet of form $S(x_1, x_2, \cdots, x_k)$, using continuous and preferably differentiable activation functions [131]. During the construction of a neuronet for the function approximation, three important problems should be settled: (1) the selection of the activation function; (2) the determination of the number of hidden-layer neurons; and (3) the calculation of connecting weights between two different layers [138].

As for the selection of the activation function, the common way is to choose a function (e.g., the sigmoid function [94, 145, 146]) which has key properties such as nonlinearity, continuity and/or differentiability. Being nonlinear and differentiable, the sine function is chosen in this chapter as the activation function. Since the sine function is periodical, by adjusting the period of the sine function, we can obtain different properties shown partially within a certain interval. Note that, in engineering applications, different complicated vibrations are composed by many simple harmonic motions with different frequencies and different amplitudes [131]. That is to say, a complicated target function can be expressed by a linear combination of a series of trigonometric functions [131].

As for the determination of the number of hidden-layer neurons, some effective algorithms have been proposed and investigated by researchers [139, 147] in view of the fact that the performance of a neuronet is greatly affected by the number of hidden-layer neurons. However, those algorithms are generally time-consuming when they are applied to approximating complex multi-input target functions. Therefore, it is important to develop a more efficient and more effective algorithm to determine the neuronet structure with an appropriate number of hidden-layer neurons for the approximation of the complex multi-input target function.

As for the calculation of connecting weights between two different layers, many efforts have been contributed and subsequently lots of algorithms have been proposed and investigated [148]. The most famous one is based on the back propagation (BP) algorithm, i.e., the so-called BP iteration algorithm [149]. However, it is not so reliable, because such an algorithm may lead to finding out the local minimum points but not a global minimum point. To avoid the problem (i.e., local-minima existence), more algorithms based on the original BP algorithm have thus been promoted and investigated. Among these algorithms, the Levenberg-Marquardt (LM) method [150, 151] is a relatively good choice in solving regression problems. Unfortunately, the LM algorithm has the issue that the iteration in such an algorithm would cost a longer time (compared with that in the original BP algorithm), which may make the LM training process also less efficient.

Focusing on the above three essential difficulties in constructing a neuronet for approximating complex multi-input target functions, it is necessary to promote an algorithm for WASD of the neuronet, and to improve its efficiency without sacrificing the accuracy. In this chapter, a single hidden-layer feed-forward neuronet activated by sine functions (or termed MISAN) is thus proposed and investigated for multi-input function approximation. Then, a TS-WASD algorithm, which is based on the WDD subalgorithm and the approximation theory of using linearly independent functions, is developed to train the proposed MISAN. Note that such a TS-WASD algorithm can efficiently and automatically obtain the optimal MISAN structure. Numerical results further illustrate the validity and efficacy of the proposed MISAN model equipped with the TS-WASD algorithm.

The remainder of this chapter is organized into four sections. In Section 12.2, the MISAN is constructed for multi-input function approximation, and then theoretical analysis is presented for such a MISAN model on function approximation. Section 12.3 develops and investigates the TS-WASD algorithm to obtain the optimal MISAN structure and hidden-layer weights efficiently and automatically. Section 12.4 illustrates the numerical results which are obtained via the proposed MISAN model equipped with the TS-WASD algorithm. Section 12.5 concludes the chapter with

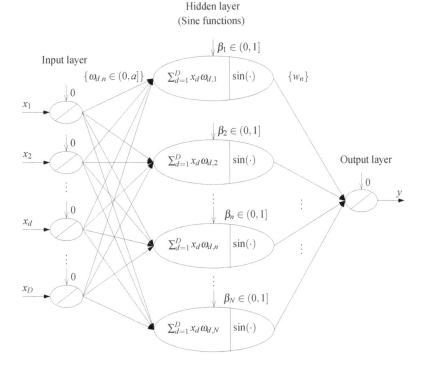

**FIGURE 12.1**: Model structure of MISAN.

final remarks. Before ending this section, it is worth mentioning the main contributions of the chapter as follows.

(1) In this chapter, a multi-input feed-forward sine-activation neuronet, i.e., the MISAN model, is constructed and investigated for multi-input function approximation.

(2) The TS-WASD algorithm is developed for the MISAN in this chapter. Note that such a TS-WASD algorithm not only can obtain the optimal hidden-layer weights of the MISAN model, but also determine the optimal (or appropriate) hidden-layer structure.

(3) Illustrative numerical results substantiate well the validity and efficacy of the proposed MISAN model equipped with the TS-WASD algorithm.

## 12.2 Neuronet Model and Theoretical Analysis

In this section, the MISAN model is first constructed and presented for multi-input function approximation. Then, theoretical analysis is presented for such a MISAN model; that is, the approaching function sets represented by hidden-layer neurons are linearly independent.

### 12.2.1    MISAN model

The MISAN model constructed for multi-input function approximation is shown in Fig. 12.1. As seen from the figure, the MISAN model adopts a conventional three-layer structure, including the input layer, the hidden layer and the output layer. For the MISAN with $D$ inputs and one output, it evidently has $D$ neurons in the input layer and one neuron in the output layer, which are activated by a simple linear identity function. The hidden-layer neurons of the MISAN are activated by the sine function (i.e., "sin" shown in Fig. 12.1), where $N$ denotes the number of hidden-layer neurons. Note that the number of hidden-layer neurons can be set manually at first, but it can be determined automatically later by using the TS-WASD algorithm (which is presented in the next section).

In addition to the above, the weight connecting the $d$th input-layer neuron (with $d = 1, 2, \cdots, D$) and the $n$th hidden-layer neuron (with $n = 1, 2, \cdots, N$) is expressed as $\omega_{d,n}$, which is generated randomly within interval $(0, a]$ to make the period of the resultant sine function different. Besides, the weight connecting the $n$th hidden-layer neuron and the output-layer neuron is expressed as $w_n$, which is determined in the next section by using the pseudoinverse-type weights determination algorithm [129, 152]. Furthermore, the bias of the $n$th hidden-layer neuron $\beta_n$ is randomly generated within interval $(0, 1]$, and the bias of the input-layer and output-layer neurons can all be fixed to be 0 simply and theoretically.

Therefore, the output of the $n$th hidden-layer neuron can be expressed in the form of a sine function as

$$\varphi_n = \sin\left(\sum_{d=1}^{D} x_d \omega_{d,n} - \beta_n\right). \tag{12.1}$$

where $x_d$ corresponds to the $d$th input-layer neuron. The output of the MISAN model can thus be expressed as $y = \sum_{n=1}^{N} w_n \varphi_n$. Note that, within a given interval, a target function can be approximated by the weighted combination of multiple sine functions. The related theoretical analysis of function approximation is presented in the ensuing subsection.

### 12.2.2    Theoretical analysis

Generally speaking, (multi-input) function approximation is closely connected to the notion of linear independence of a set of functions. In this subsection, theoretical analysis is presented to guarantee the effectiveness of the proposed MISAN model for function approximation. Specifically, every hidden-layer neuron of the MISAN is useful and effective for the target function approximation. In other words, an algorithm is presented to verify whether the approaching functions used to approximate the target function are linearly independent or not.

**Lemma 12** *Suppose that $\{\varphi_n | n = 1, 2, \cdots, N\}$ is a set of N real-valued functions (or say, approaching functions) defined on a set $\mathbb{B}$. The set of the functions is said to be linearly independent on set $\mathbb{B}$, if the following implication is valid [129]:*

$$\sum_{n=1}^{N} w_n \varphi_n(x) = 0 \text{ for all } x \in \mathbb{B} \implies \sum_{n=1}^{N} |w_n| = 0.$$

To apply this notion to the MISAN model, we should consider the finite training samples in set $\mathbb{B}$. The set of input samples denoted by $\Phi$ (for the training purpose) related to the MISAN model can thus be expressed as

$$\Phi = \{\mathbf{x}_1, \mathbf{x}_2, \cdots, \mathbf{x}_M\} \subset \mathbb{B},$$

where, with $i = 1, 2, \cdots, M$, the $i$th input sample $\mathbf{x}_i = [x_{i,1}, x_{i,2}, \cdots, x_{i,D}]^{\mathrm{T}} \in \mathbb{R}^D$. Note that superscript $^{\mathrm{T}}$ denoting the transpose of a vector/matrix. For the MISAN model, the output corresponding to input $\mathbf{x}_i$ of $\Phi$ can be interpreted as

$$y_i = \sum_{n=1}^{N} w_n \varphi_n(\mathbf{x}_i) = \sum_{n=1}^{N} w_n \sin\left(\sum_{d=1}^{D} x_{i,d} \omega_{d,n} - \beta_n\right). \tag{12.2}$$

Based on the above equation, the approaching function values (without combining coefficients $\{w_n | n = 1, 2, \cdots, N\}$) resultant from input sample $\mathbf{x}_i$ can thus be interpreted as the following row vector:

$$\Theta_i = [\varphi_1(\mathbf{x}_i), \varphi_2(\mathbf{x}_i), \cdots, \varphi_N(\mathbf{x}_i)]. \tag{12.3}$$

To show the effectiveness of the MISAN model for function approximation, what we do next is to guarantee that all the approaching function vectors (i.e., column vectors)

$$\{[\varphi_n(\mathbf{x}_1), \varphi_n(\mathbf{x}_2), \cdots, \varphi_n(\mathbf{x}_M)]^{\mathrm{T}} | n = 1, 2, \cdots, N\}$$

are linearly independent on $\Phi$.

**Lemma 13** *Multivariate homogeneous linear equation* $\Psi x = 0$ *does not have non-zero solution if and only if coefficient matrix* $\Psi$ *of dimension* $M \times N$ *(with* $M \geq N$*) has rank* $N$ *[153].*

According to (12.3) and Lemma 13, coefficient matrix $\Psi$ based on input samples of $\Phi$ can be expressed as

$$\Psi = \begin{bmatrix} \varphi_1(\mathbf{x}_1) & \varphi_2(\mathbf{x}_1) & \cdots & \varphi_N(\mathbf{x}_1) \\ \varphi_1(\mathbf{x}_2) & \varphi_2(\mathbf{x}_2) & \cdots & \varphi_N(\mathbf{x}_2) \\ \vdots & \vdots & \ddots & \vdots \\ \varphi_1(\mathbf{x}_M) & \varphi_2(\mathbf{x}_M) & \cdots & \varphi_N(\mathbf{x}_M) \end{bmatrix} \in \mathbb{R}^{M \times N}. \tag{12.4}$$

Calculating the rank of $\Psi$, i.e., rank($\Psi$), and comparing it with $N$, we can know whether all the approaching function vectors are linearly independent on $\Phi$ or not. Specifically, on one hand, if rank($\Psi$) $< N$, such approaching function vectors are not linearly independent. This implies that some hidden-layer neurons in the MISAN model are redundant (which, exactly, motivates the authors to develop an effective algorithm to determine the suitable structure of the MISAN with the appropriate number of hidden-layer neurons). On the other hand, if rank($\Psi$) $= N$, it guarantees that all the approaching function vectors are linearly independent. In other words, the outputs of hidden-layer neurons [depicted in (12.1)] of the MISAN are linearly independent at least on the training samples. That is to say, every hidden-layer neuron of the MISAN is useful and effective for the multi-input function approximation.

In summary, based on the above theoretical analysis (especially the notion of linear independence), the proposed MISAN model with the appropriate number of hidden-layer neurons would be effective for the multi-input target function approximation.

## 12.3  TS-WASD Algorithm

In this section, we first present the WDD subalgorithm to obtain the optimal connecting weights between the hidden layer and the output layer efficiently. Then, by incorporating such a subalgorithm, the so-called TS-WASD algorithm, is also developed to determine the structure of the MISAN with an appropriate number of hidden-layer neurons for multi-input function approximation.

**TABLE 12.1:**    Target functions with different values of $D$ and used in ensuing numerical studies.

| # | $D$ | Target function | # | $D$ | Target function |
|---|-----|-----------------|---|-----|-----------------|
| 1 | 2 | $f = \frac{5x_1 \cos\sqrt{100x_1^2 + 100x_2^2 + 1}}{\exp(-2x_1^2 - 2x_2^2) + 2} + 20$ | 9 | 4 | $f = \frac{\sin(2x_1 + 3x_2 + x_4)}{17x_1 + 23x_3}$ |
| 2 | 2 | $f = 10x_1x_2 \exp(-x_1^2 - x_2^2) + 10$ | 10 | 4 | $f = \frac{x_1x_2x_4}{x_1 + \exp(x_3)}$ |
| 3 | 2 | $f = \frac{2\sin(\sqrt{49x_1^2 + 100x_2^2})}{\sqrt{49x_1^2 + 100x_2^2}} + 0.5$ | 11 | 4 | $f = x_1x_4 \cos(0.2x_2x_3)$ |
| 4 | 2 | $f = 30x_1x_2 \exp(-4x_1^2 - 4x_2^2) + 20$ | 12 | 4 | $f = x_1^{x_2} + x_3^{x_4} \sin x_1 \cos x_3$ |
| 5 | 3 | $f = (x_1 + x_2 + x_3)^2 + x_1^3 x_2^5 x_3^4$ | 13 | 5 | $f = \frac{\cos(x_1 + x_2x_3) + x_5}{2x_1 + 7x_4}$ |
| 6 | 3 | $f = \sin(x_1x_3) \exp(x_2x_3)$ | 14 | 5 | $f = \frac{x_1 \cos(0.2x_2 + x_3) + x_5}{\exp(x_4x_5 + x_2)}$ |
| 7 | 3 | $f = \frac{x_1 \cos(0.2x_2 + x_3)}{\exp(x_1x_2 + x_3)}$ | 15 | 5 | $f = \exp(\sin(x_1x_2)) + x_5 \cos(x_3x_4)$ |
| 8 | 3 | $f = \exp(\cos(x_1x_2)) + x_3 \sin x_2$ | 16 | 5 | $f = \frac{\sin x_1 + \cos x_2}{x_3x_4x_5}$ |

### 12.3.1    Weights direct determination

In general, the training time of a neuronet is expected to be as short as possible. However, the BP iterative neuronet and the related neuronets (of which the training algorithms are based on the iterative algorithms) seem to be limited, because they often take a long time. Thus, in this subsection, the WDD subalgorithm incorporated into the TS-WASD algorithm is presented to replace the iterative idea and is committed to find the optimal connecting weights between the hidden layer and the output layer. Note that, based on such a WDD subalgorithm, the structure determination algorithm (i.e., the TS-WASD algorithm) presented in the ensuing subsection can find the best MISAN structure within short computation time.

To lay a basis for further discussion, the training samples are denoted by $\{(\mathbf{x}_i, \gamma_i)\}_{i=1}^{M}$, where the $i$th input sample $\mathbf{x}_i$ is defined the same as before, and $\gamma_i$ denotes the $i$th output sample (or, say, the $i$th desired output). Corresponding to the MISAN model, we define the following mean square error (MSE) ($e$):

$$e = \frac{1}{M} \sum_{i=1}^{M} \left( \gamma_i - \sum_{n=1}^{N} w_n \varphi_n(\mathbf{x}_i) \right)^2, \tag{12.5}$$

where, as mentioned before, the number of hidden-layer neurons is denoted by $N$. In addition, for all the training samples $\{(\mathbf{x}_i, \gamma_i)\}_{i=1}^{M}$, the output matrix of hidden layer is $\Psi$ which is defined in (12.4). Based on the above definitions, the vector of optimal weights connecting the hidden layer and the output layer denoted by $\mathbf{w} = [w_1, w_2, \cdots, w_N]^{\mathrm{T}} \in \mathbb{R}^N$ of the MISAN model (depicted in Fig. 12.1) can be obtained directly as

$$\mathbf{w} = (\Psi^{\mathrm{T}}\Psi)^{-1}\Psi^{\mathrm{T}}\gamma = \mathrm{pinv}(\Psi)\gamma = \Psi^{\dagger}\gamma, \tag{12.6}$$

where $\gamma = [\gamma_1, \gamma_2, \cdots, \gamma_M]^{\mathrm{T}} \in \mathbb{R}^M$ denotes the vector of desired outputs, $\mathrm{pinv}(\Psi)$ and $\Psi^{\dagger}$ both denote the pseudoinverse of matrix $\Psi$. In this chapter, (12.6) is called the WDD subalgorithm for presentation convenience. Note that such an algorithm has been proposed and completely illustrated by researchers [129, 152], now with the proof omitted here.

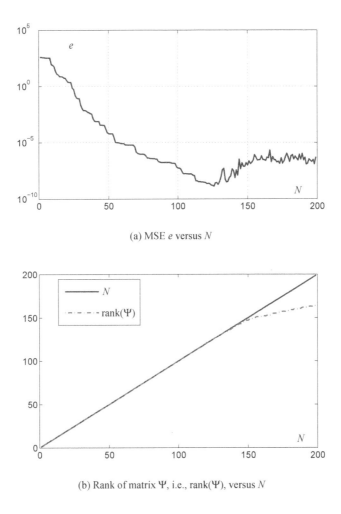

(a) MSE $e$ versus $N$

(b) Rank of matrix $\Psi$, i.e., rank($\Psi$), versus $N$

**FIGURE 12.2**: Relationships among $e \in (10^{-10}, 10^4)$, rank($\Psi$) $\in (0, 170)$ and $N \in (0, 200)$ of MISAN for target function 1 in Table 12.1.

### 12.3.2　Structure automatic determination

Based on the aforementioned WDD subalgorithm, a growing algorithm (i.e., the TS-WASD algorithm) is developed and investigated in this subsection, which can determine automatically and rapidly the optimal number of hidden-layer neurons for the proposed MISAN.

For further discussion and numerical studies, we first show Table 12.1 to list some target functions (which are chosen and used in an arbitrary manner for the numerical studies to substantiate the efficacy of the MISAN model and the TS-WASD algorithm), where $D$ denotes again the number of input variables for a target function. To show the relationships among the $e$ [via (12.5)], rank($\Psi$) and $N$ (i.e., the number of hidden-layer neurons), we take target function 1 of Table 12.1 for example. The corresponding results are illustrated in Fig. 12.2. From the figure, we can observe that, by adding the hidden-layer neurons one-by-one, the $e$ first drops and then starts to fluctuate. In addition, as seen from Fig. 12.2, if there are too many hidden-layer neurons in the MISAN model (e.g., more than 120 hidden-layer neurons), rank($\Psi$) would be smaller than $N$. According to Lemma 13, this phenomenon [i.e., rank($\Psi$) < $N$] implies that some hidden-layer neurons would be redundant in the MISAN model. Therefore, the last descending point of the $e$ is the one we need, with the dual limitation that rank$(\Psi) = N$. Besides, it is worth pointing out that, for a target function with $D > 4$, it would take a longer time to finish the training process by adding the hidden-layer neurons one-by-one (as compared with that for a target function with $D \leq 4$). Thus, by considering both the structure determination strategy and the time saving ability, a two-stage structure determination algorithm (termed the TS-WASD algorithm for presentation convenience) is developed and investigated, with its description detailed in Table 12.2.

Specifically, such a TS-WASD algorithm for finding the best point of the $e$ with rank$(\Psi) = N$ is divided into two stages. In the first stage, we add $S$ hidden-layer neurons at a time (with $S > 1$), instead of adding one-by-one; and then find out a range in which the best point of the $e$ exists. In the second stage, we search carefully in such a range by adding hidden-layer neurons one-by-one; and then the searching procedure is stopped when the $e$ starts to fluctuate. The last point found with the minimal $e$ in the second stage is the best point. Note that the number of hidden-layer neurons, corresponding to the best point with the minimal $e$, is exactly the optimal number of hidden-layer neurons for the MISAN model. That is, the TS-WASD algorithm can efficiently and automatically obtain the optimal MISAN structure. Besides, the following three aspects about the TS-WASD algorithm are discussed.

(1) Let us discuss how to choose the number of hidden-layer neurons added into the MISAN in the first stage of the TS-WASD algorithm, which is denoted by $S$. To get an acceptable choice of $S$, the MISAN is trained repeatedly by using different values of $S$, and some inspirations/conclusions are thus generated. Taking target function 5 of Table 12.1 as an example, we have the relationship between the number of hidden-layer neurons and the $e$ shown in Figs. 12.3 and 12.4, where different values of $S$ are used (i.e., $S = 1$, $S = 6$, $S = 15$ and $S = 30$). As seen from the figure, although a different number of neurons are added to the hidden layer of the MISAN at a time, the best/optimal point found in each case is almost the same; i.e., for target function 5, the optimal number of hidden-layer neurons is approximately 130. Note that, if too many neurons are added to the hidden layer at a time, the best/optimal point may become not so precise as adding the hidden-layer neurons one-by-one. This would add difficulties to the second searching stage. Thus, in order to balance the searching ability for both stages, we set the number of new hidden-layer neurons added to the MISAN as $S = 2D$.

(2) Another important factor exploited in such a TS-WASD algorithm is the searching interval of the optimal number (used at the beginning of the second stage). Empirically, it can be chosen as $I = [t_1 - D \times S, t_1 + S]$, where $t_1$ represents the optimal number of hidden-layer neurons found in the first stage by adding $S$ neurons at a time. Note that, when many neurons are added to the hidden layer at a time in the first stage, the best/optimal point may be missed in the fluctuating area, and the resultant $t_1$ may be larger than the optimal number of hidden-layer neurons in practice. This is the reason why we set the left boundary of interval $I$ as $(t_1 - D \times S)$. Based on lots of numerical tests, such a setting is effective, which is illustrated via numerical results shown in the ensuing section.

(3) It is worth noting that the pruning-while-increasing (or say, pruning-while-growing) technique is used in the TS-WASD algorithm. Specifically, in Stage 1, if the $e$ does not decrease after $S$ neurons are added to the hidden layer of the MISAN, then we delete them and re-add $S$ new neurons to the hidden layer. Besides, if the $e$ still does not decrease after the pruning process is repeated for 3 times, then we stop Stage 1 and proceed to Stage 2.

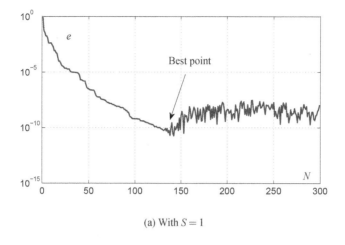

(a) With $S = 1$

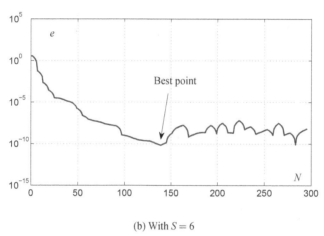

(b) With $S = 6$

**FIGURE 12.3**: Relationship between $e \in (10^{-12}, 10^2)$ and $N \in (0, 300)$ of MISAN with $S = 1$ and $S = 6$.

## 12.4 Numerical Studies

In this section, based on different target functions (i.e., from 2-input functions to 5-input functions) which are shown in Table 12.1, numerical results are illustrated to substantiate the efficacy of the proposed MISAN equipped with the TS-WASD algorithm on the multi-input function approximation. For completeness, the generalization abilities of the proposed MISAN equipped with the TS-WASD algorithm are studied as well.

Note that, for target functions 1 through 4, we generate and use 10000 training samples and 961 testing samples in the numerical studies; for target functions 5 through 8, we have 343 training samples and 216 testing samples; for target functions 9 through 12, we have 2401 training samples and 1296 testing samples; and, for target functions 13 through 16, we have 3125 training samples and 1024 testing samples.

It is also worth noting that the reason why we exhibit relatively complicated target functions

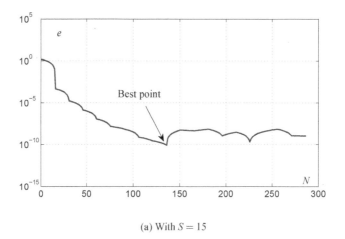

(a) With $S = 15$

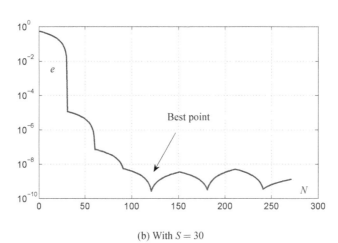

(b) With $S = 30$

**FIGURE 12.4**: Relationship between $e \in (10^{-12}, 10^2)$ and $N \in (0, 300)$ of MISAN with $S = 15$ and $S = 30$.

here is to better illustrate the efficacy of the proposed MISAN as well as the TS-WASD algorithm. In addition, as input-layer weights and hidden-layer biases are generated randomly, the final/optimal numbers of hidden-layer neurons are definitely not the same when we apply the TS-WASD algorithm more than once. The MISAN structure with a found number of hidden-layer neurons would thus be different each time. In order to test the stability of the proposed MISAN equipped with the TS-WASD algorithm, each target function is trained and then tested for 10 times, and the standard deviation of $N_{opt}$ (i.e., the optimal number of hidden-layer neurons experimentally found) for 10 times is computed, which is denoted by $\sigma(N_{opt})$. The results are shown in Table 12.3.

From the table (i.e., Table 12.3), comparing $N_{opt}$ and $\sigma(N_{opt})$ for each target function, we see that the final/optimal number of hidden-layer neurons determined by the TS-WASD algorithm is stable; i.e., the range of the value fluctuation is smaller than 6.2% of the total number. In addition, although the training $e$ and testing $e$ are different for each target function (due to its different complexity), they are rather small (i.e., of order $10^{-3} \sim 10^{-15}$). Besides, it can be seen from the column of run time, i.e., $t_{run}$, that the TS-WASD algorithm is time-saving, as compared with traditional BP-type algorithms which often cost much more time on the iteration process to get a small enough

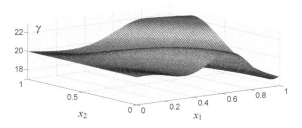

(a) Target function 1 for training

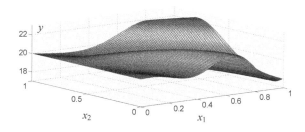

(b) Training results of MISAN

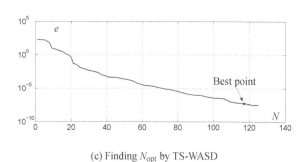

(c) Finding $N_{\text{opt}}$ by TS-WASD

**FIGURE 12.5**: Training results of MISAN equipped with TS-WASD algorithm where $e$ decreases from order $10^4$ to $10^{-8}$ for target function 1 in Table 12.1.

training (or testing) error. This is because the TS-WASD algorithm not only obtains the optimal hidden-layer weights directly (avoiding the training process of iteration type), but also determines the optimal MISAN structure automatically and efficiently. These numerical results illustrate well that the proposed MISAN equipped with the TS-WASD algorithm is effective and time-saving for multi-input target function approximation.

For better understanding, as a more specific example, Figs. 12.5 and 12.6 as well as Table 12.4 show the numerical results synthesized by the MISAN equipped with the TS-WASD algorithm for the approximation of 2-input target function 1, which intuitively and visually show the great performance (in terms of learning and generalization) of the proposed MISAN equipped with the TS-WASD algorithm. Consistent with Equation (12.2), target function 1 can be approximated by the weighted combination of multiple sine functions within a given interval. As seen specifically from Table 12.4, the optimal MISAN structure for the function approximation is obtained with $N_{\text{opt}} = 117$, and the numerical values of input-layer weights (i.e., $\{\omega_{1,n}\}$ and $\{\omega_{2,n}\}$), hidden-layer biases (i.e., $\{\beta_n\}$) and hidden-layer weights (i.e., $\{w_n\}$) can be obtained for "creating" target function 1,

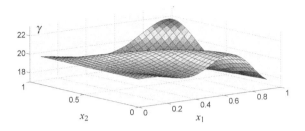

(a) Target function 1 for testing

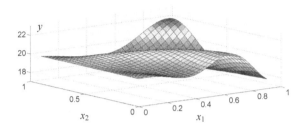

(b) Testing results of MISAN

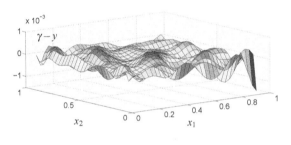

(c) Testing error in $(-1.5, 1) \times 10^{-3}$

**FIGURE 12.6**: Testing results of MISAN equipped with TS-WASD algorithm where $e$ decreases from order $10^4$ to $10^{-8}$ for target function 1 in Table 12.1.

where $n = 1, 2, \cdots, 117$. Moreover, for comparison and for further investigation, numerical results synthesized by the usually used sigmoid-activation neuronet based on Levenberg-Marquardt method are presented in Appendix F to this chapter. In summary, these numerical results have illustrated the validity and efficacy of the proposed MISAN equipped with the TS-WASD algorithm.

## 12.5 Chapter Summary

In this chapter, a MISAN with single hidden layer has been proposed and investigated for multi-input target function approximation. In addition, based on the WDD subalgorithm, TS-WASD algorithm has been developed to train the proposed MISAN model, which can automatically and efficiently obtain the optimal MISAN structure. Numerical results have further illustrated the validity and efficacy of the MISAN model and the TS-WASD algorithm.

---

## Appendix F: Comparison with Sigmoid-Activation Neuronet Based on LM Method

For comparison and for further illustration of the efficacy of the MISAN equipped with the TS-WASD algorithm, in this appendix, the 16 target functions are tested by using the traditional BP iteration algorithm; specifically, using the sigmoid-activation neuronet based on LM method. Note that, for fair comparison with existing BP iteration algorithms, we choose a relatively good (or, say, iteratively best) one, i.e., the LM algorithm which is of second order [137, 142, 148, 150, 151].

In the numerical studies, all the training and testing samples are chosen to be the same as those used in Sections 12.3 and 12.4. In addition, the desired training $e$ (as a criterion) for each target function is set to be the training $e$ shown in Table 12.3 (which is obtained by using the MISAN equipped with the TS-WASD algorithm). As aforementioned, the activation function of each hidden-layer neuron in the sigmoid-activation neuronet is the widely used sigmoid function. The corresponding numerical results are thus shown in Table 12.5 and discussed as follows.

Firstly, with the run time limitation of 600 seconds, only target functions 5 through 8 (completely) and 9 (partially) reach the corresponding accuracy of the desired training $e$. Secondly, most testing $e$ are worse than those in Table 12.3, which shows that the generalization ability of the sigmoid-activation neuronet based on the LM algorithm is relatively weaker than that of the proposed MISAN equipped with the TS-WASD algorithm. Thirdly, for different target functions, the relatively optimal numbers of hidden-layer neurons are different, which indicates that we have to try a lot to determine the final/optimal neuronet structure by using traditional BP iteration algorithm. In summary, it is evident that the performance of the MISAN equipped with the TS-WASD algorithm is better than that of the original sigmoid-activation neuronet.

**TABLE 12.2:** Description of TS-WASD algorithm for optimal MISAN structure.

---

**Definition**

- $S$: The number of hidden-layer neurons added to the MISAN at a time in the first stage (e.g., $S = 2D$).

- $D$: The number of input-layer neurons.

- $N$: The current number of hidden-layer neurons.

- $N_{opt}$: The optimal number of hidden-layer neurons.

- $e$: The MSE of the current MISAN.

- $e_{min}$: The minimal $e$ found.

**Initialization**

- Initialize $N = 1$ and $e_{min}$ large enough.

- Generate the input-layer weights (e.g., $\omega_{1,1}$ and $\omega_{2,1}$) randomly within interval $(0, a]$. Note that, in the paper, if $D \leq 2$, then $a = 10$; otherwise, $a = 1$.

- Generate the hidden-layer bias (i.e., $\beta_1$) randomly within interval $(0, 1]$.

- Compute hidden-layer weight $w_1$ using WDD subalgorithm (12.6), and initialize counter $c = 0$.

**Stage 1**
*Step 1.1*: Let $N \leftarrow N + S$.
*Step 1.2*: Randomly generate the input-layer weights and hidden-layer biases corresponding to the $S$ new neurons.
*Step 1.3*: Compute hidden-layer weights using (12.6), and obtain $e$ as well as rank($\Psi$) of the current MISAN.
*Step 1.4*: If $e_{min} > e$ and rank($\Psi$) = $N$, let $e_{min} \leftarrow e$, $N_{opt} \leftarrow N$ and $c \leftarrow 0$, and return to *Step 1.1*. Otherwise, let $c \leftarrow c + 1$, and proceed to the next step (i.e., *Step 1.5*).
*Step 1.5*: Let $N \leftarrow N - S$, and delete the corresponding input-layer weights, hidden-layer weights and hidden-layer biases. If $c < 3$, return to *Step 1.1*. Otherwise, proceed to the next step (i.e., *Step 1.6*).
*Step 1.6*: Set $t_1 = N_{opt}$, and proceed to the next stage.

**Stage 2**
*Part 2.1*: Increase $N$ one-by-one from $(t_1 - D \times S)$ to $(t_1 + S)$, and obtain the corresponding $e$.
*Part 2.2*: When $e$ begins to fluctuate [e.g., the curve over interval $(120, 200)$ shown in Fig. 12.2], stop the procedure of *Part 2.1*, let $N_{opt}$ be $N$ with the minimal $e$ (and also $e_{min} \leftarrow e$), and proceed to the next part (i.e., *Part 2.3*).
*Part 2.3*: Save and output $N_{opt}$ (the optimal number of hidden-layer neurons), $e_{min}$ (the minimal $e$) and the run time. Now terminate the program.

**TABLE 12.3:** Ten-time average results of MISAN equipped with TS-WASD algorithm for multi-input function approximation.

| Function # | $N_{opt}$ | $\sigma(N_{opt})$ | Training $e$ | Testing $e$ | $t_{run}$ (s) |
|---|---|---|---|---|---|
| 1 | 124.8 | 7.10 | $2.67 \times 10^{-08}$ | $2.34 \times 10^{-08}$ | 50.0 |
| 2 | 101.8 | 4.92 | $6.22 \times 10^{-13}$ | $5.01 \times 10^{-13}$ | 33.9 |
| 3 | 106.1 | 4.43 | $1.17 \times 10^{-10}$ | $1.87 \times 10^{-10}$ | 47.1 |
| 4 | 112.3 | 6.96 | $7.16 \times 10^{-10}$ | $6.17 \times 10^{-10}$ | 45.6 |
| 5 | 137.0 | 2.36 | $1.29 \times 10^{-09}$ | $2.05 \times 10^{-09}$ | 1.79 |
| 6 | 136.0 | 4.81 | $5.20 \times 10^{-11}$ | $1.03 \times 10^{-10}$ | 1.21 |
| 7 | 129.7 | 2.16 | $2.64 \times 10^{-12}$ | $2.94 \times 10^{-12}$ | 1.16 |
| 8 | 124.8 | 4.08 | $6.16 \times 10^{-10}$ | $2.00 \times 10^{-10}$ | 1.20 |
| 9 | 268.5 | 8.24 | $6.02 \times 10^{-12}$ | $4.49 \times 10^{-12}$ | 23.4 |
| 10 | 226.6 | 10.1 | $1.52 \times 10^{-13}$ | $1.02 \times 10^{-13}$ | 20.8 |
| 11 | 171.6 | 6.59 | $5.42 \times 10^{-15}$ | $3.88 \times 10^{-15}$ | 16.4 |
| 12 | 234.0 | 7.07 | $3.87 \times 10^{-11}$ | $4.94 \times 10^{-11}$ | 21.4 |
| 13 | 452.7 | 9.13 | $4.55 \times 10^{-12}$ | $1.10 \times 10^{-03}$ | 70.0 |
| 14 | 367.9 | 13.15 | $2.91 \times 10^{-13}$ | $2.47 \times 10^{-04}$ | 44.2 |
| 15 | 404.2 | 10.3 | $3.84 \times 10^{-12}$ | $1.26 \times 10^{-11}$ | 79.9 |
| 16 | 477.1 | 10.2 | $7.47 \times 10^{-09}$ | $4.32 \times 10^{-06}$ | 109 |

**TABLE 12.4:** Numerical values of randomly generated and well-trained parameters of MISAN equipped with TS-WASD algorithm for approximating target function 1 where $N_{opt} = 117$.

| $n$ | $\omega_{1,n}$ | $\omega_{2,n}$ | $\beta_n$ | $w_n$ |
|---|---|---|---|---|
| 1 | 1.882717757398670 | 3.241964634670396 | 0.716037342838811 | $-2.5661 \times 10^6$ |
| 2 | 5.529287085712164 | 1.422817398172573 | 0.106872780238886 | $-1.0748 \times 10^6$ |
| 3 | 3.803635594126672 | 3.965692452110417 | 0.732149758734352 | $-2.5952 \times 10^6$ |
| 4 | 5.767416956941053 | 0.194015027111201 | 0.970522786956106 | $2.2900 \times 10^3$ |
| 5 | 5.775800612694447 | 9.321960928085488 | 0.608885538697176 | $1.9367 \times 10^4$ |
| $\vdots$ | $\vdots$ | $\vdots$ | $\vdots$ | $\vdots$ |
| 50 | 4.532348181215036 | 0.747494384557664 | 0.467901722684299 | $1.2942 \times 10^6$ |
| 51 | 6.633406135933385 | 7.036516419280678 | 0.458478681919285 | $-3.5923 \times 10^4$ |
| 52 | 9.189505683082535 | 6.600719084009532 | 0.806104187449170 | $-1.7294 \times 10^1$ |
| 53 | 6.901049192816354 | 8.537236098115725 | 0.824767236231277 | $-5.3300 \times 10^4$ |
| 54 | 1.904361031878966 | 0.256732083182730 | 0.678442770367227 | $-3.0997 \times 10^6$ |
| $\vdots$ | $\vdots$ | $\vdots$ | $\vdots$ | $\vdots$ |
| 113 | 0.613777678138677 | 6.610739889322462 | 0.764640454269780 | $-9.5716 \times 10^3$ |
| 114 | 2.436839302093418 | 6.821160610495101 | 0.679517492334616 | $-9.4144 \times 10^3$ |
| 115 | 1.378545102251663 | 6.298116670255489 | 0.704121891203037 | $6.1237 \times 10^4$ |
| 116 | 8.570146926598532 | 8.997983332703601 | 0.460884056746050 | $1.0272 \times 10^3$ |
| 117 | 3.483684022318644 | 4.863101932869633 | 0.364272297195358 | $9.4078 \times 10^5$ |

**TABLE 12.5:** Numerical results of sigmoid-activation neuronet based on LM algorithm for multi-input function approximation.

| Function # | Desired training $e$ | $N$ | Training $e$ | Testing $e$ | $t_{\text{run}}$ (s) |
|---|---|---|---|---|---|
| 1 | $2.67 \times 10^{-08}$ | 50 | $4.32 \times 10^{-07}$ | $3.44 \times 10^{-07}$ | 600 |
| | | 100 | $2.69 \times 10^{-07}$ | $2.05 \times 10^{-07}$ | 600 |
| | | 150 | $7.87 \times 10^{-06}$ | $6.49 \times 10^{-06}$ | 600 |
| 2 | $6.22 \times 10^{-13}$ | 50 | $1.81 \times 10^{-08}$ | $1.96 \times 10^{-08}$ | 600 |
| | | 100 | $1.78 \times 10^{-08}$ | $1.64 \times 10^{-08}$ | 600 |
| | | 150 | $1.58 \times 10^{-07}$ | $1.28 \times 10^{-07}$ | 600 |
| 3 | $1.17 \times 10^{-10}$ | 50 | $3.39 \times 10^{-08}$ | $2.89 \times 10^{-08}$ | 600 |
| | | 100 | $6.69 \times 10^{-07}$ | $6.14 \times 10^{-07}$ | 600 |
| | | 150 | $9.82 \times 10^{-08}$ | $7.96 \times 10^{-08}$ | 600 |
| 4 | $7.16 \times 10^{-10}$ | 50 | $4.30 \times 10^{-08}$ | $4.12 \times 10^{-08}$ | 600 |
| | | 100 | $4.25 \times 10^{-08}$ | $3.93 \times 10^{-08}$ | 600 |
| | | 150 | $4.96 \times 10^{-07}$ | $4.38 \times 10^{-08}$ | 600 |
| 5 | $1.29 \times 10^{-09}$ | 50 | Achieved | $2.11 \times 10^{-06}$ | 129 |
| | | 100 | Achieved | $4.35 \times 10^{-05}$ | 15 |
| | | 150 | Achieved | $2.18 \times 10^{-04}$ | 4 |
| 6 | $5.20 \times 10^{-11}$ | 50 | Achieved | $1.24 \times 10^{-06}$ | 452 |
| | | 100 | Achieved | $1.73 \times 10^{-05}$ | 20 |
| | | 150 | Achieved | $1.77 \times 10^{-05}$ | 4 |
| 7 | $2.64 \times 10^{-12}$ | 50 | Achieved | $7.30 \times 10^{-08}$ | 324 |
| | | 100 | Achieved | $2.32 \times 10^{-06}$ | 12 |
| | | 150 | Achieved | $7.77 \times 10^{-06}$ | 4 |
| 8 | $6.16 \times 10^{-10}$ | 50 | Achieved | $7.63 \times 10^{-05}$ | 30 |
| | | 100 | Achieved | $1.03 \times 10^{-04}$ | 24 |
| | | 150 | Achieved | $1.30 \times 10^{-05}$ | 3 |
| 9 | $6.02 \times 10^{-12}$ | 100 | Achieved | $1.45 \times 10^{-11}$ | 175 |
| | | 200 | $5.02 \times 10^{-10}$ | $4.88 \times 10^{-10}$ | 600 |
| 10 | $1.52 \times 10^{-13}$ | 100 | $1.46 \times 10^{-11}$ | $1.24 \times 10^{-11}$ | 600 |
| | | 200 | $2.28 \times 10^{-07}$ | $3.87 \times 10^{-09}$ | 600 |
| 11 | $5.42 \times 10^{-15}$ | 100 | $3.60 \times 10^{-10}$ | $4.82 \times 10^{-10}$ | 600 |
| | | 200 | $3.01 \times 10^{-10}$ | $3.53 \times 10^{-07}$ | 600 |
| 12 | $3.87 \times 10^{-11}$ | 100 | $6.21 \times 10^{-10}$ | $2.09 \times 10^{-08}$ | 600 |
| | | 200 | $7.08 \times 10^{-10}$ | $1.75 \times 10^{-07}$ | 600 |
| 13 | $4.55 \times 10^{-12}$ | 100 | $1.96 \times 10^{-09}$ | $3.31 \times 10^{-09}$ | 600 |
| | | 200 | $3.66 \times 10^{-08}$ | $5.09 \times 10^{-08}$ | 600 |
| | | 300 | $2.55 \times 10^{-08}$ | $3.73 \times 10^{-08}$ | 600 |
| | | 400 | $1.67 \times 10^{-08}$ | $1.06 \times 10^{-05}$ | 600 |
| 14 | $2.91 \times 10^{-13}$ | 100 | $8.67 \times 10^{-10}$ | $2.76 \times 10^{-09}$ | 600 |
| | | 200 | $1.40 \times 10^{-08}$ | $5.48 \times 10^{-08}$ | 600 |
| | | 400 | $2.34 \times 10^{-08}$ | $2.83 \times 10^{-05}$ | 600 |
| 15 | $3.84 \times 10^{-12}$ | 100 | $3.88 \times 10^{-09}$ | $6.95 \times 10^{-09}$ | 600 |
| | | 200 | $2.67 \times 10^{-08}$ | $8.55 \times 10^{-08}$ | 600 |
| | | 400 | $2.67 \times 10^{-07}$ | $5.73 \times 10^{-06}$ | 600 |
| 16 | $7.47 \times 10^{-09}$ | 100 | $1.50 \times 10^{-07}$ | $5.35 \times 10^{-05}$ | 600 |
| | | 200 | $5.19 \times 10^{-05}$ | $2.20 \times 10^{-04}$ | 600 |
| | | 400 | $3.20 \times 10^{-04}$ | $6.98 \times 10^{-04}$ | 600 |

# Part V

# Population Applications Using Chebyshev-Activation Neuronet

# Chapter 13

## Application to Asian Population Prediction

Function data approximation and prediction are important in many domains. As computing power improves, artificial intelligence (AI) methods such as the weights-and-structure-determination (WASD) neuronet become more operable. Although the WASD neuronet has been applied to several other issues, its application on function data approximation needs to be explored and discussed more specifically. This chapter is committed to introducing the WASD neuronet activated by Chebyshev polynomials of Class 1 for function data approximation and to exploring its capability of prediction. The learning-testing method and the concept of global minimum point are introduced to improve the prediction performance and extend the application of the WASD neuronet. Applying such a model to Asian population prediction substantiates its excellent performance. With numerical studies showing the prediction performance and a final prediction based on historical data, this chapter presents a reasonable tendency of Asian population.

## 13.1    Introduction

Population has become one of the most important factors in policymaking and education, among other fields. Accurate prediction of population may help governments make reasonable decisions. Thus, such a topic continuously attracts consideration [154–156]. The prediction of population is challenging and highly uncertain [156]. Population is affected by many factors (e.g., natural environment, policy, culture and disease [155]). Thus, correctly and accurately foreseeing the population is difficult [157]. Many researchers who focus on the prediction of population have presented corresponding results based on different methods [154, 157–162]. For example, an empirical method was used by Whelpton to calculate future population [158]. In [159], Raftery et al. developed a Bayesian method for probabilistic population predictions for all countries. In addition, the Department of Economic and Social Affairs of the United Nations (UN) publishes World Population Prospects (WPP)

**TABLE 13.1:**    Asian population data used in this chapter for learning and prediction.

| Year | 400 BC | 200 BC | 1 | 200 | 400 | 600 | 800 |
|---|---|---|---|---|---|---|---|
| Data (million) | 83 | 105 | 115 | 130 | 130 | 140 | 155 |
| Year | 1000 | 1100 | 1200 | 1300 | 1400 | 1500 | 1600 |
| Data (million) | 185 | 230 | 250 | 230 | 235 | 280 | 375 |
| Year | 1650 | 1700 | 1750 | 1800 | 1850 | 1900 | 1950 |
| Data (million) | 370 | 415 | 495 | 625 | 795 | 970 | 1437.565 |
| Year | 1951 | 1952 | 1953 | 1954 | 1955 | 1956 | 1957 |
| Data (million) | 1457.356 | 1481.176 | 1507.747 | 1536.389 | 1567.779 | 1600.222 | 1634.936 |
| Year | 1958 | 1959 | 1960 | 1961 | 1962 | 1963 | 1964 |
| Data (million) | 1670.070 | 1700.455 | 1720.291 | 1738.433 | 1771.595 | 1817.957 | 1865.852 |
| Year | 1965 | 1966 | 1967 | 1968 | 1969 | 1970 | 1971 |
| Data (million) | 1911.899 | 1959.304 | 2006.426 | 2055.548 | 2107.053 | 2158.832 | 2211.536 |
| Year | 1972 | 1973 | 1974 | 1975 | 1976 | 1977 | 1978 |
| Data (million) | 2263.391 | 2314.691 | 2365.205 | 2413.261 | 2459.464 | 2505.640 | 2551.516 |
| Year | 1979 | 1980 | 1981 | 1982 | 1983 | 1984 | 1985 |
| Data (million) | 2599.373 | 2644.088 | 2698.256 | 2749.595 | 2802.260 | 2854.216 | 2907.474 |
| Year | 1986 | 1987 | 1988 | 1989 | 1990 | 1991 | 1992 |
| Data (million) | 2962.207 | 3019.589 | 3077.310 | 3134.012 | 3190.508 | 3242.239 | 3296.275 |
| Year | 1993 | 1994 | 1995 | 1996 | 1997 | 1998 | 1999 |
| Data (million) | 3348.566 | 3400.365 | 3452.081 | 3503.208 | 3552.609 | 3600.732 | 3648.068 |
| Year | 2000 | 2001 | 2002 | 2003 | 2004 | 2005 | 2006 |
| Data (million) | 3694.628 | 3740.930 | 3786.739 | 3831.708 | 3876.151 | 3920.235 | 3964.762 |
| Year | 2007 | 2008 | 2009 | 2010 | 2011 | 2012 | 2013 |
| Data (million) | 4008.948 | 4052.503 | 4095.935 | 4138.919 | 4181.579 | 4223.675 | 4265.292 |
| Year | 2014 | | | | | | |
| Data (million) | 4306.690 | | | | | | |

every two years according to its widespread research. In [162], the department presented the most recent prediction result, which is widely used by researchers, international organizations, and governments, especially groups with less developed statistical systems. The WPP is viewed as the de facto standard [159], on which prediction is built on the standard cohort-component method by considering several individual factors (e.g., fertility, mortality, and migration rates) [160].

Historical data are the significant foundation in population prediction because they contain the general regularity of the population development. These data are also a comprehensive reflection of population development under the influence of all factors (e.g., natural environment, policy, and culture). Although population prediction methods vary considerably, collecting accurate population data is always a priority. By learning the tendency inside the historical data, people are able to make a comprehensive prediction without specifically analyzing each factor that affects population growth. In this chapter, specifically for the Asian population, all of the experiments for prediction are based on a certain group of Asian population data. That is, before the year 1900, the population data come from *the Atlas of Word Population History* [163]; and after 1900, the population data come from the International Programs Data [154]. The Asian population data are presented in Table 13.1.

In addition, based on previous work [154, 161, 164], the WASD neuronet is an AI model with excellent learning and prediction capabilities. In terms of population prediction, the WASD neuronet allows for all relevant factors that influence population development [161]. Such a method is quite different from the aforementioned demographic methods [157–159, 162], which use several complicated parameters. Specifically, unlike other demographic methods, the WASD neuronet does not involve analysis of fertility rate, mortality rate, migration rate, age structure, and sex structure.

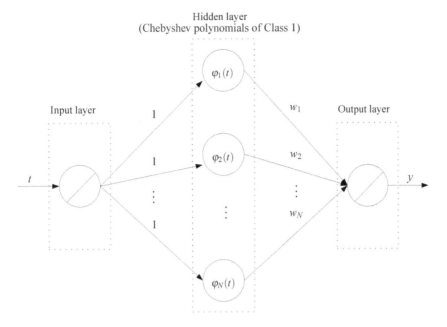

**FIGURE 13.1**: Model structure of single-input Chebyshev-activation neuronet for Asian population prediction.

Thus, this method is more suitable and applicable for population prediction. Another strength of the WASD neuronet for population prediction is that all the experiments are repeatable. In this chapter, we introduce the WASD neuronet activated by Chebyshev polynomials of Class 1 for function data approximation, and further exploit such a model for the prediction of Asian population.

## 13.2 Neuronet Model and WASD Algorithm

The WASD neuronet is derived from the error back-propagation (BP) neuronet that, theoretically, can approximate any nonlinear continuous function with arbitrary accuracy as a universal approximator [119]. Such a WASD neuronet overcomes the weaknesses of the classic BP neuronet, such as relatively slow convergence and local-minima existence [66, 164]. In this section, we introduce a model of the WASD neuronet (for the final purpose of the Asian population prediction), the model structure of which is shown in Fig. 13.1.

### 13.2.1 Chebyshev-activation neuronet

Orthogonal polynomials (such as Chebyshev polynomials and Bernoulli polynomials) have been widely applied as the activation functions of the neuronet [165]. As for the hidden-layer neurons of the WASD neuronet, different groups of activation functions lead to different performances. In previous work [164], the great capability of Chebyshev polynomials (used as the activation functions) has been illustrated and investigated. Therefore, we choose Chebyshev polynomials of class 1 in this chapter, and the resultant neuronet shown in Fig. 13.1 is termed Chebyshev-activation neuronet.

The Chebyshev polynomials is a series of recursive polynomials [66, 164] with the domain being $[-1, 1]$. The Chebyshev polynomials of Class 1 exploited in this chapter are formulated as $\varphi_1(t) = 1$, $\varphi_2(t) = t, \cdots, \varphi_k(t) = 2t\varphi_{k-1}(t) - \varphi_{k-2}(t)$ with $k = 3, 4, \cdots$, where $t$ corresponds to the input of Chebyshev-activation neuronet. From the above formulation, two hidden-layer neurons are presented when initializing the neuronet construction (which implies that the number of hidden-layer neurons $N \geq 2$), and the expressions of these two initial hidden-layer neurons correspond to $\varphi_1(t)$ and $\varphi_2(t)$. During the learning process, the number of hidden-layer neurons $N$ can automatically be determined by using the WASD algorithm presented in the subsequent section. Furthermore, as for Chebyshev-activation neuronet shown in Fig. 13.1, the output $y$ is obtained as $y = \sum_{i=1}^{N} w_i \varphi_i(t)$, with $t$ being the input of the neuronet and $\{w_1, \cdots, w_N\}$ being the weights that connect the hidden layer and the output layer. Thus, the computations of applying such a Chebyshev-activation neuronet require the calculation to obtain the activation values of all hidden-layer neurons and the final weighted summation of these activation values. According to Chebyshev-polynomial formula, the numbers of operations of additions and multiplications for constructing Chebyshev polynomials are required as $N - 2$ and $2(N - 2)$, respectively. Therefore, based on the input-output relationship, the numbers of operations of additions and multiplications in applying Chebyshev-activation neuronet once are obtained as $2N - 3$ and $3N - 4$, respectively.

### 13.2.2    WASD algorithm

In this subsection, as for the presented Chebyshev-activation neuronet, the WASD algorithm is given to determine the number of hidden-layer neurons $N$ and the corresponding weights $\{w_1, \cdots, w_N\}$ that connect the hidden layer and the output layer.

For further discussion, we give $\{(t_i, p_i)|_{i=1}^{M}\}$ as the data-set of $M$ sample pairs for the training of Chebyshev-activation neuronet, where $t_i \in \mathbb{R}$ denotes the $i$th input and $p_i \in \mathbb{R}$ denotes the $i$th desired output. The WASD algorithm [66, 164] determines the vector of optimal weights for Chebyshev-activation neuronet as

$$\mathbf{w} = (\mathbf{\Psi}^T \mathbf{\Psi})^{-1} \mathbf{\Psi}^T \mathbf{p}, \tag{13.1}$$

where superscript $^T$ denotes the transpose operator. In addition, optimal weight vector $\mathbf{w} = [w_1, \cdots, w_N]^T \in \mathbb{R}^N$; $\mathbf{\Psi} \in \mathbb{R}^{M \times N}$ is the input activation matrix with the $i$th row defined as $\mathbf{\Psi}_i = [\varphi_1(t_i), \cdots, \varphi_N(t_i)]$; desired-output vector $\mathbf{p} = [p_1, \cdots, p_M]^T \in \mathbb{R}^M$; and $(\mathbf{\Psi}^T \mathbf{\Psi})^{-1} \mathbf{\Psi}^T$ represents the pseudoinverse of matrix $\mathbf{\Psi}$.

To determine the optimal number of hidden-layer neurons (e.g., with the best learning performance), after calculating the weights via (13.1), the output result of Chebyshev-activation neuronet is compared with the desired result. The WASD algorithm uses the following mean square error (MSE) to evaluate the difference between the neuronet output and the desired output:

$$e = \frac{1}{M} \sum_{i=1}^{M} \left( p_i - \sum_{j=1}^{N} w_j \varphi_j(t_i) \right)^2, \tag{13.2}$$

where $e$ represents the MSE value when the number of hidden-layer neurons is $N$. Different $N$ values lead to different MSE values, showing that $N$ is important to Chebyshev-activation neuronet's performance.

More specifically, the neuronet performance may become poor when the number of hidden-layer neurons (i.e., $N$) is insufficient. However, too many neurons might lead to the over-fitting problem. Therefore, we use the following procedure to obtain the optimal structure of Chebyshev-activation neuronet (e.g., corresponding to $N$ with the best learning performance). Besides, $N_{\text{opt}}$ denotes the optimal number of hidden-layer neurons, and $e_{\text{min}}$ denotes the minimal MSE that was found.

*Step 1.* The data-set of sample pairs $\{(t_i, p_i)|_{i=1}^{M}\}$ is obtained for training. The structure of Chebyshev-activation neuronet is initialized with $N = 2$, and set $N_{\text{opt}} = 2$. Furthermore, $e_{\text{min}}$ is set initially large enough (e.g., $e_{\text{min}} = 10^3$).

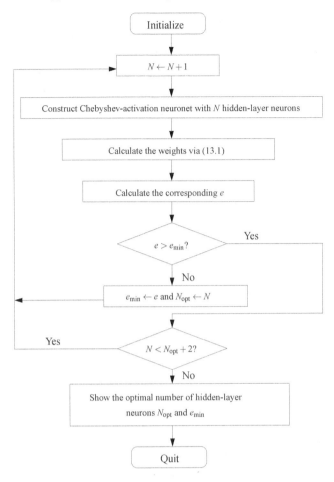

**FIGURE 13.2**: Flowchart of WASD algorithm for Chebyshev-activation neuronet applied to Asian population prediction.

*Step 2.* $N \leftarrow N + 1$, Chebyshev-activation neuronet is constructed.

*Step 3.* The weights between the hidden-layer and output-layer neurons are calculated via (13.1), and the corresponding $e$ is calculated via (13.2).

*Step 4.* If $e > e_{min}$, then *Step 5* commences. Otherwise, $e_{min} \leftarrow e$ and $N_{opt} \leftarrow N$, and *Step 2* commences.

*Step 5.* If $N < N_{opt} + 2$, then *Step 2* commences. Otherwise, *Step 6* commences.

*Step 6.* The optimal number of hidden-layer neurons $N_{opt}$ and $e_{min}$ are output and saved. The procedure is terminated.

We provide the related flowchart in correspondence with the above six steps to make the WASD algorithm easy to understand, as shown in Fig. 13.2. Based on the above analysis and on Fig. 13.2, the optimal number of hidden-layer neurons (or, say, the optimal model structure) of Chebyshev-activation neuronet with $e_{min}$ can be determined via the WASD algorithm.

In previous work [166], Chebyshev-activation neuronet equipped with the WASD algorithm has been theoretically proven to approximate any target function with infinitesimal error. Furthermore, Chebyshev-activation WASD neuronet with a multiple-input-single-output structure has been applied to pattern classification in [166], where the comparative results of such a neuronet, conventional multi-layer perceptron, radial-basis-function neuronet, and support vector machine have been presented as well. Additional details may be found in [166].

With Chebyshev-activation neuronet well trained via the WASD algorithm, it can thus be applied to the prediction of Asian population. In this case, the input of Chebyshev-activation WASD neuronet corresponds to the year (e.g., 2014). The domain of the input for Chebyshev-activation WASD neuronet is $[-1, 1]$. Thus, the data that are used as the neuronet input need to be normalized. In this chapter, the normalization interval is $[0, \alpha]$ with the normalization factor $\alpha \in (0, 1)$. Based on [164], we find that $\alpha$ also plays an important role in the learning performance of Chebyshev-activation WASD neuronet. Therefore, finding a proper $\alpha$ value becomes necessary. For a specific value of $\alpha$, we have the corresponding MSE via (13.2). If we find the $\alpha$ value that corresponds to the best learning performance, then a reasonable method is obtained to compare the MSE for each $\alpha$ and obtain the $\alpha$ value that corresponds to the minimum MSE. This method can be named the complete-learning method. The Chebyshev-activation WASD neuronet presented in this chapter aims at not only function data approximation, but also prediction. Thus, to evaluate both capabilities, the learning-testing method is introduced as follows.

We reconsider the data-set $\{(t_i, p_i)|_{i=1}^{M}\}$ with $M$ sample pairs. To examine the prediction capability of Chebyshev-activation WASD neuronet, not all sample pairs are used for learning. The learning-testing method requires, for example, that the data in $\{(t_i, p_i)|_{i=1}^{M-Q}\}$ are used for learning, while the rest of the data in $\{(t_i, p_i)|_{i=M-Q+1}^{M}\}$ are used for testing, where $Q$ is a positive integer and should be set as $1 < Q \ll M$. Then, the prediction error for Chebyshev-activation WASD neuronet is obtained as

$$\varepsilon_{\text{pre}} = \frac{1}{Q} \sum_{j=1}^{Q} \left| \frac{y_{M-Q+j} - p_{M-Q+j}}{p_{M-Q+j}} \right| \times 100\%, \tag{13.3}$$

where $y_{M-Q+j}$ is the $(M-Q+j)$th output of Chebyshev-activation WASD neuronet corresponding to the input $t_{M-Q+j}$, and $|\cdot|$ denotes the absolute value of a scalar. With a fixed $Q$, based on the (population) data in the normalization interval $[0, \alpha]$, we obtain the error $\varepsilon_{\text{pre}}$ via (13.3). We then compare the error $\varepsilon_{\text{pre}}$ for each $\alpha$ (changing from 0.001 to 0.999), and obtain the $\alpha$ value corresponding to the error $\varepsilon_{\text{pre}}$ achieving the global minimum. Such an $\alpha$, together with $\varepsilon_{\text{pre}}$, is named the global minimum point, which is also the focus of this chapter. Theoretically, Chebyshev-activation WASD neuronet that corresponds to the global minimum point has the best capability in terms of learning and prediction.

In addition, the choice of a proper $Q$ is worth investigating. On the one hand, if $Q$ is too small, then the resultant Chebyshev-activation WASD neuronet may have less prediction capability. On the other hand, if $Q$ is too large, then the resultant Chebyshev-activation WASD neuronet may be quite different from the neuronet constructed by using data-set $\{(t_i, p_i)|_{i=1}^{M}\}$, which also results in less prediction capability. Selecting an appropriate value of $Q$ for Chebyshev-activation WASD neuronet is thus necessary. The numerical results shown in Fig. 13.3, Fig. 13.4 and Table 13.2 show that Chebyshev-activation WASD neuronet is effective in function prediction, particularly in nearby prediction. In addition, with the selection of different $Q$ values (e.g., $Q = 2$, 3, and 4), the related numerical results show that Chebyshev-activation WASD neuronet with $Q = 3$ achieves superior performance (with small prediction error). The choice of $Q = 3$ also means that the resultant Chebyshev-activation WASD neuronet can predict the population for the next 3 years (at least). Thus, based on these experimental results, focusing on population prediction, we choose $Q = 3$ for Chebyshev-activation WASD neuronet in this chapter.

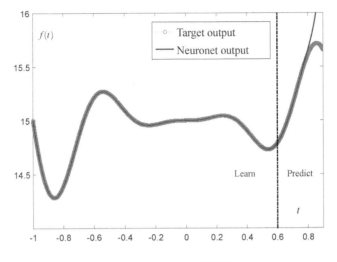

(a) Using Chebyshev-activation WASD neuronet

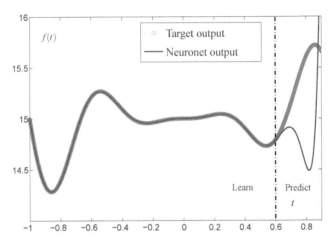

(b) Using Bernoulli-activation WASD neuronet

**FIGURE 13.3**: Approximation and prediction results of Chebyshev-activation and Bernoulli-activation neuronets for target function (13.4).

## 13.3 Function Data Approximation and Prediction

In this section, two different polynomials are used as the activation functions for the WASD neuronet. Then, the performances of the WASD neuronets activated by these two different activation functions are investigated by approximating two target functions and predicting the function values.

In previous work [164], comparative results have been summarized and presented for the WASD neuronet by choosing different activation functions (i.e., Legendre polynomials, Hermite polynomials, Chebyshev polynomials of Class 1, Chebyshev polynomials of Class 2, Bernoulli polynomials and power functions). Based on these results, we use the Bernoulli polynomials as the activation functions for the WASD neuronet. The Bernoulli polynomials is an orthogonal polynomial, which

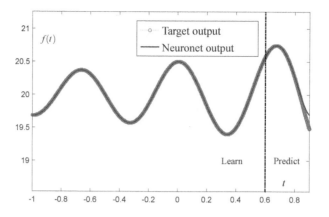

(a) Using Chebyshev-activation WASD neuronet

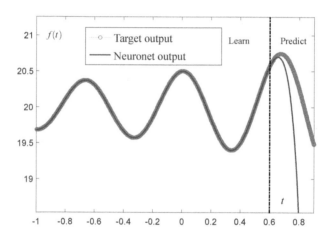

(b) Using Bernoulli-activation WASD neuronet

**FIGURE 13.4**: Approximation and prediction results of Chebyshev-activation and Bernoulli-activation neuronets for target function (13.5).

is formulated as follows:

$$\begin{cases} \varphi_1(t) = 1, \\ \varphi_{k+1}(t) = t^k - \frac{1}{k+1}\sum_{i=0}^{k}\left(\frac{\varphi_j(t)(k+1)!}{(j-1)!(k+2-j)!}\right), \ k = 1,2,\cdots. \end{cases}$$

In this group of numerical studies, the Bernoulli-activated WASD neuronet and Chebyshev-activation WASD neuronet are used to learn and predict the target functions as follows:

$$f(t) = t^2\sin(3\pi t) + 5, \tag{13.4}$$

$$f(t) = \frac{\cos(3\pi t)\exp(t)}{\sin(t) + 2} + 20. \tag{13.5}$$

The domain of the input for Chebyshev-activation WASD neuronet is $[-1, 1]$. The data-set for the approximations of both functions (13.4) and (13.5) is set to be $\{(t_i, f(t_i))|_{i=1}^{1601}\}$ with

**TABLE 13.2:** Numerical results of Chebyshev-activation (CA) and Bernoulli-activation (BA) neuronets for target functions (13.4) and (13.5).

| Target function | Activation function | $N$ | $t_{\text{tra}}$ (ms) | Approximation $e_{\min}$ | $e_{\text{pre}}$ in $t \in (0.6, 0.7]$ | $e_{\text{pre}}$ in $t \in (0.7, 0.8]$ | $e_{\text{pre}}$ in $t \in (0.8, 0.9]$ |
|---|---|---|---|---|---|---|---|
| (13.4) | CA | 22 | 27.35 | $4.139 \times 10^{-16}$ | $4.2234 \times 10^{-8}$ | 0.0003 | 0.2345 |
|  | BA | 13 | 91.24 | $3.8108 \times 10^{-6}$ | 0.0113 | 0.4627 | 0.9175 |
| (13.5) | CA | 20 | 49.73 | $3.9175 \times 10^{-16}$ | $8.0521 \times 10^{-9}$ | $2.3982 \times 10^{-5}$ | 0.0091 |
|  | BA | 14 | 41.48 | $4.2123 \times 10^{-8}$ | 0.0038 | 0.7703 | 36.8911 |

**TABLE 13.3:** Global minimum points and optimal hidden-neuron numbers via Chebyshev-activation WASD neuronet with respect to different learning-testing data-sets.

| Learning-testing last year | 1993 | 1994 | 1995 | 1996 | 1997 | 1998 |
|---|---|---|---|---|---|---|
| Global minimum point | 0.539 | 0.790 | 0.705 | 0.772 | 0.763 | 0.712 |
| Optimal hidden-neuron number $N$ | 26 | 35 | 35 | 33 | 33 | 35 |
| Learning-testing last year | 1999 | 2000 | 2001 | 2002 | 2003 | 2004 |
| Global minimum point | 0.705 | 0.718 | 0.719 | 0.750 | 0.553 | 0.551 |
| Optimal hidden-neuron number $N$ | 35 | 30 | 30 | 31 | 22 | 22 |

$t_i = -1.001 + 0.001i$. After the neuronet learning, the neuronet is used to predict the data in interval $x \in (0.6, 0.9]$ with the data gap equaling 0.0005. The corresponding experimental results are shown in Figs. 13.3 and 13.4. Figures 13.3 and 13.4 show that Chebyshev-activation WASD neuronet has been learned well in interval $t \in [-1, 0.6]$ and has shown excellent prediction performance in interval $t \in (0.6, 0.8]$. By contrast, the prediction performance of the Bernoulli-activation WASD neuronet is not satisfactory, especially when predicting function (13.4). This result shows that the Bernoulli polynomials may not be suitable as the activation function of the WASD neuronet (when it is applied to function data approximation and prediction). In addition, Table 13.2 provides more detailed results about the above studies. The $e_{\text{pre}}$ in Table 13.2 represents the prediction MSE in a specific data interval, which is defined as $e_{\text{pre}} = \sum_{i=1}^{M} (f(t_i) - y_i)^2 / M$, where $y_i$ is the neuronet output that corresponds to the input $t_i$, and $M$ is the total data number in the data-set. In addition, CA and BA in Table 13.2 denote the neuronets using Chebyshev activation and Bernoulli activation, respectively. As shown in Table 13.2, Chebyshev-activation WASD neuronet fits the function much better than the Bernoulli-activation WASD neuronet (considering a smaller value of the function data approximation $e_{\min}$). Moreover, the $e_{\text{pre}}$ of Chebyshev-activation WASD neuronet in interval $t \in (0.6, 0.8]$ is low. The prediction errors of both neuronets increase as the prediction interval increases (e.g., in this numerical study, the prediction error of Chebyshev-activation WASD neuronet remarkably increases when $t > 0.8$). Therefore, choosing a proper prediction interval is important to ensure prediction accuracy (which will be investigated in the subsequent section).

In summary, Fig. 13.3, Fig. 13.4 and Table 13.2 have indicated that Chebyshev polynomials is an ideal activation function for the WASD neuronet in function data approximation and prediction.

**TABLE 13.4:**    Prediction errors of Asian population via Chebyshev-activation WASD neuronet using global minimum points in Table 13.3.

| Learning-testing last year | +8 (Years after last) | +9 | +10 | +11 | +12 | +13 | +14 | +15 |
|---|---|---|---|---|---|---|---|---|
| 1993 | 0.98% | 1.25% | 1.57% | 1.96% | 2.41% | 2.97% | 3.61% | 4.33% |
| 1994 | 4.03% | 5.11% | 6.37% | 7.85% | 9.56% | 11.55% | 13.87% | 16.55% |
| 1995 | 0.64% | 0.80% | 0.97% | 1.15% | 1.35% | 1.60% | 1.88% | 2.22% |
| 1996 | 1.20% | 1.47% | 1.76% | 2.09% | 2.49% | 2.94% | 3.47% | 4.09% |
| 1997 | 1.30% | 1.56% | 1.86% | 2.21% | 2.62% | 3.10% | 3.66% | 4.32% |
| 1998 | 1.02% | 1.21% | 1.43% | 1.69% | 2.00% | 2.37% | 2.81% | 3.33% |
| 1999 | 0.93% | 1.11% | 1.31% | 1.56% | 1.86% | 2.23% | 2.67% | 3.18% |
| 2000 | 0.87% | 1.08% | 1.31% | 1.55% | 1.82% | 2.09% | 2.38% | |
| 2001 | 0.95% | 1.16% | 1.39% | 1.63% | 1.88% | 2.14% | | |
| 2002 | 0.90% | 1.09% | 1.27% | 1.46% | 1.66% | | | |
| 2003 | 2.54% | 3.14% | 3.82% | 4.59% | | | | |
| 2004 | 3.12% | 3.80% | 4.55% | | | | | |
| Average $\varepsilon_{pre}$ | 1.54% | 1.90% | 2.30% | 2.52% | 2.76% | 3.44% | 4.29% | 5.43% |
| Maximum $\varepsilon_{pre}$ | 4.03% | 5.11% | 6.37% | 7.85% | 9.56% | 11.55% | 13.87% | 16.55% |

## 13.4    Asian Population Prediction

In this subsection, Asian population data are used to evaluate the prediction performance of Chebyshev-activation WASD neuronet with the global minimum point chosen. In addition, as mentioned previously, a proper prediction interval may ensure prediction accuracy. Thus, the proper prediction interval of Asian population prediction based on global minimum point is explored in this application. To present a persuasive prediction on Asian population, we need to evaluate the prediction performance of Chebyshev-activation WASD neuronet using the global minimum point. Thus, 12 numerical studies are conducted, with the corresponding results shown in Table 13.3. The learning-testing last year "1993" in the table means that the data in 1991, 1992, and 1993 are used for prediction testing (or, say, prediction-type testing). Other years shown in the table are similar in meaning. As shown in Table 13.3, the global minimum point for each year is obtained, and they are different from each other. In addition, Table 13.3 shows that the optimal number of hidden-layer neurons for Chebyshev-activation WASD neuronet of each year is relatively small, which illustrates the feasibility of such a neuronet for Asian population prediction. Note that the WASD neuronet is both used in the function data approximation and population learning in the research. The nomenclature of approximation and learning refers to the traditional function approximation theory and machine learning [80,81]. As for the WASD neuronet, the essence of approximation and learning is the same.

For further investigation, based on the results given in Table 13.3, more numerical studies are conducted. The corresponding results are shown in Table 13.4 and Fig. 13.5 through Fig. 13.7. Table 13.4 is explained as follows. We take the value "0.0098" in Table 13.4 as an example: it is the prediction error at the year 2001 (i.e., 8 years after 1993), which is synthesized by Chebyshev-activation WASD neuronet with the global minimum point being 0.539 (see Table 13.3). Other prediction errors shown in Table 13.4 are thus similarly obtained and understood. For the results shown in Table 13.4 and Fig. 13.5 through Fig. 13.7, more analyses are presented in the subsequent subsection.

Specifically, Table 13.4 shows prediction errors for Asian population that are synthesized by Chebyshev-activation WASD neuronet using the global minimum points shown in Table 13.3. From Table 13.4, we observe that most of the prediction errors are small, showing the great prediction capability of Chebyshev-activation WASD neuronet. As the best case, the results that correspond to

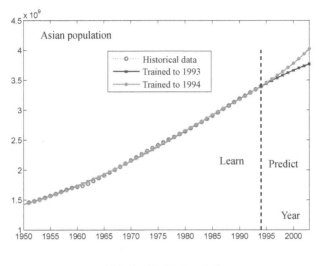

(a) Trained to 1993 or 1994

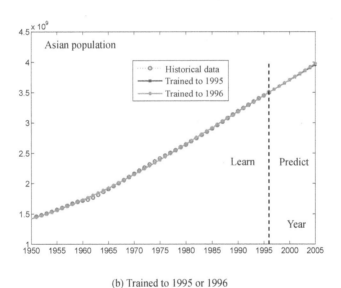

(b) Trained to 1995 or 1996

**FIGURE 13.5**: Numerical results of Asian population prediction via Chebyshev-activation WASD neuronet with learning-testing last years being 1993 through 1996.

the year 1995 show a maximally 2.2% prediction error even in 15-year-long prediction. In addition, the average prediction errors show that, although the error increases as the predicted years lengthen, the error remains within a small magnitude. Furthermore, the 14-year-long prediction shows the average prediction error being less than 5%, which is practically acceptable. More importantly, Table 13.4 implies that Chebyshev-activation WASD neuronet successfully achieves the purpose of 9-year-long prediction within a 1.9% error on average. As for the maximum prediction error, the worst situation of Chebyshev-activation WASD neuronet prediction may be implied. The table shows that the maximum prediction error that corresponds to 9-year-long prediction is 5.11%, which is also quite acceptable (in view of a 5% error standard). Thus, by summarizing the results of the

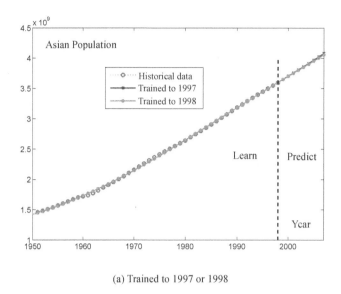

(a) Trained to 1997 or 1998

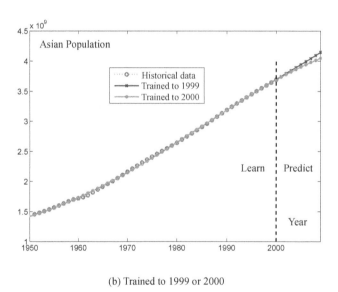

(b) Trained to 1999 or 2000

**FIGURE 13.6**: Numerical results of Asian population prediction via Chebyshev-activation WASD neuronet with learning-testing last years being 1997 through 2000.

average and maximum prediction errors, we conclude that Chebyshev-activation WASD neuronet for Asian population has an excellent 9-year-long prediction capability (i.e., within 1.9% error on average).

Moreover, Figs. 13.5 through 13.7 illustrate the numerical results synthesized by Chebyshev-activation WASD neuronet for 9-year-long prediction. The output results of the neuronet learn the data well. In addition, different prediction results are indicated by Chebyshev-activation WASD neuronet, which correspond to different learning-testing data-sets (or, say, different learning-testing last years shown in Table 13.3). Evidently, Figs. 13.5 through 13.7 visually and intuitively show the superior performances of Chebyshev-activation WASD neuronet in terms of learning and prediction.

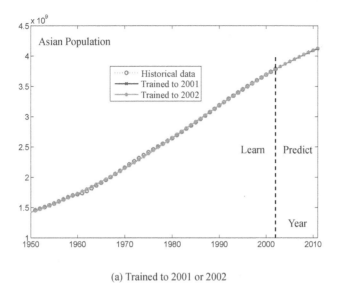

(a) Trained to 2001 or 2002

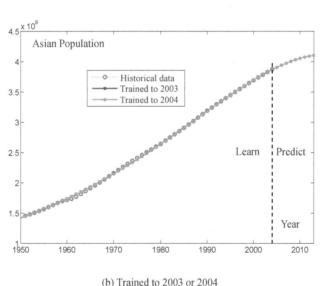

(b) Trained to 2003 or 2004

**FIGURE 13.7**: Numerical results of Asian population prediction via Chebyshev-activation WASD neuronet with learning-testing last years being 2001 through 2004.

In summary, the above results shown in Tables 13.3 and 13.4 as well as Figs. 13.5 through 13.7 have substantiated that Chebyshev-activation WASD neuronet has great capabilities in learning historical data and prediction. More importantly, these results have shown that Chebyshev-activation WASD neuronet has an excellent capability in 9-year-long prediction.

Based on the previous results, Chebyshev-activation WASD neuronet is applied to the 9-year-long prediction of Asian population as follows.

The learning-testing method is used to find the global minimum point for Chebyshev-activation WASD neuronet. Therefore, we use population data from 400 BC to 2011 for learning, and the population data from 2012 to 2014 are used for testing. Then, Fig. 13.8(a) shows the relationship

**TABLE 13.5:**    Prediction results of Asian population via Chebyshev-activation WASD neuronet using $\alpha = 0.817$ (global minimum point) in the next 9 years.

| Year | 2015 | 2016 | 2017 | 2018 | 2019 | 2020 | 2021 | 2022 | 2023 |
|---|---|---|---|---|---|---|---|---|---|
| Population (billion) | 4.361 | 4.411 | 4.464 | 4.520 | 4.580 | 4.646 | 4.717 | 4.795 | 4.880 |

**TABLE 13.6:**    Prediction results of Asian population via Chebyshev-activation WASD neuronet using $\alpha = 0.744$ and $\alpha = 0.921$ in the next 9 years.

| Year | 2015 | 2016 | 2017 | 2018 | 2019 | 2020 | 2021 | 2022 | 2023 |
|---|---|---|---|---|---|---|---|---|---|
| Prediction (billion) on 0.744 | 4.351 | 4.395 | 4.442 | 4.49 | 4.541 | 4.595 | 4.652 | 4.714 | 4.780 |
| Prediction (billion) on 0.921 | 4.342 | 4.378 | 4.412 | 4.444 | 4.472 | 4.496 | 4.515 | 4.527 | 4.532 |

between the normalization factor $\alpha$ and the prediction error $\varepsilon_{\mathrm{pre}}$ via (13.3). As shown in Fig. 13.8(a), many local minimum points and one global minimum point (i.e., the marked one) are presented. For the local minimum points, detailed discussion will be given in the next section. With the global minimum point (i.e., $\alpha = 0.817$) used, the resultant Chebyshev-activation WASD neuronet is thus applied to the final prediction of Asian population. The corresponding prediction results are shown in Fig. 13.8(b) and Table 13.5.

As seen from Fig. 13.8(b), Chebyshev-activation WASD neuronet is well trained based on the historical data of Asian population. In addition, such a well-trained neuronet succeeds in learning the (sparse) data before the year 1950. With the well-trained Chebyshev-activation WASD neuronet, we thus obtain the corresponding prediction for Asian population in the next 9 years. That is, from Fig. 13.8(b), we see that, as synthesized by the neuronet, the population of Asian is predicted to increase continuously from 2015 to 2023. For better understanding, Table 13.5 shows the detailed prediction data of Asian population in the next 9 years, which are indicated by Chebyshev-activation WASD neuronet. As seen from the table, with a steady growth rate, the Asian population is predicted to increase to 4.880 billion in 2023. According to the analyses in Subsection 13.4, Chebyshev-activation WASD neuronet may have a 1.9% error on average for the 9-year-long prediction of Asian population. Therefore, based on the data shown in Table 13.5, we obtain the prediction that the Asian population in 2023 could be in the range of $[4.880 \times (1 \pm 1.9\%)] = [4.787, 4.973]$ billion. Moreover, as presented in the WPP [162], the Asian population is expected to continue to grow in the next 9 years. Specifically, based on the low-variant prediction, the Asian population is predicted to increase to 4.528 billion in 2023. Based on medium-variant prediction, the Asian population is predicted to increase to 4.686 billion in 2023. Based on high-variant prediction, the Asian population is predicted to increase to 4.843 billion in 2023. In other words, as for the prediction of Asian population, the WPP [162] present a population interval from 4.528 to 4.843 billion in 2023. Comparing the prediction results via the neuronet and those given in the WPP shows that they are similar to each other. This numerical comparison shows that the prediction synthesized by Chebyshev-activation WASD neuronet is reasonable to some extent.

## 13.5    Additional Prediction Results

The population prediction concerns the future, which is full of uncertainty [156]. Thus, providing several prediction tendencies, if possible, is reasonable. For example, the WPP [162] present three different potential population tendencies for the Asian population (based on low-variant, medium-variant and high-variant predictions). Thus, in this section, for a more comprehensive prediction, we present other different potential tendencies of the Asian population by choosing different local minimum points (or, say, different $\alpha$ values) for Chebyshev-activation WASD neuronet.

From Fig. 13.8(a), many local minimum points can be observed. A local minimum point also shows a prediction possibility of Chebyshev-activation WASD neuronet for the Asian population. Given result similarity and space limitation, only two local minimum points (i.e., $\alpha = 0.744$ and $\alpha = 0.921$) are chosen as the representative examples. The corresponding results are shown in Fig. 13.9 and Table 13.6. As seen from Fig. 13.9, Chebyshev-activation WASD neuronet fits the historical population data well. The Asian population is predicted to increase continuously in the next 9 years. Furthermore, Table 13.6 provides the detailed prediction data of Asian population from 2015 to 2023. The table shows that, as indicated by Chebyshev-activation WASD neuronet with $\alpha = 0.744$ and $\alpha = 0.921$, the Asian population is predicted to increase to 4.780 billion and 4.532 billion in 2023, respectively. A comparison between these prediction values (i.e., 4.780 and 4.532) and the values in the WPP based on the low-variant and high-variant predictions (i.e., 4.843 and 4.528) shows that they are quite consistent. Considering that Fig. 13.8(b) and Fig. 13.9(a) and Fig. 13.9(b) are prediction possibilities via Chebyshev-activation WASD neuronet, we may conclude that the neuronet prediction in this chapter could incorporate the prediction of the WPP (in terms of a few years).

In summary, the results shown in Figs. 13.8 and 13.9 and Tables 13.5 and 13.6 have provided a comprehensive view of the prediction of Asian population in the next 9 years.

---

## 13.6 Chapter Summary

Current AI methods have gained increasing attention given their increasing efficiency and accuracy. Such methods have been effectively applied in function data approximation and prediction, which makes them a powerful tool for population research. This chapter has investigated the capabilities of Chebyshev-activation neuronet (being an AI method) in the learning and prediction of the Asian population. As a Chebyshev-activation neuronet, the WASD algorithm has been shown to determine the optimal number of hidden-layer neuron numbers and the corresponding weights automatically. In addition, the learning-testing method has been developed to find the proper normalization factor $\alpha$ for the application of Chebyshev-activation WASD neuronet to Asian population prediction. The learning-testing method may provide an efficient way for researchers who do not necessarily know the mathematical principle inside the neuronet. Comparative studies have also been illustrated to show the considerable performance of Chebyshev polynomials as the activation function. Furthermore, twelve experiments have shown that Chebyshev-activation WASD neuronet with the learning-testing method is capable of 9-year-long prediction. The final application of the neuronet has shown that the Asian population will increase continuously with a steady growth rate in the next 9 years. In addition, other potential growth tendencies of Asian population have been presented and analyzed. However, a detail that is worth mentioning is that population prediction may be continuously challenging because of many uncertainties in the future, such as unexpected wars, natural disasters, and infectious diseases of high mortality. Note that the Asian population data from 2015 to 2017 (the time that we prepared this chapter in the book) in WPP 2017 [167] are 4419.898 million, 4462.677 million and 4504.428 million, respectively. For the convenience of readers, the above population data can be used to further compare with the population prediction results reported in this chapter.

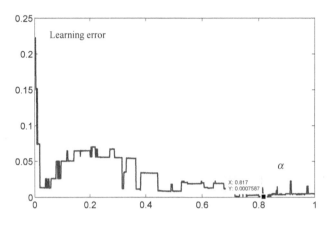

(a) Learning error of neuronet

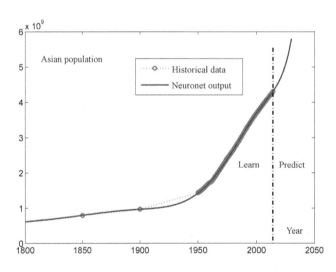

(b) Predicted tendency of Asian population

**FIGURE 13.8**: Numerical results of Asian population prediction via Chebyshev-activation WASD neuronet using historical data from 400 BC to 2014.

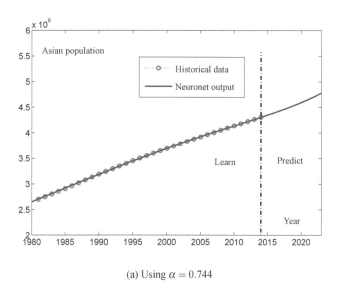

(a) Using $\alpha = 0.744$

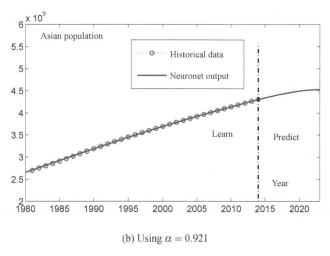

(b) Using $\alpha = 0.921$

**FIGURE 13.9**: Numerical results of Asian population prediction via Chebyshev-activation WASD neuronet using different values of $\alpha$.

# Chapter 14

# Application to European Population Prediction

With the world population increasing rapidly, the conflicts between the population and limited resources have become more and more severe. Population growth is a root cause of many environmental and social problems. Therefore, it is of vital importance to make population predictions. However, predictions based on standard cohort-component method fail to consider all relevant impact factors and may neglect some important uncertainty factors. To overcome the inherent limitations, in this chapter, we present a Chebyshev-activation weights-and-structure-determination (WASD) neuronet approach for the population prediction. This neuronet algorithm is applied to predicting European population, with numerous numerical studies conducted as a research basis to guarantee the feasibility and validity of our approach. It is predicted with the most possibility that European population will decrease in the near future.

## 14.1   Introduction

Population problem is closely related to the development of the human society. With the world becoming more and more crowded, the conflicts between human subsistence and the increasing population are very severe. Owing to these facts, the prediction of European population, which can be used for decision making and scientific research, is becoming more and more important and necessary [169–174]. Policymakers and planners around the world use population predictions to evaluate future demands for food, water, energy and service, and to forecast future demographic characteristics. Population predictions can also alert policymakers to major trends that may affect economic development, and help policymakers craft policies that can be adapted for various prediction scenarios [180].

However, as we all know, the population is affected by many factors, such as policy, environment, culture and economy [170–175]. It is impossible to take all the factors into account explicitly, which means that the population researches merely based on fertility, mortality and other individual factors may lead to the lack of all-sidedness in the prediction results [180]. To solve these

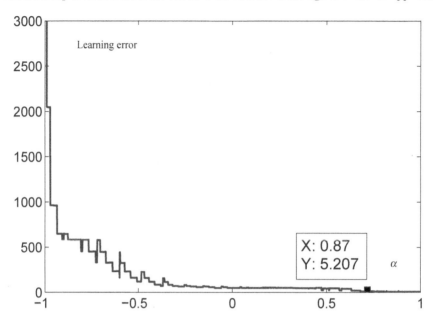

**FIGURE 14.1**: Learning error of Chebyshev-activation WASD neuronet with $\alpha = 0.870$ being global minimum point.

problems, we may think differently: the historical population data are the most direct indicator of all the explicit and implicit factors which have impacts on the population changing. Therefore, the prediction based on them is more reliable and convincing. In this chapter, we construct a three-layer feed-forward neuronet equipped with the WASD algorithm to make population predictions. With the neuronet trained by the historical population data, we successfully predict the near future population of Europe.

## 14.2   Neuronet Model and Preliminaries

As a branch of artificial intelligence, artificial neuronets (AN) have attracted considerable attention as candidates for novel computational systems nowadays. Due to the inherent nonlinearity and outstanding learning ability, various AN have been developed and applied widely in many scientific and engineering fields. In these studies, the feed-forward neuronet is applied as a class of typical AN. According to the in-depth researches, the feed-forward neuronet have now been involved in many real-world applications, such as system identification, pattern classification and stock prediction. The details of the structure and mechanism of the neuronet are presented in literatures [164, 176]. In order to find the internal mechanism and make effective predictions, we adopt this algorithm to the population research. With the neuronet well trained by the historical data, a number of neurons are properly generated and thus a feed-forward neuronet which is suitable for predictions is constructed. All in all, by means of a suitable training procedure, such a neuronet would have the marvelous approximation, generalization and prediction abilities. Theoretically speaking, a three-layer feed-forward neuronet can approximate any nonlinear continuous function with an excellent accuracy, and thus makes itself suitable for population prediction.

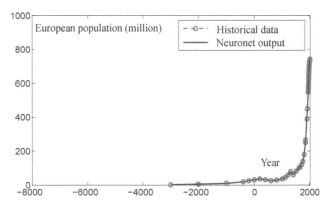

(a) Learning result of neuronet

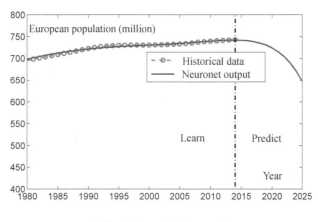

(b) Prediction result of neuronet

**FIGURE 14.2**: Learning and prediction results of European population via Chebyshev-activation WASD neuronet using $\alpha = 0.870$ (global minimum point).

Traditionally, the neuronets used for predictions are based on the error back-propagation (BP) algorithm (i.e., the so-called BP neuronet) [168, 177]. However, BP neuronets have some inherent weaknesses, such as relatively slow convergence, unclear local-minima existence, and structural uncertainty about the optimal number of hidden-layer neurons [176, 177]. Thereby, these neuronets are less applicable to the prediction of population. To compensate for the weaknesses of BP neuronets, we exploit linearly independent or orthogonal activation functions (e.g., Chebyshev polynomials of Class 1), and our successful experience indicates the validity of this algorithm in [176].

As we know, the performance of a neuronet is greatly affected by the number of the hidden-layer neurons. Specifically, the neuronet with a few hidden-layer neurons may fail to achieve the expected learning accuracy, whereas excessive hidden-layer neurons may result in the over-fitting phenomena, poor generalization ability and high computational complexity [46, 178, 179]. The WASD algorithm is thus introduced for neuronets. Such a WASD algorithm can (1) determine effectively the optimal weights connecting the hidden-layer neurons and the output-layer neuron, and (2) obtain automatically the optimal structure of the neuronet. These two aims are achieved by finding the minimal error. Therefore, the neuronet equipped with the WASD algorithm, which is named as

**TABLE 14.1:**    European historical population data from 3000 BC to 2014 AD (with unit of population data being million).

| Year | -3000 | -2000 | -1000 | -400 | -200 | 1 |
|------|-------|-------|-------|------|------|---|
| Data | 2 | 5 | 10 | 20 | 26 | 31 |
| Year | 200 | 400 | 600 | 800 | 1000 | 1100 |
| Data | 36 | 31 | 26 | 29 | 36 | 44 |
| Year | 1200 | 1300 | 1400 | 1500 | 1600 | 1650 |
| Data | 58 | 79 | 60 | 81 | 100 | 105 |
| Year | 1700 | 1750 | 1800 | 1845 | 1850 | 1900 |
| Data | 120 | 140 | 180 | 250 | 265 | 390 |
| Year | 1914 | 1950 | 1951 | 1952 | 1953 | 1954 |
| Data | 450 | 547.140 | 552.693 | 558.066 | 563.779 | 569.432 |
| Year | 1955 | 1956 | 1957 | 1958 | 1959 | 1960 |
| Data | 575.279 | 581.242 | 587.170 | 593.245 | 599.440 | 605.611 |
| Year | 1961 | 1962 | 1963 | 1964 | 1965 | 1966 |
| Data | 611.953 | 618.407 | 624.411 | 630.148 | 635.453 | 640.370 |
| Year | 1967 | 1968 | 1969 | 1970 | 1971 | 1972 |
| Data | 644.784 | 649.159 | 653.573 | 657.943 | 662.606 | 666.952 |
| Year | 1973 | 1974 | 1975 | 1976 | 1977 | 1978 |
| Data | 671.070 | 674.970 | 678.636 | 682.015 | 685.449 | 688.720 |
| Year | 1979 | 1980 | 1981 | 1982 | 1983 | 1984 |
| Data | 691.968 | 695.225 | 698.342 | 700.978 | 703.511 | 706.098 |
| Year | 1985 | 1986 | 1987 | 1988 | 1989 | 1990 |
| Data | 708.709 | 711.460 | 714.141 | 716.878 | 719.756 | 722.638 |
| Year | 1991 | 1992 | 1993 | 1994 | 1995 | 1996 |
| Data | 724.923 | 726.826 | 728.138 | 729.228 | 730.000 | 730.389 |
| Year | 1997 | 1998 | 1999 | 2000 | 2001 | 2002 |
| Data | 730.555 | 730.545 | 730.499 | 730.598 | 730.836 | 731.171 |
| Year | 2003 | 2004 | 2005 | 2006 | 2007 | 2008 |
| Data | 731.627 | 732.332 | 733.119 | 733.930 | 735.346 | 737.045 |
| Year | 2009 | 2010 | 2011 | 2012 | 2013 | 2014 |
| Data | 738.322 | 739.343 | 740.300 | 741.226 | 742.131 | 743.008 |

WASD neuronet, has superior performance on approximation and prediction. To learn more about the WASD algorithm and neuronet, please refer to literatures [176, 177, 180].

Before starting the population prediction of Europe, we need to give some necessary explanations as follows. Used in this chapter, the historical population data of Europe ranging from 3000 BC to 2014 AD are shown in Table 14.1 [163, 180]. In addition, for the three-layer feed-forward neuronet exploited in this chapter, the input and output of the neuronet correspond to the year and population datum, respectively. Moreover, the hidden layer of the feed-forward neuronet is activated by a group of Chebyshev polynomials of Class 1, which means that the domain of the input is $[-1, 1]$. Thus it is necessary to normalize the year data that are used as the neuronet input. Specifically, in this chapter, the time interval $[-3000, 2014]$ is normalized to the interval $[-1, \alpha]$ with the normalization factor $\alpha \in (-1, 1)$. Based on the above data processing, we have the data-set for the training of the neuronet. With the neuronet being well trained, we can apply it to the population prediction of Europe.

Moreover, it is necessary to point out that different values of $\alpha$ lead to different learning performances of the feed-forward neuronet, thus producing different prediction results. For better understanding, Fig. 14.1 presents the relationship between the normalization factor $\alpha$ and the learning

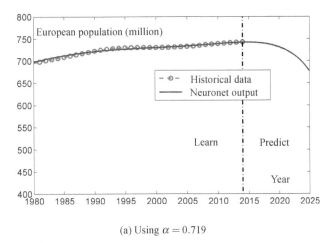

(a) Using $\alpha = 0.719$

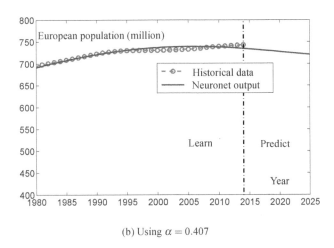

(b) Using $\alpha = 0.407$

**FIGURE 14.3**: Different prediction results of Chebyshev-activation WASD neuronet for European population prediction using $\alpha = 0.719$ and $\alpha = 0.407$.

error of the neuronet. To some extent, this relationship could be an important guide for determining the suitable value of $\alpha$ for the prediction. The $\alpha$ value corresponding to the minimal learning error is most likely to produce the prediction of the highest possibility.

From Fig. 14.1, we observe that there are some local minimum points and one global minimum point. Besides, both the global and local minimum points correspond to very small learning errors, showing that they are suitable for the prediction of European population. With different values of $\alpha$ used, we will get various prediction results which indicate different possibilities of the future population. The prediction given by the global minimum point is regarded as the most possible one, and simultaneously the predictions given by local minimum points are also noteworthy. In view of these, we conduct lots of numerical experiments and get the following predictions of European population.

After the neuronet is trained by the historical population data of Europe, we get the result that $\alpha = 0.870$ is the global minimum point. Since it has the minimal learning error of all values of $\alpha$, the corresponding prediction can be seen as the most possible one. The corresponding prediction results of the neuronet with $\alpha = 0.870$ are shown in Fig. 14.2. Specifically, from Fig. 14.2(a), we can see

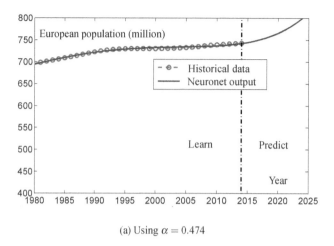

(a) Using $\alpha = 0.474$

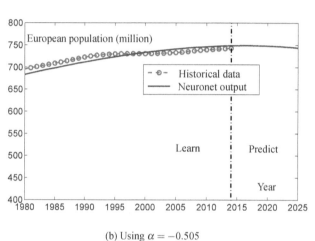

(b) Using $\alpha = -0.505$

**FIGURE 14.4**: Different prediction results of Chebyshev-activation WASD neuronet for European population prediction using $\alpha = 0.474$ and $\alpha = -0.505$.

that the neuronet output is very similar to the historical data, which indicates that the neuronet is well trained. In addition, Fig. 14.2(b) shows the prediction result (including the population decreasing trend) of the WASD neuronet with the most possibility.

## 14.3    Population Prediction and Discussion

Based on the built WASD neuronet model, we apply it to dealing with the population prediction problem. As we notice, every (global or local) minimum point in Fig. 14.1 represents its own prediction possibility for the future trend of European population. The $\alpha$ values corresponding to all minimum points are shown in the figure. At the same time, numerical experiments corresponding to all the minimum points in the figure are conducted to investigate all the possibilities for European population trends in the next decade.

**TABLE 14.2:** Different trends of European population in the next decade predicted via all of 33 minimum points shown in Fig. 14.1.

| $\alpha$ | -0.907 | -0.899 | -0.806 | -0.725 | -0.600 | -0.505 |
|---|---|---|---|---|---|---|
| Trend | ↗ | ↗ | ↗ | ↗ | ↗ | ↗↘ |
| $\alpha$ | -0.380 | -0.288 | -0.187 | -0.093 | -0.043 | 0.063 |
| Trend | ↘ | ↘ | ↘ | ↘ | ↘ | ↘ |
| $\alpha$ | 0.119 | 0.164 | 0.174 | 0.186 | 0.207 | 0.220 |
| Trend | ↘ | ↘ | ↘ | ↘ | ↘ | ↘ |
| $\alpha$ | 0.234 | 0.324 | 0.330 | 0.407 | 0.441 | 0.474 |
| Trend | ↘ | ↘ | ↘ | ↘ | ↘ | ↗ |
| $\alpha$ | 0.514 | 0.579 | 0.719 | 0.768 | 0.812 | 0.815 |
| Trend | ↗ | ↗ | ↘ | ↘ | ↘ | ↘ |
| $\alpha$ | 0.827 | **0.870** (global) | 0.882 | | | |
| Trend | ↗ | ↘ | ↘ | | | |

## 14.3.1 Results

As mentioned previously, Table 14.2 shows the different prediction trends of European population in the next decade using all the different $\alpha$ values corresponding to all the minimum points in Fig. 14.1. It is easy to see that there are 23 minimum points (about 69.7% of total 33 minimum points in Fig. 14.1) presenting the decreasing trends in the next decade, 9 minimum points (about 27.2% of total 33 minimum points in Fig. 14.1) presenting the increasing trends in the next decade, and one minimum point where $\alpha = -0.505$ presenting the trend that will increase slightly and then decrease in the next decade. In summary, with 69.7% possibility (exceeding the other two kinds of possibilities), European population will show a decreasing trend, which strongly consolidates the prediction result in Fig. 14.2(b) using $\alpha = 0.870$ corresponding to the global minimum point.

Because of the ageing population as well as the increasingly lower fertility, European population will decrease with a relatively gentle rate, which is also shown in Fig. 14.3(a) and Fig. 14.3(b). Not only $\alpha = 0.870$ (which is the global minimum point in Fig. 14.1) shows the decreasing trend as the most possible one, but also the experiments and statistics of 69.7% minimum points in Fig. 14.1 shows that European population is predicted to have a decreasing trend. On the other hand, governments in some Nordic countries (e.g., Sweden) have made the policies for encouraging local residents' fertility and attracting more immigrants to alleviate the problem of manpower lack [181]. These policies may take effect in the ensuing decade. The increasing trend shown in Fig. 14.4(a) might indicate the effect of these policies. On July 1st, 2014, Sweden's government announced the permanent residence permit to all PhD students after the completion of 4 years of research studies. Just as the population growth stimulation strategy carried out by the efficient governments in history, these new policies may accelerate the growth of population. Under the influence of these different restraint policies, it is also possible that the population may have a small amount of increasing or decreasing in the future (i.e., a stabilizing trend), as $\alpha = -0.505$, $\alpha = -0.600$, $\alpha = 0.407$ and $\alpha = 0.441$ correspond to (and show). For instance, the trend shown in Fig. 14.4(b) may indicate that those long-term systematic policies made by the government are effective in controlling the population. With these effective policies, European population might be well under control. All the $\alpha$ values mentioned in Fig. 14.4(b) are the different local minimum points and thus representing the different prediction results.

## 14.3.2 Discussion

Look again at the most possible prediction results that the European population will decrease in the near future. Owing to the fact that the European countries suffer a population ageing problem

[182–185], we are not surprised at the prediction results. The European Union (EU) currently has to cope with demographic decline, low natural growth, and ageing population, which further suggest the economic contraction or even a possible economic crisis [182, 183, 185, 186]. Some media and governments have noted the 'baby crisis' in the EU; and the United Nations (UN) as well as other multinational authorities continue to warn of a possible crisis [171]. All these facts indicate a future decline of the European population, which is in accordance with our most possible prediction results that the population of Europe will decrease in the near future.

In summary, the three-layer feed-forward neuronet equipped with WASD algorithm can predict the population of Europe reasonably and effectively. This WASD neuronet could give the most possible prediction, which will then give more appropriate indications for policymakers and planners to adjust their schemes properly for the future demands.

## 14.4   Chapter Summary

In terms of population prediction, compared with the standard algorithm, the WASD neuronet algorithm allows for all relevant factors influencing population development. Besides, the WASD neuronet model offers more efficient, complete and exact solution than traditional BP neuronets do. Extended to the population prediction of other countries and the world, the WASD algorithm may provide a new perspective as well as approach for population researches. Through providing the trend prediction of a country or region, it can help the government(s) to make more efficacious population policies as well as take prevention measures (if necessary). Note that the European population data from 2015 to 2017 (the time that we prepared this chapter in the book) in WPP 2017 [167] are 740.813 million, 741.447 million and 742.073 million, respectively. For the convenience of readers, the above population data can be used to further compare with the population prediction results reported in this chapter.

# Chapter 15

# Application to Oceanian Population Prediction

With growing economic and political influence in the world, the important role played by Oceania in population issues should not be neglected. So it is very important and urgent to find an effective way to make proper population predictions. Nonetheless, the traditional algorithms focused on fertility and mortality may lead to the lack of all-sidedness in prediction results. We realize that the historical data contain the internal mechanism of the population development, and the neuronet performs well with nonlinear data and the multifactor system. Therefore, in this chapter, we construct a three-layer feed-forward neuronet activated by a group of Chebyshev polynomials of Class 1 and equipped with a weights-and-structure-determination (WASD) algorithm (or, say, Chebyshev-activation neuronet with WASD algorithm) to learn the historical data and predict the population. With the neuronet well trained by over 1000-year historical data, we successfully predict that the future Oceanian population will keep a steady increasing trend in the coming 15 years.

## 15.1  Introduction

Population is closely related to the development of the human society [187]. With the world becoming more and more crowded, the conflicts between human subsistence and the increasing population are very severe [188–190]. Although Oceania is often neglected by the demographers (for its small population size), its vast land and abundant resources make Oceanian population increase in the near future.

**TABLE 15.1:** Prediction results of Chebyshev-activation neuronet using $\alpha = 0.014$ (global minimum point) with neuronet output data being in the thousands.

| Year | 2014 | 2015 | 2016 | 2017 | 2018 | 2019 | 2020 |
|---|---|---|---|---|---|---|---|
| Neuronet output | 38833 | 39413 | 40001 | 40593 | 41194 | 41801 | 42416 |
| Growth rate (%) | 1.4974 | 1.4948 | 1.4893 | 1.4803 | 1.4810 | 1.4726 | 1.4709 |

Owing to these facts, the prediction of Oceanian population, which can be used for decision making and scientific research, is becoming more and more important and necessary. Policymakers around the world use population predictions to evaluate future demands for food, water, energy and service, and to forecast future demographic characteristics. Population predictions can help policymakers craft policies that can be adapted for various prediction scenarios.

Literature [162] published by the United Nations (UN) is viewed as the de facto standard of population prediction. Based on the fertility, mortality and migration rates, the UN makes different assumptions about these factors (such as high, medium or low fertility) and thus get different prediction results. It is noted that these prediction results are based on the specific constant assumptions about the changing components (e.g., fertility, mortality and migration rates).

In addition, as we know, the population is affected by many factors, such as policy, environment, culture and economy. It is impossible to take all the factors into account explicitly, which means that the population research merely based on fertility, mortality and other individual factors may lead to the lack of all-sidedness in the prediction results [191]. To solve these issues, a new perspective is considered: the historical population data is the most direct indicator of all the factors which have impacts on the population changing. Therefore, the predictions based on them are more reliable and convincing. In this chapter, a three-layer feed-forward neuronet equipped with a weights-and-structure-determination (WASD) algorithm is constructed to make population predictions [192–196]. With the neuronet trained by the historical data (shown in Appendix G to this chapter), we successfully predict the future population of Oceania.

## 15.2   Chebyshev-Activation Neuronet for Population Prediction

The feed-forward neuronet is a class of typical artificial neuronets (AN). According to the in-depth research, the feed-forward neuronets have now been involved in many real-world applications, such as system identification and pattern classification. The details of the structure and mechanism of the neuronet are presented in Appendix H to this chapter.

Now we adopt this approach to the population research and to make effective predictions. With the neuronet well trained by the historical data, a number of neurons are connected and thus a feed-forward neuronet which is suitable for predictions is constructed. All in all, by means of a suitable training procedure, such a neuronet would have the marvelous approximation, generalization and prediction abilities. Theoretically speaking, a three-layer feed-forward neuronet can approximate any nonlinear continuous function with an excellent accuracy [129,187,195], thus making it suitable for population prediction.

Traditionally, the neuronet used for predictions is based on the error back-propagation (BP) algorithm (i.e., the so-called BP neuronet) [197]. However, BP neuronets have some inherent weaknesses [196], thereby making these neuronets less applicable to the prediction of population. To remedy the weaknesses of BP neuronets, we use linearly independent or orthogonal activation functions (e.g., Chebyshev polynomials of Class 1 in this chapter), and our successful experience indicates the validity of this Chebyshev-activation neuronet [196].

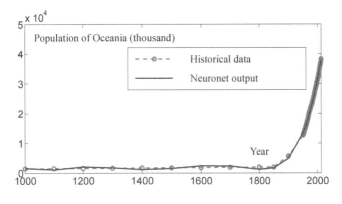

(a) Training result of neuronet

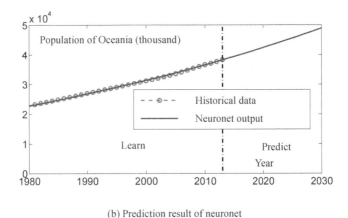

(b) Prediction result of neuronet

**FIGURE 15.1**: Training and prediction results of Oceanian population via Chebyshev-activation neuronet with WASD algorithm using $\alpha = 0.014$ (global minimum point).

As we know, the performance of a neuronet is greatly affected by the number of the hidden-layer neurons [187, 196]. Specifically, the neuronet with a fewer hidden-layer neurons may fail to achieve the expected learning accuracy, whereas excessive hidden-layer neurons may result in the over-fitting phenomenon, poor generalization and high computational complexity. The WASD algorithm [187, 196] is thus introduced for the neuronet. Such a WASD algorithm (1) determines effectively the optimal weights connecting the hidden-layer neurons and the output-layer neurons, and (2) obtains automatically the optimal structure of the neuronet. These two aims are achieved by finding the minimum error. Therefore, the neuronet activated by a group of Chebyshev polynomials of Class 1 and equipped with the WASD algorithm, which is also named as Chebyshev-activation neuronet with WASD algorithm, has superior performance on learning and prediction.

Before starting the population prediction of Oceania, we give some necessary explanations as follows. Generally, for the three-layer feed-forward neuronet exploited in this chapter, the input and output of the neuronet correspond to the year and population data, respectively. In addition, the hidden-layer neurons of the neuronet are activated by a group of Chebyshev polynomials of Class 1 (i.e., Chebyshev-activation neuronet), which means that the domain of the input is $[-1, 1]$. The historical population data of Oceania ranges from 1000 AD to 2013 AD [198]. Thus it is necessary

**TABLE 15.2:**  Evaluation results of Oceanian population via Chebyshev-activation neuronet with WASD algorithm.

| Year | 1999 | 2001 | 2003 | 2005 | 2007 | 2009 |
|---|---|---|---|---|---|---|
| Testing error of prediction (%) | 0.7471 | 0.6626 | 0.2754 | 0.2069 | 0.1440 | 0.0791 |

to normalize the data so as to be used as the neuronet input. Specifically, in this chapter, the time interval $[1000, 2013]$ is normalized to the interval $[0, \alpha]$ with the normalization factor $\alpha \in (0, 1)$. Based on the above data preprocessing, we have the data-set for the training of the neuronet. With the neuronet being well trained, we can apply it to the population prediction of Oceania.

Moreover, it is necessary to point out that different values of $\alpha$ lead to different training performances of the feed-forward neuronet, thus producing different prediction results. For better understanding, Appendix I to this chapter presents the relationship between the normalization factor $\alpha$ and the testing error of the neuronet.

From Fig. 15.5 in Appendix I to this chapter, we can further observe that there are some local minimum points and one global minimum point. Such local minimum points and global minimum point can be used for the prediction of Oceanian population. From the figure, we can tell that both the global and local minimum points have very small testing errors, showing that they are suitable for the prediction. With different values of $\alpha$ used, we get various prediction results which indicate different possibilities of the future population. The prediction given by the global minimum point is regarded as the most possible one, and simultaneously the predictions given by other local minima of $\alpha$ are also noteworthy. We conduct numerous studies and get the following predictions of Oceanian population.

## 15.3   Prediction of Oceanian Population

After the neuronet is trained by the 1000-year population data of Oceania, we get the result that $\alpha = 0.014$ is the global minimum point. Since it has the minimum testing error among all values of $\alpha$, the corresponding prediction can be seen as the most possible one. The corresponding results of the neuronet simulation with $\alpha = 0.014$ are shown in Fig. 15.1. From Fig. 15.1(a), we can see that the neuronet output is very similar to the historical data which indicates that the neuronet is well trained. Besides, the prediction result of Chebyshev-activation neuronet with WASD algorithm is shown in Fig. 15.1(b), and the numerical results of prediction from 2014 to 2020 are listed in Table 15.1. According to them, the population of Oceania will keep increasing with a relatively steady rate in the coming 15 years and reach 42.416 million in 2020. Given that the result is produced by the global minimum point, we regard it as the most possible prediction.

### 15.3.1   More possible prediction results

As previously stated, the global minimum point is not the only point that could make suitable prediction. The testing errors of local minimum points in Appendix I to this chapter, though greater than the global minimum one, are still relatively small among other values of $\alpha$, which indicates that the prediction results based on them are also considerable and may be valid. For instance, we choose different values of $\alpha$ (i.e., 0.014, 0.03, 0.02 and 0.012) and show their typical predictions. The results are in Fig. 15.2 and Fig. 15.3.

It is worth pointing out that, to make the presentation of results more pellucid and obvious, the neuronet predictions are further compared with UN's predictions [162]. From Fig. 15.2 and Fig.

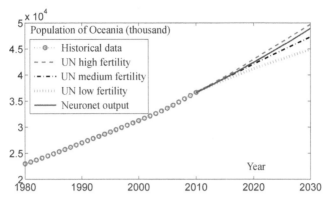

(a) Using $\alpha = 0.014$ (global minimum point)

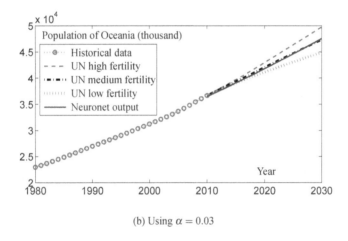

(b) Using $\alpha = 0.03$

**FIGURE 15.2**: Different prediction results of Oceanian population via Chebyshev-activation neuronet with WASD algorithm using $\alpha = 0.014$ and $\alpha = 0.03$.

15.3, we can find that, although the growth rates corresponding to different values of $\alpha$ differ, all the predictions are similar in trend (i.e., the increasing trend in the next 15 years or even longer). According to the comparison of the predictions with UN's predictions [162], all predictions indicate that the population of Oceania will keep growing. The trend similarity between the neuronet's and the UN's predictions indicates the rationality and validity of Chebyshev-activation neuronet with WASD algorithm.

Moreover, compared with the UN's predictions, Chebyshev-activation neuronet with WASD algorithm gives many possible results (i.e., the predictions via the global minimum point and local minimum points) rather than a vague range based on fertility and other assumptions. On the other hand, although the prediction results are all indicating a growth of the population, there are some slight differences between them. Using the UN's predictions as references, we find that the results of Fig. 15.2 and Fig. 15.3 are different in terms of growth rate. Specifically, (1) the predictions of Fig. 15.2(a) and Fig. 15.3(b) are similar to the UN's high-variant prediction; (2) the prediction of Fig. 15.2(b) is similar to the UN's medium-variant prediction, and the two predictions are nearly overlapped; and (3) the prediction of Fig. 15.3(a) is between the UN's high-variant and medium-

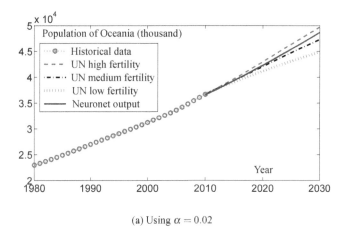

(a) Using $\alpha = 0.02$

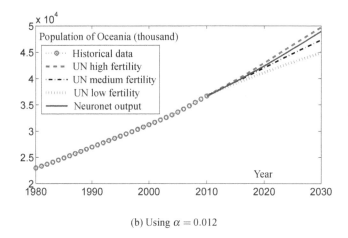

(b) Using $\alpha = 0.012$

**FIGURE 15.3**: Different prediction results of Oceanian population via Chebyshev-activation neuronet with WASD algorithm using $\alpha = 0.02$ and $\alpha = 0.012$.

variant predictions. Based on the comparative results, the predictions made by Chebyshev-activation neuronet with WASD algorithm are acceptable and effective.

To make the results more reliable and convincing, some extra evaluations of Chebyshev-activation neuronet with WASD algorithm are conducted. Owing to the fact that the future population data is unknown, we cannot use them to validate our predictions. But we can use the historical data to inspect and verify. For instance, we use the historical population data from years 1000 to 1999 to train the neuronet and then make predictions for years 2000 to 2013. The actual population data from years 2000 to 2013 are known and thus used to test the predicting ability of Chebyshev-activation neuronet with WASD algorithm. The evaluation results are shown in Table 15.2, where the "Year" in the table means the last year of the neuronet training. For example, year "2001" means that we use the population data interval $[1000, 2001]$ to train the neuronet and use the interval $[2002, 2013]$ to compute the testing error of prediction. It is worthy noting that all the prediction intervals end at 2013.

From Table 15.2, we can find that all the testing errors of prediction are relatively small, which indicates the excellent prediction ability of Chebyshev-activation neuronet with WASD algorithm. Besides, the more population data the neuronet is trained with, the smaller the errors are (in other

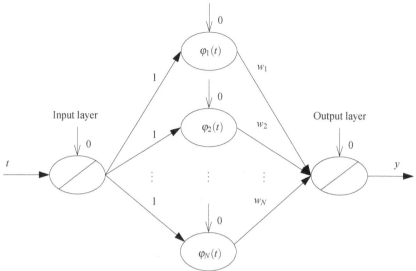

**FIGURE 15.4**: Model structure of three-layer Chebyshev-activation neuronet for learning and prediction of Oceanian population.

words, the more precise the predictions are). This fact shows that the training procedures of the neuronet are valid and credible; and thus manifests that Chebyshev-activation neuronet with WASD algorithm in predicting the population is convincing and effective. In addition, note that, for the most possible prediction shown in Fig. 15.2(a) (corresponding to the global minimum point), the testing error of prediction is 0.02745% (where year 2010 is used as the last year of the neuronet training, and thus the interval $[2011, 2013]$ is used for the prediction-type testing).

### 15.3.2 Further discussion

Using Chebyshev-activation neuronet with WASD algorithm, the predictions of Oceanian population are successfully produced. Rather than giving a vague range of the future population, the goal of our prediction is to give several predictions of high possibility. As mentioned before, many governments make and adjust their policies according to the received predictions. The policies made by a vague and wide range of population prediction, though rounded, may additionally cost a huge amount of money and resources. It is obviously more reasonable and economical to process the accurate high-possibility predictions in priority. That is the reason why we give the numerically specific predictions of different possibilities (especially the most possible one) rather than a possible vague and wide range.

Furthermore, different from the traditional approaches, Chebyshev-activation neuronet with WASD algorithm does not need to make any assumptions on fertility, mortality, etc. With too many man made factors added to the predictions, the objectivity of the results may be weakened and even lead to inaccuracy. To avoid the hidden errors introduced by the man made factors, Chebyshev-activation neuronet with WASD algorithm just focuses on the historical population data. Owing to the fact that the historical data contain the overall internal mechanism of the population system, they (i.e., the data) are the most direct indicator of all the factors which have impacts on the population

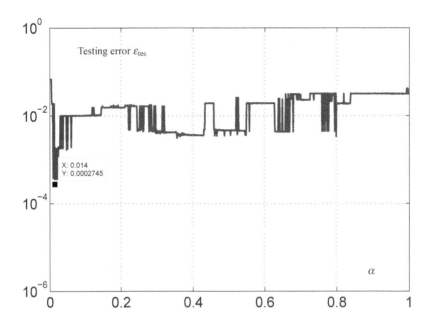

**FIGURE 15.5**: Testing error of Oceanian population prediction via Chebyshev-activation neuronet with WASD algorithm using $\alpha = 0.014$ (global minimum point).

changing. The study based on historical population data with fewer assumptions should be more reliable and effective.

Despite the difference of growth rate, the predictions made by Chebyshev-activation neuronet with WASD algorithm all indicate the increase of Oceanian population. The prediction comparison between the UN and the neuronet shows the validity of the presented neuronet. As we know, Australia occupies the largest portion of Oceanian population, which means that Australia has a big impact on Oceanian population. We are thus not surprised at the potential increase of the population of Oceania. Specifically, in order to attract more immigrants, the Australia government has changed its immigration policy to be immigrant-friendly and thus may lead to a remarkable growth in the population of Oceania, which matches up with our predictions and supports the rationality of neuronet [187].

## 15.4 Chapter Summary

With numerical studies on function data approximation and prediction shown in Appendix J to this chapter, the three-layer feed-forward neuronet equipped with the WASD algorithm can further predict the population of Oceania reasonably and effectively. Not to replace the cohort-component prediction algorithm, this chapter is intended to predict the total population on the basis of the available historical total-population data. So, we do not require the information about age structure, spatial distribution or sex distribution that may be missing, and this detachment is actually an advantage of our proposed method. By exploiting Chebyshev-activation neuronet with WASD algorithm,

**TABLE 15.3:** Oceanian historical population data from 1000 AD to 2013 AD.

| Year | 1000 | 1100 | 1200 | 1300 | 1400 | 1500 | 1600 |
|---|---|---|---|---|---|---|---|
| Data (thousand) | 1478 | 1524 | 1575 | 1631 | 1694 | 1765 | 1837 |
| Year | 1700 | 1800 | 1850 | 1900 | 1950 | 1951 | 1952 |
| Data (thousand) | 1936 | 1953 | 1976 | 5676 | 12675 | 12996 | 13294 |
| Year | 1953 | 1954 | 1955 | 1956 | 1957 | 1958 | 1959 |
| Data (thousand) | 13582 | 13871 | 14167 | 14474 | 14792 | 15118 | 15448 |
| Year | 1960 | 1961 | 1962 | 1963 | 1964 | 1965 | 1966 |
| Data (thousand) | 15775 | 16100 | 16424 | 16757 | 17111 | 17494 | 17909 |
| Year | 1967 | 1968 | 1969 | 1970 | 1971 | 1972 | 1973 |
| Data (thousand) | 18351 | 18805 | 19253 | 19681 | 20084 | 20466 | 20827 |
| Year | 1974 | 1975 | 1976 | 1977 | 1978 | 1979 | 1980 |
| Data (thousand) | 21168 | 21492 | 21795 | 22081 | 22361 | 22653 | 22968 |
| Year | 1981 | 1982 | 1983 | 1984 | 1985 | 1986 | 1987 |
| Data (thousand) | 23310 | 23678 | 24066 | 24466 | 24872 | 25284 | 25702 |
| Year | 1988 | 1989 | 1990 | 1991 | 1992 | 1993 | 1994 |
| Data (thousand) | 26125 | 26548 | 26969 | 27388 | 27803 | 28217 | 28633 |
| Year | 1995 | 1996 | 1997 | 1998 | 1999 | 2000 | 2001 |
| Data (thousand) | 29052 | 29476 | 29905 | 30339 | 30779 | 31224 | 31672 |
| Year | 2002 | 2003 | 2004 | 2005 | 2006 | 2007 | 2008 |
| Data (thousand) | 32125 | 32593 | 33090 | 33623 | 34198 | 34808 | 35437 |
| Year | 2009 | 2010 | 2011 | 2012 | 2013 | | |
| Data (thousand) | 36059 | 36659 | 37136 | 37703 | 38289 | | |

we have the final prediction result that the population of Oceania will increase steadily in the coming 15 years and Oceania will be a new area with growing population of the world. As a future research direction, we may exploit such a neuronet or its variants to conduct and present more predictions of other areas if possible. Note that the Oceanian population data from 2014 to 2017 (the time that we prepared this chapter in the book) in WPP 2017 [167] are 38970 thousand, 39542 thousand, 40117 thousand and 40690 thousand, respectively. For the convenience of readers, the above population data can be used to further compare with the population prediction results reported in this chapter.

---

## Appendix G: Historical Data of Oceania from 1000 AD to 2013 AD for Learning and Testing

Based on the past 1000-year data, Chebyshev-activation neuronet with WASD algorithm is constructed and investigated in this chapter for the prediction of the Oceanian population. The data from 1000 AD to 1900 AD are from [198]; the data from 1950 to 2010 are from [162]; and the data from 2011 to 2013 are from [187]. For completeness and further investigation, these data are presented in Table 15.3.

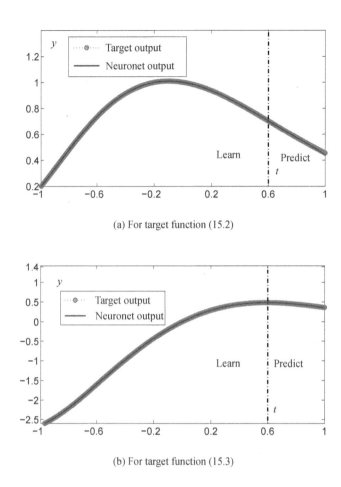

(a) For target function (15.2)

(b) For target function (15.3)

**FIGURE 15.6**: Approximation and prediction results of Chebyshev-activation neuronet with WASD algorithm for target functions (15.2) and (15.3).

## Appendix H: Model Structure of Chebyshev-Activation Neuronet for Prediction of Oceanian Population

As mentioned in this chapter, a three-layer feed-forward Chebyshev-activation neuronet is applied to the prediction of the Oceanian population. For completeness and for better understanding, the model structure of such a neuronet is shown in Fig. 15.4, where $t$ denotes the model input and $y$ denotes the model output. We show the structure of the three-layer feed-forward neuronet, where the neurons of the hidden layer are activated by Chebyshev polynomials, i.e., $\varphi_j$ (with $j = 1, 2, \cdots, N$). All the connecting weights from the input layer to the hidden layer are fixed to be 1. Besides, the connecting weights from the hidden layer to the output layer, denoted as $w_j$, need to be determined or adjusted. Moreover, while guaranteeing the effectiveness of the neuronet, all neuronal thresholds are fixed to be 0, and these settings can simplify the complexities of the neuronet structure design, analysis and computation [176].

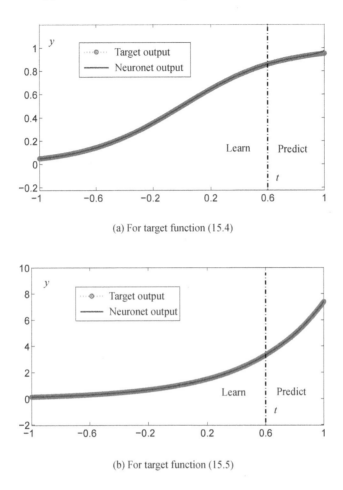

(a) For target function (15.4)

(b) For target function (15.5)

**FIGURE 15.7**: Approximation and prediction results of Chebyshev-activation neuronet with WASD algorithm for target functions (15.4) and (15.5).

## Appendix I: Evaluation of Prediction Ability with Different $\alpha$

Note that the time interval $[1000, 2013]$ needs to be normalized to the interval $[0, \alpha]$ with the normalization factor $\alpha \in (0, 1)$. The learning and prediction performances of the neuronets with different values of $\alpha$ are shown in Fig. 15.5 via testing error.

Before Chebyshev-activation neuronet is used for prediction, the neuronet needs to be trained by the historical population data. Thus, we give $\{(t_i, p_i)|_{i=1}^{M}\}$ as the data-set for the training of the neuronet, where $M$ denotes the total number of sample pairs. For the $i$th sample pair, $t_i \in \mathbb{R}$ denotes the input and $p_i \in \mathbb{R}$ denotes the historical data (i.e., the target output). While training the neuronet, the input and output of the neuronet correspond to the date (e.g., 1995 AD) and population (e.g., 29052 thousand) data, respectively. To make the neuronet well trained and to reach the best neuronet structure, we define the mean square error (MSE) as follows:

$$e = \frac{1}{M} \sum_{i=1}^{M} \left( p_i - \sum_{k=1}^{N} w_k \varphi_k(t_i) \right)^2, \tag{15.1}$$

**TABLE 15.4:** Approximation and prediction results of Chebyshev-activation neuronet with WASD algorithm for target functions (15.2) through (15.5).

| Target function | (15.2) | (15.3) | (15.4) | (15.5) |
|---|---|---|---|---|
| $e_{min}$ | $2.2157 \times 10^{-19}$ | $2.4100 \times 10^{-23}$ | $1.1166 \times 10^{-19}$ | $1.8624 \times 10^{-23}$ |
| $\varepsilon_{pre}^{1}$ | $5.3281 \times 10^{-13}$ | $3.8905 \times 10^{-20}$ | $3.7015 \times 10^{-13}$ | $3.6589 \times 10^{-20}$ |
| $\varepsilon_{pre}^{2}$ | $1.5097 \times 10^{-9}$ | $1.2974 \times 10^{-17}$ | $1.5739 \times 10^{-9}$ | $1.1547 \times 10^{-17}$ |
| $\varepsilon_{pre}^{3}$ | $5.6031 \times 10^{-7}$ | $9.6216 \times 10^{-16}$ | $7.6225 \times 10^{-7}$ | $8.5938 \times 10^{-16}$ |
| $\varepsilon_{pre}^{4}$ | $7.1318 \times 10^{-5}$ | $3.2785 \times 10^{-14}$ | $1.1750 \times 10^{-4}$ | $2.9550 \times 10^{-14}$ |

where $e$ represents the MSE value when the number of hidden-layer neurons is $N$. Based on $e$, the optimal weights and structure of the neuronet are determined by the WASD algorithm. For detailed description of WASD algorithm, please refer to [176].

After the neuronet being well trained, we can evaluate its prediction performance by using the whole data-set of Oceanian population, i.e., the data-set $\{(t_i, p_i)|_{t_i=1000}^{2013}\}$. It is worth pointing out that the data $\{(t_i, p_i)|_{t_i=1000}^{2010}\}$ are used for the neuronet learning, while the data $\{(t_i, p_i)|_{t_i=2011}^{2013}\}$ are used for the neuronet testing. The testing error that is exploited to evaluate the prediction performance of the neuronet is defined as follows:

$$\varepsilon_{tes} = \frac{1}{H} \sum_{m=1}^{H} \left| \frac{y_m - p_m}{p_m} \right|,$$

where $H$ is the total number of the data for testing (specifically, $H = 3$ in this research), and $y_m$ denotes the $m$th neuronet output corresponding to the input $t_m$. Generally speaking, the smaller testing error $\varepsilon_{tes}$ is, the better prediction performance of the neuronet achieves.

The normalization factor $\alpha$ and its corresponding testing error $\varepsilon_{tes}$ are shown in Fig. 15.5. As seen from the figure, most of the testing errors are relatively small, which results from the optimal structure of the neuronet achieved. Moreover, the $\alpha$ with the smallest testing error, which is the global minimum point, indicates the most possible situation for the Oceanian population prediction. Except for the global minimum point, the local minimum points in Fig. 15.5 represent other possible prediction results. Using the global minimum point and local minimum points, the corresponding predictions of Oceanian population can thus be made.

# Appendix J: Numerical Studies of Function Data Approximation and Prediction via Chebyshev-Activation Neuronet

To test the function data approximation and prediction ability of Chebyshev-activation neuronet with WASD algorithm, the following four target functions as examples are used for verification and illustration:

$$f(x) = \frac{1}{(1.2 + x)^x}, \tag{15.2}$$

$$f(x) = \frac{\sin(1.8x)}{\exp(x)}, \tag{15.3}$$

$$f(x) = \frac{1}{1 + 20^{-x}}, \tag{15.4}$$

$$f(x) = \exp(2x). \tag{15.5}$$

For all the target functions above, we use the interval $[-1, 0.6]$ to generate the data-set

$\{(t_i, p_i)|_{i=1}^{1601}\}$ (with $f = p$ and $x = t$ for target functions to generate the data-set) for the approximation. Additionally, the neuronet will generate the data-set $\{(t_i, y_i)|_{i=1}^{800}\}$ corresponding to the interval $(0.6, 1]$.

The detailed results of the function data approximation and prediction ability of Chebyshev-activation neuronet with WASD algorithm are shown in Table 15.4, Fig. 15.6 and Fig. 15.7. Note that $e_{min}$ represents the minimum MSE corresponding to the optimal hidden-layer neuron numbers. In addition, $\varepsilon_{pre}^1$, $\varepsilon_{pre}^2$, $\varepsilon_{pre}^3$ and $\varepsilon_{pre}^4$ denote the prediction errors for intervals $(0.6, 0.7]$, $(0.7, 0.8]$, $(0.8, 0.9]$ and $(0.9, 1]$, respectively. From Table 15.4, we can find that the minimum errors (i.e., $e_{min}$) for function approximation are tiny, which shows the excellent approximation ability of Chebyshev-activation neuronet with WASD algorithm. With the optimal structure (i.e., the structure corresponding to $e_{min}$), the neuronet can be used for function prediction on the interval $(0.6, 1]$. As shown in Table 15.4, the prediction errors for nearby predicting interval, e.g., $(0.6, 0.7]$, are tiny, and thus indicating the superior prediction ability of the neuronet. Moreover, from Fig. 15.6 and Fig. 15.7 we can see the excellent prediction performance of Chebyshev-activation neuronet with WASD algorithm visually.

# Chapter 16

## Application to Northern American Population Prediction

The recovery and prediction of Northern American population data, which are closely related to the future development of Northern America and even the whole world, have become significant subjects and captured great attention among sociologists as well as scientists. However, most of the relevant researches are just based on fertility, mortality or other individual quantifiable factors by traditional statistical models and thus lack all-sidedness in their results. As we know, the historical population data are the comprehensive reflection of the population development under the influence of all factors. In this chapter, based on the past 513-year population data, a feed-forward neuronet equipped with the weights-and-structure-determination (WASD) algorithm is thus constructed for the recovery and prediction of Northern American population data. Besides, the neuronet is activated by a group of Chebyshev polynomials of Class 1, which is named Chebyshev-activation neuronet in this chapter. Moreover, the optimal normalization factor is found and utilized to improve the neuronet's performance. Due to the marvelous learning and generalization abilities of the presented Chebyshev-activation neuronet, we recover the missing population data from 1500 AD to 1950 AD as well as draw up the Northern American population prediction for the next few decades.

## 16.1    Introduction

The population of Northern America has changed a lot since 1500 AD. According to the relevant researches [199, 200], Northern American population is over 350 million in 2013 AD, being hundreds of times larger than the population in 1500 AD. In fact, the size of the population always makes a great impact on political, economic and other aspects of society. Northern America is such a region that occupies an important position in the world consisting of two influential and powerful developed countries (i.e., Canada and the United States) and other countries (i.e., Bermuda,

Greenland, Saint-Pierre and Miquelon). The historical population data are significant sources for historical overview of Northern America and can reflect the evolutionary history of the continent. So it is meaningful to recover the missing population data of Northern America, which means to recover the actually existing but non-recorded data, from 1500 AD to 1950 AD. Besides, the proper prediction of population growth is an important decision factor for governments' policies, like immigration policy and education policy. Therefore, researches on recovery and prediction of Northern American population data have attracted the great attention of sociologists and scientists in the relevant fields, and thus have become a significant subject.

In previous researches, recovery and prediction of Northern American population data were investigated by using some traditional statistical methods, based on fertility, mortality, immigration, emigration and/or other several quantifiable factors [201, 202]. However, the Northern American population is also actually affected by many factors which are hard to be quantified, such as culture, wars, policies and some sudden disasters. Ignoring such key factors may make the results hard to ensure their comprehensiveness, and even lead to substantial deviation from the actual situation. As realized, the general regularity of population development could be found in a large number of historical population data, which makes historical data the significant foundation in recovery and prediction. In other words, the historical data are the comprehensive reflection of the population development under the influence of all factors (explicit and implicit), and thus are the significant foundation in population research. In order to make recovery and prediction more efficient and closer to the general regularity of population development, a model considering all influencing factors explicitly or implicitly should be built on the basis of enough historical population data.

Due to the remarkable features, such as approximation, generalization and adaptive self-learning capability, artificial neuronets (AN) have attracted considerable attention as candidates for novel computational systems in recent years [203–205]. Through the development of over 50 years, various AN have been developed and applied widely in many scientific and engineering fields [2–4, 56, 197]. Especially, with the simple structure, the feedforward neuronets are first devised and applied in more widely practical fields.

In this chapter, by supplying historical population data from 1500 AD to 2013 AD (i.e., spanning 513 years) of Northern America, a three-layer feedforward neuronet is constructed for the recovery and prediction of Northern American population data. According to the theory of function approximation and polynomial interpolation, linearly independent or orthogonal polynomials can be used as activation functions of hidden-layer neurons to construct polynomial neuronets [166]. Our previous works [2–4, 203] have investigated the neuronet performances of different groups of activation functions, and substantiated that Chebyshev polynomials of Class 1 as the activation functions have excellent performance. To guarantee the efficacy and accuracy of recovery and prediction results, a group of Chebyshev polynomials of Class 1 are thus applied in this chapter.

This chapter is organized as follows. We first briefly introduce the weights-and-structure-determination (WASD) neuronet model, which is derived from the error back-propagation (BP) neuronet. Then the numerical tests are conducted to show the outstanding learning capacity of Chebyshev-activation neuronet. Moreover, the numerical studies for the recovery and prediction of Northern American population data are conducted, with the relevant results well illustrated. Finally, based on the results, we have a further discussion about the Northern American population.

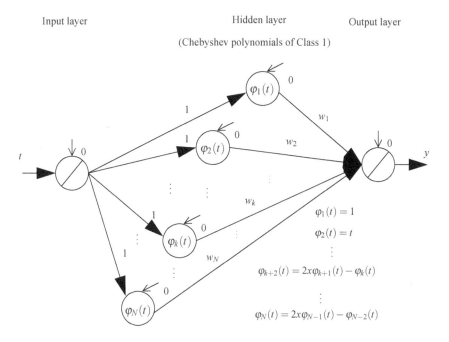

**FIGURE 16.1**: Model structure and activation functions of Chebyshev-activation neuronet.

## 16.2 Neuronet Model and WASD Algorithm

For better understanding the neuronet model, the structure of the constructed Chebyshev-activation neuronet is shown in Fig. 16.1. In the neuronet, the hidden layer has $N$ neurons activated by a group of Chebyshev polynomials $\varphi_k(t)$, with $k = 1, 2, \cdots, N$ and $N \geq 2$. Besides, the input layer or the output layer of Chebyshev-activation neuronet each has a neuron activated by the linear function. In order to simplify the neuronet model as well as its complexities of computation and analysis, we design that the connecting weights from the input-layer neuron to the hidden-layer neurons are all fixed to be 1. In addition, we use $\{w_1, \cdots, w_N\}$, which are to be decided or adjusted, to denote the connecting weights from the hidden-layer neurons to the output-layer neuron. It is also important to point out that thresholds of the neuronet are all set to be zero [129, 176].

For a three-layer neuronet, its performance can be greatly affected by the number of hidden-layer neurons. Specifically, too few hidden-layer neurons may fail to achieve the expected learning accuracy, while excess hidden-layer neurons may lead to over-fitting phenomenon, poor generalization and high computational complexity. On the basis of the analysis above, the WASD algorithm is thus presented for Chebyshev-activation neuronet [129, 176].

For further discussion, we offer $\{(t_i, p_i)|_{i=1}^M\}$ as the training data-set of Chebyshev-activation neuronet, where $t_i$ denotes the $i$th input and $p_i$ denotes the $i$th desired output (or to say, the $i$th target output). Please note that $M$ denotes the quantity of sample pairs in the data-set for the training of Chebyshev-activation neuronet. It should also be mentioned that, in this chapter, when Chebyshev-activation neuronet equipped with the WASD algorithm is applied to recovering and predicting Northern American population data, the input corresponds to the year and the output corresponds to the population data. Besides, the optimal weight vector $\mathbf{w} = [w_1, \cdots, w_N]^T \in \mathbb{R}^N$ can then be determined as

$$\mathbf{w} = (\Psi^T \Psi)^{-1} \Psi^T \mathbf{p} = \text{pinv}(\Psi)\mathbf{p}, \tag{16.1}$$

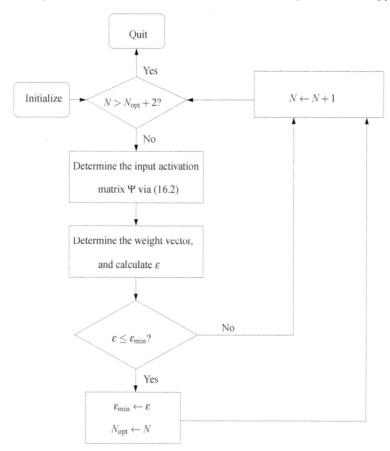

**FIGURE 16.2**: Flowchart of WASD algorithm for Chebyshev-activation neuronet.

where superscript $^T$ means the transpose operator, pinv($\Psi$) means the pseudoinverse of matrix $\Psi$, and the input activation matrix $\Psi$ is defined as

$$
\Psi = \begin{bmatrix}
\varphi_1(t_1) & \varphi_2(t_1) & \cdots & \varphi_N(t_1) \\
\varphi_1(t_2) & \varphi_2(t_2) & \cdots & \varphi_N(t_2) \\
\vdots & \vdots & \ddots & \vdots \\
\varphi_1(t_M) & \varphi_2(t_M) & \cdots & \varphi_N(t_M)
\end{bmatrix} \in \mathbb{R}^{M \times N}. \tag{16.2}
$$

The mean relative error (i.e., $\varepsilon$) for Chebyshev-activation neuronet with $N$ hidden-layer neurons, which is used to evaluate the performance of the neuronet, is defined correspondingly as follows:

$$
\varepsilon = \frac{1}{M} \sum_{i=1}^{M} \left| \frac{p_i - \sum_{k=1}^{N} w_k \varphi_k(t_i)}{p_i} \right|. \tag{16.3}
$$

The related $\varepsilon$ for Chebyshev-activation neuronet with a fixed number of hidden-layer neurons can be calculated via (16.3), and thus the relationship between mean relative error and the number of hidden-layer neurons can be determined by increasing the number of hidden-layer neurons one-by-one. So the WASD algorithm is developed to determine the optimal structure of Chebyshev-activation neuronet. The brief description of WASD algorithm is shown in Fig. 16.2. Note that, in the "Initialize" part, $N$ and $N_{\text{opt}}$ are both set to be 2. Besides, based on the formulations shown in Fig. 16.1, the expressions of such two initial hidden-layer neurons correspond to the first two

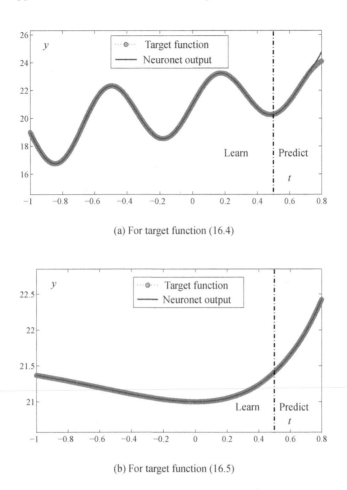

(a) For target function (16.4)

(b) For target function (16.5)

**FIGURE 16.3**: Approximation and prediction results of Chebyshev-activation neuronet with WASD algorithm for target functions (16.4) and (16.5).

formulations in Chebyshev polynomials of Class 1. In addition, $\varepsilon_{\min}$ should be initialized as large as possible; for example, in MATLAB running environment, it is set to be "inf" (i.e., infinity).

The WASD algorithm can determine directly the weights connecting the hidden-layer neurons and the output-layer neuron, and obtain automatically the optimal structure of Chebyshev-activation neuronet, i.e., the optimal number of neurons in the hidden layer. Therefore, Chebyshev-activation neuronet equipped with the WASD algorithm has excellent performance on learning and prediction, and can be used for our such research.

## 16.3    Numerical Studies and Population Prediction

In this chapter, based on the 513-year historical population data, a Chebyshev-activation neuronet equipped with the WASD algorithm is constructed for the recovery and prediction of Northern American population. Before giving the detailed results, some numerical tests are first made to

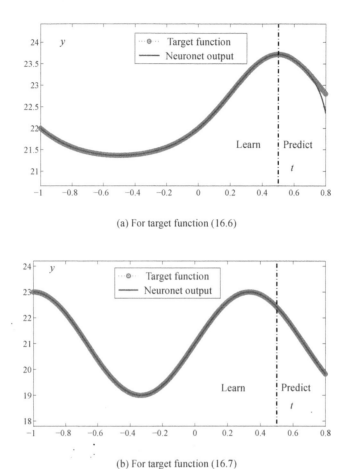

(a) For target function (16.6)

(b) For target function (16.7)

**FIGURE 16.4**: Approximation and prediction results of Chebyshev-activation neuronet with WASD algorithm for target functions (16.6) and (16.7).

substantiate the excellent performance of Chebyshev-activation neuronet equipped with the WASD algorithm in terms of recovery and prediction.

### 16.3.1 Numerical studies

To well illustrate the efficacy of Chebyshev-activation neuronet equipped with the WASD algorithm on recovery and prediction, a variety of target functions are used to make numerical tests. Due to result similarity, the test results are given only for the following four target functions (with $x \in [-1, 1]$), which show obvious differences between each other:

$$f(x) = 2\sin(3\pi x)\exp(-0.3x) + 2x + 21, \tag{16.4}$$

$$f(x) = x^2 \exp(x) + 21, \tag{16.5}$$

$$f(x) = \exp(\sin(\pi x)) + 21, \tag{16.6}$$

$$f(x) = 2\sin(1.5\pi x) + 21. \tag{16.7}$$

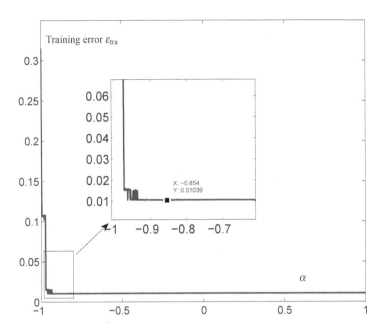

**FIGURE 16.5**: Relationship between normalization factor $\alpha$ and training error $\varepsilon_{\text{tra}}$ of Chebyshev-activation neuronet with optimal structure.

Note that all the numerical studies shown in this chapter are performed on a personal digital computer with a CPU of Pentium(R) Dual-Core E5300 @2.60GHZ and 2GB memory.

For the target functions shown above, we sample uniformly over the region $[-1, 0.5]$ with the step being 0.001 to generate data-set $\{(t_i, p_i)|_{i=1}^{1500}\}$ as the training set for Chebyshev-activation neuronet (with $p = f$ and $x = t$ for target functions to generate the data-set). Besides, for testing the prediction ability, another data-set $\{(t_i, p_i)|_{i=1}^{1000}\}$ is generated by sampling uniformly over the untrained region $(0.5, 1]$ with the gap size being 0.0005. The numerical results for the approximation and prediction of the target function are shown in Fig. 16.3 and Fig. 16.4. By comparing the target outputs with the neuronet outputs in Figs. 16.3 and 16.4, it can be observed that the neuronet outputs learn the target outputs well in both the approximation and prediction regions for all these different functions, which thus substantiates that Chebyshev-activation neuronet has excellent abilities on recovery and prediction.

### 16.3.2 Data normalization

According to the analysis above, Chebyshev-activation neuronet equipped with the WASD algorithm is a good choice to recover and predict the Northern American population data. For Chebyshev polynomials of Class 1, the domain of input data is $[-1, 1]$, so it is necessary to make the normalization of the data at first. In this chapter, the time interval $[1500, 2013]$ is normalized to the interval $[-1, \alpha]$, with the normalization factor $\alpha$ belonging to $(-1, 1)$. During our research, it is found out that, while using different $\alpha$, the corresponding recovery and prediction results are different, which means that the values of $\alpha$ affect the performances of Chebyshev-activation neuronet on the Northern American population data recovery and prediction.

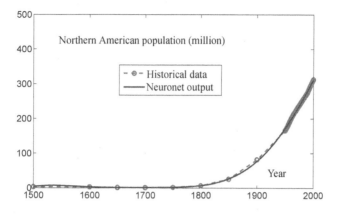

(a) Population data recovery from 1500 AD to 1950 AD

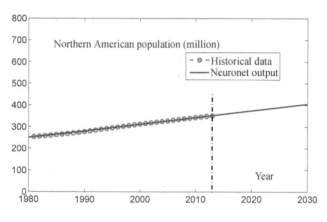

(b) Population data prediction in the next 15 years

**FIGURE 16.6**: Northern American population data recovery and prediction results of Chebyshev-activation neuronet with WASD algorithm.

To determine the best suitable normalization factor $\alpha$ and ensure the best performance of Chebyshev-activation neuronet, we make a numerical study to find out the relationship between the normalization factor $\alpha$ and the training error of Chebyshev-activation neuronet with the optimal structure. When the data normalization interval is $[-1, \alpha]$, the training error (i.e., $\varepsilon_{\text{tra}}$) of Chebyshev-activation neuronet equipped with the WASD algorithm is defined as

$$\varepsilon_{\text{tra}} = \frac{1}{M} \sum_{i=1}^{M} \left| \frac{y_i - p_i}{p_i} \right|, \tag{16.8}$$

where, again, $p_i$ denotes the $i$th target output and $y_i$ denotes the $i$th actual output of Chebyshev-activation neuronet. The set of normalization factor $\alpha$ is generated by sampling uniformly over the region $[-0.999, 0.999]$ with the gap size being 0.001. The corresponding training error $\varepsilon_{\text{tra}}$ can be calculated via (16.8). The results are displayed in Fig. 16.5, which clearly show the relationship between the normalization factor $\alpha$ and the training error $\varepsilon_{\text{tra}}$.

From the figure, the global minimum point is determined to be $\alpha_{\text{glo}} = -0.854$, which corresponds to the most possible result of the Northern American population learning and prediction via

**TABLE 16.1:** Part of recovered Northern American population data from 1500 AD to 1950 AD.

| Year | 1500 | 1505 | 1510 | 1515 | 1520 | 1525 | 1530 |
|---|---|---|---|---|---|---|---|
| Population (million) | 3.005 | 4.269 | 5.251 | 5.986 | 6.506 | 6.839 | 7.013 |
| Year | **1534** | 1535 | 1540 | 1545 | 1550 | 1560 | 1590 |
| Population (million) | **7.055** | 7.054 | 6.982 | 6.819 | 6.583 | 5.957 | 3.694 |
| Year | 1600 | 1630 | 1650 | **1671** | 1690 | 1700 | 1730 |
| Population (million) | 3.021 | 1.633 | 1.227 | **1.113** | 1.161 | 1.215 | 1.503 |
| Year | 1750 | 1800 | 1830 | 1850 | 1900 | 1930 | 1950 |
| Population (million) | 1.985 | 7.084 | 16.300 | 26.970 | 77.300 | 128.400 | 172.200 |

**TABLE 16.2:** Prediction results of Northern American population in the next few decades.

| Year | 2015 | 2016 | 2017 | 2018 | 2019 | 2020 | 2021 | 2022 | 2023 |
|---|---|---|---|---|---|---|---|---|---|
| Population (million) | 358.6 | 361.7 | 364.9 | 368 | 371.1 | 374.2 | 377.4 | 380.5 | 383.6 |
| Year | 2024 | 2025 | 2026 | 2027 | 2030 | 2035 | 2040 | 2045 | 2050 |
| Population (million) | 386.7 | 389.8 | 392.9 | 395.9 | 405.1 | 420.2 | 434.8 | 448.9 | 462.5 |

Chebyshev-activation neuronet equipped with the WASD algorithm; and the minimal training error $\varepsilon_{\text{tra}} = 0.01039$ (i.e., 1.039%), which also shows the great learning performance of this Chebyshev-activation neuronet model. So we choose $\alpha_{\text{glo}} = -0.854$ as the normalization factor for Chebyshev-activation neuronet to recover and predict the population data of Northern America in the following parts.

### 16.3.3 Recovery and prediction of population data

To recover and predict the population data of Northern America, we use Chebyshev-activation neuronet equipped with the WASD algorithm, which is based on the historical data of the Northern American population from 1500 AD to 2013 AD. With $\alpha_{\text{glo}} = -0.854$ as the normalization factor, the time interval $[1500, 2013]$ is normalized to the interval $[-1, \alpha_{\text{glo}}]$, and then the training set $\{(t_i, p_i)|_{i=1}^{M}\}$ is generated. By applying the training set to the neuronet presented above, the recovery and prediction results are generated and shown in Fig. 16.6.

As seen from Fig. 16.6(a), Chebyshev-activation neuronet equipped with the WASD algorithm completes the population data which was missing (or to say, had not been recorded in detail) from 1500 AD to 1950 AD. The recovery results indicate the brief population development situation from 1500 AD to 1950 AD. Specifically, Northern American population increased in the early 16th century, and then decreased; i.e., had a fluctuation. The population fluctuation lasted over 171 years, and finally the population kept increasing. The detailed data can be seen from Table 16.1. Besides, the prediction result shown in Fig. 16.6(b) indicates that the trend of the Northern American population in the next 15 years is increasing steadily. The detailed prediction population data from 2015 AD to 2050 AD is further shown in Table 16.2.

## 16.4 Discussion

Based on the historical population data from 1500 AD to 2013 AD, we have effectively developed and applied Chebyshev-activation neuronet equipped with the WASD algorithm for the recovery of the missing population data of Northern America from 1500 AD to 1950 AD and the prediction of Northern American population in the next few decades.

As we know, because of the lack of fidelity of the statistics [200], the population of Northern America from 1500 AD to 1950 AD is uncertain and contentious, which causes great challenges for the research on the evolution and history of human population. For example, during the late 15th and 16th centuries, reports about America, including Northern America, and the people's lives there, filtered back to Europe, which was the center of the world at that time. These incomplete reports often filled with imagination instead of information are always inaccurate [206]. However, Chebyshev-activation neuronet with great generalization and adaptive learning abilities successfully fills the gap in the historical demography of Northern America. The result shows Northern American population trends from 1500 AD to 1950 AD. More specifically, from 1500 AD to 1534 AD, population kept increasing, and population was up to 7.055 million in 1534; but it then decreased throughout the next 13 decades. Since 1671, the population has turned to growth. In view of the effects of immigration, wars and other historical factors, such results are highly consistent with the course of Northern American history [200, 206]. For example, before the European found and developed Northern America in the 15th and early 16th centuries, the local people lived in tribal style, meaning that their population could maintain steady growth but was hard to reach a huge size. Such a historical information matches the results presented above. As another example, when a growing number of people, especially the European, emigrated to Northern America in the 16th century, the conflicts between these immigrants and local people broke out. The decreasing situation of the recovered population data may reflect these conflicts (such as wars for land or illness brought by immigrants). These historical records, from another aspect, actually confirm the numerical results which we have presented in this chapter.

Meanwhile, the prediction results of Northern American future population have also been shown. According to Fig. 16.6(b) and Table 16.2, Chebyshev-activation neuronet predicts that the population of Northern America keeps increasing but with a gentle growth rate in the next few decades. Comparing with the prediction model from the Department of Economic and Social Affairs of the United Nations (UN) [199], the results of these two prediction models for population development trends are similar, though there are a few differences in practice. For example, Chebyshev-activation neuronet indicates that the population will reach 405.1 million in 2030, while the prediction model from UN reports that the population in 2030 is 403.4 million. Besides, it may be realized that the prediction about the future is always full of uncertainties. However, as mentioned above, Chebyshev-activation neuronet equipped with the WASD algorithm is based on the historical population data which contain the general regularity of the human development. So the prediction results actually include the influence of all factors, both explicit and implicit, and may be more comprehensive, reasonable and acceptable than some prediction models using traditional statistical methods.

## 16.5    Chapter Summary

As a developed and impressive region in the world, Northern America deserves a detailed and intensive study, especially in terms of human evolution and population development. In this chapter, based on the historical population data from 1500 AD to 2013 AD, spanning 513 years, Chebyshev-activation neuronet equipped with the weights-and-structure-determination (WASD) algorithm has been established to recover the missing population data of Northern America from 1500 AD to 1950 AD and make the prediction for the next few decades. With this effective and innovative method, a new vision for the research on Northern American population and human evolution has been presented. The results provide useful information for further research and will be an important supplement for local governments to adopt suitable policies. Note that the Northern American population data from 2014 to 2017 (the time that we prepared this chapter in the book) in WPP 2017 [167] are 353.448 million, 356.003 million, 358.593 million and 361.207 million, respectively. For the convenience of readers, the above population data can be used to further compare with the population prediction results reported in this chapter.

# Chapter 17

# Application to Indian Subcontinent Population Prediction

The population prediction of the Indian subcontinent, which is closely related to the future development of this region and even the whole world, has caught great attention among sociologists as well as scientists. However, most of the former researches are just based on fertility, mortality or other individual quantifiable factors by using some traditional statistical models and thus may lack all-sidedness in their results. The historical population data are the comprehensive reflection of population development under the influence of all factors. Based on the historical population data over 2000 years, a feed-forward neuronet equipped with the weights-and-structure-determination (WASD) algorithm aided by twice-pruning (TP) technique is constructed. Besides, by introducing the cubic spline and error evaluation methods, the neuronet shows great performance in the population prediction. Due to the marvelous learning and generalization abilities of the presented TP-aided WASD neuronet, we successfully draw up the population prediction for the Indian subcontinent.

## 17.1 Introduction

The Indian subcontinent, which lies in South Asia, is an important and powerful region in the world. Because of its long history, unique culture and fast development in recent years, it attracts wide attention from all over the world. Among all research subjects about the Indian subcontinent, the population prediction is one of the hottest [207–209]. According to the relevant researches, population in this region is nearly up to 1600 million in 2014 AD, which is over 21 percent of the world population [210]. Moreover, the countries in the Indian subcontinent, for example, India, Pakistan, and Bangladesh, play important roles in the international affairs, because two of these countries are nuclear states. Meanwhile, conflicts among these countries draw extensive attention from the international community and cause serious impacts on regional and international security. Under the circumstances, it is meaningful and necessary to make a prediction for the population growth in this region, since population will actually affect decisions of local governments in all kinds of policies, such as economy policy, education policy and foreign policy [155].

However, most of the former researches about this subject preferred to utilize some traditional statistical methods, only based on some individual quantifiable factors, for example, fertility and mortality, to make the predictions [202, 211]. As we know, the development of population in a region is affected by many factors, including both explicit and implicit ones [212]. Besides, the historical population data, of which the quantity is large enough, are the comprehensive reflections of all influent factors. Building a model is a common and effective method for solving population problems [213, 214]. In order to make a prediction closer to the real development situation, a new model that can reflect the influence of all factors should be built. Based on the consideration above, the new model, which utilizes the historical population data as samples, is presented for making the population prediction of the Indian subcontinent.

In recent years, the neuronet, an increasingly important branch of artificial intelligence, has been widely applied to engineering and computation areas [4, 215, 216]. In order to overcome the problems existing in the traditional back-propagation algorithm, a weights-and-structure-determination (WASD) algorithm for a three-layer feed-forward neuronet was proposed in the authors' former research and has been successfully applied in many areas, such as classification and medical researches [4, 215, 216]. Such a neuronet is thus named the WASD neuronet. Moreover, according to the previous studies about WASD algorithm, the twice-pruning (TP) technique is applied to improve the performance of the WASD neuronet.

In order to make an appropriate population prediction of the Indian subcontinent, a TP-aided WASD neuronet is constructed. The input data are the historical population data from 200 BC to 2014 AD, which span over 2000 years. The activation functions of such a neuronet are the Chebyshev polynomials of Class 1. Theories of function approximation via polynomials have proved that linearly independent or orthogonal polynomials can be utilized as activation functions of hidden-layer neurons to construct polynomial neuronets. The authors' previous studies present the great performance of the WASD neuronet which utilizes Chebyshev polynomials of Class 1 as its activation functions [2, 4]. Therefore, the neuronet which is discussed utilizes Chebyshev polynomials of Class 1 as the activation functions. Besides, in order to reduce the computational complexity and improve the predicting ability of the neuronet, the neurons which are less important are pruned by using the TP technique. Moreover, some other methods, such as the cubic spline method and learning-and-predicting error evaluation method, are also introduced for getting more accurate prediction results.

The rest of the chapter is organized as follows. Firstly, the TP-aided WASD neuronet and other helpful methods which include the cubic spline method and learning-and-predicting error evaluation method, are introduced. Then the population prediction of the Indian subcontinent are conducted with results well presented and illustrated. Finally, based on the different possible prediction results, a further discussion is proposed.

---

## 17.2 Spline and Neuronet

In this section, the WASD algorithm aided by TP technique is illustrated in detail. The cubic spline method and learning-and-predicting error evaluation method are also proposed to improve

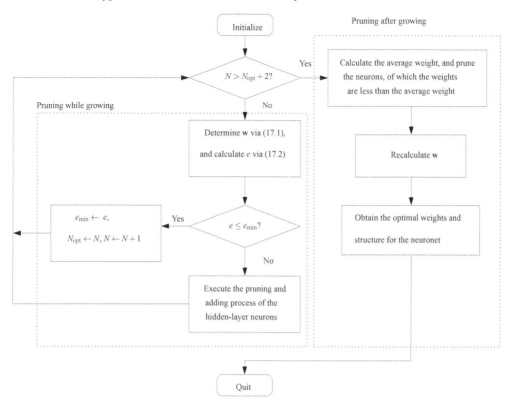

**FIGURE 17.1**: Flowchart of WASD algorithm aided by TP technique for neuronet.

the performance of the TP-aided WASD neuronet.

### 17.2.1 Cubic spline method

Before giving the detailed description of the neuronet, the cubic spline method should be mentioned at first. As we know, due to the technology limitation, war, disaster and other reasons, the population records about the Indian subcontinent in some years, especially the years before 1950 AD, are missing, which means that the population records are inconsecutive [207]. In other words, the gap between every adjacent historical data is unfixed. When these data are directly utilized as the training data-set for a neuronet, the learning abilities in different intervals of the neuronet are significantly different. Specifically, the neuronet often learns well in the intervals with small data gaps, while learns not well enough in the intervals with larger gaps.

For solving this problem and ensuring the great performance of the neuronet, the cubic spline method is applied to the data preprocessing. Since the cubic spline method can learn and restore data well [217], after getting the initial data-set $\{(t_i, p_i)|_{i=1}^{Q_1}\}$, we utilize this method to restore the missing data and then generate a new spline data-set $\{(t_i^{\mathrm{spl}}, p_i^{\mathrm{spl}})|_{i=1}^{Q_2}\}$ with a fixed and even gap between adjacent data. This new spline data-set is thus applied as the actual training data-set for the WASD neuronet. Besides, $t_i$ and $p_i$ respectively denote the $i$th initial input and the $i$th initial desired output (or to say, the $i$th initial target output), while $t_i^{\mathrm{spl}}$ and $p_i^{\mathrm{spl}}$ respectively denote the actual $i$th input and desired output for the neuronet after applying the cubic spline method. Besides, $Q_1$ and $Q_2$ represent the quantities of data pairs in the corresponding data-sets. Such a method can be easily implemented in MATLAB by using the spline function [18].

### 17.2.2    WASD algorithm aided by TP technique

Based on the above spline data-set, of which the quantity is $Q_2$ in addition to a fixed and even gap, the TP-aided WASD neuronet can thus be constructed more readily. Since the neuronet model aims at getting an ideal prediction result, in order to balance the learning and predicting performance of the neuronet, the leading $Q_3$ (with $Q_3 < Q_2$) data pairs in the spline data-set are selected to construct the learning data-set, while the rest $(Q_2 - Q_3)$ data pairs form the spline data-set to construct the predicting-testing data-set.

For better understanding the model, let us review the neuronet shown in Fig. 17.1. In such a neuronet, the quantity of the hidden-layer neurons is $N$. As mentioned, the hidden-layer neurons are activated by a group of Chebyshev polynomials denoted by $\varphi_k(t)$, with $k = 1, 2, \cdots, N$ and $N \geq 2$. Besides, the linear identity function, $h(t) = t$, is utilized as the activation function for each neuron in both input and output layers of this neuronet. In order to simplify the neuronet model as well as its complexities of computation and analysis, the connecting weights from the input-layer neuron to the hidden-layer neurons are all designed to be one. In addition, the vector $\mathbf{w} = [w_1, \cdots, w_N]^{\mathrm{T}} \in \mathbb{R}^N$ is utilized to denote the connecting weights from the hidden-layer neurons to the output-layer neuron, with its determination discussed in the ensuing part. It is also important to mention that the thresholds of the neuronet are all set to be zero [2, 4].

The partial spline data-set $\{(t_i^{\mathrm{spl}}, p_i^{\mathrm{spl}})|_{i=1}^{Q_3}\}$ is utilized as the actual learning data-set for the aforementioned neuronet. Specifically, when the TP-aided WASD neuronet is applied to the population prediction of the Indian subcontinent, the input data correspond to the year data, and the output data correspond to the population data. Then, the weight vector $\mathbf{w} = [w_1, \cdots, w_N]^{\mathrm{T}}$ can be determined as

$$\mathbf{w} = (\Psi^{\mathrm{T}}\Psi)^{-1}\Psi^{\mathrm{T}}\mathbf{p}^{\mathrm{spl}} = \mathrm{pinv}(\Psi)\mathbf{p}^{\mathrm{spl}}, \tag{17.1}$$

where superscript $^{\mathrm{T}}$ means the vector or matrix transpose operator, and $\mathrm{pinv}(\Psi)$ means the pseudoinverse of matrix $\Psi$. Besides, vector $\mathbf{p}^{\mathrm{spl}} = [p_1^{\mathrm{spl}}, p_2^{\mathrm{spl}}, \cdots, p_{Q_3}^{\mathrm{spl}}]^{\mathrm{T}} \in \mathbb{R}^{Q_3}$ corresponds to the desired outputs of the neuronet. In addition, the input activation matrix $\Psi \in \mathbb{R}^{Q_3 \times N}$ is defined as

$$\Psi = \begin{bmatrix} \varphi_1(t_1^{\mathrm{spl}}) & \cdots & \varphi_j(t_1^{\mathrm{spl}}) & \cdots & \varphi_N(t_1^{\mathrm{spl}}) \\ \varphi_1(t_2^{\mathrm{spl}}) & \cdots & \varphi_j(t_2^{\mathrm{spl}}) & \cdots & \varphi_N(t_2^{\mathrm{spl}}) \\ \vdots & \vdots & \vdots & \vdots & \vdots \\ \varphi_1(t_{Q_3}^{\mathrm{spl}}) & \cdots & \varphi_j(t_{Q_3}^{\mathrm{spl}}) & \cdots & \varphi_N(t_{Q_3}^{\mathrm{spl}}) \end{bmatrix}.$$

According to (17.1), the weight vector of the neuronet can be determined directly.

Moreover, for a three-layer neuronet, the quantity of hidden-layer neurons greatly affects its learning and predicting performance. Specifically speaking, too few hidden-layer neurons may be hard to achieve the expected learning accuracy, while excess hidden-layer neurons may lead to over-fitting phenomenon, poor generalization and high computational complexity. According to the analysis, the WASD algorithm aided by TP technique is proposed for the neuronet.

In detail, the absolute error of the root mean square form for the neuronet with $N$ hidden-layer neurons, which is applied to evaluate the performance of the neuronet in the twice-pruning process, is defined correspondingly as

$$e = \sqrt{\frac{1}{Q_3} \sum_{i=1}^{Q_3} \left( p_i^{\mathrm{spl}} - \sum_{k=1}^{N} w_k \varphi_k(t_i^{\mathrm{spl}}) \right)^2}. \tag{17.2}$$

**TABLE 17.1:** Most possible prediction results with $t_{\text{gap}} = 1$ and $\alpha = 0.992$.

| Year | 2015 | 2016 | 2017 | 2018 |
|---|---|---|---|---|
| Population (million) | 1620.32 | 1642.25 | 1665.16 | 1690.00 |
| Growth Rate (%) | 1.342 | 1.353 | 1.395 | 1.491 |
| Year | 2019 | 2020 | 2021 | 2022 |
| Population (million) | 1718.40 | 1753.18 | 1798.97 | 1863.16 |
| Growth Rate (%) | 1.681 | 2.024 | 2.611 | 3.569 |

In the first pruning (or, say, pruning while growning) subprocess, the hidden-layer neurons are selected to obtain the minimal $e$. Based on the result of the first pruning subprocess, the second pruning starts and aims at pruning the less important neurons for less computational complexity and for better predicting performance of the neuronet. The description of the WASD algorithm aided by TP technique is shown in Fig. 17.1. In the "Initialize" part, $N_{\text{opt}}$ and $N$ are both set to be two. Besides, $e_{\text{min}}$ is initialized as large as possible, for example, infinity in the MATLAB running environment.

The neuronet is applied to making a population prediction based on the historical population data. So, after the neuronet is well trained with the WASD algorithm aided by TP technique, its predicting ability and the learning ability both should be presented. Thus the learning-and-predicting error evaluation method is proposed. The relative error (RE) of the root mean square form for showing the learning ability of the neuronet is defined as

$$\varepsilon_{\text{lea}} = \sqrt{\frac{1}{Q_3} \sum_{i=1}^{Q_3} \left( \frac{p_i^{\text{spl}} - y_i}{p_i^{\text{spl}}} \right)^2}, \tag{17.3}$$

where $y_i$ denotes the $i$th actual output of the TP-aided WASD neuronet. Analogously, since there are $(Q_2 - Q_3)$ data pairs constructing the predicting-testing data-set, the RE for showing the predicting ability of the neuronet is defined as

$$\varepsilon_{\text{pre}} = \sqrt{\frac{1}{Q2 - Q3} \sum_{j=1}^{Q_2 - Q_3} \left( \frac{p_{Q_3+j}^{\text{spl}} - y_{Q_3+j}}{p_{Q_3+j}^{\text{spl}}} \right)^2}. \tag{17.4}$$

As investigated abundantly, in order to balance the learning ability and predicting ability of the neuronet, the final evaluation error criterion can be defined as

$$\varepsilon_{\text{eva}} = (\varepsilon_{\text{lea}})^2 \varepsilon_{\text{pre}}. \tag{17.5}$$

By calculating the evaluation error $\varepsilon_{\text{eva}}$ via (17.5) and comparing different $\varepsilon_{\text{eva}}$ corresponding to different neuronets (of which the structures and weights are different), the neuronet with the best learning and predicting performance can thus be found.

## 17.3 Results

Based on the historical population data from 200 BC to 2014 AD, which span over 2000 years, by exploiting the introduced and presented methods, the approach of TP-aided WASD neuronet is finally established for the population prediction of the Indian subcontinent.

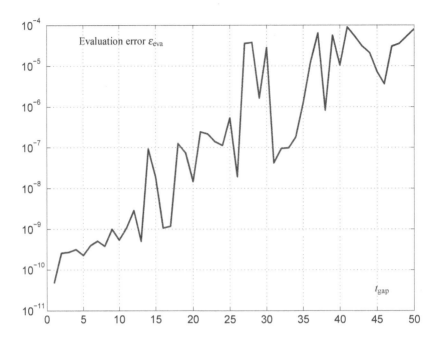

**FIGURE 17.2**: Relationship between spline gap $t_{gap}$ and evaluation error $\varepsilon_{eva}$ of TP-aided WASD neuronet.

### 17.3.1    Spline gap determination and data normalization

According to the analysis above, a spline data-set with spline gap $t_{gap}$ can be generated. Besides, for Chebyshev polynomials of Class 1 of the first kind, the domain of input data is $[-1, 1]$. The time interval $[-200, 2014]$ is normalized onto the interval $[-1, \alpha]$, with the normalization factor $\alpha$ belonging to $(-1, 1)$. So, it is necessary to find out the best suitable spline gap $t_{gap}$ and normalization factor $\alpha$. A group of numerical studies are thus conducted in order to find out the relationship among $t_{gap}$, $\alpha$ and the evaluation error $\varepsilon_{eva}$ of the neuronet with the optimal structure via (17.5), with partial results displayed in Fig. 17.2.

By applying the cubic spline method presented to numerical studies, the results show that, when $t_{gap} = 1$ and $\alpha = 0.992$, the corresponding evaluation error $\varepsilon_{eva}$ shown in Fig. 17.2 is globally the smallest one, meaning the most possible population prediction result of the Indian subcontinent via the TP-aided WASD neuronet. So, we choose $t_{glo} = 1$ and $\alpha_{glo} = 0.992$, respectively, as the spline gap and normalization factor for the neuronet to make the prediction as follows.

### 17.3.2    Most possible prediction results

As mentioned, when using different $t_{gap}$ and $\alpha$, the corresponding evaluation errors $\varepsilon_{eva}$ are accordingly different. The prediction results with the smallest evaluation error are the most possible results that may come closest to the real situation. Such results can be seen in Fig. 17.3, and more detailed data can be seen in Table 17.1. Specifically, from the figure and table, it can be found out that, in the next few years, the population as well as the growth rate will keep increasing; and that the population in the Indian subcontinent will break through 1700 million in 2019.

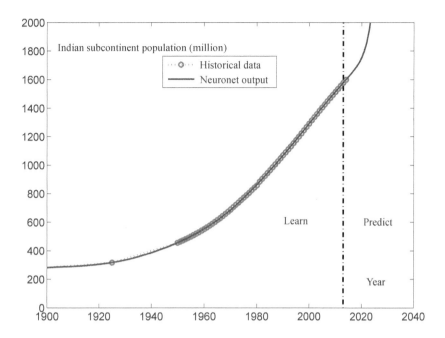

**FIGURE 17.3**: Most possible prediction results of Indian subcontinent population via TP-aided WASD neuronet with spline gap $t_{\mathrm{gap}} = 1$ and normalization factor $\alpha = 0.992$.

### 17.3.3 Other possible prediction results

Since the population growth in the future is full of uncertainty, in order to make a more comprehensive prediction, other possible prediction results (with small but relatively larger evaluation errors) are also presented. Such prediction results are of less possibility than the aforementioned results (corresponding to the globally smallest evaluation error). Due to the space limitation and similarity among some results, only two groups of other possible prediction results are presented, of which the corresponding evaluation errors are larger than the one shown above but smaller than the rest; i.e., please see Fig. 17.4, Table 17.2 and Table 17.3.

Specifically, the possible prediction results with the second smallest evaluation error correspond to the neuronet outputs which utilize $t_{\mathrm{gap}} = 5$ and $\alpha = 0.961$. The population development tendency can be seen in Fig. 17.4(a), and part of the detailed population data can be seen in Table 17.2. Similar to the most possible prediction results, these results show that the population in the Indian subcontinent will keep rising in the future. However, the population growth rate in this group of results presents a fluctuation. More specifically, the growth rate may decrease during 2015 AD to 2024 AD, and reach the minimum in 2025. After 2026 AD, the growth rate may turn to increasing.

Furthermore, the possible prediction results with the third smallest evaluation error correspond to the neuronet output which utilizes $t_{\mathrm{gap}} = 2$ and $\alpha = 0.97$. These results show that, in the next decade, the population in the Indian subcontinent may keep rising and reach the highest point, which is 1750.00 million. But, after that, the population may turn to decreasing.

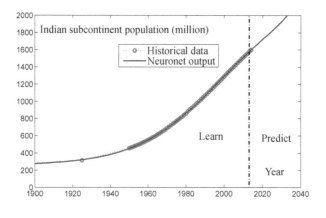

(a) With $t_{gap} = 5$ and $\alpha = 0.961$

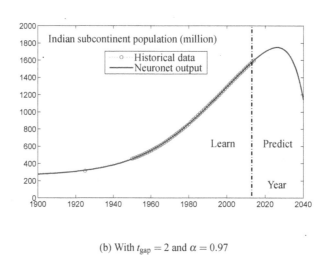

(b) With $t_{gap} = 2$ and $\alpha = 0.97$

**FIGURE 17.4**: Other possible prediction results about Indian subcontinent population.

## 17.4    Discussion

Based on the historical population data from 200 BC to 2014 AD, the TP-aided WASD neuronet is successfully applied to the population prediction of the Indian subcontinent, and three groups of possible prediction results are shown.

As we know, countries in the Indian subcontinent, especially India, are developing fast in economy. Though India was the first country proposing the population control policy in the whole world, the actual results are not notable. The traditional, cultural and social problems, existing in the Indian subcontinent for thousands of years, have been greatly against the official work for controlling population [207–209]. For example, the Indian subcontinent is a region where religions mix, in addition to the complicated caste system existing. It can be found that the population there is hard to be affected by macro-control from local governments. So, it is realistic that the population keeps

**TABLE 17.2:** Detailed results of second possible prediction with $t_{gap} = 5$ and $\alpha = 0.961$.

| Year | 2015 | 2016 | 2017 | 2018 |
|---|---|---|---|---|
| Population (million) | 1619.68 | 1640.32 | 1660.80 | 1681.12 |
| Growth Rate (%) | 1.302 | 1.274 | 1.248 | 1.224 |
| Year | 2019 | 2020 | 2021 | 2022 |
| Population (million) | 1701.32 | 1721.14 | 1741.45 | 1761.45 |
| Growth Rate (%) | 1.201 | 1.181 | 1.164 | 1.149 |
| Year | 2023 | 2024 | **2025** | 2026 |
| Population (million) | 1781.49 | 1801.61 | **1821.89** | 1842.40 |
| Growth Rate (%) | 1.137 | 1.129 | **1.125** | 1.126 |
| Year | 2027 | 2028 | 2029 | 2030 |
| Population (million) | 1863.23 | 1884.49 | 1906.28 | 1928.75 |
| Growth Rate (%) | 1.131 | 1.141 | 1.157 | 1.179 |

**TABLE 17.3:** Detailed results of another possible prediction with $t_{gap} = 2$ and $\alpha = 0.97$.

| Year | 2015 | 2016 | 2017 | 2018 |
|---|---|---|---|---|
| Population (million) | 1616.91 | 1635.58 | 1653.43 | 1670.35 |
| Growth Rate (%) | 1.213 | 1.155 | 1.092 | 1.023 |
| Year | 2019 | 2020 | 2021 | 2022 |
| Population (million) | 1686.18 | 1700.78 | 1713.94 | 1725.48 |
| Growth Rate (%) | 0.948 | 0.865 | 0.774 | 0.673 |
| Year | 2023 | 2024 | 2025 | **2026** |
| Population (million) | 1735.14 | 1742.65 | 1747.72 | **1750.00** |
| Growth Rate (%) | 0.560 | 0.433 | 0.291 | **0.130** |
| Year | 2027 | 2028 | 2029 | 2030 |
| Population (million) | 1749.10 | 1744.56 | 1735.90 | 1722.56 |
| Growth Rate (%) | -0.052 | -0.259 | -0.496 | -0.769 |

steadily growing. According to the relevant researches, the best prediction result presented above shows similarity with the actual population situation in the Indian subcontinent [207–209].

Meanwhile, due to the high uncertainty of social and population development, such as the complicated politics, culture environments, serious sudden wars and/or disasters, the population of the Indian subcontinent may increase with fluctuations, and even suffer negative growth. These situations can be reflected by the possible prediction results shown above.

## 17.5 Chapter Summary

As an impressive and fast developing region in the world, the Indian subcontinent deserves a detailed and intensive study, especially in terms of population development and evolution. Based on the historical population data from 200 BC to 2014 AD, which span over 2000 years, the TP-aided WASD neuronet has been constructed to make the population prediction for the future. With this effective and creative method, a new vision for the research on the Indian subcontinent population has been presented. The results provide useful information for further research and offer a powerful reference for local policymakers. Improving the WASD algorithm further and applying it to more and more fields are the directions of our future researches. Note that the Indian subcontinent population data from 2015 to 2017 (the time that we prepared this chapter in the book) in WPP 2017 [167] are 1710.21 million, 1731.33 million and 1752.29 million, respectively. For the convenience of readers, the above population data can be used to further compare with the population prediction results reported in this chapter.

# Chapter 18

## Application to World Population Prediction

The population of the world attracts considerable attention, as it is closely related to the development of human society. The prediction of the world population, which can be used for planning and research, is becoming more and more important. In this chapter, we present a neuronet approach for world population prediction. Note that the historical population data contain the general regularity of the population development, and are also the comprehensive reflection of the population development under the influence of all factors (e.g., natural environment, policy and economy). Thus, using the past 10000-year rough data, a three-layer feed-forward neuronet equipped with the weights-and-structure-determination (WASD) algorithm is constructed for the prediction of the world population in this chapter. Via various numerical studies, such a neuronet with WASD algorithm indicates that there are several possibilities of the change of the world population in the future. With the most possibility, the trend of the world population in the next decade is to rise, peak in 2020, and then decline.

## 18.1 Introduction

Two hundred and sixteen years ago, a curate named Thomas Malthus published a sobering pamphlet in which he argued that the human population will always tend to grow [218]. Believe it or not, since Malthus's time, the population of the world has risen sevenfold to more than 7 billion; or specifically, 7.162199 billion estimated by the United Nations (UN) [162]. Evidently, with the rapid increase of human population, there arise lots of problems that the world has to face [218]. The population problem has been one of the major problems that influences and restricts the development of human society [218].

**TABLE 18.1:**    World population data in the past 10000 years for learning and prediction.

| Year | −8000 | −7000 | −6000 | −5000 | −4000 | −3000 | −2000 |
|---|---|---|---|---|---|---|---|
| Data (million) | 5.00 | 7.00 | 10.00 | 15.00 | 20.00 | 25.00 | 35.00 |
| Year | −1000 | −500 | 1 | 200 | 400 | 500 | 600 |
| Data (million) | 50.00 | 100.00 | 200.00 | 223.00 | 198.00 | 198.00 | 203.00 |
| Year | 700 | 750 | 800 | 900 | 1000 | 1200 | 1250 |
| Data (million) | 208.50 | 215.50 | 222.00 | 240.00 | 310.00 | 404.00 | 408.00 |
| Year | 1300 | 1340 | 1400 | 1500 | 1600 | 1650 | 1700 |
| Data (million) | 396.80 | 443.00 | 362.00 | 475.71 | 562.00 | 510.71 | 633.60 |
| Year | 1750 | 1800 | 1804 | 1850 | 1900 | 1910 | 1920 |
| Data (million) | 791.00 | 978.00 | 1000.00 | 1262.00 | 1650.00 | 1750.00 | 1860.00 |
| Year | 1927 | 1940 | 1950 | 1955 | 1960 | 1965 | 1970 |
| Data (million) | 2000.00 | 2300.00 | 2525.779 | 2761.651 | 3026.003 | 3329.122 | 3691.173 |
| Year | 1974 | 1975 | 1980 | 1985 | 1987 | 1990 | 1995 |
| Data (million) | 4000.00 | 4071.02 | 4449.049 | 4863.602 | 5000.00 | 5320.817 | 5741.822 |
| Year | 1999 | 2000 | 2005 | 2010 | 2011 | 2013 | |
| Data (million) | 6000.00 | 6127.70 | 6514.095 | 6916.183 | 7000.00 | 7162.119 | |

Because the world population is closely related to the development of human society, the prediction of the world population, which can be used for planning and research, is becoming more and more important [162, 218, 219]. It is conducted by many organizations, including national and local governments and private companies [162, 219], for economy and infrastructure planning, social and health research, and so on. Among these organizations, the UN produces the updated prediction for the world population every two years [162]. Then, the WPP is reported, which is viewed as the de facto standard [220]. In this chapter, we refer to the 2012 revision of the WPP as WPP 2012. Besides, it is worth pointing out that the prediction of the world population conducted in this section is partly based on the data given in WPP 2012 (see Table 18.1 for details).

As we know, the world population is affected by many factors, such as natural environment, policy, economy and culture, thereby making it difficult to forecast the change of the world population. Generally speaking, the population studies based just on fertility, mortality and other individual factors [162, 219] may lead to the lack of all-sidedness in the prediction results that differ sharply from the actual population of the world. In addition, the population studies based just on the data in recent decades (e.g., the data provided by the UN) [159, 162] may miss the consideration of sudden disasters that may happen in the future, thereby making the prediction results of the world population less comprehensive [218]. As we may realize, the historical population data contain the general regularity of the population development, and are also the comprehensive reflection of the population development under the influence of all factors (e.g., natural environment, policy and economy). Based on the historical population data, we may have the overall view on the trend of the world population from the past to the future, as well as the information of sudden disasters that happened in the history (e.g., epidemics and wars). Therefore, it makes good sense if we can build a model that uses the historical population data as many times as possible for the prediction of the world population in the future, e.g., the feed-forward neuronet that is presented and investigated in this section.

Nowadays, as a branch of artificial intelligence, artificial neuronets (AN) have attracted considerable attention as candidates for novel computational systems [203]. Benefiting from inherent nonlinearity and learning ability, various AN have been developed and applied widely in many scientific and engineering fields [56, 203]. In these studies, the feed-forward neuronet is a class of typical AN [56, 176]. Due to the in-depth researches, the feed-forward neuronets have now been involved in many real-world applications, such as, system identification, pattern classification and stock prediction. In general, with a number of artificial neurons connected, a feed-forward neuronet can be constructed [203], e.g., the one shown in Fig. 15.4 of Chapter 15. Then, by means of a suitable training procedure, such a neuronet would have the marvelous learning, generalization and prediction abilities. Theoretically speaking, a three-layer feed-forward neuronet can approximate any nonlinear continuous function with an arbitrary accuracy [203].

In view of the aforementioned superiority, the approach based on feed-forward neuronets can thus be developed and investigated for the prediction of the world population. The common neuronet can readily be the one based on the error back-propagation (BP) algorithm [56], i.e., the so-called BP neuronet. However, BP-type neuronets have some inherent weaknesses, such as, relatively slow convergence, local-minima existence, and uncertainty about the optimal number of hidden-layer neurons [176], thereby making these neuronets less applicable to the prediction of the world population. Differing from algorithmic improvements in the BP training procedure, using linearly independent or orthogonal activation functions (e.g., Chebyshev polynomials of Class 1 [176]) to remedy the weaknesses of BP-type neuronets can be a better way, which is reflected in our successful experience [176].

Therefore, in this section, based on the past 10000-year rough data (i.e., the data from 8000 BC to 2013 which are obtained via the website provided by the Wikipedia [218] as well as WPP 2012 [162]), a three-layer feed-forward neuronet activated by a group of Chebyshev polynomials (specifically, of Class 1, which is named the Chebyshev-activation neuronet for presentation convenience) is constructed for the prediction of the world population.

## 18.2 Chebyshev-Activation WASD Neuronet

In this section, the Chebyshev-activation neuronet is firstly constructed. Then, as for such a neuronet, the WASD algorithm is presented.

### 18.2.1 Chebyshev-activation neuronet

In this subsection, based on the past 10000-year rough data which are shown in Table 18.1, a three-layer feed-forward neuronet activated by a group of Chebyshev polynomials of Class 1 (i.e., the Chebyshev-activation neuronet) is constructed for the prediction of the world population. Specifically, Fig. 15.4 of Chapter 15 shows the model structure of such a Chebyshev-activation neuronet, which, in the hidden layer, has $N$ neurons activated by a group of Chebyshev polynomials $\varphi_j(x)$ (with $j = 1, 2, \cdots, N$). In addition, the input layer or the output layer each has one neuron activated by the linear function. Moreover, the connecting weights from the input layer to the hidden layer are all fixed to be 1, whereas the connecting weights from the hidden layer to the output layer, denoted as $w_j$, are to be decided or adjusted. Besides, all neuronal thresholds are fixed to be 0. Note that, theoretically guaranteeing the efficacy of the Chebyshev-activation neuronet, these settings can simplify the complexities of the neuronet structure design, analysis and computation [176].

### 18.2.2 WASD algorithm

As we know, the neuronets' performance is greatly affected by the number of the hidden-layer neurons [176]. Specifically, the neuronet with too few hidden-layer neurons may fail to achieve the expected learning accuracy, whereas excessive hidden-layer neurons may result in an over-fitting phenomenon, poor generalization ability and high computational complexity. In this subsection, based on the weights-direct-determination (WDD) subalgorithm, the WASD algorithm [176] is thus

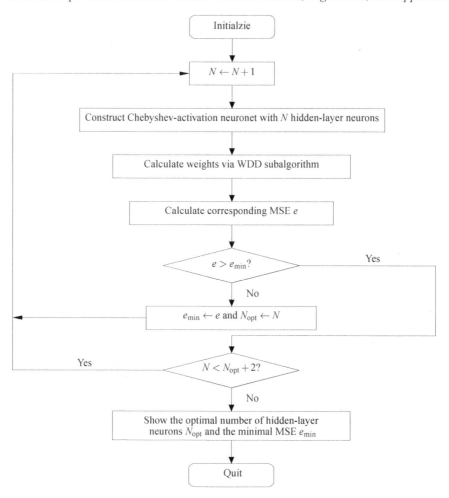

**FIGURE 18.1**: Flowchart of WASD algorithm for Chebyshev-activation neuronet applied to world population prediction.

introduced for the Chebyshev-activation neuronet. Such a WASD algorithm can (1) determine effectively the weights connecting the hidden layer and the output layer, and (2) obtain automatically the optimal structure of the Chebyshev-activation neuronet. These two aims are achieved by finding the smallest training error.

To lay a basis for further discussion, we give $\{(t_i, p_i)|_{i=1}^{M}\}$ as the data-set of sample pairs for the training of the Chebyshev-activation neuronet, where $t_i \in \mathbb{R}$ denotes the $i$th input and $p_i \in \mathbb{R}$ denotes the $i$th desired output (or, say, target output). Then, the mean square error (MSE) for the Chebyshev-activation neuronet is defined as follows:

$$e = \frac{1}{M} \sum_{i=1}^{M} \left( p_i - \sum_{k=1}^{N} w_k \varphi_k(t_i) \right)^2. \tag{18.1}$$

Evidently, for the Chebyshev-activation neuronet with a fixed number of hidden-layer neurons, we can obtain the related MSE (i.e., the training error) via Equation (18.1). By increasing the number of hidden-layer neurons one-by-one, we can finally have the relationship between the MSE and the number of hidden-layer neurons [176]. The WASD algorithm is thus developed to determine

**TABLE 18.2:** Prediction results of world population via Chebyshev-activation neuronet corresponding to different values of $\beta$.

| $\beta$ | 1980 | 1985 | 1990 | 1995 | 2000 | 2005 | 2010 |
|---|---|---|---|---|---|---|---|
| $\varepsilon_{tes}$ | 0.1958 | 0.1532 | 0.1277 | 0.1004 | 0.0550 | 0.0346 | 0.0141 |

the optimal structure of the Chebyshev-activation neuronet (i.e., with the number of hidden-layer neurons determined corresponding to the smallest MSE).

For better understanding, the description of such a WASD algorithm is shown in Fig. 18.1. The WASD algorithm involves the following variables: $e$ denotes the MSE of the current Chebyshev-activation neuronet, $e_{min}$ denotes the minimal MSE found, $N$ denotes the current number of hidden-layer neurons and $N_{opt}$ denotes the optimal number of hidden-layer neurons.

## 18.3 Application to World Population

In this section, based on the past 10000-year rough data, we utilize such a Chebyshev-activation neuronet to approximate and predict the world population with several possible tendencies of the world population in the future presented. Note that, as for the Chebyshev-activation neuronet, the input corresponds to the year and the output is the world-population data.

### 18.3.1 Learning of world population

Based on the previous analysis, the Chebyshev-activation neuronet equipped with the WASD algorithm is applied to the learning of the world population data in the past 10000 years. Note that, for Chebyshev polynomials of Class 1, the domain is $[-1, 1]$, thereby making the normalization of the data necessary. Specifically, in this letter, the time interval $[-8000, 2013]$ is normalized to the interval $[-1, \alpha]$ with the normalization factor $\alpha \in (0, 1)$. For illustration and investigation, $\alpha = 0.461$ is chosen here as an example, and the data-set for training is thus generated. On the basis of such a data-set, we can investigate the learning ability of the Chebyshev-activation neuronet equipped with the WASD algorithm, and the corresponding numerical results are shown in Fig. 18.2(a). As seen from this figure, there is little difference between the target output and the neuronet output, showing the excellent learning ability of the Chebyshev-activation neuronet. Besides, for such a Chebyshev-activation neuronet, the number of hidden-layer neurons determined automatically by the WASD algorithm is 28. In addition, the total run time is about 0.04 s, showing the feasibility of the Chebyshev-activation neuronet. In summary, these results substantiate the efficacy of the Chebyshev-activation neuronet equipped with the WASD algorithm on the learning of the world population.

### 18.3.2 Prediction of world population

In this subsection, to further show the efficacy of the Chebyshev-activation neuronet equipped with the WASD algorithm, we have conducted a series of numerical studies on its prediction ability, which are based on the past 10000-year data of the world population. That is, the data corresponding to the time interval $[-8000, \beta]$ (with $\beta < 2013$) are used to train the Chebyshev-activation neuronet, and the other data are used for the prediction study of the Chebyshev-activation neuronet. Here we choose $\beta = 1980, 1985, 1990, 1995, 2000, 2005$ and $2010$ for investigation, and the corresponding prediction results are presented in Table 18.2. Note that the testing error shown in the table is defined

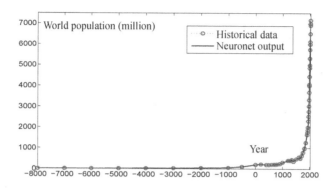

(a) Learning result

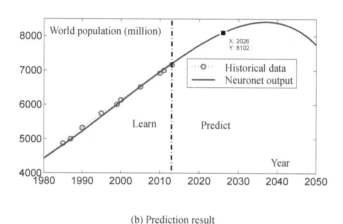

(b) Prediction result

**FIGURE 18.2**: Learning and prediction results of world population via Chebyshev-activation WASD neuronet.

as follows:

$$\varepsilon_{\text{tes}} = \frac{1}{H} \sum_{m=1}^{H} \left| \frac{y_m - p_m}{p_m} \right|,$$

where $H$ is the total number of the other data for testing, and $y_m$ and $p_m$ denote, respectively, the neuronet output and the world-population data at the $m$th testing point. From Table 18.2, we can find that, (1) with different values of $\beta$ used (i.e., using different data-set for training), all of the testing errors are small, and (2) the testing error $\varepsilon_{\text{tes}}$ is decreasing as the data for training increase. These results show the excellent prediction ability of the Chebyshev-activation neuronet equipped with the WASD algorithm, which thus motivates us to exploit such a neuronet for world population prediction.

As for the trained Chebyshev-activation neuronet based on the past 10000-year data of the world population, we can apply it to predicting the population of the world in the next few decades. The corresponding numerical results are shown in Fig. 18.2(b), which indicates that the trend of the world population in the next 40 years is to rise, peak, and then decline. Specifically, in the next 20 years, the world population is still increasing, but with a gentle growth rate. Then, at 2037, the

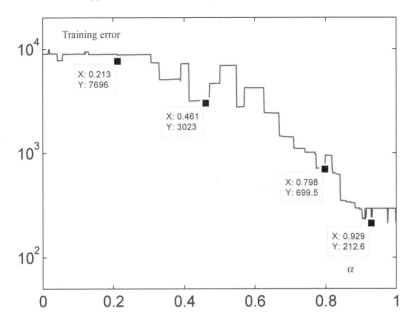

**FIGURE 18.3**: Relationship between normalization factor $\alpha$ and training error of Chebyshev-activation neuronet with optimal structure.

world population reaches the summit with the population being 8.416 billion. After the summit (or, say, from 2038), the world population decreases gradually. Besides, it is worth pointing out that the prediction results illustrated in Fig. 18.2(b) show that the world population is predicted to increase to 8.1 billion in 2026. By contrast, from WPP 2012, we know that the world population is predicted to increase to 8.1 billion in 2025, which is based on the medium-variant prediction. This numerical comparison, to some extent, illustrates that the predication of the world population via the Chebyshev-activation neuronet is acceptable and reliable (i.e., the Chebyshev-activation neuronet equipped with the WASD algorithm has the ability to predict the population of the world).

### 18.3.3 More possible situations of population prediction

Note that, as mentioned previously, the time interval $[-8000, 2013]$ is normalized to the interval $[-1, \alpha]$. Evidently, different values of $\alpha$ lead to different learning results of the Chebyshev-activation neuronet equipped with the WASD algorithm. For better understanding, Fig. 18.3 shows the relationship between the normalization factor $\alpha$ and the training error of the Chebyshev-activation neuronet with the optimal structure [i.e., the smallest MSE via Equation (18.1)]. As shown in the figure, superior learning performance of the Chebyshev-activation neuronet can be achieved by choosing a suitable value of $\alpha$. More importantly, from the figure, we can observe that there exist several local minimum points and a global minimum point, such as the marked ones, which correspond to different values of $\alpha$. Such local and global minimum points indicate the possible situations of the world population prediction via the Chebyshev-activation neuronet, and the global minimum point further implies the most possible situation. Note that $\alpha = 0.461$ is a local minimum point that is shown in Fig. 18.3. This is the reason why we choose $\alpha = 0.461$ as an illustrative example (for learning and prediction of the world population) in the previous parts.

Based on the results shown in Fig. 18.3, different values of $\alpha$ can thus be used for the Chebyshev-activation neuronet to predict the population of the world. Due to results similarity and space limitation, Figs. 18.4 and 18.5 show the prediction results via the Chebyshev-activation

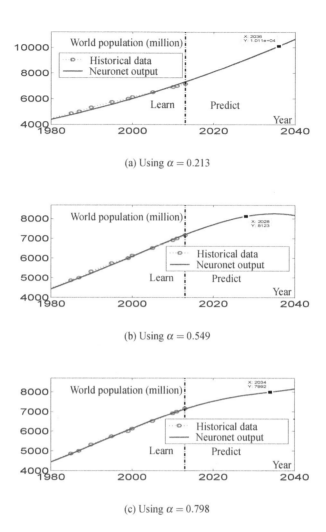

(a) Using $\alpha = 0.213$

(b) Using $\alpha = 0.549$

(c) Using $\alpha = 0.798$

**FIGURE 18.4**: Different prediction results via Chebyshev-activation WASD neuronet using $\alpha = 0.213$, $\alpha = 0.549$ and $\alpha = 0.798$.

neuronet (equipped with the WASD algorithm) using $\alpha = 0.213, 0.549, 0.798, 0.929, 0.976$ and $0.999$ only. From Fig. 18.4, we can observe that there are six different prediction results for the world population, but all of the results tell the rise of the world population in the next few years. In addition, comparing the trends of the prediction results shown in Figs. 18.4(a) through 18.4(c) with those given in WPP 2012, we find that they have something in common. Specifically, (1) the prediction in Fig. 18.4(a) is similar to that in WPP 2012 based on the high-variant prediction; (2) the prediction in Fig. 18.4(b) is similar to that in WPP 2012 based on the low-variant prediction; and (3) the prediction in Fig. 18.4(c) is similar to that in WPP 2012 based on the medium-variant prediction. Considering that each of Fig. 18.4(a) through 18.4(c) is a prediction possibility via the Chebyshev-activation neuronet, we may have the conclusion that the neuronet prediction in this letter could incorporate the WPP 2012 prediction (in terms of a few decades/years). Besides, as seen from Figs. 18.5(a) through 18.5(c), the world population is predicted to increase to the summit in about 2020 and then decline, which is quite different from the prediction results shown in Figs. 18.4(a) through 18.4(c) (and those in WPP 2012). Note that $\alpha = 0.929$ is the global minimum point, and $\alpha = 0.976$

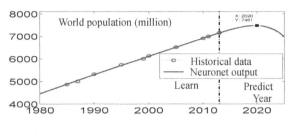

(a) Using $\alpha = 0.929$

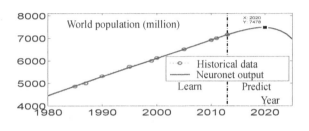

(b) Using $\alpha = 0.976$

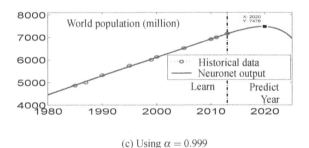

(c) Using $\alpha = 0.999$

**FIGURE 18.5**: Different prediction results via Chebyshev-activation WASD neuronet using $\alpha = 0.929$, $\alpha = 0.976$ and $\alpha = 0.999$.

and $\alpha = 0.999$ are the two sub global minimum points shown in Fig. 18.3. This is the reason why the prediction results in Figs. 18.5(b) and 18.5(c) coincide well with those in Fig. 18.5(a), except for the summit values being slightly different. More importantly, as for the global minimum point (i.e., $\alpha = 0.929$), it means that Fig. 18.5(a) shows the prediction results with the most possibility. Thus, we would like to accept such prediction results showing the probable future of the world population, though with a little surprise ("Why? Well controlled?") and also worry ("Disaster? War?").

## 18.4 Discussion

As mentioned previously, the world population increases year-by-year, and to 7.162199 billion in 2013 (estimated by the UN). The population problem has now been a very appealing topic that influences and restricts the development of human society. As we know, the population of the developing countries is a vital component of the world population. The (rapid) growth of the population in such countries, especially in China and India, has a large influence on the change of the world population. In recent years, some developing countries (e.g., China, India and Brazil) have made the corresponding policies for handling the population problem. Note that these policies may not have much of an effect on the huge population within a short period. In addition, the policies for the childbirth encouragement are carried out in some other countries (e.g., Russia, Canada and Japan). Thus, as for Fig. 18.5(a), it predicts that the population of the world increases continually (but with a gentle growth rate) in the next few years, which is reasonable and acceptable. After 7 years (i.e., in 2020), the world population will reach its summit with the value being 7.481 billion, thereby showing from one viewpoint that the policies made by governments are indeed effective and efficient on the overall control of the population growth. With the successful policies, the world population is well under control and then decreases slowly as shown in Fig. 18.5(a). In addition to the government policies, what we cannot ignore is that the fertility rates in some developing countries are becoming low recently, resulting in the (potential) decrease of the population in the future. Besides, under the influence of the economic recession as well as immigration, many developed countries are also facing the same situation that the fertility rates are declining (which is also the reason why these countries prefer to make the policies for childbirth encouragement). The low fertility rates in such developed countries may limit considerably the population growth, and even lead to the decrease of the population. Therefore, by considering the recent situations of the developing and developed countries, it is reasonable that the world population shown in Fig. 18.5(a) is predicted to decline in the future (with the most possibility).

Besides, it is also worth pointing out here that each of Fig. 18.2(b) and Figs. 18.4(a) through 18.4(c) indicates a possibility of the world population in the future. This implies that the current population policies carried out in some (developing) countries may be less effective on the population-growth control. In addition, Figs. 18.5(b) and 18.5(c) show the prediction results using the Chebyshev-activation neuronet with $\alpha = 0.976$ and 0.999 (being two sub global minimum points in Fig. 18.3). As seen from such two subfigures, the population of the world is predicted to increase as well in the next few years, and then reach its summit in 2020 with the value being 7.478 billion [which is smaller than the one shown in Fig. 18.5(a)]. Note that the change of the historical population data (shown in Table 18.1) generally contains the information of sudden disasters that happened in history (e.g., epidemics and wars), as these data are the comprehensive reflection of the population development under the influence of all factors. Thus, from another viewpoint, the prediction results corresponding to the two sub global minimum points, together with Fig. 18.5(a), may possibly imply that some disasters including wars may happen, thereby resulting in the decrease of the world population. Therefore, by realizing several possibilities of the change of the future world population, governments may need to make more effective policies to control the still-increasing population of the world and also take measures for preventing the possibility of sudden disasters.

## 18.5 Chapter Summary

In this section, the Chebyshev-activation neuronet equipped with the WASD algorithm has been presented and investigated. Then, the Chebyshev-activation neuronet equipped with the WASD algorithm has been applied to predicting the world population in the next few decades based on the past 10000-year rough data. The related numerical results have further illustrated the efficacy of the Chebyshev-activation neuronet equipped with the WASD algorithm on the prediction of the world population. That is, using the past 10000-year rough data, such a neuronet can predict the world population effectively and reasonably. As indicated by the Chebyshev-activation neuronet equipped with the WASD algorithm, there are several possibilities of the change of the world population in the future, which could incorporate the WPP 2012 prediction based on the low-variant, medium-variant and high-variant predictions. As the most possible situation, the trend of the world population in the next decade is to rise, peak in 2020, and then decline. Note that the world population data from 2014 to 2017 (the time that we prepared this chapter in the book) in WPP 2017 [167] are 7298.453 million, 7383.008 million, 7466.964 million and 7550.262 million, respectively. For the convenience of readers, the above population data can be used to further compare with the population prediction results reported in this chapter.

At the end of this section, the authors would like to emphasize the importance of the above prediction approach based on the WASD neuronet as follows. Since ancient ancestors, the human has developed over millions of years. However, for the scientific research on human evolution, it is just a start. It seems that the requirements on enough data and the sophisticated computational tools have not yet been reached, thereby making scientists less capable of predicting the world population. In comparison, a WASD neuronet and the rough population data may turn this difficult situation around. Using the WASD neuronet and the related population data, several human process models can thus be constructed and further investigated to evaluate their reliability and optimality. With the continuous and in-depth research on world population and human evolution, more perfecting answers and pictures are expected to present.

# Part VI

# Population Applications Using Power-Activation Neuronet

# Chapter 19

## Application to Russian Population Prediction

In recent years, the serious situation of the Russian population caused concerns for the government, which also attracts the great attention of researchers from all over the world. The research on Russian population can help the government to make positive policies for solving the crisis and boosting economic growth. In this chapter, implicitly considering almost all factors that influence population development, we present a three-layer feed-forward power-activation neuronet equipped with the weights-and-structure-determination (WASD) algorithm for the estimation, correction and prediction of the Russian population. Many numerical tests are conducted via power-activation neuronet using past 2013-year Russian population data. We estimate the Russian population from 1000 AD to 1800 AD, correct it around 1897 AD, and further indicate several possibilities of Russian population in the future. With the most possibility, the Russian population is predicted to decrease steadily in the next decade; while it is still possible that it will (finally) increase.

## 19.1 Introduction

In 1996, the United Nations (UN) released a forecast about the Russian population saying that it would decrease to 138 million by 2015, and would be down to 114 million by 2050 [221, 222]. A report published in 2011 by the financial services company, Standard & Poor, said that the Russian population might shrink from roughly 140 to 116 million people by the middle of the century [221]. Although we now may not be able to estimate the accuracy of the predictions about the future, it is a fact that Russia is the country that has the largest decreases of population in the last 10 years. This shocks and worries all the world. Russia may face a deep demographic crisis that threatens the country's very existence and future [221].

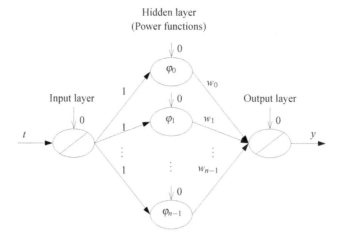

**FIGURE 19.1**: Model structure of three-layer power-activation neuronet for Russian population prediction.

In fact, the Russian population has been declining since the disintegration of the Soviet Union. The population problem has been the biggest threat to the survival and development of the Russian nation. Successive Russian governments attach great importance to the potential demographic crisis and draw up numerous measures [221]. Many organizations, including companies, universities and research institutes, also pay increasing attention to the research of Russian population for economy planning and social research, and so on [221–223]. Traditional researches on population predictions use the standard cohort-component method based on several limited factors (e.g., fertility, mortality and migration rates) [160, 224]. It may lead to the lack of all-sidedness in the prediction results. We realize that historical data contain the general regularity under the influence of all factors. So, we may make the prediction with all factors considered implicitly if we can build a model with preferable ability for learning from historical data.

Note that artificial neuronets (AN) are simplified systems, which emulate the organization structures, signal processing methods and system functions of biological neuronets [99]. With parallel-processing nature, distributed storage, self-adaptive and self-learning abilities, AN, especially with error back-propagation (BP) training algorithms, has been investigated and applied widely in many scientific, engineering and practical fields [176]. However, the conventional BP algorithms have some inherent shortages, e.g., local minima, slow convergence, and inability to determine the optimal number of hidden-layer neurons [129, 176], which make it difficult to build an extremely accurate model. To overcome these shortages, through a large number of experiments, the authors find that some linearly independent activation functions (e.g., the power activation function exploited in this chapter) can help improve the performance of the neuronet [176].

## 19.2   Neuronet Model and WASD Algorithm

In this section, a three-layer feed-forward power-activation neuronet model with $n$ hidden-layer neurons is firstly constructed for the research of the Russian population. Then, we introduce the weights-and-structure-determination (WASD) algorithm to train the power-activation neuronet model.

### 19.2.1 Power-activation neuronet model

In this research, we collect the 2013-year Russian population data from 1 AD to 2013 AD (including the period of the Soviet Union, in which the demographic data of Russian republic is used). Based on these data, we construct a three-layer feed-forward power-activation neuronet, of which the model structure is shown in Fig. 19.1. As illustrated in Fig. 19.1, the hidden layer has $n$ neurons activated by a group of order-increasing power functions $\varphi_j(t) = t^j$ with $j = 0, 1, \cdots, n-1$, and each of the input layer and the output layer has one neuron using linear activation function. In addition, to simplify the structure, we set all thresholds of the neuronet to be zero and fix all connecting weights from the input-layer to the hidden-layer to be one. Then, the input-output relation is $y = \sum_{j=0}^{n-1} w_j \varphi_j(t)$, where $w_j$ denotes the connecting weight from the $j$th hidden-layer neuron to the output-layer neuron.

### 19.2.2 WASD algorithm

We define $\left\{ (t_i, p_i)|_{i=1}^{m} \right\}$ to be data-set of sample pairs, and, in this chapter, $t_i \in \mathbb{R}$ corresponding to the year datum is the $i$th input, and $p_i \in \mathbb{R}$ corresponding to the Russian population datum is the $i$th target output. The mean square error (MSE) is thus defined as

$$e = \frac{1}{m} \sum_{i=1}^{m} \left( p_i - \sum_{j=0}^{n-1} w_j \varphi_j(t_i) \right)^2. \tag{19.1}$$

Being different from conventional iterative-training algorithms, the weights-direct-determination (WDD) subalgorithm [99, 176] can be used to train the power-activation neuronet, which avoids the lengthy and possibly oscillating iterative-training procedure.

Let us respectively define the following input activation matrix $\Psi$, weight vector $\mathbf{w}$, and target-output vector $\mathbf{p}$ as

$$\Psi = \begin{bmatrix} t_1^0 & t_1^1 & \cdots & t_1^{n-1} \\ t_2^0 & t_2^1 & \cdots & t_2^{n-1} \\ \vdots & \vdots & \ddots & \vdots \\ t_m^0 & t_m^1 & \cdots & t_m^{n-1} \end{bmatrix} \in \mathbb{R}^{m \times n}, \ \mathbf{w} = \begin{bmatrix} w_0 \\ w_1 \\ \vdots \\ w_{n-1} \end{bmatrix} \in \mathbb{R}^n, \ \mathbf{p} = \begin{bmatrix} p_1 \\ p_2 \\ \vdots \\ p_m \end{bmatrix} \in \mathbb{R}^m.$$

Then, the optimal weight vector is determined directly as

$$\mathbf{w} = (\Psi^T \Psi)^{-1} \Psi^T \mathbf{p} = \text{pinv}(\Psi)\mathbf{p} = \Psi^\dagger \mathbf{p}, \tag{19.2}$$

where $\text{pinv}(\Psi)$ and $\Psi^\dagger$ both denote the pseudoinverse of the matrix $\Psi$.

Based on the above WDD subalgorithm (19.2), the WASD algorithm [176] is thus developed, of which the flowchart is shown in Fig. 19.2. Note that $e_{\min}$ and $n_{\text{opt}}$ are set initially as $e_{\min} = 10^9$ (or preferably "inf" in MATLAB computing environment) and $n_{\text{opt}} = 1$. As seen from the figure, the WASD algorithm not only can determine directly the optimal weights connecting the hidden layer and the output layer, but also obtain automatically the optimal structure for the power-activation neuronet shown in Fig. 19.1.

### 19.3 Estimation, Correction and Prediction

In this section, we firstly conduct the numerical experiments via the built power-activation neuronet model with the 2013-year Russian population data. Then, based on these experimental results, the abilities of the power-activation neuronet model are investigated in depth in terms of estimation, correction and prediction.

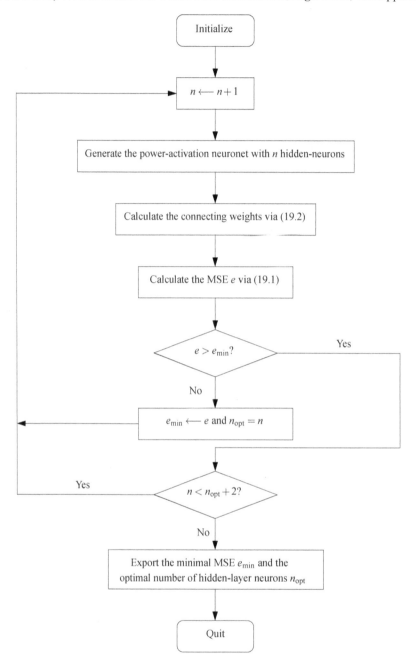

**FIGURE 19.2**: Flowchart of WASD algorithm for training power-activation neuronet.

## 19.3.1 Data normalization

Data normalization is a progress that makes the data satisfy certain constraints. It is to improve the performance and fasten the calculations [225]. In this chapter, time interval $[1, 2013]$ is normalized onto the interval $[0, \alpha]$. For further analysis, a numerical study is conducted, and the related results are shown in Fig. 19.3, which makes us better understand the relationship between normalization factor $\alpha$ and training error $e_{\text{tra}}$ of power-activation neuronet built with the optimal structure

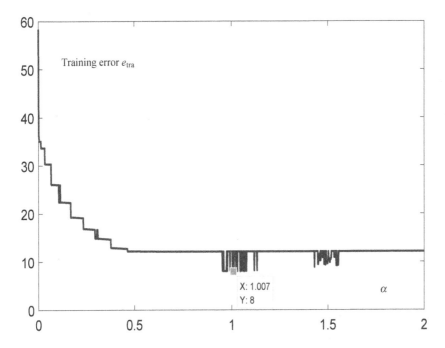

**FIGURE 19.3**: Relationship between normalization factor $\alpha$ and training error $e_{\text{tra}}$ of power-activation neuronet equipped with WASD algorithm.

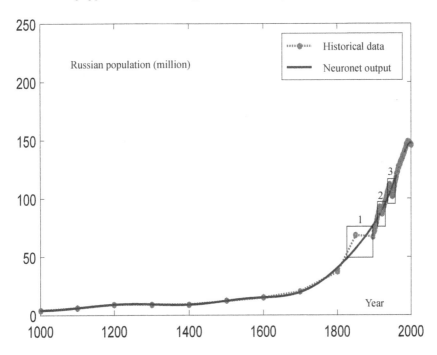

**FIGURE 19.4**: Estimation and correction performance for Russian population data via power-activation neuronet using $\alpha = 1.007$ (global minimum point).

[i.e., with the minimal MSE (19.1)]. Evidently, Fig. 19.3 indicates that the learning abilities of power-activation neuronet with different $\alpha$ values are different. Besides, as seen from the figure,

**TABLE 19.1:** Estimation results of Russian population data from 1000 AD to 1800 AD via power-activation neuronet using $\alpha = 1.007$ (global minimum point).

| Year | Population (million) | Year | Population (million) | Year | Population (million) |
|------|------|------|------|------|------|
| 1000 | 4.1 | 1280 | 9.5 | 1560 | 14.5 |
| 1020 | 4.2 | 1300 | 9.3 | 1580 | 14.9 |
| 1040 | 4.6 | 1320 | 9.1 | 1600 | 15.2 |
| 1060 | 5.0 | 1340 | 8.9 | 1620 | 15.6 |
| 1080 | 5.5 | 1360 | 8.8 | 1640 | 16.0 |
| 1100 | 6.2 | 1380 | 8.8 | 1660 | 16.8 |
| 1120 | 6.8 | 1400 | 9.0 | 1680 | 18.0 |
| 1140 | 7.5 | 1420 | 9.4 | 1700 | 19.8 |
| 1160 | 8.1 | 1440 | 9.9 | 1720 | 22.4 |
| 1180 | 8.6 | 1460 | 10.6 | 1740 | 25.8 |
| 1200 | 9.0 | 1480 | 11.5 | 1760 | 30.0 |
| 1220 | 9.4 | 1500 | 12.3 | 1780 | 34.9 |
| 1240 | 9.5 | 1520 | 13.2 | 1800 | 40.6 |
| 1260 | 9.6 | 1540 | 13.9 | | |

**TABLE 19.2:** Correction result of Russian population data from 1885 AD to 1904 AD via power-activation neuronet using $\alpha = 1.007$ (global minimum point).

| Year | Population (million) | Year | Population (million) | Year | Population (million) |
|------|------|------|------|------|------|
| 1885 | 71.4 | 1892 | 74.6 | 1899 | 78.0 |
| 1886 | 71.9 | 1893 | 75.1 | 1900 | 78.6 |
| 1887 | 72.3 | 1894 | 75.6 | 1901 | 79.1 |
| 1888 | 72.8 | 1895 | 76.1 | 1902 | 79.6 |
| 1889 | 73.2 | 1896 | 76.6 | 1903 | 80.1 |
| 1890 | 73.7 | 1897 | 77.1 | 1904 | 80.6 |
| 1891 | 74.2 | 1898 | 77.5 | | |

there exists a global minimum point, i.e., $\alpha = 1.007$, where the power-activation neuronet has the best learning performance, i.e., the minimal MSE is 8. In addition, there exist many local minimum points, especially the ones with $\alpha = 0.3041$, 0.9601 and 1.43, which may show sub-best learning performance.

## 19.3.2 Estimation and correction

Based on the above analysis, the power-activation neuronet model using $\alpha = 1.007$ (i.e., the global minimum point) is thus exploited firstly for the learning of Russian population data, with the corresponding results shown in Fig. 19.4. As seen from the figure, the power-activation neuronet model learns well the Russian population data from 1000 AD to 1800 AD. That is, the fitting curve generated via power-activation neuronet is smooth and well consistent with the historical data, thereby showing the excellent learning performance of the power-activation neuronet model for Russian population data. Table 19.1 shows part of the estimated Russian population data from 1000 AD to 1800 AD.

Besides, from Fig. 19.4, we can observe that there are three rectangle areas (i.e., *Rectangle 1*, *Rectangle 2* and *Rectangle 3*) with interesting sudden changes, where the power-activation neuronet appears to make "bad learning". Let us look into them.

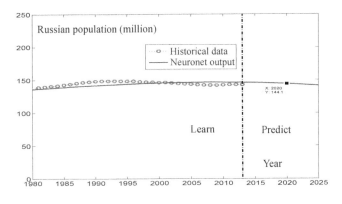

(a) Using $\alpha = 0.3041$

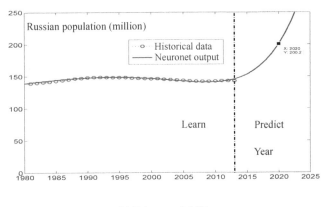

(b) Using $\alpha = 0.9601$

**FIGURE 19.5**: Different prediction trends of Russian population via power-activation neuronet using $\alpha = 0.3041$ and $\alpha = 0.9601$.

*Rectangle 1:* The first sudden change happens around 1897 AD. According to textual research [226], Russia took its first census of demography at 1897 AD, and thus the accuracy of Russian population data was relatively poor before 1897 AD. However, it follows from the Russian history that, in this period, the Industrial Revolution boosted greatly Russian economical development, which accelerated the increase of the Russian population. Therefore, as for accuracy, *Rectangle 1* can be viewed as a contradiction domain (or termed, connection domain). That is, the data before 1897 AD are with relatively poor accuracy; and the data after 1897 AD are with relatively high accuracy. On the other hand, when collecting Russian population data, we cannot find a whole data source providing all the 2013-year data. In addition, we are faced with many different data sources, such as Russian Federal State Statistics Service, UN, and Utrecht University Library. Thus, we adopt the data based on the priority ranking of data sources built according to their authorities. Note that *Rectangle 1* is just the joint of two inconsistent data sources. Fortunately, the power-activation neuronet model recognizes the inconsistency and makes a correction. Table 19.2 shows part of the corrected Russian population data from 1885 AD to 1904 AD via power-activation neuronet (corresponding to the results shown in Fig. 19.4). As a matter of fact, in the field of sociological research, the inconsistency of data sources is usually a perplexing problem, but now it can be solved readily by the power-activation neuronet model due to its excellent correction ability.

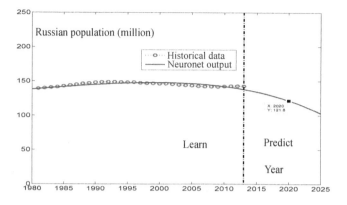

(a) Using $\alpha = 1.007$ (global minimum point)

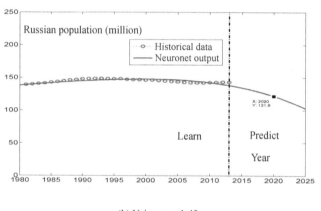

(b) Using $\alpha = 1.43$

**FIGURE 19.6**: Different prediction trends of Russian population via power-activation neuronet using $\alpha = 1.007$ and $\alpha = 1.43$.

**TABLE 19.3:**   Prediction results of Russian population data in 2020 AD with four possibilities corresponding to Figs. 19.5 and 19.6.

| $\alpha$ | 0.3041 | 0.9601 | **1.007** (global) | 1.43 |
|---|---|---|---|---|
| Population (million) | 144.1 | 200.2 | **121.8** | 121.9 |

**TABLE 19.4:**   Prediction results of Russian population data in the next decade via power-activation neuronet using $\alpha = 1.007$ (global minimum point).

| Year | 2014 | 2015 | 2016 | 2017 | 2018 |
|---|---|---|---|---|---|
| Population (million) | 136.4 | 134.5 | 132.4 | 130.1 | 127.5 |
| Year | 2019 | 2020 | 2021 | 2022 | 2023 |
| Population (million) | 124.8 | 121.8 | 118.5 | 115.0 | 111.3 |

**TABLE 19.5:** Different prediction trends of Russian population in the next decade predicted at all of 44 minimum points shown in Fig. 19.3.

| $\alpha$ | 0.1061 | 0.3041 | 0.9521 | 0.9551 | 0.9571 | 0.9601 | 0.9681 | 0.9761 |
|---|---|---|---|---|---|---|---|---|
| Trend | ↗ | → | ↘ | ↗ | ↘ | ↗ | ↘ | ↘ |
| $\alpha$ | 0.9911 | 1.004 | **1.007** (global) | 1.011 | 1.022 | 1.024 | 1.026 | 1.044 |
| Trend | ↗ | ↘ | ↘ | ↘ | ↗ | ↘ | ↗ | ↗ |
| $\alpha$ | 1.052 | 1.061 | 1.065 | 1.067 | 1.076 | 1.117 | 1.131 | 1.43 |
| Trend | ↗ | ↗ | ↗ | ↗ | ↗ | ↗ | ↗ | ↘ |
| $\alpha$ | 1.449 | 1.455 | 1.46 | 1.462 | 1.472 | 1.474 | 1.476 | 1.48 |
| Trend | ↘ | ↘ | ↘ | ↘ | ↘ | ↘ | ↘ | ↘ |
| $\alpha$ | 1.486 | 1.488 | 1.49 | 1.499 | 1.501 | 1.511 | 1.515 | 1.534 |
| Trend | ↘ | ↘ | ↘ | ↘ | ↘ | ↘ | ↘ | ↗ |
| $\alpha$ | 1.54 | 1.543 | 1.547 | 1.554 | | | | |
| Trend | ↘ | ↘ | ↘ | ↘ | | | | |

*Rectangle 2:* World War I, civil war, foreign intervention, famine and high emigration resulted in the slump of the Russian population back then [226, 227]. According to Russian researchers' estimation, between 1917 AD and 1922 AD, the lost population of the Soviet Union was more than 12 million [226]. After that, the government launched many policies which promoted the steady growth of economics and population.

*Rectangle 3:* In the late 1930s, the Great Purge encompassed the entire Soviet Union, and millions of people were subjected to persecution (5 million, 7 million, 11 million or more? There are no official statistics) [228]. According to the estimation of historian Michael Ellman, in 1937∼1938, about 950,000∼1,200,000 Soviet people were killed, including those executed and those dead as a result of ill-treatment in captivity or detention [228]. Then, World War II cost 13% of the country's (the Soviet Union) population, to about 27 million, which was the greatest cataclysm for Russia (or the Soviet Union) of the 20th century [228].

As the slumps of *Rectangle 2* and *Rectangle 3* seriously violate the nature rule of population development, the power-activation neuronet model processes them as noises. Instead of neglecting them, the power-activation neuronet equipped with WASD algorithm just passes through the slumps of the short dynamics and shows the trend of the long dynamics. The losses of population above are not the only consequences of the several events. These events led to serious gender disparity and slow-increased fertility trend, which affected more the population potential [227]. In fact, up to now, the population of the countries of the former Soviet Union has still been under the impact of the several events.

## 19.3.3 Prediction

As substantiated previously, different values of $\alpha$ lead to different learning abilities of the power-activation neuronet equipped with WASD algorithm, thereby making the resultant predictions different. Owing to space limitation and results similarity, Fig. 19.5 and Fig. 19.6 show four different trends of Russian population predicted via power-activation neuronet equipped with WASD algorithm using different $\alpha$ values (i.e., $\alpha = 0.3041, 0.9601, 1.007$ and $1.43$). Specifically, from Fig. 19.5(a), we see that Russian population is predicted to keep relatively stable in the next decade. Compared to the down trends predicted in Fig. 19.6, the trend predicted in Fig. 19.5(a) is relatively optimistic, which may be the results of positive population policies or attractive immigration policies that Russian government made, makes or will make. Besides, Fig. 19.5(b) shows that Russian population is predicted to increase in an accelerated manner, which is quite different from other organizations' and/or researchers' predictions [221, 222, 226, 227]. Why? Recovery? Immigration?

Expansion? ... It seems astonishing, but it is possible in view of the long-dynamics passing-through situation of *Rectangle 2* and *Rectangle 3*. For the four possibilities, Table 19.3 further shows the predicted Russian population data in 2020 AD via power-activation neuronet equipped with WASD algorithm. Note that $\alpha = 1.007$ is the global minimum point which means that the predicted results in Fig. 19.6(b) are with the most possibility. Thus, in Table 19.4, we present the Russian population data per year of the next decade predicted via power-activation neuronet equipped with WASD algorithm at the global minimum point.

As we notice, minimum points (local or global) lead to different possibilities of Russian population trend in the next decade. From Fig. 19.3, we count that there are 44 minimum points, and every minimum point represents its own possibility of Russian population trend in the next decade. At every minimum point, corresponding numerical experiment is made to predict Russian population in the next decade. Then, Table 19.5 shows the next-decade trends of Russian population indicated by power-activation neuronet equipped with WASD algorithm using different $\alpha$ values at all minimum points. It follows from the table that, compared to 15 minimum points presenting the up-trend, 28 minimum points present the down-trend in the next decade, and only 1 minimum point presents a relatively stable trend. So, by simple calculation of Table 19.5, with 63.6% possibility the Russian population will decrease in the next decade, with 34.1% possibility it will increase, and with only 2.3% possibility it keeps relatively stable.

## 19.4   Chapter Summary

This chapter has constructed a power-activation neuronet equipped with WASD algorithm for the research of the Russian population. Based on the 2013-year Russian population data, via the constructed neuronet, the Russian population from 1000 AD to 1800 AD has been well estimated, some inconsistent population data around 1897 have been corrected, and the future trends of Russian population in the next decade have been predicted. As researchers in information technology, we try to propose a new perspective and method for sociological research such as population investigation. In addition, the research can provide a large quantity of high-quality population data and results supporting sociological researchers for their deeper study. It is also worth pointing out that the proposed model can be extended to the population analysis of other countries or the world, which will be our future research items.

# Chapter 20

# WASD Neuronet versus BP Neuronet Applied to Russian Population Prediction

Russian population problem attracts great concerns to the future trend of population and the development of the nation. Conventional researches on Russian population prediction are usually based on the standard cohort-component method. Such a method only allows for several factors (fertility, mortality and migration rates), and then leads to the lack of all-sidedness in the prediction results. With outstanding generalization ability, the feed-forward neuronet is considered to be a more appropriate substitute. Besides, the back-propagation (BP) is of the most widely used feed-forward neuronet. As the conventional BP neuronet has some inherent weaknesses, in this chapter, two types of improved feed-forward neuronet are constructed for the Russian population prediction. More specifically, a type of three-layer power-activation neuronet equipped with the BP algorithm and a type of three-layer power-activation neuronet equipped with the weights-and-structure-determination (WASD) algorithm are built on the basis of the 2013-year (from 1 AD to 2013 AD) historical population data for the Russian population prediction. By a lot of numerical studies, the future declining trend of Russian population in the next decade is predicted with the highest possibility. In addition, via the Russian population prediction, the comparisons on the performance between the WASD neuronet and BP neuronet are conducted and summarized.

## 20.1  Introduction

Benefiting from the inherent generalization ability, artificial neuronets (AN) have attracted considerable attention, and have thus been developed and applied widely in many scientific and engineering fields [229–232]. In these studies, the feed-forward neuronet with the error back-propagation (BP) training algorithm is now viewed as the most important neuronet, and has been involved widely in many theoretical and practical fields [142]. The main idea of the algorithm is to adjust the AN weights with a gradient-based descent direction until the neuronet input/output behavior gets a desired mapping [21,229]. However, the BP neuronet has many natural weaknesses, such as unknown local minima, slow convergence, and uncertainties about the optimal structure [21,123]. Such weaknesses of BP neuronet are serious impediments to the further development and applications in some practical fields. To remedy these weaknesses, two types of improvement have been developed and investigated based on the authors' previous work [21, 123]. On one hand, some orthogonal or linearly independent activation functions (e.g., power functions) are used to achieve better performance. On the other hand, a weights-and-structure-determination (WASD) algorithm is developed and applied, which can efficaciously determine the optimal weights and numbers of hidden-layer neurons [229].

Since the disintegration of the Soviet Union, Russian population has been declining. It is beyond dispute that Russia has the largest decrease of population in the world during the last two decades [222,226]. The country is confronted with a serious demographic crisis, which has been one of the biggest threat to the strong existence and future of the Russian nation [222]. Many researchers and organizations pay very close attention to the prediction of Russian population for the economy planning, social research and so on [222,223]. However, most of these population predictions use a standard cohort-component method, which is based on several limited factors (e.g., fertility, mortality and migration rates) [160,224]. As we know, the population development is subjected to the influence of multiple complicated factors (explicit or implicit ones). The conventional method may thus lead to the lack of all-sidedness in the prediction results [229]. We realize that the large amounts of historical population data contain the objective law of population development under the influence of all factors. So, with good generalization ability, the BP neuronet may be an option.

To remedy the weaknesses of the conventional BP neuronet and to overcome the drawbacks of the standard cohort-component method, two types of improved feed-forward neuronet are constructed for Russian population prediction. More specifically, a type of three-layer power-activation neuronet equipped with the BP algorithm and a type of three-layer power-activation neuronet equipped with the WASD algorithm are built on the basis of the 2013-year (from 1 AD to 2013 AD) historical population data for the Russian population prediction.

## 20.2    Neuronet Model and Algorithms

In this section, a three-layer power-activation neuronet model is built for the general purpose of Russian population prediction with main parameters assumed. Then, the BP algorithm and WASD algorithm are introduced to train the power-activation neuronet model, correspondingly.

### 20.2.1    Power-activation neuronet model

Based on the collected 2013-year historical population data, a three-layer (i.e., one input layer, one hidden layer, and one output layer) power-activation neuronet model is constructed with the structure shown in Fig. 20.1. In such a neuronet model, $t$ (denoting the year datum) is the neuronet input, and $y$ is the output of the neuronet. As illustrated in the figure, the hidden layer has $n$ neurons activated by a group of power functions $\varphi_j(t) = t^{j-1}$ with $j = 1, 2, \cdots, n$ denoting the $j$th hidden-layer neuron. Each of the input layer and output layer has one only neuron activated by the linear identity function, respectively. Besides, to simplify the structure, all thresholds of the neuronet are

**TABLE 20.1:** Russian population data in past 2013 years for learning and prediction.

| Year (AD) | 1 | 200 | 400 | 600 | 800 | 1000 | 1100 | 1200 | 1300 |
|---|---|---|---|---|---|---|---|---|---|
| Data (million) | 2.10 | 2.60 | 3.10 | 3.10 | 3.60 | 4.10 | 6.12 | 9.14 | 9.16 |
| Year (AD) | 1400 | 1500 | 1600 | 1700 | 1800 | 1850 | 1897 | 1900 | 1901 |
| Data (million) | 9.18 | 12.20 | 15.20 | 20.30 | 37.00 | 68.50 | 67.47 | 71.16 | 72.54 |
| Year (AD) | 1902 | 1903 | 1904 | 1905 | 1906 | 1907 | 1908 | 1909 | 1910 |
| Data (million) | 73.93 | 75.34 | 76.76 | 78.18 | 79.61 | 81.05 | 82.50 | 83.96 | 85.43 |
| Year (AD) | 1911 | 1912 | 1913 | 1914 | 1915 | 1916 | 1917 | 1918 | 1919 |
| Data (million) | 86.91 | 88.40 | 89.90 | 91.50 | 93.00 | 92.00 | 91.00 | 90.00 | 89.00 |
| Year (AD) | 1920 | 1921 | 1922 | 1923 | 1924 | 1925 | 1926 | 1927 | 1928 |
| Data (million) | 88.00 | 87.00 | 87.76 | 89.90 | 91.00 | 92.20 | 93.46 | 94.59 | 95.73 |
| Year (AD) | 1929 | 1930 | 1931 | 1932 | 1933 | 1934 | 1935 | 1936 | 1937 |
| Data (million) | 96.89 | 98.07 | 99.25 | 100.45 | 101.67 | 102.90 | 104.14 | 105.40 | 106.68 |
| Year (AD) | 1938 | 1939 | 1940 | 1941 | 1942 | 1943 | 1944 | 1945 | 1946 |
| Data (million) | 107.97 | 108.38 | 110.10 | 111.50 | 112.00 | 110.00 | 108.00 | 106.00 | 105.00 |
| Year (AD) | 1947 | 1948 | 1949 | 1950 | 1951 | 1952 | 1953 | 1954 | 1955 |
| Data (million) | 104.00 | 103.00 | 102.00 | 102.80 | 103.91 | 105.74 | 107.63 | 109.53 | 111.40 |
| Year (AD) | 1956 | 1957 | 1958 | 1959 | 1960 | 1961 | 1962 | 1963 | 1964 |
| Data (million) | 113.22 | 114.97 | 116.67 | 117.53 | 119.05 | 120.77 | 122.00 | 123.30 | 124.70 |
| Year (AD) | 1965 | 1966 | 1967 | 1968 | 1969 | 1970 | 1971 | 1972 | 1973 |
| Data (million) | 126.31 | 127.19 | 126.82 | 128.00 | 129.00 | 129.94 | 130.70 | 131.44 | 132.19 |
| Year (AD) | 1974 | 1975 | 1976 | 1977 | 1978 | 1979 | 1980 | 1981 | 1982 |
| Data (million) | 132.90 | 134.13 | 134.69 | 135.60 | 136.50 | 137.41 | 138.29 | 139.03 | 139.82 |
| Year (AD) | 1983 | 1984 | 1985 | 1986 | 1987 | 1988 | 1989 | 1990 | 1991 |
| Data (million) | 140.77 | 141.48 | 142.82 | 143.84 | 145.11 | 146.34 | 147.02 | 148.04 | 148.54 |
| Year (AD) | 1992 | 1993 | 1994 | 1995 | 1996 | 1997 | 1998 | 1999 | 2000 |
| Data (million) | 148.70 | 148.60 | 148.37 | 148.25 | 148.30 | 147.31 | 146.91 | 146.62 | 146.00 |
| Year (AD) | 2001 | 2002 | 2003 | 2004 | 2005 | 2006 | 2007 | 2008 | 2009 |
| Data (million) | 146.30 | 145.40 | 144.65 | 144.07 | 143.52 | 142.75 | 142.22 | 142.00 | 141.90 |
| Year (AD) | 2010 | 2011 | 2012 | 2013 | | | | | |
| Data (million) | 142.40 | 142.90 | 143.00 | 142.83 | | | | | |

set to be 0, and all weights connecting the input-layer neuron and hidden-layer neurons are fixed to be 1. Then, the relationship between input $t$ and output $y$ is established and denoted as

$$y = \sum_{j=1}^{n} w_j \varphi_j(t),$$

where $w_j$ denotes the weight connecting the $j$th hidden-layer neuron and the output-layer neuron.

## 20.2.2 BP algorithm

In 1986, one book [56] raised great concerns to the BP algorithm and promoted the development and applications of BP neuronets in scientific and engineering fields. As to the power-activation neuronet model constructed above, by the iterative BP training procedure, such a model may obtain the optimal connecting weights and make a good learning from the historical population data. In mathematics, the classical error back-propagation algorithm (or, say, weight-updating formula) can

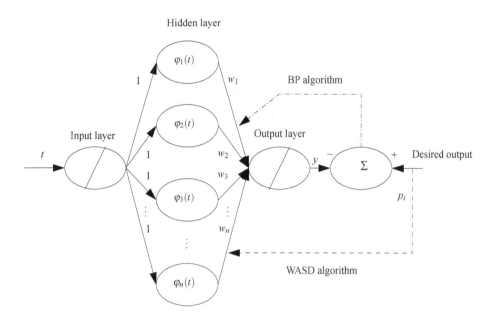

**FIGURE 20.1**: Model structure of three-layer power-activation neuronet with BP algorithm or WASD algorithm.

be simply denoted as [142]:

$$\mathbf{w}(k+1) = \mathbf{w}(k) + \Delta\mathbf{w}(k) = \mathbf{w}(k) - \eta \frac{\partial u(\mathbf{w})}{\partial \mathbf{w}}\bigg|_{\mathbf{w}=\mathbf{w}(k)},$$

where $\mathbf{w}$ denotes the vector of connecting weights, i.e., $\mathbf{w} = [w_1, w_2, \cdots, w_n]^{\mathrm{T}} \in \mathbb{R}^n$, and $k = 0, 1, 2, \cdots$ denotes the iteration index during the training procedure. Besides, $\Delta\mathbf{w}(k)$ denotes the weight-updating increment at the $k$th iteration; and, with $\eta$ denoting the learning rate (i.e., learning step size), $\eta$ should be small enough [229]. In addition, $u(\mathbf{w})$ denotes the performance indicator of the neuronet.

Moreover, we define $(t_i, p_i)\,|_{i=1}^m$ to be the data-set of sample pairs, where, in addition to $t_m = 2013$, we know that $p_i$ (denoting the collected Russian population datum in year $t_i$) is the $i$th desired output. Besides, the input vector $\mathbf{t}$, the desired output vector $\mathbf{p}$, and the activation matrix $\Psi$ are respectively defined as

$$\mathbf{t} = \begin{bmatrix} t_1 \\ t_2 \\ \vdots \\ t_m \end{bmatrix} \in \mathbb{R}^m, \ \mathbf{p} = \begin{bmatrix} p_1 \\ p_2 \\ \vdots \\ p_m \end{bmatrix} \in \mathbb{R}^m, \ \Psi = \begin{bmatrix} \varphi_1(t_1) & \varphi_2(t_1) & \cdots & \varphi_n(t_1) \\ \varphi_1(t_2) & \varphi_2(t_2) & \cdots & \varphi_n(t_2) \\ \vdots & \vdots & \ddots & \vdots \\ \varphi_1(t_m) & \varphi_2(t_m) & \cdots & \varphi_n(t_m) \end{bmatrix} \in \mathbb{R}^{m \times n}.$$

Then, let us define the root-mean-square error (RMSE) to denote the neuronet learning error as follows:

$$\varepsilon(\mathbf{w}) = \sqrt{\frac{\sum\limits_{i=1}^m \left( p_i - \sum\limits_{j=1}^n w_j \varphi_j(t_i) \right)^2}{m}} = \frac{\|\Psi\mathbf{w}(k) - \mathbf{p}\|_2}{\sqrt{m}}. \tag{20.1}$$

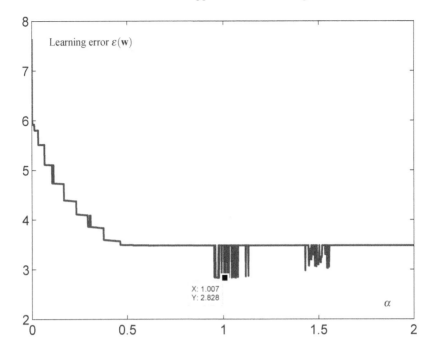

**FIGURE 20.2**: Learning error of power-activation neuronet with WASD algorithm for Russian population prediction.

In this chapter, for the convenience of deriving, the performance indicator of the power-activation neuronet with BP algorithm is further defined as

$$u(\mathbf{w}) = \frac{1}{2}\sum_{i=1}^{m} \left( p_i - \sum_{j=1}^{n} w_j \varphi_j(t_i) \right)^2 = \frac{\|\Psi\mathbf{w}(k) - \mathbf{p}\|_2^2}{2}. \qquad (20.2)$$

Furthermore, based on literatures [142, 229], the weight-updating formula of the power-activation neuronet with BP algorithm for Russian population prediction can be obtained as

$$\mathbf{w}(k+1) = \mathbf{w}(k) - \eta \Psi^{\mathrm{T}}(\Psi\mathbf{w}(k) - \mathbf{p}), \qquad (20.3)$$

where we initially set $\eta = 0.5/\sqrt{\mathrm{trace}(\Psi^{\mathrm{T}}\Psi)}$ in this chapter [229]. It is also worth pointing out that, based on Equations (20.1) and (20.2), the relationship between $\varepsilon(\mathbf{w})$ and $u(\mathbf{w})$ is built up: $\varepsilon(\mathbf{w}) = \sqrt{2u(\mathbf{w})/m}$.

Note that the conventional BP neuronet is activated by sigmoid functions and/or linear functions [142], which can greatly impact the performance of the neuronet in the problem solving. Meanwhile, to the best of the authors' knowledge, there had been relatively little work in the systematic manner to investigate the activation functions. Since the mid-2000s, the authors' team has been investigating the linearly independent or orthogonal activation functions in the feed-forward neuronet framework, showing excellent improvement [21, 123]. So, in this chapter, the three-layer BP neuronet activated by a group of power functions is constructed for Russian population prediction.

### 20.2.3 WASD algorithm

Based on the aforementioned thought and improvement, since 2007, the authors' team has gradually opened up a new perspective to improve the performance of the neuronet, and finally developed

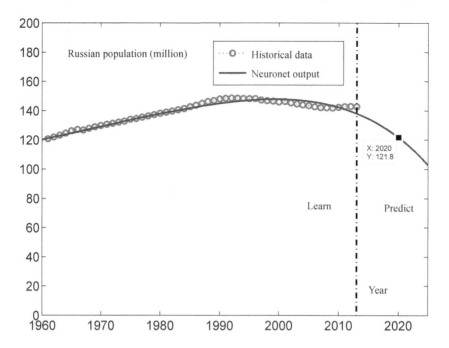

**FIGURE 20.3**: Learning and prediction results of power-activation neuronet with WASD algorithm using $\alpha = 1.007$ (global minimum point).

the WASD algorithm [123]. Such an algorithm, using the pseudo inverse principle, can directly determine the optimal weights and automatically obtain the optimal structure (i.e., the number of hidden-layer neurons with the minimal RMSE) of the feed-forward neuronet.

According to the studies [123, 176], the optimal weights-direct-determination (WDD) formula of the power-activation neuronet with WASD algorithm can be given immediately as

$$\mathbf{w} = (\mathbf{\Psi}^T \mathbf{\Psi})^{-1} \mathbf{\Psi}^T \mathbf{p} = \text{pinv}(\mathbf{\Psi})\mathbf{p}, \qquad (20.4)$$

where $\text{pinv}(\mathbf{\Psi})$ denotes the pseudoinverse of the activation matrix $\mathbf{\Psi}$, and other variables or parameters are defined as before.

Based on the optimal weight vector determined by the WDD formula (20.4), the optimal neuronet structure can be automatically obtained by the WASD algorithm. For the convenience of understanding, the detailed operation flow of the WASD algorithm is as follows.

*Step 1:* Obtain the data-set of sample pairs $\{(t_i, p_i)|_{i=1}^m\}$ for training. Initialize the structure of the power-activation neuronet with $n = 1$, and set $n_{\text{opt}} = 1$. Besides, $\varepsilon_{\text{min}}$ is set initially large enough (e.g., $\varepsilon_{\text{min}} = 10^3$ or "inf" in MATLAB).

*Step 2:* Let $n \longleftarrow n + 1$. Then construct the power-activation neuronet.

*Step 3:* Calculate the weights between the hidden-layer and output-layer neurons via WDD formula (20.4), and calculate the corresponding RMSE $\varepsilon$.

*Step 4:* If $\varepsilon > \varepsilon_{\text{min}}$, proceed to *Step 5*. Otherwise, let $\varepsilon_{\text{min}} \longleftarrow \varepsilon$ and $n_{\text{opt}} \longleftarrow n$, and proceed to *Step 2*.

*Step 5:* If $n < n_{\text{opt}} + 2$, then proceed to *Step 2*. Otherwise, proceed to *Step 6*.

*Step 6:* Output and save the optimal number of hidden-layer neurons $n_{\text{opt}}$, the minimal RMSE $\varepsilon_{\text{min}}$ and the run time. Then terminate the procedure.

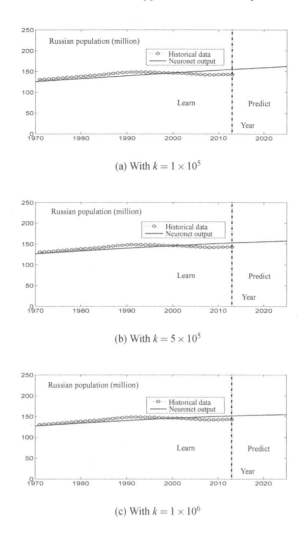

(a) With $k = 1 \times 10^5$

(b) With $k = 5 \times 10^5$

(c) With $k = 1 \times 10^6$

**FIGURE 20.4**: Learning and prediction results of power-activation neuronet with BP algorithm for Russian population prediction with iteration index $k = 1 \times 10^5$, $5 \times 10^5$ and $1 \times 10^6$, respectively.

## 20.3 Further Comparisons via Russian Population Prediction

In this section, the power-activation neuronet models with WASD and BP algorithms are applied to predicting Russian population based on the 2013-year historical population data, respectively. Meanwhile, via Russian population prediction, the comparisons of performance between the WASD neuronet and the BP neuronet are conducted and summarized.

### 20.3.1 Prediction results of WASD algorithm

Based on the previous analysis, the power-activation neuronet model with WASD algorithm is applied to learning the historical Russian population data in the past 2013 years shown in Table 20.1, and then predicting the future trend. Note that, in this chapter, to improve the performance

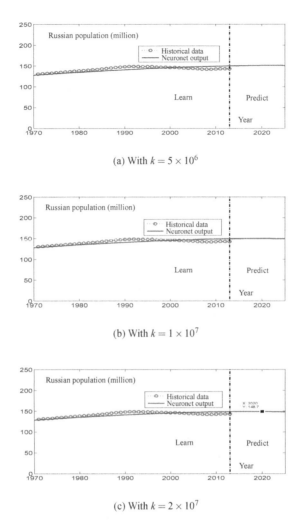

(a) With $k = 5 \times 10^6$

(b) With $k = 1 \times 10^7$

(c) With $k = 2 \times 10^7$

**FIGURE 20.5**: Learning and prediction results of power-activation neuronet with BP algorithm for Russian population prediction with iteration index $k = 5 \times 10^6$, $1 \times 10^7$ and $2 \times 10^7$, respectively.

and to fasten the calculations [225], the time interval $[1, 2013]$ is normalized to the interval $[0, \alpha]$, although the domain of the power-activation function is $\mathbb{R}$. To better investigate the relationship between the normalization factor $\alpha$ and the neuronet performance (i.e., the learning error of WASD-power-activation neuronet in the form of RMSE), numerical studies are performed with the related results shown in Fig. 20.2. Evidently, the figure indicates that different $\alpha$ values lead to different learning abilities of the neuronet. Besides, as seen from the figure, there exists a global minimum point $\alpha = 1.007$, using which the neuronet has the best learning performance with the minimal $\varepsilon_{min} = 2.828$ (i.e., relative error 1.98% to Russian population datum in 2013). It is worth pointing out that, corresponding to the global minimum point (i.e., $\alpha = 1.007$), the number of hidden-layer neurons is 28.

Based on the obtained optimal structure, the numerical study is performed to predict the Russian population via power-activation neuronet with WASD algorithm using $\alpha = 1.007$, and the related results are shown in Fig. 20.3. As shown in the figure, with the highest possibility, Russian population will keep a slowly declining trend in the next decade, and decline to 121.8 million by 2020.

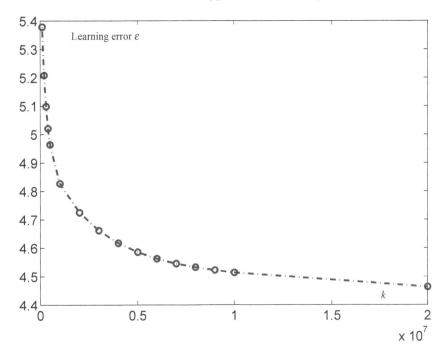

**FIGURE 20.6**: Relationship between iteration index $k$ and learning RMSE $\varepsilon$ of power-activation neuronet with BP algorithm.

Note that the predicted results above correspond to the error (i.e., RMSE) of 2.828 million, and the run time of the numerical study is 0.249 s.

### 20.3.2 Prediction results of BP algorithm

Based on the optimal structure (i.e., 28 hidden-layer neurons) obtained previously, the power-activation neuronet with BP algorithm model is used to predicting the Russian population. Since the iteration index $k$ can greatly impact the neuronet performance, in this chapter, we choose $k = 1 \times 10^5$, $2 \times 10^5$, $3 \times 10^5$, $4 \times 10^5$, $5 \times 10^5$, $1 \times 10^6$, $2 \times 10^6$, $3 \times 10^6$, $4 \times 10^6$, $5 \times 10^6$, $6 \times 10^6$, $7 \times 10^6$, $8 \times 10^6$, $9 \times 10^6$, $1 \times 10^7$ and $2 \times 10^7$ to run the power-activation neuronet with BP algorithm model for the Russian population prediction. For the convenience of comparison and analysis, the results with representative values of $k$, i.e., $k = 1 \times 10^5$, $5 \times 10^5$, $1 \times 10^6$, are shown in Fig. 20.4, and $k = 5 \times 10^6$, $1 \times 10^7$ and $2 \times 10^7$, are shown in Fig. 20.5. Besides, to better understand the relationship between the $k$ values and the RMSE (or, say, learning and prediction performance), Fig. 20.6 is generated and presented with the X-axis denoting $k$ and the Y-axis denoting the neuronet learning error (in the form of RMSE). As seen from Figs. 20.4 through 20.6, the bigger $k$ value leads to the smaller learning error, which also means the better prediction performance. Evidently, among several selected $k$ values mentioned above, $k = 2 \times 10^7$ is used to achieve the relatively optimal prediction results of Russian population via the power-activation neuronet with BP algorithm model. As shown in Fig. 20.5(c), with the relatively highest possibility, Russian population will decline with a very small rate in the next decade. Note that such a prediction result has an RMSE error of 4.463 (i.e., relative error 3.12% to the Russian population datum in 2013), and the run time of the numerical study is 1392860.871 s (or, say, 386.9 hours or 16.1 days).

**TABLE 20.2:** Learning and prediction results of power-activation neuronet via BP algorithm with different values of iteration index $k$ for Russian population prediction.

| $k$ | $1 \times 10^5$ | $2 \times 10^5$ | $3 \times 10^5$ | $4 \times 10^5$ | $5 \times 10^5$ |
|---|---|---|---|---|---|
| $\varepsilon$ | 5.378 | 5.208 | 5.099 | 5.020 | 4.963 |
| $t_{\text{run}}$ (s) | 51.712 | 170.498 | 376.038 | 650.555 | 1031.440 |
| $k$ | $1 \times 10^6$ | $2 \times 10^6$ | $3 \times 10^6$ | $4 \times 10^6$ | $5 \times 10^6$ |
| $\varepsilon$ | 4.827 | 4.725 | 4.662 | 4.617 | 4.586 |
| $t_{\text{run}}$ (s) | 3624.968 | 15739.720 | 36861.764 | 52648.378 | 88034.123 |
| $k$ | $6 \times 10^6$ | $7 \times 10^6$ | $8 \times 10^6$ | $9 \times 10^6$ | $1 \times 10^7$ |
| $\varepsilon$ | 4.563 | 4.546 | 4.532 | 4.522 | 4.513 |
| $t_{\text{run}}$ (s) | 120985.387 | 175831.555 | 228705.070 | 295452.607 | 351688.364 |
| $k$ | $2 \times 10^7$ | $3 \times 10^7$ (estimate) | $4 \times 10^7$ (estimate) | | |
| $\varepsilon$ | 4.462 | 4.411 | 4.360 | | |
| $t_{\text{run}}$ (s) | 1392860.871 | 2434033.378 | 3475205.885 | | |

### 20.3.3 Discussion

To compare the performance between these two types of neuronet, the run time and neuronet learning errors (i.e., RMSEs) of the power-activation neuronet with WASD and BP algorithms with all selected $k$ values are listed in Table 20.2. From the table, we can find that the power-activation neuronet with WASD algorithm has the shortest run time and minimal error, or say, the most excellent efficiency and accuracy. In practical applications, with the run time limited, $k$ cannot be an infinite value. So, as for the learning error, the power-activation neuronet with WASD algorithm has a certainly better performance than the power-activation neuronet with BP algorithm. In terms of the power-activation neuronet with BP algorithm, from Fig. 20.7, we may find the relationship between run time and $k$ values: with the increase of $k$ value, the related run time of the power-activation neuronet with BP algorithm increases with a great rate. This is also the reason why we select the $k$ values up to $2 \times 10^7$. In contrast, the procedure of WASD-power-activation neuronet for Russian population prediction only needs a run time of 0.249 s with the RMSE $\varepsilon$ being 3.478.

In summary, the power-activation neuronet with WASD algorithm is illustrated to be a better one than the power-activation neuronet with BP algorithm for Russian population prediction. With the highest possibility, as shown in Fig. 20.3 [and substantiated further by Fig. 20.5(c), though slightly different], Russian population will keep a gently declining trend in the next decade and may decrease to 121.8 million by 2020.

## 20.4 Chapter Summary

In this chapter, the basic theories and developments of the neuronet with BP and WASD algorithms have been introduced. To solve the problem of Russian population prediction, two types of improved neuronet respectively equipped with the BP algorithm and the WASD algorithm have been constructed. Using these two neuronet models, Russian population has been successfully predicted with acceptable errors. Furthermore, via the Russian population prediction, the performances

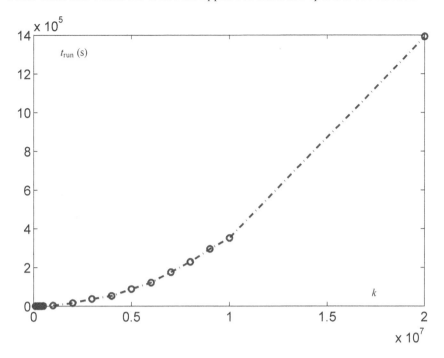

**FIGURE 20.7**: Relationship between iteration index $k$ and run time $t_{run}$ of power-activation neuronet with BP algorithm.

of the power-activation neuronet models with WASD and BP algorithms have been compared and analyzed, showing that the neuronet with WASD algorithm is much more efficient and accurate than the one with BP algorithm. It is reasonable to further think that the power-activation neuronet with WASD algorithm may also be a preeminent method for the population prediction of other countries or regions. Note that the Russian population data from 2014 to 2017 (the time that we prepared this chapter in the book) in WPP 2017 [167] are 143.76 million, 143.88 million, 143.96 million and 143.98 million, respectively. For the convenience of readers, the above population data can be used to further compare with the population prediction results reported in this chapter.

# Chapter 21

## Application to Chinese Population Prediction

As one of the most important factors influencing the development potential of the country, Chinese population attracts considerable attention. Some official organizations regularly publish the predictions of Chinese population every calendar year. However, most of the predictions use the standard cohort-component method, which does not allow for all relevant impact factors and may lose sight of some important uncertainty factors. To overcome the aforementioned limitations, in this chapter, we present a three-layer feed-forward neuronet approach equipped with a weights-and-structure-determination (WASD) algorithm for the population prediction of China. Numerical studies further substantiate the feasibility of such an approach and indicate that there are three kinds of possibilities for the progress of Chinese population in the next decade. With the highest possibility, Chinese population will keep continual increase with a gentle growth rate.

## 21.1 Introduction

Population analysis plays a significant role in various social fields, such as policy planning, social and health research, and development monitoring [159, 162, 233]. China has the biggest population size and relatively complicated demographics structure in the world. The population of China is faced with constantly intensifying old problems and newly emerging challenges, such as a shrinking labor force, aging population and sex-selective abortion [188, 189]. Evidently, the population problem has been one of the critical problems that influence and restrict the development of China [233].

The United Nations (UN) publishes prediction of the population of China every two years as a report called the WPP [162]. We refer to the 2012 revision as WPP 2012 here. This prediction is widely used by researchers, international organizations and governments, especially the groups with less developed statistical systems. It is the de facto standard [220]. The prediction is built on the standard cohort-component method, which relates to the number of births, the number of

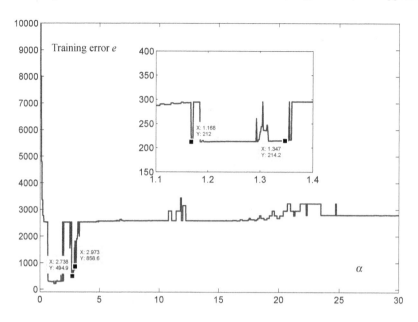

**FIGURE 21.1**: Relationship between normalization factor $\alpha$ and training error $e$ of power-activation WASD neuronet with optimal structure and weights.

immigrants, the number of deaths, and the number of emigrants [162, 233, 234]. Such a method loses sight of various uncertain factors' influence on population development, and may thus lead to larger errors of the prediction results. Taking WPP 2012 for example, we see that the annual error between its prediction result and the actual Chinese population is over 20 million. Compared with around 6 million people of annual increment in recent years, this larger error may discount the reference value. As we realize, the historical data contain the general regularity of the population development, and comprehensively reflect the population development under the influence of almost all impact factors [233]. Based on the historical population data, we can get the overall view on the progress of Chinese population from the past to the future. Therefore, it makes good sense if we can build a model using historical population data and the general regularity within them, for the prediction of Chinese population.

## 21.2    Power-Activation Neuronet Model

Inspired by the neural system in human body, artificial neuronets (AN) have attracted considerable attention as candidates for novel computational systems [176]. Benefiting from the inherent nonlinearity and learning ability, the feed-forward neuronets have been developed and applied widely in many scientific and engineering fields [235–237]. From our previous work [176], a three-layer feed-forward neuronet can approximate/estimate the nonlinear continuous equations with high accuracy. With a host of experiments and years of testing, we have found out that linearly independent or orthogonal activation equations (e.g., power equations) can help to improve the performance of neuronet models [176].

Theoretically guaranteeing the efficacy of the neuronet model, we make some simplifications here to reduce the complexity of the neuronet structure design, analysis and computation. In the

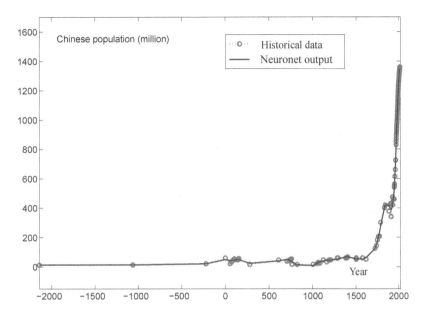

**FIGURE 21.2**: Learning results of power-activation neuronet with WASD algorithm for Chinese population prediction using $\alpha = 1.168$ (global minimum point).

chapter, based on the rough data of 4153 years (i.e., the data from 2140 BC to 2013 AD), a three-layer feed-forward power-activation neuronet is used and investigated for the prediction of Chinese population, with the structure shown in Fig. 19.1 of Chapter 19. Specifically, the hidden layer has $n$ neurons activated by a group of power functions denoted as $\{\varphi_j(t)\}$ with $j = 1, 2, \cdots, n$. In addition, the input layer and the output layer each have one neuron activated by the linear identity equation. We set the connecting weights from the input layer to the hidden layer to be 1; and the connecting weights from the hidden layer to the output layer, which are denoted as $\{w_j\}$, are to be determined or adjusted in the learning process.

One of the most difficult parts of applying AN models in dealing with practical prediction is to determine the number of the hidden-layer neurons. In general, the neuronet with too few hidden-layer neurons may fail to achieve the expected learning accuracy, whereas excessive hidden-layer neurons may cause the over-fitting phenomenon, poor generalization ability and high computational complexity [65, 142]. We thus introduce the weights-and-structure-determination (WASD) algorithm for the feed-forward power-activation neuronet [176]. Such a WASD algorithm can determine effectively the weights connecting the hidden layer and the output layer, and obtain automatically the optimal structure of the power-activation neuronet model. Such a model equipped with the WASD algorithm can find the smallest training error between the output value and the exact value, thereby making it an excellent alternative for learning and prediction. More specifically, $\{(t_i, p_i)|_{i=1}^{M}\}$ denotes the sample pairs of the training data-set for the WASD neuronet, where $t_i \in \mathbb{R}$ denotes the $i$th input (the year), $p_i \in \mathbb{R}$ denotes the $i$th desired output (the population of China in the year $t_i$), and $M$ denotes the total number of sample pairs. Then, we have the mean square error (MSE) equation for the WASD neuronet defined as follows:

$$e = \frac{1}{M} \sum_{i=1}^{M} \left( p_i - \sum_{j=1}^{n} w_j \varphi_j(t_i) \right)^2. \tag{21.1}$$

For every given number of hidden-layer neurons, we can get its related training MSE via (21.1). By traversing all the possible numbers of hidden-layer neurons, we can finally obtain the mapping

**TABLE 21.1:**   Testing errors of power-activation neuronet with WASD algorithm for Chinese population prediction using different values of $\beta$ and $\alpha$ at global minimum points.

| $\beta$ | 2012 | 2011 | 2010 | 2009 | 2008 | 2007 | 2006 | 2005 |
|---|---|---|---|---|---|---|---|---|
| $\alpha$ | 1.185 | 1.202 | 1.204 | 1.219 | 1.234 | 1.235 | 1.243 | 1.244 |
| 2013 | 0.00796 | 0.0104 | 0.01659 | 0.01246 | 0.01389 | 0.01582 | 0.01103 | 0.01188 |
| 2012 | | 0.00739 | 0.01224 | 0.00941 | 0.01076 | 0.01235 | 0.00868 | 0.00941 |
| 2011 | | | 0.00846 | 0.00668 | 0.00796 | 0.00925 | 0.00652 | 0.00715 |
| 2010 | | | | 0.00450 | 0.00571 | 0.00673 | 0.00479 | 0.00534 |
| 2009 | | | | | 0.00389 | 0.00467 | 0.00338 | 0.00385 |
| 2008 | | | | | | 0.00019 | 0.00148 | 0.00101 |
| 2007 | | | | | | | 0.00283 | 0.00243 |
| 2006 | | | | | | | | 0.00763 |

relationship between the MSE and the number of hidden-layer neurons. The optimal structure of neuronet corresponds to the smallest MSE, and thus we can define the optimal structure and weights for the power-activation neuronet model.

## 21.3   Numerical Studies

In our analysis, the population data of China are partly based on literatures [233, 238]. In this chapter, based on the Chinese demographic data of 4153 years, a three-layer power-activation neuronet equipped with a WASD algorithm is constructed and investigated for the prediction of Chinese population.

### 21.3.1   Data normalization

Before applying the power-activation neuronet equipped with the WASD algorithm (i.e., power-activation WASD neuronet) to learn Chinese population data, to improve the performance and fasten the calculations [235], the time interval $[-2140, 2013]$ is normalized to the interval $[0, \alpha]$ with $\alpha$ denoting the normalization factor. The data-set for learning is thus generated. Then, on the basis of the generated data-set, the learning ability of power-activation WASD neuronet is investigated. For illustration, $\alpha = 1.168$ is chosen here as an example (see also Fig. 21.1), and the learning results via power-activation WASD neuronet using $\alpha = 1.168$ are illustrated in Fig. 21.2. Specifically, as shown in the figure, power-activation WASD neuronet has a good performance in data learning, since there is little difference between the neuronet output data and the historical data. For such a power-activation WASD neuronet model, the number of hidden-layer neurons determined automatically by the WASD algorithm is 61. In addition, the minimum training error is 211.954 (i.e., the smallest MSE $14.5586^2$), which also means that the relative error corresponding to Chinese population data in 2013 is 0.0107 (i.e., 1.07%), showing the feasibility of the power-activation WASD neuronet on the learning of Chinese population.

### 21.3.2   Testing results

As mentioned previously, the time interval $[-2140, 2013]$ is normalized to the interval $[0, \alpha]$. Through the WASD algorithm, the optimal structure and weights for any given $\alpha$ are automatically determined, and different values of $\alpha$ lead to different learning and prediction results of the

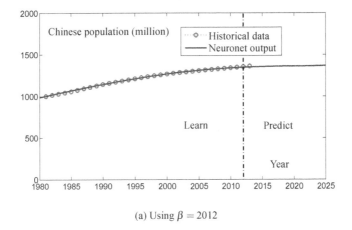

(a) Using $\beta = 2012$

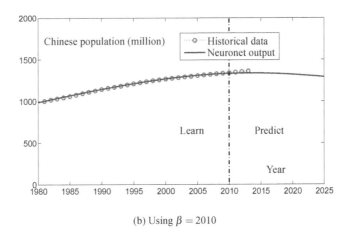

(b) Using $\beta = 2010$

**FIGURE 21.3**: Different testing results of power-activation neuronet with WASD algorithm for Chinese population prediction at global minimum points using $\beta = 2012$ and $\beta = 2010$ corresponding to two columns in Table 21.1.

power-activation WASD neuronet. For better understanding, Fig. 21.1 shows the relationship between the normalization factor $\alpha$ and the training error of power-activation WASD neuronet with the optimal structure (i.e., the smallest MSE). As shown in the figure, superior learning and prediction performance of power-activation WASD neuronet can be achieved by choosing a suitable value of $\alpha$. More importantly, from the figure, we can observe that there exist some local minimum points and a global minimum point, such as the marked ones, which correspond to different values of $\alpha$. Such local and global minimum points indicate the possible situations on Chinese population prediction via power-activation WASD neuronet, and the global minimum point further implies the most possible situation. Note that $\alpha = 1.168$ is the global minimum point that is shown in Fig. 21.1. This is the reason why we choose $\alpha = 1.168$ as an illustrative example for learning and prediction of Chinese population in the previous part. For every normalization factor $\alpha$, we have the corresponding best structure and weights of power-activation WASD neuronet. To further investigate and substantiate the effectiveness of the power-activation WASD neuronet, a host of numerical studies on its prediction ability are performed based on Chinese population data. We take the population data of China in the time interval $[-2140, \beta]$, with $\beta < 2013$, to train the power-activation WASD

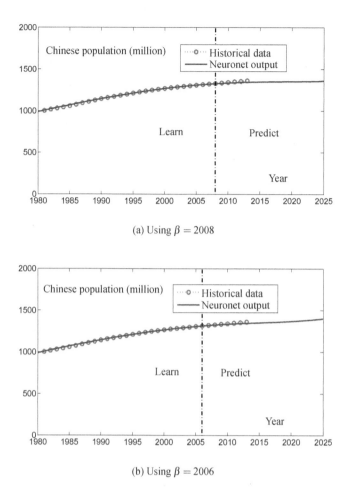

(a) Using $\beta = 2008$

(b) Using $\beta = 2006$

**FIGURE 21.4**: Different testing results of power-activation neuronet with WASD algorithm for Chinese population prediction at global minimum points using $\beta = 2008$ and $\beta = 2006$ corresponding to two columns in Table 21.1.

neuronet model, and then use the other data for the prediction-type testing of the model. It is worth pointing out that the $\alpha$ values at the global minimum points are chosen for the prediction-type testing of different $\beta$ values. Due to the space limitation, this chapter chooses $\beta = 2006, 2007, 2008,$ 2009, 2010, 2011 and 2012 to test the model, with the results presented in Table 21.1. The difference between the actual value and prediction value of the $i$th year is $\varepsilon_i = |(y_i - p_i)/p_i|$, where $y_i$ and $p_i$ denote the power-activation WASD neuronet output and the actual Chinese population of the $i$th year, respectively. As seen from Fig. 21.3 and Fig. 21.4 as well as Table 21.1, the prediction-type testing errors are quite small throughout the test cases, which further substantiates the excellent performance of the power-activation WASD neuronet model.

### 21.3.3    Prediction results

Based on the constructed power-activation WASD neuronet model, we can now apply it to dealing with the population prediction problem. Due to the result similarity and space limitation, Fig. 21.5 shows the prediction results via power-activation WASD neuronet model using $\alpha = 1.168$,

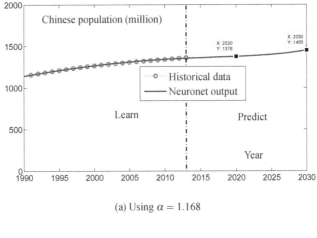

(a) Using $\alpha = 1.168$

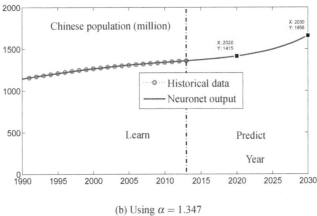

(b) Using $\alpha = 1.347$

**FIGURE 21.5**: Different prediction results of power-activation neuronet with WASD algorithm for Chinese population prediction using $\alpha = 1.168$ and $\alpha = 1.347$ with each subfigure corresponding to local or global minimum point in Fig. 21.1.

1.347, 2.738 and 2.973 only. From the figure, we can observe that there are four different prediction results for Chinese population. As seen from Fig. 21.5(a) and Fig. 21.5(b), Chinese population is predicted to increase gradually, which could incorporate the high-variant prediction of the WPP 2012 [162]. Note that $\alpha = 1.168$ is the global minimum point in Fig. 21.1, which means that Fig. 21.5(a) shows the prediction result with the highest possibility. Besides, there exists a surprising prediction in Fig. 21.6(a) that Chinese population will go down gradually from 2014, and we are trying to find the clues and evidence for this possible result later. In addition, it is worth pointing out that Fig. 21.6(b) shows the turning point of the population development, i.e., there may exist a peak of Chinese population at some point in the next decade.

As we notice, every (global or local) minimum point in Fig. 21.1 represents its own prediction possibility for the future trend of Chinese population. The $\alpha$ values corresponding to all minimum points in the figure are thus found. Meanwhile, numerical studies corresponding to all the minimum points in the figure are conducted to investigate all the possibilities for Chinese population trends in the next decade. Table 21.2 shows the different prediction trends of Chinese population in the next decade using the $\alpha$ values corresponding to all the minimum points in Fig. 21.1. According to

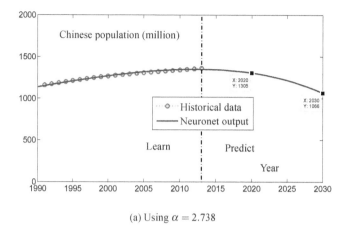

(a) Using $\alpha = 2.738$

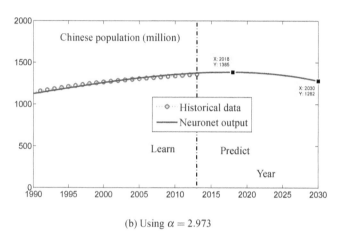

(b) Using $\alpha = 2.973$

**FIGURE 21.6**: Different prediction results of power-activation neuronet with WASD algorithm for Chinese population prediction using $\alpha = 2.738$ and $\alpha = 2.973$ with each subfigure corresponding to local or global minimum point in Fig. 21.1.

our statistics, there are 42 minimum points (about 47.7% of total 88 minimum points) presenting the step-up trends in the next decade, 34 minimum points (about 38.6%) presenting the step-down trends in the next decade, and 12 minimum points (about 13.6%) presenting the up-down trends in the next decade. That is to say, with 47.7% possibility exceeding other two kinds of possibilities, Chinese population will keep a step-up trend, which also cross-validates the prediction results in Fig. 21.5(a) using $\alpha = 1.168$ corresponding to the global minimum point (i.e., with the highest possibility).

## 21.4    Discussion

Due to the large population base and the historical trend of continuous growth, the Chinese population will keep increasing with a relatively gentle rate, as shown in Fig. 21.5(a) and Fig.

**TABLE 21.2:** Different prediction trends of power-activation neuronet with WASD algorithm for Chinese population prediction in the next decade using values of $\alpha$ corresponding to all (global or local) minimum points in Fig. 21.1.

| $\alpha$ | 0.8291 | 0.8331 | 0.8411 | 0.8521 | 0.8951 | 0.9121 | 0.9191 | 0.9421 | 0.9531 |
|---|---|---|---|---|---|---|---|---|---|
| Trend | ↘ | ↘ | ↘ | ↘ | ↘ | ↘ | ↘ | ↘ | ↘ |
| $\alpha$ | 0.9801 | 1.004 | 1.042 | 1.083 | 1.098 | 1.116 | 1.134 | 1.168 | 1.185 |
| Trend | ↘ | ↘ | ↘ | ↘ | ↘ | ↘ | ↘ | ↗ | ↗ |
| $\alpha$ | 1.192 | 1.197 | 1.232 | 1.234 | 1.237 | 1.242 | 1.294 | 1.312 | 1.316 |
| Trend | ↗ | ↗ | ↗ | ↗ | ↗ | ↗ | ↗ | ↗↘ | ↗↘ |
| $\alpha$ | 1.347 | 1.354 | 1.359 | 1.446 | 1.531 | 1.551 | 1.726 | 1.737 | 1.768 |
| Trend | ↗ | ↗ | ↘ | ↘ | ↘ | ↘ | ↘ | ↘ | ↘ |
| $\alpha$ | 1.771 | 1.779 | 1.787 | 1.899 | 1.969 | 1.998 | 2.527 | 2.559 | 2.587 |
| Trend | ↘ | ↘ | ↘ | ↘ | ↘ | ↘ | ↗ | ↗ | ↗ |
| $\alpha$ | 2.604 | 2.685 | 2.708 | 2.738 | 2.763 | 2.789 | 2.818 | 2.846 | 2.877 |
| Trend | ↘ | ↘ | ↘ | ↘ | ↗↘ | ↘ | ↗↘ | ↗↘ | ↗↘ |
| $\alpha$ | 2.909 | 2.918 | 2.938 | 2.959 | 2.968 | 2.973 | 2.992 | 3.003 | 3.052 |
| Trend | ↗↘ | ↗↘ | ↗↘ | ↗ | ↗↘ | ↗↘ | ↗ | ↗ | ↗ |
| $\alpha$ | 3.079 | 3.085 | 3.105 | 3.165 | 3.304 | 3.195 | 3.335 | 4.917 | 6.225 |
| Trend | ↗↘ | ↗ | ↗ | ↗ | ↗ | ↗ | ↗ | ↗ | ↗ |
| $\alpha$ | 6.501 | 6.711 | 7.144 | 11.05 | 11.87 | 12.24 | 15.58 | 16.15 | 16.75 |
| Trend | ↗ | ↗ | ↗ | ↗ | ↗ | ↗ | ↗ | ↗ | ↗ |
| $\alpha$ | 17.45 | 17.99 | 18.79 | 19.85 | 21.21 | 22.25 | 23.47 | | |
| Trend | ↗ | ↗ | ↗ | ↗ | ↗ | ↗ | ↗ | | |

21.5(b). Note that Fig. 21.5(a) presents a step-up trend of Chinese population with the highest possibility, since $\alpha = 1.168$ is the global minimum point in Fig. 21.1. Besides, according to the statistics of all minimum points in Fig. 21.1, with 47.7% possibility (i.e., the highest possibility), the Chinese population is predicted to keep a step-up trend. As a matter of fact, Chinese government has made the policies for controlling the rapid growth of the population since the 1970s. This so-called one-child policy, which has been viewed as a basic national policy of China since 1982, has been taking effect in the past decades and will continually take effect in the next decade (without ruling out unexpected events, e.g., disasters, wars) [236]. The downward trend shown in Fig. 21.6(a) might indicate the effect of this policy. In November 2013, Chinese government passed an amendment on urban population and family planning that the couples can have a second child if either of the parents is an only child. Just as the population growth stimulation strategy carried out by the effective governments in the history, this new policy might spur the growth of population. Under the influence of these two mutual restraint policies, it is possible that the population will increase gently and then peak at some year in the future as shown in Fig. 21.6(b). Thereby, those long-term systematic policies made by the government are indeed effective and efficient in controlling the population growth. With the successful policies, the Chinese population is well under control. Predictably, by estimating several possibilities for the future trends of Chinese population, more effective policies might be imperious to control the still-increasing population of China and also prevent or make full preparations for the down-trend of population development caused by family planning and other reasons.

## 21.5   Chapter Summary

In terms of population prediction, the power-activation WASD neuronet has allowed for all relevant factors influencing population development. Compared with WPP 2012, the proposed method has not involved the analysis of fertility rate, mortality rate, migration rate, age structure and sex structure. However, from a new and simple perspective, more accurate prediction results for gross population have been generated via generalizing the historical rule of Chinese population development. According to the research, with the highest possibility, Chinese population will keep increasing at a gentle rate in the next decade.

# Chapter 22

# WASD Neuronet versus BP Neuronet Applied to Chinese Population Prediction

Population is one of the most significant factors affecting the social and economic development of a country. Currently, China is facing a big challenge of population aging. It is important for the Chinese government to pay continuous attention to the population situation and take measures so as to keep the economic growth. Undoubtedly, the effectiveness of these measures depends crucially on the accurate prediction of Chinese population. Many methods, including the feed-forward neuronet equipped with back-propagation (BP) algorithm, have been proposed in order to improve the prediction accuracy. However, these methods possibly have their inherent limitations. In this chapter, we construct an enhanced feed-forward neuronet, i.e., a three-layer feed-forward power-activation neuronet equipped with the weights-and-structure-determination (WASD) algorithm, to predict the Chinese population. Numerical studies show that the Chinese population will continue to increase at a low rate in the next decade. The authors also compare the WASD algorithm with the BP algorithm for the power-activation neuronet, with numerical results showing the excellent performance of the former.

## 22.1    Introduction

China has not only the second biggest economy, but also the largest population in the world. Population (especially working-age population) is an important factor related to the potential of economic growth [162, 239, 240]. Currently, China is facing a big challenge of population aging. It is urgent for the Chinese government to adjust the population policy and take measures so as to keep the economic growth. Therefore, an accurate prediction for Chinese population is necessary to ensure the effectiveness of the population policy and measures.

The United Nations publishes the prediction of Chinese population every two years in a report. The prediction is based on the standard cohort-component method [162,234]. It is impossible to take all the factors into account explicitly, which will lead to the lack of all-sidedness in the prediction results. Taking the Chinese population in 2014 as an example, we can see that the actual population reported in [241] is 1369.436 million; however, the predicted one is 1385.567 million in [162]. The annual error between the predicted result and the actual population is more than 16 million.

The large prediction error that cohort-component method produces is caused by the omission of some important factors. These factors are implicitly contained in historical population data [239]. That is, to overcome the limitations of cohort-component method, we need to find some other methods which are able to model the implicit information in historical data. Fortunately, some sophisticated techniques, such as artificial neuronets (AN) with back-propagation (BP) algorithm, have been developed and widely used in academia and industry [239]. The BP algorithm is used to adjust the weights between neurons with a gradient-based descent strategy until the input/output behavior of neurons reaches a desired mapping [242]. Nevertheless, BP neuronet has several weaknesses such as unknown local minima, uncertainties about the optimal structure, and slow convergence [243]. Even worse, such weaknesses greatly prevent the further applications of BP neuronet. To remedy the forenamed weaknesses, an enhanced feed-forward neuronet has been proposed [123,176], which is called weights-and-structure-determination (WASD) neuronet [239]. The WASD neuronet has two advanced features compared with the conventional BP neuronet. Firstly, WASD neuronet employs orthogonal or linearly independent activation functions, such as power functions. Secondly, WASD can directly determine the optimal weights and the optimal number of hidden-layer neurons.

By making progress along the direction of Chinese population prediction in Chapter 21, this chapter employs the WASD neuronet to predict the Chinese population. Specifically, we develop a three-layer power-activation neuronet equipped with weights-and-structure-determination algorithm, which is then used to predict Chinese population in the next decade. The historical population data from 2140 BC to 2014 AD is used for neuronet model training. Furthermore, we also construct a conventional BP neuronet, for comparison purposes. Based on the historical data, we conduct a series of numerical experiments. The numerical results show that the Chinese population will continue to increase at a low rate in the next decade. The authors also found that the prediction performance of the neuronet with WASD algorithm is much better than that of the neuronet with BP algorithm.

## 22.2    Neuronet Model and Algorithms

In this section, a three-layer power-activation neuronet model is constructed for the general purpose of Chinese population prediction. Then, the BP and WASD algorithms for power-activation neuronet model are developed in details. The algorithms are applied to the subsequent numerical studies on the prediction of Chinese population.

### 22.2.1    Power-activation neuronet model

Firstly, we construct a three-layer (input layer, hidden layer, and output layer) power-activation neuronet model as shown in Fig. 20.1 of Chapter 20.

Then, we define $\left\{ (t_i, p_i) \,|_{i=1}^{m} \right\}$ as the set of input data (year) and desired output data (actual population size) for the neuronet, where $m$ denotes the number of training pairs. Thus, the input data vector $\mathbf{t}$ and the desired output data vector $\mathbf{p}$ can be written as

$$\mathbf{t} = [t_1, t_2, \cdots, t_m]^{\mathrm{T}} \in \mathbb{R}^m, \ \mathbf{p} = [p_1, p_2, \cdots, p_m]^{\mathrm{T}} \in \mathbb{R}^m.$$

**TABLE 22.1:** Notations for Equations (22.3) and (22.4).

| Symbol | Description |
|--------|-------------|
| $\mathbf{w}$ | Connection weight vector |
| $\Delta\mathbf{w}(k)$ | Weight-updating increment at the $k$th iteration |
| $\eta$ | Learning rate |
| $u(\mathbf{w})$ | Performance indicator |

In the neuronet model, we use power functions as the activation functions of neurons in hidden layer:

$$\varphi_j(t_i) = t_i^{j-1}, \tag{22.1}$$

where $t$ is the neuronet input with $j = 1, 2, \cdots, n$ and $i = 1, 2, \cdots, m$. A neuronet output $y_i$ is defined as the accumulation of the output from hidden layer. That is, $y_i$ can be further represented as the sum of the product of activation functions $\{\varphi_j(t_i)\}$ and connection weights $\{w_j\}$:

$$y_i = \sum_{j=1}^{n} w_j \varphi_j(t_i). \tag{22.2}$$

### 22.2.2 BP algorithm

We develop the corresponding BP algorithm to obtain the optimal connection weights between hidden neurons and output neuron. Mathematically, the BP algorithm (weight-updating formula) [142] is denoted as

$$\mathbf{w}(k+1) = \mathbf{w}(k) + \Delta\mathbf{w}(k), \tag{22.3}$$

where

$$\Delta\mathbf{w}(k) = -\eta \frac{\partial u(\mathbf{w})}{\partial \mathbf{w}}\bigg|_{\mathbf{w}=\mathbf{w}(k)}. \tag{22.4}$$

Note that the corresponding notations for Equations (22.3) and (22.4) are presented in Table 22.1. According to (22.1), the activation matrix $\Psi$ can be defined as

$$\Psi = \begin{bmatrix} \varphi_1(t_1) & \varphi_2(t_1) & \cdots & \varphi_n(t_1) \\ \varphi_1(t_2) & \varphi_2(t_2) & \cdots & \varphi_n(t_2) \\ \vdots & \vdots & \ddots & \vdots \\ \varphi_1(t_m) & \varphi_2(t_m) & \cdots & \varphi_n(t_m) \end{bmatrix} \in \mathbb{R}^{m \times n}.$$

After that, we define the following root-mean-square error (RMSE) to indicate the learning error of neuronet:

$$\varepsilon(\mathbf{w}) = \sqrt{\frac{\sum_{i=1}^{m}\left(p_i - \sum_{j=1}^{n} w_j \varphi_j(t_i)\right)^2}{m}} = \frac{\|\Psi\mathbf{w}(k) - \mathbf{p}\|_2}{\sqrt{m}}. \tag{22.5}$$

Besides, for the convenience of computing, derived from the definition of RMSE, indicator is introduced to denote the performance of power-activation neuronet:

$$u(\mathbf{w}) = \frac{1}{2}\sum_{i=1}^{m}\left(p_i - \sum_{j=1}^{n} w_j \varphi_j(t_i)\right)^2 = \frac{\|\Psi\mathbf{w}(k) - \mathbf{p}\|_2^2}{2}. \tag{22.6}$$

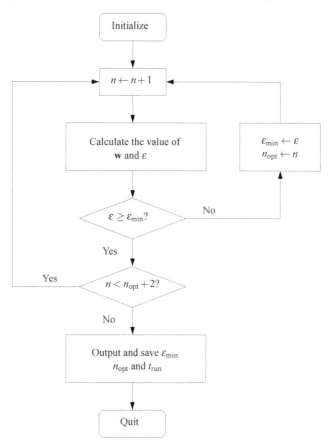

**FIGURE 22.1**: Flowchart of WASD algorithm for power-activation neuronet applied to Chinese population prediction.

Moreover, according to Equation (22.4) and Equation (22.6), we can rewrite Equation (22.3) as follows:

$$\mathbf{w}(k+1) = \mathbf{w}(k) - \eta \Psi^{T}(\Psi \mathbf{w}(k) - \mathbf{p}), \tag{22.7}$$

where $\eta = 0.5/\text{trace}(\Psi^{T}\Psi)$ is set in this chapter [239].

It is worthwhile pointing out that, in light of Equation (22.5) and Equation (22.6), the relationship between $\varepsilon(\mathbf{w})$ and $u(\mathbf{w})$ can be derived as follows:

$$\varepsilon(\mathbf{w}) = \sqrt{2u(\mathbf{w})/m}. \tag{22.8}$$

It is also worthwhile pointing out that the neurons in the conventional BP neuronet are activated by sigmoid functions or linear functions [142], which usually results in poor performance in solving practical problems [244]. Nevertheless, systematical researches have seldom been conducted on activation functions. Since the mid-2000s, we have been focusing on the study of linearly independent and orthogonal activation functions. The findings show that these kinds of activation functions perform better than the conventional sigmoid functions in the feed-forward neuronet framework [123, 176]. Consequently, in this chapter, we adopt power functions as the activation functions during the construction of the three-layer BP neuronet for Chinese population prediction.

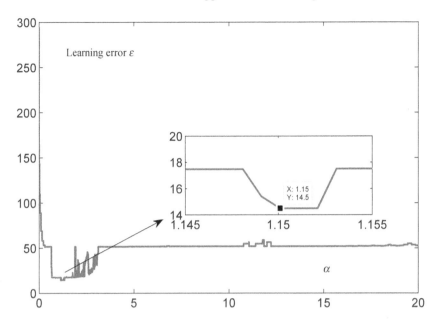

**FIGURE 22.2**: Learning error of power-activation neuronet with WASD algorithm for Chinese population prediction.

### 22.2.3   WASD algorithm

In light of the above mentioned idea, we have been making effort to achieve an innovative breakthrough to enhance the performance of the neuronet, and eventually developed WASD algorithm [123, 176]. By utilizing the pseudoinverse principle, the WASD algorithm is capable of determining the optimal weights and structure (or say, the optimal number of neurons in hidden-layer with the minimal RMSE) of the feed-forward neuronet.

Different from the conventional iterative-training algorithms, the WDD subalgorithm [123, 176] can obtain the optimal weights directly, which avoids the lengthy and potentially oscillating iterative-training procedure. In accordance with the previous studies, the WDD formula of power-activation neuronet can be given as follows:

$$\mathbf{w} = (\mathbf{\Psi}^T \mathbf{\Psi})^{-1} \mathbf{\Psi}^T \mathbf{p} = \text{pinv}(\mathbf{\Psi})\mathbf{p}, \tag{22.9}$$

where $\text{pinv}(\mathbf{\Psi})$ refers to the pseudoinverse of the activation matrix $\mathbf{\Psi}$ [239].

Furthermore, based on the WDD formula, the optimal structure of the neuronet can be obtained through the procedure of WASD algorithm, which is presented in Fig. 22.1, where initially $n \leftarrow 1$, $n_{\text{opt}} \leftarrow 1$, $\varepsilon_{\text{min}} \leftarrow \inf$, and $t_{\text{run}}$ indicates program run time.

---

## 22.3   Further Comparisons via Chinese Population Prediction

In this section, according to historical population data, the WASD and BP algorithms are employed in power-activation neuronets to predict the Chinese population respectively. The corresponding performance comparison between WASD algorithm and BP algorithm is also presented.

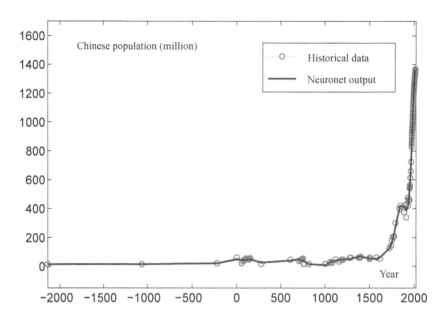

**FIGURE 22.3**: Learning result of power-activation neuronet with WASD algorithm for Chinese population prediction using $\alpha = 1.15$ (global minimum point).

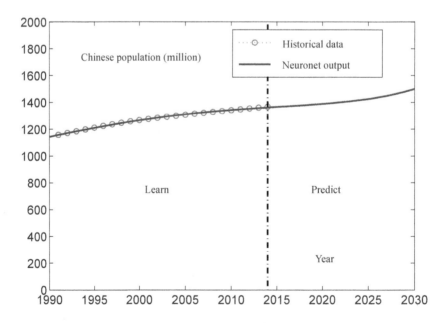

**FIGURE 22.4**: Learning and prediction results of power-activation neuronet with WASD algorithm for Chinese population prediction using $\alpha = 1.15$ (global minimum point).

**TABLE 22.2:** Learning and prediction results of power-activation neuronet via BP algorithm with different values of iteration index $k$ for Chinese population prediction.

| $k$ | $1 \times 10^5$ | $2 \times 10^5$ | $3 \times 10^5$ | $4 \times 10^5$ | $5 \times 10^5$ | $6 \times 10^5$ |
|---|---|---|---|---|---|---|
| $\varepsilon$ (million) | 67.61 | 66.80 | 66.06 | 65.40 | 64.80 | 64.26 |
| $t_{run}$ (s) | 7.04 | 13.79 | 20.07 | 26.53 | 32.25 | 39.68 |
| $k$ | $7 \times 10^5$ | $8 \times 10^5$ | $9 \times 10^5$ | $1 \times 10^6$ | $2 \times 10^6$ | $3 \times 10^6$ |
| $\varepsilon$ (million) | 63.78 | 63.34 | 62.94 | 62.59 | 60.48 | 59.59 |
| $t_{run}$ (s) | 46.11 | 51.44 | 58.20 | 66.02 | 130.52 | 196.63 |
| $k$ | $4 \times 10^6$ | $5 \times 10^6$ | $6 \times 10^6$ | $7 \times 10^6$ | $8 \times 10^6$ | $9 \times 10^6$ |
| $\varepsilon$ (million) | 59.15 | 58.85 | 58.59 | 58.36 | 58.14 | 57.94 |
| $t_{run}$ (s) | 268.22 | 324.01 | 393.80 | 459.47 | 516.48 | 585.73 |
| $k$ | $1 \times 10^7$ | $1.5 \times 10^7$ | $2 \times 10^7$ | $2.5 \times 10^7$ | $3 \times 10^7$ | $4 \times 10^7$ |
| $\varepsilon$ (million) | 57.74 | 56.86 | 56.15 | 55.58 | 55.12 | 54.44 |
| $t_{run}$ (s) | 650.70 | 980.26 | 1309.23 | 1613.30 | 1952.67 | 2546.42 |
| $k$ | $5 \times 10^7$ | $6 \times 10^7$ | $7 \times 10^7$ | $8 \times 10^7$ | $9 \times 10^7$ | $1 \times 10^8$ |
| $\varepsilon$ (million) | 53.98 | 53.66 | 53.44 | 53.27 | 53.13 | 53.02 |
| $t_{run}$ (s) | 3223.72 | 4320.46 | 4642.36 | 5373.40 | 6984.25 | 7620.63 |

### 22.3.1 Prediction results of WASD algorithm

On the basis of previous works, power-activation neuronet with the WASD algorithm is applied to approximating the Chinese population data in the past 4154 years. It is also worthwhile pointing out that, in order to fasten the calculations [235], the time interval $[-2140, 2014]$ is normalized to the interval $[0, \alpha]$, where $\alpha$ denotes the normalization factor. Then, we can use the normalized data-set to train the neuronet. Furthermore, to investigate the relationship between the normalization factor $\alpha$ and the performance (i.e., learning error in the form of RMSE) of the neuronet, numerical studies with different $\alpha$ values are conducted and the corresponding results are presented in Fig. 22.2. Apparently, as shown in Fig. 22.2, the performance of power-activation neuronet with the WASD algorithm varies with different values of $\alpha$, and there exists a (relatively) global minimum point with $\varepsilon = 14.50$ and $\alpha = 1.15$. That is, the optimal weights and structure of neuronet are obtained by setting $\alpha = 1.15$. It is the reason why we choose $\alpha = 1.15$ as the normalization factor for the numerical studies of Chinese population prediction. The training results of the neuronet with $\alpha = 1.15$ are shown in Fig. 22.3. It can be easily observed that the neuronet performs very well in data learning, since the error between the neuronet output data and the desired output is narrow. Note that, for the optimal power-activation neuronet (i.e., with $\alpha = 1.15$), the number of neurons in hidden-layer determined by WASD algorithm is 63. By applying the above trained power-activation neuronet with the WASD algorithm to the prediction of Chinese population, the trend of Chinese population growth after 2014 can be depicted in Fig. 22.4. As shown in Fig. 22.4, with the highest possibility, the Chinese population will keep on increasing at a low rate in the next decade, and will reach 1500 million by 2030.

### 22.3.2 Prediction results of BP algorithm

In the case of power-activation neuronet with BP algorithm, the number of hidden-layer neurons adopted in studies is 63 (i.e., the same as that in the optimal power-activation neuronet with WASD

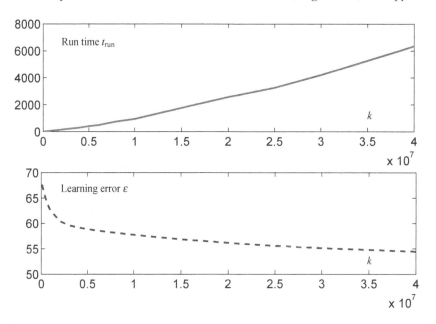

**FIGURE 22.5**: Relationships between iteration index $k$ and run time $t_{run}$ as well as learning error $\varepsilon$ of power-activation neuronet with BP algorithm for Chinese population prediction.

algorithm). Since the performance (i.e., learning error in the form of RMSE) of power-activation neuronet with BP algorithm can be influenced tremendously by iteration index $k$, it is necessary to choose a large enough value of $k$ to obtain satisfactory learning results with a relatively small RMSE value. Also, considering the run time of BP algorithm, we finally choose $k$ equal to $1 \times 10^5$, $2 \times 10^5$, $3 \times 10^5$, $4 \times 10^5$, $5 \times 10^5$, $6 \times 10^5$, $7 \times 10^5$, $8 \times 10^5$, $9 \times 10^5$, $1 \times 10^6$, $2 \times 10^6$, $3 \times 10^6$, $4 \times 10^6$, $5 \times 10^6$, $6 \times 10^6$, $7 \times 10^6$, $8 \times 10^6$, $9 \times 10^6$, $1 \times 10^7$, $1.5 \times 10^7$, $2 \times 10^7$, $2.5 \times 10^7$, $3 \times 10^7$, $4 \times 10^7$, $5 \times 10^7$, $6 \times 10^7$, $7 \times 10^7$, $8 \times 10^7$, $9 \times 10^7$ and $1 \times 10^8$ to build the power-activation neuronet with BP algorithm neuronet, respectively. The RMSE and corresponding run time $t_{run}$ spent under these $k$ values can be found in Table 22.2. In addition, the relationship between $k$ and RMSE, $k$ and run time $t_{run}$ can be found in Fig. 22.5. The minimal RMSE (i.e., 53.02 million) is achieved at $k = 1 \times 10^8$, where the run time $t_{run}$ is 7620.63 s (i.e., about two hours). Fig. 22.6 shows the learning and prediction results of the power-activation neuronet via BP algorithm with iteration index $k = 1 \times 10^8$ for Chinese population prediction. It can be seen from Fig. 22.6 that Chinese population is most likely to increase at a low rate in the next decade. That is, the prediction results gotten by power-activation neuronet with BP algorithm are consistent with those by power-activation neuronet with WASD algorithm in general. Even so, we can discover obviously from Fig. 22.4 and Fig. 22.6 that power-activation neuronet with WASD algorithm is superior to power-activation neuronet with BP algorithm in terms of prediction performance. The more details about the performance comparison between power-activation neuronets with WASD and BP algorithms are to be discussed in the next section.

### 22.3.3    Discussion

The most important performance criteria for a population prediction model are prediction accuracy and prediction efficiency. In this study, RMSE is used to measure prediction accuracy, and the run time of model is used to measure prediction efficiency. For power-activation neuronet with WASD algorithm model, as illustrated in Fig. 22.2 in Section 22.3.1, the optimal RMSE (i.e.,

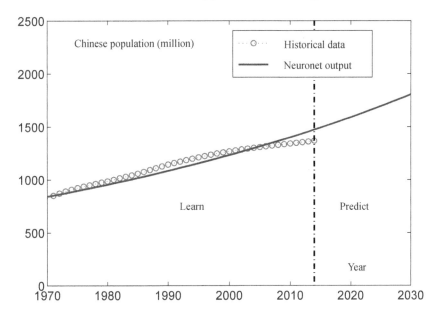

**FIGURE 22.6**: Learning and prediction results of power-activation neuronet with BP algorithm for Chinese population prediction with iteration index $k = 10^8$.

learning error) is 14.50 million (i.e., relative error is 1.06% to the datum in 2014), and the corresponding run time $t_{run}$ of the model is 0.254652 s. For power-activation neuronet with BP algorithm model, the optimal RMSE is 53.02 million (i.e., relative error is 3.88% to the datum in 2014), and the corresponding run time of the model is 7620.63 s (i.e., about two hours), which can be found in Table 22.2 in Section 22.3.2. According to the performance evaluation, it can be concluded that power-activation neuronet with WASD algorithm outperforms power-activation neuronet with BP algorithm in terms of both prediction accuracy and prediction efficiency. Specifically, power-activation neuronet with WASD algorithm gains 73% improvement in RMSE compared with the one with BP algorithm, and the run time needed is just 0.25 s (note that power-activation neuronet with BP algorithm needs two hours).

## 22.4 Chapter Summary

The authors have established power-activation neuronets based on the theories of WASD and BP algorithms to predict Chinese population. Historical Chinese population data from 2140 BC to 2014 AD (i.e., spanning 4154 years in Table 22.3) has been used to train the power-activation neuronets models successfully. Then, the trained models have been applied to the prediction of the Chinese population. Prediction results show that the Chinese population will continue to increase at a low rate in the next decade. Furthermore, through the comparisons between the prediction performance (i.e., in terms of RMSE and run time criteria) of power-activation neuronets models, the proposition that WASD algorithm is much more efficient and accurate than the BP algorithm is reproved. Thus, we are confident that the mentioned power-activation neuronet with WASD algorithm model can be employed in population prediction for other countries or regions. Note that the Chinese population data from 2015 to 2017 (the time that we prepared this chapter in the book) in WPP 2017 [167] are

**TABLE 22.3:**    Chinese population data in the past 4154 years used for learning and prediction.

| Year | 2140 (BC) | 1063 (BC) | 220 (BC) | 2 | 57 | 75 | 88 |
|---|---|---|---|---|---|---|---|
| Data (million) | 13.55 | 13.71 | 20.00 | 59.59 | 21.01 | 34.13 | 43.36 |
| Year | 105 | 125 | 140 | 144 | 145 | 146 | 156 |
| Data (million) | 53.26 | 48.69 | 49.15 | 49.73 | 49.52 | 47.57 | 56.48 |
| Year | 280 | 609 | 705 | 726 | 732 | 740 | 742 |
| Data (million) | 16.16 | 46.02 | 37.14 | 41.42 | 45.43 | 48.14 | 48.91 |
| Year | 754 | 755 | 760 | 764 | 820 | 1006 | 1053 |
| Data (million) | 52.88 | 52.92 | 16.99 | 16.90 | 15.76 | 16.28 | 22.29 |
| Year | 1066 | 1083 | 1122 | 1162 | 1187 | 1207 | 1281 |
| Data (million) | 29.09 | 24.97 | 46.73 | 33.11 | 44.71 | 45.82 | 58.83 |
| Year | 1291 | 1381 | 1393 | 1403 | 1502 | 1504 | 1578 |
| Data (million) | 59.85 | 59.87 | 60.54 | 66.60 | 50.91 | 60.11 | 60.69 |
| Year | 1620 | 1724 | 1741 | 1751 | 1764 | 1776 | 1790 |
| Data (million) | 51.66 | 126.11 | 143.41 | 181.81 | 205.50 | 208.10 | 301.49 |
| Year | 1834 | 1844 | 1887 | 1901 | 1911 | 1913 | 1928 |
| Data (million) | 401.01 | 419.44 | 377.64 | 426.45 | 341.42 | 432.00 | 474.78 |
| Year | 1931 | 1935 | 1947 | 1949 | 1950 | 1951 | 1955 |
| Data (million) | 421.07 | 462.15 | 461.00 | 541.67 | 551.96 | 563.00 | 614.65 |
| Year | 1960 | 1965 | 1970 | 1971 | 1972 | 1973 | 1974 |
| Data (million) | 662.07 | 725.38 | 829.92 | 852.29 | 871.77 | 892.11 | 908.59 |
| Year | 1975 | 1976 | 1977 | 1978 | 1979 | 1980 | 1981 |
| Data (million) | 924.20 | 937.17 | 949.74 | 962.59 | 975.42 | 987.05 | 1000.72 |
| Year | 1982 | 1983 | 1984 | 1985 | 1986 | 1987 | 1988 |
| Data (million) | 1016.54 | 1030.08 | 1043.57 | 1058.51 | 1075.07 | 1093.00 | 1110.26 |
| Year | 1989 | 1990 | 1991 | 1992 | 1993 | 1994 | 1995 |
| Data (million) | 1127.04 | 1143.33 | 1158.23 | 1171.71 | 1185.17 | 1198.50 | 1211.21 |
| Year | 1996 | 1997 | 1998 | 1999 | 2000 | 2001 | 2002 |
| Data (million) | 1223.89 | 1236.26 | 1247.61 | 1257.86 | 1267.43 | 1276.27 | 1284.53 |
| Year | 2003 | 2004 | 2005 | 2006 | 2007 | 2008 | 2009 |
| Data (million) | 1292.27 | 1299.88 | 1307.56 | 1314.48 | 1321.29 | 1328.02 | 1334.50 |
| Year | 2010 | 2011 | 2012 | 2013 | 2014 | | |
| Data (million) | 1340.91 | 1347.35 | 1354.04 | 1360.72 | 1367.82 | | |

1397.02 million, 1403.50 million and 1409.51 million, respectively. For the convenience of readers, the above population data can be used to further compare with the population prediction results reported in this chapter.

# Part VII

# Other Applications

# Chapter 23

## Application to USPD Prediction

Recently, the total public debt outstanding (TPDO) of the United States has increased rapidly, and to more than $17 trillion on October 18, 2013, when our research group began this work. It is important and necessary to conduct the TPDO prediction for better policymaking and more effective measurements taken. In this chapter, we present the ten-year prediction for the public debt of the United States (termed also the United States public debt, USPD) via a three-layer feed-forward neuronet. It is worth mentioning here that this research work used the USPD data as of October 2013, and our research group reported the main prediction results of the USPD as of November 2015. Specifically, using the calendar year data on the USPD, the Chebyshev-activation neuronet is trained, and then is applied to prediction. Via a series of numerical studies, we find that there are several possibilities of the change of the USPD in the future, which are classified into two categories in terms of prediction trend: the continuous-increase trend and the increase-peak-decline trend. In the most possible situation, the neuronet indicates that the TPDO of the United States is predicted to increase, and it will double in 2019 and double again in 2024.

## 23.1    Introduction

The USPD is the amount owed by the federal government of the United States [245]. It consists of two components: (1) the debt held by the public, and (2) the intra-governmental debt holdings [245, 246]. Without doubt, the USPD as a share of the gross domestic product (GDP) plays an important role in the development of the United States. Because of this important role, many studies have been reported on the USPD. It follows from the public debt reports provided in [245] that the

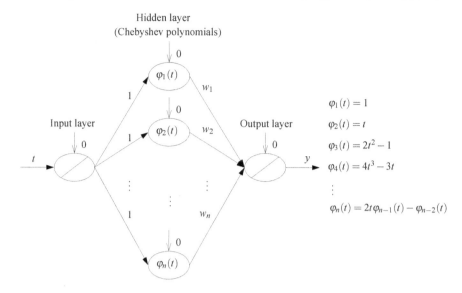

**FIGURE 23.1**: Model structure and activation functions of Chebyshev-activation neuronet.

TPDO of the United States on January 1, 1790 was $71.0605085 million. Since then, the TPDO of the United States has risen to more than $17 trillion on October 18, 2013 (though, historically, it declined in some short time periods). Specially, the USPD has recently increased with a rapid growth rate (mainly because of the financial crisis) [245]. With the rapid increase of the public debt, there may arise lots of problems that the United States government has to face (e.g., the risks to economic growth and the potential existence of inflation) [245, 247–249]. The USPD has been a very appealing topic that influences the development of the United States.

Because the debt is closely related to the development of the United States, the prediction of the USPD, which can be used for planning and research (e.g., for the federal budget), is becoming urgent and important. It is conducted by many organizations, including national and local governments and private companies [245, 250–253], for better policymaking and more effective measurements taken. For example, the congressional budget office (CBO) of the United States releases its annual report in 2013, which covers a ten-year window [245]. As shown in the report, for the 2014–2023 period, the debt held by the public is predicted to remain above 70 percent of GDP. In addition to the above short-term prediction, the CBO also predicts the USPD as part of its annual report (referred to [245]). In such a report, the CBO forecasts that the debt held by the public will reach 100 percent of GDP in 2038. Another office, i.e., the Government Accountability Office (GAO) of the United States, also does some research and provides the related reports on the USPD prediction [245]. According to the GAO, the debt-to-GDP ratio will be doubled in 2040, and doubled again in 2060, reaching 600% in 2080.

As for the USPD, the Department of the Treasury provides the fiscal year reports [245], from which the historical TPDO of the United States during 1790 ∼ 2013 can be found and can also be viewed as the de facto standard. Note that the historical data contain the general regularity of change of the USPD, and are also the comprehensive reflection of change of the USPD under the influence of all factors (e.g., natural environment, policy, economy and culture). Based on the historical data, we can have the overall view on the trend of the USPD from the past to the future. Therefore, in this chapter, based on the calendar year data from the department of the treasury, we conduct the ten-year prediction (termed also as the short-term prediction) of the USPD using a three-layer feed-forward neuronet [66].

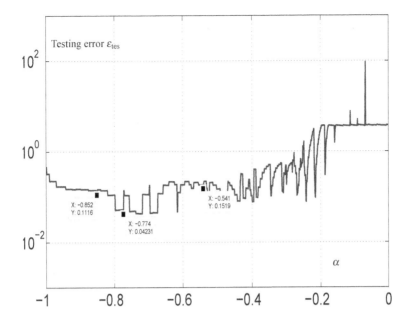

**FIGURE 23.2**: Relationship between normalization factor $\alpha$ and testing error $\varepsilon_{\text{tes}}$ of Chebyshev-activation neuronet with optimal structure.

## 23.2 Neuronet Model and Data Normalization

Benefiting from parallel processing capability, inherent nonlinearity, distributed storage and adaptive learning capability, neuronet has been widely used in many areas [245, 254–259]. In this section, the neuronet model for the prediction of the USPD is developed and investigated. Specifically, based on the past 224-year data (i.e., from January 1, 1790 to October 18, 2013), a three-layer feed-forward neuronet model is constructed and then applied to the prediction of the USPD. Note that, in this chapter, the USPD data are obtained from the Department of the Treasury.

### 23.2.1 Model structure

The three-layer feed-forward neuronet used for the prediction of the USPD is constructed in this subsection. The model structure of such a neuronet is detailed as follows.

For the convenience of the readers, Fig. 23.1 intuitively shows the structure of the three-layer feed-forward neuronet, which, in the hidden layer, has $n$ neurons activated by a group of Chebyshev polynomials $\varphi_j(\cdot)$ (with $j = 1, 2, \cdots, n$). In addition, the input layer or the output layer each has one neuron activated by the linear function. Moreover, the connecting weights from the input layer to the hidden layer are all fixed to be 1, whereas the connecting weights from the hidden layer to the output layer, denoted as $w_j$, are to be decided or adjusted. Besides, all neuronal thresholds are fixed to be 0. Note that, theoretically guaranteeing the efficacy of the neuronet, these settings can simplify the complexities of the neuronet structure design, analysis and computation. Furthermore, we exploit the algorithm of weights-and-structure-determination (WASD) that can determine effectively the weights connecting the hidden layer and the output layer, and obtain automatically the optimal structure of the neuronet. Please refer to the authors' previous works [66, 245] for more details about the WASD algorithm, of which the neuronet is termed WASD neuronet.

### 23.2.2   Data normalization

In this subsection, to lay a basis for further discussion, we give some necessary explanations as follows. For the three-layer feed-forward neuronet exploited in this chapter, the input corresponds to date (e.g., January 1, 1790), and the output is the treasury datum (i.e., the TPDO of the United States). In addition, the hidden-layer neurons of such a neuronet are activated by a group of Chebyshev polynomials of Class 1, which means that the domain of the input is $[-1,1]$. It is thus necessary to normalize the data that are used as the neuronet input. Specifically, in this chapter, the time interval $[1790, 2013]$ is normalized to the interval $[-1, \alpha]$ with the normalization factor $\alpha \in (-1,0)$. Note that "1790" and "2013" here represent January 1, 1790 and October 18, 2013 (i.e., the day the TPDO of the United States reached \$17 trillion), respectively. Therefore, using the calendar year data on the USPD, we have the data-set (of sample pairs) for the training of the feed-forward neuronet. Then, with the neuronet well trained, it is applied to the prediction of the USPD.

## 23.3   Learning and Testing Results

As mentioned above, the time interval $[1790, 2013]$ is normalized to the interval $[-1, \alpha]$ with the normalization factor $\alpha \in (-1,0)$. In this section, different values of $\alpha$ are used to test the learning and prediction performances of the neuronet shown in Fig. 23.1.

To lay a basis for further discussion, we give $\{(t_i, p_i)|_{i=1}^M\}$ as the data-set of sample pairs for the training of the neuronet, where, for the $i$th sample pair, $t_i \in \mathbb{R}$ denotes the input and $p_i \in \mathbb{R}$ denotes the desired output (or to say, target output). As mentioned in this chapter, the input corresponds to date (e.g., January 1, 1790), and the output is the treasury datum (i.e., the TPDO of the United States). Then, the mean square error (MSE) for the neuronet is defined as follows:

$$e = \frac{1}{M}\sum_{i=1}^{M}\left(p_i - \sum_{j=1}^{n} w_j \varphi_j(t_i)\right)^2 . \tag{23.1}$$

Note that, for the neuronet with a fixed number of hidden-layer neurons, we can obtain the related MSE (i.e., the training error) via (23.1). By increasing the number of hidden-layer neurons one-by-one, we can finally have the relationship between the MSE and the number of hidden-layer neurons. The WASD algorithm can thus be developed to determine the optimal structure of the neuronet (i.e., with the number of hidden-layer neurons determined corresponding to the smallest MSE). With the optimal structure obtained, the training procedure is finished, and the learning performance of the resultant neuronet is evaluated.

Based on the well-trained neuronet, we can investigate its prediction performance using the calendar year data on the USPD from 1790 to 2013. Specifically, the data corresponding to the time interval $[1790, 2010]$ are used to train the neuronet, and the other data are used for the testing of USPD prediction. Note that the time interval $[1790, 2010]$ also needs to be normalized to the interval $[-1, \alpha]$. Besides, the testing error that is exploited to evaluate the prediction performance of the neuronet is defined as follows:

$$\varepsilon_{\text{tes}} = \frac{1}{H}\sum_{m=1}^{H}\left|\frac{y_m - p_m}{p_m}\right|,$$

where $H$ is the total number of the other data for test, and $y_m$ and $p_m$ denote respectively the neuronet output and the public debt datum at the $m$th test point. Generally speaking, the smaller the testing error $\varepsilon_{\text{tes}}$ is, the better the prediction performance of the neuronet achieves.

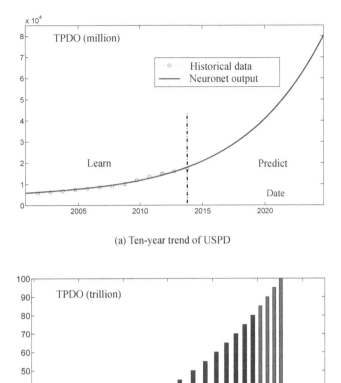

(a) Ten-year trend of USPD

(b) Histogram of selected data

**FIGURE 23.3**: USPD prediction results of Chebyshev-activation neuronet using $\alpha = -0.774$ (global minimum point).

Via a series of numerical studies, we find that different values of $\alpha$ lead to different prediction results of Chebyshev-activation neuronet. For better understanding, Fig. 23.2 shows the relationship between the normalization factor $\alpha$ and the testing error $\varepsilon_{\text{tes}}$ of Chebyshev-activation neuronet with the optimal structure. As shown in the figure, superior prediction performance of the neuronet can be achieved by choosing a suitable value of $\alpha$. More importantly, from the figure, we can observe that there exist several local minimum points and a global minimum point, such as the marked ones, which correspond to different values of $\alpha$. Such local and global minimum points indicate the possible situations of the public debt prediction via the neuronet, and the global minimum point further implies the most possible situation. Based on the results shown in Fig. 23.2, different $\alpha$ values are thus used for the neuronet to predict the USPD in 10 years (specifically, 2014 to 2024), with the corresponding prediction results presented in the ensuing section.

**TABLE 23.1:**    Actual datum of August 31, 2014 and numerical results corresponding to Fig. 23.3(b) for USPD prediction.

| Date | TPDO (trillion) | Date | TPDO (trillion) |
|---|---|---|---|
| August 31, 2014 | $17.75 (actual) | August 30, 2014 | $20 |
| May 24, 2016 | $25 | October 2, 2017 | $30 |
| November 16, 2018 | $35 | November 1, 2019 | $40 |
| September 2, 2020 | $45 | June 1, 2021 | $50 |
| February 1, 2022 | $55 | September 13, 2022 | $60 |
| April 7, 2023 | $65 | October 14, 2023 | $70 |
| April 9, 2024 | $75 | September 22, 2024 | $80 |
| February 26, 2025 | $85 | July 24, 2025 | $90 |
| December 11, 2025 | $95 | April 24, 2026 | $100 |

## 23.4    Prediction Results

As presented above, different values of $\alpha$ lead to different training performances of the feed-forward neuronet, thereby making the prediction results of the USPD different. Thus, in this section, such different $\alpha$ values (or more specifically, the local and global minimum points marked in Fig. 23.2) are used for the neuronet to predict the USPD in 10 years (specifically, to September 30, 2024). The related prediction results of the USPD via the neuronet numerical studies are presented as follows.

### 23.4.1    Most possibility for prediction of USPD

As shown in Fig. 23.2, $\alpha = -0.774$ is the global minimum point, which indicates the situation with the most possibility for the prediction of the USPD using Chebyshev-activation neuronet. The corresponding prediction results via the neuronet with $\alpha = -0.774$ are illustrated in Fig. 23.3 and Table 23.1. Specifically, Fig. 23.3(a) intuitively and visually shows the learning and prediction results, which tells the rise of the USPD in 10 years. In addition, as shown in Fig. 23.3(b) and Table 23.1, the TPDO of the United States is predicted to increase to $20 trillion (actually, to $17.749172 trillion) on August 30, 2014, and it will double in 2019 and double again in 2024 (i.e., reaching $80 trillion on September 22, 2024). Moreover, from Fig. 23.3(b) and Table 23.1, we can observe that the growth rate of the USPD is increasing. With such a growth trend, as indicated by the numerical study, the TPDO of the United States will increase further to $90 trillion on July 24, 2025, and then to $100 trillion on April 24, 2026 (see also Fig. 23.3 and Table 23.1).

### 23.4.2    More possibilities for prediction of USPD

Differing from the global minimum point in Fig. 23.2, the local minimum point that indicates a possible situation of the debt prediction is worth being investigated as well. Fig. 23.4 and Fig. 23.5 show the prediction results of the USPD via the neuronet using $\alpha = -0.719, -0.852, -0.575$ and $-0.541$. As seen from Fig. 23.4(a), the USPD is predicted to increase in 10 years. Note that such a prediction result coincides with Fig. 23.3(a) that is related to the global minimum point (with $\alpha = -0.774$), except for the values being slightly different. Besides, Fig. 23.4(b) also shows the continually increasing trend of the USPD in 10 years, but with a gentle growth rate. As for Fig. 23.4(b), the corresponding numerical study shows that the TPDO of the United States is predicted to increase to $20 trillion on June 13, 2015 (actually, to $18.152852 trillion on May 31, 2015), to

**TABLE 23.2:** Relatively realistic monthly results corresponding to Fig. 23.5(b) for USPD prediction.

| Date | TPDO (trillion) | Date | TPDO (trillion) |
|---|---|---|---|
| October 31, 2013 | $17.187655 | October 31, 2015 | $16.613578 |
| November 30, 2013 | $17.244600 | November 30, 2015 | $16.469235 |
| December 31, 2013 | $17.298451 | December 31, 2015 | $16.306543 |
| January 31, 2014 | $17.346936 | January 31, 2016 | $16.129521 |
| February 28, 2014 | $17.385905 | **February 29, 2016** | $15.950718 |
| March 31, 2014 | $17.423112 | March 31, 2016 | $15.744864 |
| April 30, 2014 | $17.453283 | April 30, 2016 | $15.530741 |
| May 31, 2014 | $17.477971 | May 31, 2016 | $15.293400 |
| June 30, 2014 | $17.495326 | June 30, 2016 | $15.047667 |
| July 31, 2014 | $17.506394 | **July 31, 2016** | $14.776580 |
| **August 31, 2014** | **$17.509866** | August 31, 2016 | $14.487729 |
| September 30, 2014 | $17.505957 | September 30, 2016 | $14.190557 |
| October 31, 2014 | $17.493863 | **October 31, 2016** | $13.864486 |
| November 30, 2014 | $17.474147 | November 30, 2016 | $13.530212 |
| December 31, 2014 | $17.445095 | December 31, 2016 | $13.164693 |
| January 31, 2015 | $17.406600 | **January 31, 2017** | $12.778280 |
| February 28, 2015 | $17.363987 | February 28, 2017 | $12.410525 |
| March 31, 2015 | $17.307264 | **March 31, 2017** | $11.982011 |
| April 30, 2015 | $17.242524 | April 30, 2017 | $11.545547 |
| **May 31, 2015** | $17.165411 | May 31, 2017 | $11.071140 |
| June 30, 2015 | $17.079894 | **June 30, 2017** | $10.588983 |
| **July 31, 2015** | $16.980503 | July 31, 2017 | $10.065911 |
| August 31, 2015 | $16.869273 | **August 31, 2017** | $9.516749 |
| September 30, 2015 | $16.749625 | **September 30, 2017** | $8.959872 |

$30 trillion on September 17, 2019, to $40 trillion on September 10, 2022, and finally to $48.813838 trillion on September 30, 2024.

Here, it is worthwhile noting that the trends of the prediction results shown in Fig. 23.5(a) and Fig. 23.5(b) are quite different from those shown in Fig. 23.4(a) and Fig. 23.4(b). That is, instead of increasing continuously, the prediction of the USPD is also found with possibilities to rise, peak and then decline, as shown in Fig. 23.5(a) and Fig. 23.5(b). More specifically, on the one hand, as for Fig. 23.5(a), the related numerical study shows that the total public debt outstanding of the United States is predicted to increase to $20 trillion on January 7, 2015 (actually, to $18.082294 trillion on January 31, 2015), reach the summit on June 3, 2020 with the value being $27.413432 trillion, and then decrease gradually. On the other hand, as for Fig. 23.5(b), the related numerical study shows that the TPDO of the United States is predicted to reach the summit on August 30, 2014 with the value being $17.51 trillion, and then decrease gradually and further to less than $10 trillion on August 4, 2017. Besides, according to the report provided by the Department of the Treasury (referred to [245]), the TPDO of the United States on October 31, 2013, November 30, 2013, December 31, 2013, January 31, 2014, and February 28, 2014 are $17.156117 trillion, $17.217152 trillion, $17.351971 trillion, $17.293020 trillion, and $17.463229 trillion, respectively. By contrast, the numerical study corresponding to Fig. 23.5(b) shows that the TPDO of the United States is predicted to increase to $17.187655 trillion on October 31, 2013, to $17.244600 trillion on November 30, 2013, to $17.298451 trillion on December 31, 2013, then to $17.346936 trillion on January 31, 2014, and further to $17.385905 trillion on February 28, 2014. Evidently, the differences are tiny; specifically, $0.031538 trillion (i.e., 0.183829%), $0.027448 trillion (i.e., 0.159422%),

**TABLE 23.3:**    Actual USPD data from October 31, 2013 to May 31, 2015.

| Date | TPDO (trillion) | Date | TPDO (trillion) |
|------|-----------------|------|-----------------|
| October 31, 2013 | $17.156117 | **August 31, 2014** | $17.749172 |
| November 30, 2013 | $17.217152 | September 30, 2014 | $17.824071 |
| December 31, 2013 | $17.351971 | October 31, 2014 | $17.937160 |
| January 31, 2014 | $17.293020 | November 30, 2014 | $18.005549 |
| February 28, 2014 | $17.463229 | December 31, 2014 | $18.141444 |
| March 31, 2014 | $17.601227 | **January 31, 2015** | $18.082294 |
| April 30, 2014 | $17.508437 | February 28, 2015 | $18.155854 |
| May 31, 2014 | $17.516958 | March 31, 2015 | $18.152056 |
| June 30, 2014 | $17.632606 | April 30, 2015 | $18.152560 |
| July 31, 2014 | $17.687137 | **May 31, 2015** | $18.152852 |

$0.053510 trillion (i.e., 0.308380%), $0.053916 trillion (i.e., 0.311779%), and $0.077324 trillion (i.e., 0.442782%), respectively. In view of this point, we thus pay more attention to Fig. 23.5(b) that may show the relatively realistic prediction for the USPD.

### 23.4.3    Relatively realistic prediction of USPD

Corresponding to Fig. 23.5(b), Table 23.2 shows the relatively realistic monthly prediction results of the USPD. From the table, we can observe that the USPD is predicted to increase continuously until August 2014. Then, the TPDO of the United States is predicted to decrease to $17 trillion in July 2015 (actually, it is $18.152852 trillion on May 31, 2015), to $15 trillion in July 2016 and to less than $10 trillion in August 2017. Note that the Department of the Treasury is authorized to issue the debt needed to fund the United States government operations (as authorized by each federal budget) up to a statutory debt limit. However, the Congress in October 2013 had not stated the debt limit, but approved the Department of the Treasury to continue the borrowing until February 7, 2014. In the day after that the newly increased TPDO of the United States was $0.328 trillion. Thus, as for Table 23.2, the still-increasing prediction of the USPD in few months (or at least, until February 2014) is acceptable and reliable. With the corresponding policies made (in or after February 2014), the USPD may be well under control. Then, it was hopeful that, in August 2014, the USPD reaches the summit, showing that the related measurements are taken effectively; and that, after the summit (or say, from September 2014), the USPD decreases gradually, as predicted in Table 23.2 [245]. Besides, for comparison, the actual USPD data from October 31, 2013 to May 31, 2015 are shown in Table 23.3, which, together with the latest data listed at the end of the chapter, however, show that the hoped relatively realistic prediction of USPD is actually still less realistic.

### 23.5    Further Discussion

The above numerical results synthesized by the neuronet show that there are two different trends of the prediction of the USPD in the future, i.e., the continuous-increase trend and the increase-peak-decline trend. As mentioned previously, the TPDO of the United States increases year-by-year, and to more than $17 trillion in October 2013 (provided by the treasury report). Thus, the United States government has made the policies for handling the rapid growth of the public debt. Note that these policies may not have much of an effect on such a huge TPDO within a short period. Therefore, as for Figs. 23.3, 23.4 and 23.5 as well as Tables 23.1 and 23.2, it is predicted that the USPD increases

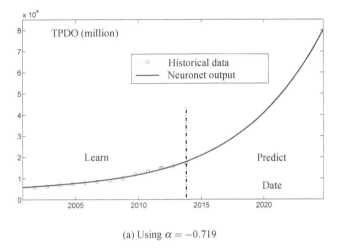

(a) Using $\alpha = -0.719$

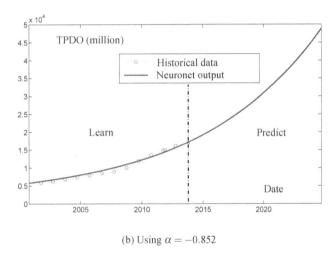

(b) Using $\alpha = -0.852$

**FIGURE 23.4**: Different USPD prediction results of Chebyshev-activation neuronet using $\alpha = -0.719$ and $\alpha = -0.852$.

continually in 10 years/months, which is reasonable and acceptable. On the one hand, as indicated by Fig. 23.3 and Table 23.1 as well as Fig. 23.4(a) and Fig. 23.4(b), for the huge TPDO that is still increasing, it may become more and more difficult for the United States government to handle, but just keep it up (which can also be viewed as a vicious cycle). In this sense, Fig. 23.3 and Table 23.1, showing the prediction results of the USPD with the most possibility, imply that the current policies carried out by the government may be less effective on the debt-growth control. On the other hand, as indicated by Fig. 23.5(a) and Fig. 23.5(b) and Table 23.2, the USPD will reach its summit and then decrease gradually, thereby showing from one viewpoint the delayed effectiveness of those policies made by the United States government on controlling the public debt growth. As noted from another viewpoint [245], these prediction results may also possibly imply that some events including wars may happen, thereby resulting in the decrease of the USPD. Thus, by realizing these possibilities of the change of the future public debt, the United States government together with other governments may need to make more effective policies to control the still-increasing TPDO and also take measures for handling the possibility of sudden events.

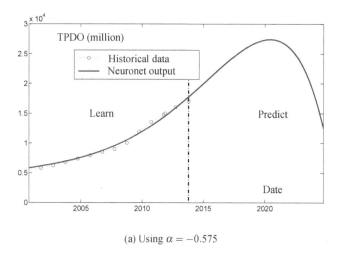

(a) Using $\alpha = -0.575$

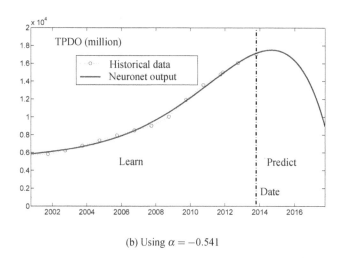

(b) Using $\alpha = -0.541$

**FIGURE 23.5**: Different USPD prediction results of Chebyshev-activation neuronet using $\alpha = -0.575$ and $\alpha = -0.541$.

## 23.6    Chapter Summary

This chapter has presented the neuronet prediction for the USPD, showing different possibilities of the change of the USPD in the future. It is worth mentioning here that this research work used the USPD data as of October 2013, and the main prediction results of the USPD as of November 2015 was reported by our research group in [245]. Based on this work, we expect to do more and deeper research on the USPD, such as the trend of the debt held by the public and the debt-to-GDP ratio of the United States. Besides, we anticipate this work to be a starting point for proposing and developing many more sophisticated prediction models of the USPD. Future works lie in the further tests using the present data of the USPD to substantiate the effectiveness of the presented Chebyshev-activation neuronet with the WASD algorithm for the prediction. For the convenience of readers, we have presented the actual USPD data from June 30, 2015 to October 31, 2017 (the time

**TABLE 23.4:**  Actual USPD data from June 30, 2015 to October 31, 2017.

| Date | TPDO (trillion) | Date | TPDO (trillion) |
|---|---|---|---|
| June 30, 2015 | $18.151998 | September 30, 2016 | $19.573445 |
| July 31, 2015 | $18.151323 | October 31, 2016 | $19.805715 |
| August 31, 2015 | $18.151150 | November 30, 2016 | $19.948065 |
| September 30, 2015 | $18.150618 | December 31, 2016 | $19.976827 |
| October 31, 2015 | $18.152982 | January 31, 2017 | $19.937261 |
| November 30, 2015 | $18.827323 | February 28, 2017 | $19.959594 |
| December 31, 2015 | $18.922179 | March 31, 2017 | $19.846420 |
| January 31, 2016 | $19.012828 | April 30, 2017 | $19.846129 |
| February 29, 2016 | $19.125455 | May 31, 2017 | $19.845942 |
| March 31, 2016 | $19.264939 | June 30, 2017 | $19.844554 |
| April 30, 2016 | $19.187387 | July 31, 2017 | $19.844909 |
| May 31, 2016 | $19.265452 | August 31, 2017 | $19.844533 |
| June 30, 2016 | $19.381591 | September 30, 2017 | $20.244900 |
| July 31, 2016 | $19.427695 | October 31, 2017 | $20.442474 |
| August 31, 2016 | $19.510296 | | |

that we prepared this chapter in the book) in Table 23.4, which can be used to further compare with the prediction results reported in this chapter.

# Chapter 24

## Application to Time Series Prediction

In this chapter, a weights-and-structure-determination (WASD) algorithm is presented for a power-activation neuronet to solve monthly time series learning and prediction problems. Besides, a simple and effective data preprocessing approach is employed. Based on the weights-direct-determination (WDD) subalgorithm and the relationship between the structure and the performance of the power-activation neuronet, the WASD algorithm can determine the weights and the optimal structure (i.e., the optimal numbers of input-layer and hidden-layer neurons) of the power-activation neuronet. Numerical studies further substantiate the superiority of the power-activation neuronet equipped with the WASD algorithm to predict monthly time series.

## 24.1 Introduction

Prediction has practical applications in many different fields [260–265], such as traffic flow prediction [262], river flow prediction [263], and stock price prediction [264]. Therefore, time series prediction has been studied extensively [265].

In recent years, neuronets have been powerful tools for solving the prediction problem. Compared with statistics-based prediction techniques, the following several unique characteristics of neuronets make them valuable and attractive for time series prediction [265, 266]. First, neuronets are data-driven self-adaptive method and have no requirement for a priori assumptions about the underlying models. Second, neuronets have powerful generalization capability. Last, neuronets are universal approximators; i.e., it has been proved that a three-layer feed-forward neuronet can approximate any nonlinear continuous function with an arbitrary accuracy.

In this chapter, a power-activation feed-forward neuronet with the three-layer structure is constructed for time series learning and prediction. For the time series prediction problem, the number of input-layer neurons corresponds to the number of lagged observations. However, the appropriate number of input-layer neurons is not easy to be determined [265, 266] (or, say, lacking a systematic approach to determine). Besides, in light of previous work [28, 99, 260], the number of hidden-layer neurons (or, say, hidden neurons) influences greatly the overall performance of neuronets. Specifically, an inappropriate number of hidden-layer neurons results in the unsatisfied learning or prediction performance of the neuronet. Thus, how to determine the optimal structure of the neuronet is especially important and meaningful.

Motivated by this reason, a WASD algorithm is presented for the power-activation neuronet to solve time series learning and prediction problems in this chapter. According to related works [265–268], appropriate data preprocessing is necessary to neuronets for time series prediction. Therefore, we employ a simple and effective data preprocessing approach for the better prediction performance. Numerical studies substantiate the efficacy of the power-activation neuronet equipped with the WASD algorithm to predict the monthly time series.

---

## 24.2   Data Preprocessing

In this section, we employ a simple and effective data preprocessing approach to adjust the time series which may contain various patterns, such as trend and seasonality. More specifically, the preprocessing includes pattern adjustment and normalization.

Firstly, we consider the trend factor of time series which can be fitted via a linear function. Then we remove the estimated trend factor from the series. After that, deseasonalization is done by employing the method of season factor based on four-point moving averages and centered moving averages, following the classic multiplication decomposition [267,268]. The detailed steps of pattern adjustment can be referred to [260].

After performing the pattern adjustment, data points are normalized to a range of $[-0.5, -0.25]$ using the following linear transformation based on the minimum and maximum values of the adjusted series [265, 268], i.e.,

$$x_{\text{nor}} = \frac{x_{\text{adj}} - x_{\text{min}}}{4x_{\text{max}} - 4x_{\text{min}}} - 0.5,$$

where $x_{\text{nor}}$ and $x_{\text{adj}}$ denote the normalized and adjusted data, respectively; and $x_{\text{min}}$ and $x_{\text{max}}$ are the minimum and maximum values of the adjusted data $x_{\text{adj}}$, respectively.

In order to process the original data for generating suitable inputs of power-activation neuronet, we use the techniques of data pattern adjustment and normalization via the steps of aforementioned data preprocessing. Similarly, the output data of power-activation neuronet need inverse process after the neuronet prediction, so that we can obtain the target prediction values. We refer to this inverse process as data postprocessing. To be more illustrative, the diagram of the complete prediction approach is shown in Fig. 24.1. It is worth mentioning that all time series data used in this chapter have been processed by the proposed data preprocessing, and additionally all output data need to be processed by the aforementioned data postprocessing.

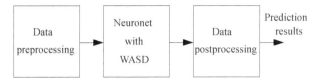

**FIGURE 24.1**: Block diagram of prediction approach for power-activation WASD neuronet.

## 24.3 Power-Activation Neuronet Model

In this chapter, time series learning and prediction via neuronet are investigated. For a time series prediction problem, the inputs are typically lagged observations and the output is the future value [265]. Note that the problem of time series prediction investigated in this chapter is multi-interval-ahead prediction. Then, the problem of time series prediction via neuronet is considered as obtaining the relationship of the observation at target time instant $t + l$ and observations at previous time instants, i.e., the following function:

$$x_{t+l} = f_l(x_t, x_{t-1}, x_{t-2}, x_{t-3}, x_{t-4}, \cdots, x_{t-q+1}), \tag{24.1}$$

where $x_{t+l}$ denotes the observation at time instant $t + l$, with $l \geq 1$ typically being (maximally) 18 and denoting the number of intervals ahead of time instant $t$, and with $q \geq 1$ being the number of lagged observations of the series (or, say, the number of inputs).

We aim at constructing the power-activation neuronet for mapping (or, say, approximating) function (24.1). Firstly, the theorem of multivariate Taylor polynomial approximation [260] is tailored as follows.

For a target function $f(x_g, \cdots, x_1)$ with $g$ variables and $g \geq 1$, which has the $(K+1)$th-order continuous partial derivatives in a neighborhood of the origin $(0, \cdots, 0)$, the $K$-order Taylor series $P_K(x_g, \cdots, x_1)$ about the origin is

$$P_K(x_g, \cdots, x_1) = \sum_{i=0}^{K} \sum_{i_g + \cdots + i_1 = i} \frac{x_g^{i_g} \cdots x_1^{i_1}}{i_g! \cdots i_1!} \left( \frac{\partial^{i_g + \cdots + i_1} f(0, \cdots, 0)}{\partial x_g^{i_g} \cdots \partial x_1^{i_1}} \right), \tag{24.2}$$

where $i_g, \cdots, i_1$ are nonnegative integers.

Based on the above, we use the following function $P_K(x_t, x_{t-1}, x_{t-2}, x_{t-3}, x_{t-4}, \cdots, x_{t-q+1})$ to map (24.1), i.e.,

$$P_K(x_t, \cdots, x_{t-q+1}) = \sum_{i=0}^{K} \sum_{i_1 + \cdots + i_q = i} \frac{x_t^{i_1} \cdots x_{t-q+1}^{i_q}}{i_1! \cdots i_q!} \left( \frac{\partial^{i_1 + \cdots + i_q} f_l(0, \cdots, 0)}{\partial x_t^{i_1} \cdots \partial x_{t-q+1}^{i_q}} \right). \tag{24.3}$$

In addition, $P_K(x_t, \cdots, x_{t-q+1})$ can be rewritten in the compact notation as

$$P_K(x_t, \cdots, x_{t-q+1}) = \sum_{n=0}^{N-1} w_n \varphi_n, \tag{24.4}$$

where the basis function $\varphi_n$ denotes a power function of all inputs, i.e.,

$$\varphi_n = x_t^{i_1} \cdots x_{t-q+1}^{i_q}, \tag{24.5}$$

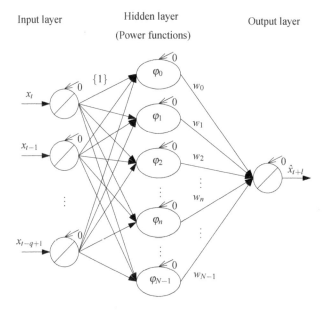

**FIGURE 24.2**: Model structure of multi-input power-activation neuronet.

and the weight (or coefficient) for $\varphi_n$ can be expressed as

$$w_n = \frac{1}{i_1! \cdots i_q!} \left( \frac{\partial^{i_1 + \cdots + i_q} f_l(0, \cdots, 0)}{\partial x_t^{i_1} \cdots \partial x_{t-q+1}^{i_q}} \right). \tag{24.6}$$

Thus, the underlying model of time series $f_l(x_t, \cdots, x_{t-q+1})$ can be mapped via the optimal weights $\{w_n | n = 0, 1, \cdots, N-1\}$ corresponding to an appropriate number $N$ of the inputs and basis functions $\{\varphi_n | n = 0, 1, \cdots, N-1\}$. Besides, the basis functions $\{\varphi_n | n = 0, 1, \cdots, N-1\}$ are sequenced by the graded lexicographic order [64] in this chapter.

According to the above analysis and (24.4), the power-activation neuronet is constructed with its structure shown in Fig. 24.2. As seen from the figure, the power-activation neuronet has a conventional three-layer structure: input layer, hidden layer and output layer. The input-layer and output-layer neurons are activated by linear identity functions. In addition, the input layer has $q$ neurons, corresponding to the number of lagged observations; and the hidden layer has $N$ neurons (i.e., $N$ hidden neurons), which are activated by a group of power functions (i.e., basis functions $\{\varphi_n | n = 0, 1, \cdots, N-1\}$). The weights linking the input-layer and hidden-layer neurons are set to be 1; and, shown in Fig. 24.2, the weights linking the hidden-layer and output-layer neurons are denoted by $\{w_n | n = 0, 1, \cdots, N-1\}$, which need to be determined. In order to simplify the computational complexity, all neuronal thresholds in the model of the power-activation neuronet can be and are actually set to be 0.

## 24.4 WASD Algorithm

In order to achieve the superior performance of the constructed power-activation neuronet model in terms of time series learning and prediction, the WASD algorithm is presented in this section.

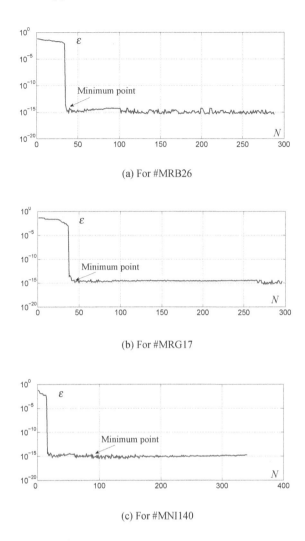

(a) For #MRB26

(b) For #MRG17

(c) For #MNI140

**FIGURE 24.3**: Relationship between number $N$ of hidden-layer neurons and SMAPE $\varepsilon$.

The WASD algorithm can obtain the optimal weights from hidden layer to output layer directly by utilizing the so-called WDD subalgorithm. Moreover, the WASD algorithm can determine the optimal structure (i.e., the optimal numbers of input-layer and hidden-layer neurons) of the power-activation neuronet adaptively by searching the structure with the best testing performance (i.e., the structure with the minimal generalization error) and good learning performance.

For the purpose of illustration, we suppose that the total number of observations for training is $D$; in other words, there are $D$ observations, i.e., $x_1, x_2, \cdots, x_D$, in the training set. Additionally, $l$-interval-ahead prediction problem is mainly investigated. Thus, we have $M$ training samples, with $M = D - q - l + 1$, when the number of inputs is given as $q$, with $q \leq D - l$. Therefore, we can define a set of training samples as $\{(\mathbf{x}_m, \gamma_m) | m = 1, 2, \cdots, M\}$, in which, $\mathbf{x}_m = [x_{m+q-1}, \cdots, x_{m+1}, x_m]^T$ with superscript $^T$ denoting the transpose of a vector or a matrix and $\gamma_m = x_{m+q+l-1}$. To be more specific, the first training sample $(\mathbf{x}_1, \gamma_1)$ consists of an input vector $\mathbf{x}_1 = [x_q, \cdots, x_2, x_1]^T$ and the corresponding desired output $\gamma_1 = x_{q+l}$; the second training sample $(\mathbf{x}_2, \gamma_2)$ consists of an input vector $\mathbf{x}_2 = [x_{q+1}, \cdots, x_3, x_2]^T$ and the corresponding desired output $\gamma_2 = x_{q+l+1}$; and the last training

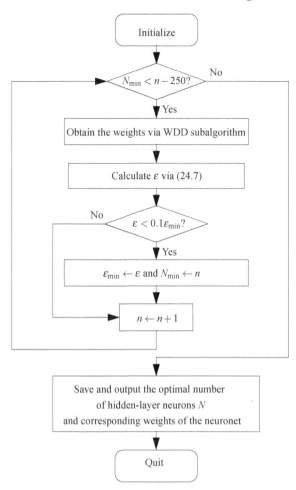

**FIGURE 24.4**: Flowchart of determining optimal structure for power-activation neuronet.

sample $(\mathbf{x}_M, \gamma_M)$ consists of an input vector $\mathbf{x}_M = [x_{D-l}, \cdots, x_{D-q-l+2}, x_{D-q-l+1}]^{\mathrm{T}}$ (or equivalently written as $\mathbf{x}_M = [x_{M+q-1}, \cdots, x_{M+1}, x_M]^{\mathrm{T}}$) and the corresponding desired output $\gamma_M = x_D$.

### 24.4.1  Performance measure

In order to evaluate the prediction performance of the power-activation WASD neuronet, we employ the symmetric mean absolute percentage error (SMAPE) $\varepsilon$ as the metric, which is defined as

$$\varepsilon = \frac{1}{H} \sum_{j=1}^{H} \frac{|x_j - \hat{x}_j|}{(x_j + \hat{x}_j)/2} \times 100\%, \tag{24.7}$$

where $x_j$ and $\hat{x}_j$ are the target value and the predicted value, respectively, with $H$ being the number of predicted values. Since SMAPE is a relative error measure, we can compare errors computed for different series so as to find which time series can be mapped into the underlying model better.

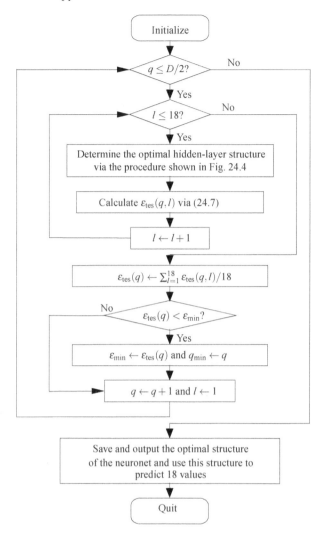

**FIGURE 24.5**: Flowchart of WASD algorithm for power-activation neuronet applied to time series prediction.

### 24.4.2   WDD subalgorithm

For the power-activation neuronet shown in Fig. 24.2, the optimal weights from hidden-layer to output-layer neurons can be determined directly via the following so-called WDD subalgorithm [260]:

$$\mathbf{w} = (\mathbf{\Psi}^{\mathrm{T}}\mathbf{\Psi})^{-1}\mathbf{\Psi}^{\mathrm{T}}\gamma, \tag{24.8}$$

where the weight vector $\mathbf{w}$, the desired-output vector $\gamma$ and the input-activation matrix $\mathbf{\Psi}$ are defined respectively as

$$\mathbf{w} = \begin{bmatrix} w_0 \\ w_1 \\ \vdots \\ w_{N-1} \end{bmatrix} \in \mathbb{R}^N, \ \gamma = \begin{bmatrix} \gamma_1 \\ \gamma_2 \\ \vdots \\ \gamma_M \end{bmatrix} \in \mathbb{R}^M, \ \mathbf{\Psi} = \begin{bmatrix} \varphi_0(\mathbf{x}_1) & \varphi_1(\mathbf{x}_1) & \cdots & \varphi_{N-1}(\mathbf{x}_1) \\ \varphi_0(\mathbf{x}_2) & \varphi_1(\mathbf{x}_2) & \cdots & \varphi_{N-1}(\mathbf{x}_2) \\ \vdots & \vdots & \ddots & \vdots \\ \varphi_0(\mathbf{x}_M) & \varphi_1(\mathbf{x}_M) & \cdots & \varphi_{N-1}(\mathbf{x}_M) \end{bmatrix} \in \mathbb{R}^{M \times N}.$$

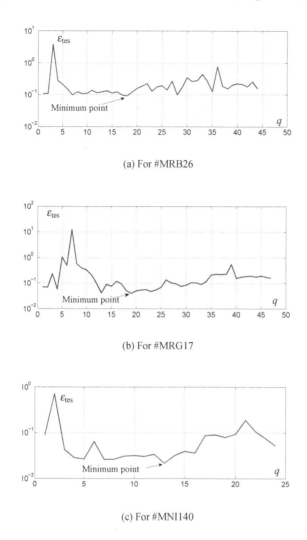

(a) For #MRB26

(b) For #MRG17

(c) For #MNI140

**FIGURE 24.6**: Relationship between number $q$ of input-layer neurons and mean testing SMAPE $\varepsilon_{tes}$.

As $(\Psi^{T}\Psi)^{-1}\Psi^{T}$ is the pseudoinverse of $\Psi$, the WDD subalgorithm (24.8) can be rewritten as $\mathbf{w} = \text{pinv}(\Psi)\gamma$, where $\text{pinv}(\Psi)$ denotes the pseudoinverse of $\Psi$ and it can be easily achieved by calling MATLAB routine "pinv$(\cdot)$".

### 24.4.3   Structure automatic determination

In light of literatures [265, 266], the numbers of input-layer and hidden-layer neurons influence greatly the overall performances of neuronets in time series prediction. Thus, it is important and meaningful to determine the optimal structure of the power-activation neuronet, that is, the optimal numbers of input-layer and hidden-layer neurons. Motivated by this reason, a novel WASD algorithm is designed in this chapter to obtain the optimal structure of the power-activation neuronet, which can self-adaptively search the smallest structure with the best generalization performance according to the relationship between the performance of the power-activation neuronet and the numbers of input-layer neurons and hidden-layer neurons.

**TABLE 24.1:** Training, testing and prediction results of power-activation WASD neuronet applied to time series prediction.

| Data-set | Mean $\varepsilon_{tra}$ | Mean $\varepsilon_{tes}$ | Mean $\varepsilon_{pre}$ |
|----------|--------------------------|--------------------------|--------------------------|
| #MRB26   | $3.930 \times 10^{-15}$  | 9.269%                   | 18.113%                  |
| #MRG17   | $5.457 \times 10^{-14}$  | 3.965%                   | 6.555%                   |
| #MNI140  | $1.573 \times 10^{-15}$  | 2.143%                   | 4.088%                   |

Before proposing the WASD algorithm, we firstly investigate the relationship between the SMAPE $\varepsilon$ and the number of hidden-layer neurons $N$ of the power-activation neuronet with every possible number of input-layer neurons given. Furthermore, we repeat such investigation via a variety of time series. For the purpose of better illustration, in this chapter, we use three monthly time series examples: #MRB26, #MRG17 and #MNI140 [260].

Due to the similarity of results, Fig. 24.3 only provides the relationship between $\varepsilon$ and the number of hidden-layer neurons $N$, in which the number of input-layer neurons $q$ is given as half of the number of training set $D$ and the 9-interval-ahead value is predicted (i.e., $q = D/2$ and $l = 9 < D - q = D/2$). As seen from Fig. 24.3, every curve has a minimum point $(N_{min}, \varepsilon_{min})$, which has the minimum number of hidden-layer neurons $N_{min}$ with the relatively superior learning performance (i.e., the minimal SMAPE of training). It is worth mentioning that such characteristics can be found in the training process of many other time series. It means that there exists a hidden-layer structure of the power-activation neuronet with the relatively superior learning performance for the fixed input-layer structure. In addition, we can obtain the minimum point $(N_{min}, \varepsilon_{min})$ via the following simple procedure as a part of the WASD algorithm. First, increase the number of hidden-layer neurons one-by-one. Second, when the SMAPE $\varepsilon$ for training is less than $0.1\varepsilon_{min}$ (with $\varepsilon_{min}$ denoting the minimum $\varepsilon$ found so far), record this new point as $(N_{min}, \varepsilon_{min})$. Otherwise, without loss of generality, search for 250 more hidden-layer neurons to make sure that $(N_{min}, \varepsilon_{min})$ is found correctly. For better understanding, the flowchart of this procedure for determining the optimal hidden-layer structure is shown in Fig. 24.4.

In addition to the relationship between the number of hidden-layer neurons and the learning performance of the power-activation neuronet, we further investigate the relationship between the number of input-layer neurons and the generalization performance of the power-activation neuronet. As we know from $M = D - q - l + 1$, too many input-layer neurons (with their number being $q$) lead to a small number of training samples, i.e., $M$, which may result in a bad generalization performance. Thus, we set the maximum of the number of input-layer neurons as half of the number of the observations (i.e., $D/2$). As a result, based on the procedure shown in Fig. 24.4, we can determine the optimal hidden-layer structure with minimal training error for power-activation neuronet with the number of input-layer neurons changing from 1 to $D/2$. Furthermore, by testing the $l$-interval-ahead values (with $l = 1, 2, \cdots, 18$), we can obtain a group of testing SMAPEs (or, say, generalization SMAPEs) $\varepsilon_{tes}$, and calculate the mean of testing SMAPEs, via the procedure shown in Fig. 24.5. Finally, the relationship between the mean of testing SMAPEs and the number of input-layer neurons is investigated and shown in Fig. 24.6. As seen from Fig. 24.6, there exists an optimal input-layer structure which can achieve the best generalization performance.

Finally, we can obtain the optimal structure of the power-activation neuronet via the proposed WASD algorithm. It is worth mentioning that the complete WASD algorithm shown in Fig. 24.5 runs the procedure shown in Fig. 24.4 for $(D/2) \times 18$ times to find the optimal structure with the best generalization performance.

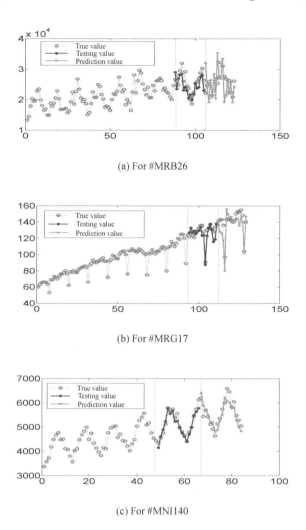

(a) For #MRB26

(b) For #MRG17

(c) For #MNI140

**FIGURE 24.7**: Testing and prediction results of power-activation WASD neuronet for three time series.

## 24.5    Numerical Studies

We use the monthly time series from M forecasting competition, which contain seasonality or trend for numerical experiments. Besides, the last 18 data points of the firstly published of each data series are retained to constitute the testing data-set which is used to measure the generalization performance of the power-activation WASD neuronet.

To assess the learning, testing and prediction performances of the proposed power-activation neuronet equipped with the WASD algorithm, we have conducted a large number of numerical experiments. Some numerical results are shown only for the aforementioned time series, #MRB26, #MRG17 and #MNI140, due to space limitation and results similarity. It is worth mentioning that the 18 points of the secondly published (or, say, of the complete data-set) are predicted for these three presented time series.

### 24.5.1 Learning and testing

To verify the superior learning and generalization ability of the power-activation neuronet equipped with the WASD algorithm, numerical results about the time series are presented in Table 24.1 and Fig. 24.7. As shown in the table, all of the means of training SMAPEs (i.e., Mean $\varepsilon_{tra}$) are very tiny (i.e., less than $10^{-13}$), and all of the means of testing SMAPEs (i.e., Mean $\varepsilon_{tes}$) of the three presented time series are less than 10%. Besides, Fig. 24.7 shows more illustratively that the shape of the curve of testing values predicted by power-activation WASD neuronet closely resembles the curve of true values (or, say, target values, desired values or real values). Thus, we can conclude from Table 24.1 and Fig. 24.7 that the power-activation neuronet equipped with the WASD algorithm possesses excellent learning ability and good generalization ability. It is worth mentioning that such good characteristics can be found in the numerical results of many other monthly time series.

### 24.5.2 Prediction

Following the above numerical studies about the testing ability, we further investigate the prediction ability of the power-activation neuronet equipped with the WASD algorithm. The corresponding numerical results of #MRB26, #MRG17 and #MNI140 are also shown in Table 24.1 and Fig. 24.7. As seen from the table, all of the means of prediction SMAPEs (i.e., $\varepsilon_{pre}$) are less than 20%, which substantiates the efficacy of the proposed power-activation WASD neuronet on prediction. Moreover, Fig. 24.7 shows that the power-activation WASD neuronet can accurately predict the variation tendency of future values.

In summary, we can conclude that the proposed power-activation WASD neuronet achieves good performances in terms of learning, generalization and prediction.

---

## 24.6 Chapter Summary

In order to explore the abilities of neuronets in monthly time series learning and prediction, a power-activation neuronet has been presented, constructed and investigated in this chapter. Then, the relationship between the number of hidden-layer neurons and the learning performance as well as the relationship between the number of input-layer neurons and the testing performance have been fully investigated on the basis of the WDD subalgorithm. In light of the above investigation, a WASD algorithm has been proposed to determine the optimal weights and the optimal structure of the power-activation neuronet. Numerical results have further substantiated the superiority of the power-activation neuronet equipped with the WASD algorithm in terms of monthly time series learning and prediction. Moreover, based on the work of this chapter, more types of WASD neuronet models to predict various time series can be a possible research direction in the future.

# Chapter 25

## Application to GFR Estimation

By combining the weights-direct-determination (WDD) subalgorithm and Levenberg-Marquardt (LM) method, this chapter presents an algorithm called weights-and-structure-determination (WASD) for a three-layer feed-forward neuronet. Note that the pruning-while-growing (PWG) and twice-pruning (TP) techniques are developed and exploited in the WASD algorithm with the aim of achieving a neuronet with a simple and economical structure. In order to verify the WASD efficacy and to address the problem of chronic kidney disease (CKD) for clinical applications in China, numerical studies about estimating glomerular filtration rate (GFR) by the WASD neuronet and traditional GFR-estimation equations are conducted and compared. Numerical results show that the WASD training speed is fast and that the estimating accuracy via the WASD neuronet is around 20% higher than those via traditional GFR-estimation equations. The WASD efficacy is thus substantiated with a significant value in GFR estimation of CKD for clinical applications.

## 25.1  Introduction

Note that artificial neuronets (AN) have been widely used in many fields because of the special properties and capabilities such as parallel distributed processing, learning and generalization. Many researchers [269–272] have proven that feed-forward neuronets, even with three layers (i.e., only one hidden layer), are capable of approximating any function with any desired accuracy, provided that associated conditions are satisfied. Hence the class of feed-forward neuronets is perhaps the most commonly used neuronet and has been applied to address a lot of problems such as multi-class classification and estimation arising from a wide variety of subjects included in environmental science, economics, medicine, etc.

The training algorithm for a feed-forward neuronet plays a significant role in determining the performance of the neuronet. In general, what a training algorithm does is to tune all parameters (including weights and biases) of a feed-forward neuronet such that the trained neuronet can achieve an acceptable performance of generalization. For a feed-forward neuronet with a given structure, there exist many algorithms that can be used in practical applications. Roughly speaking, they can usually be divided into 2 types: (i) gradient-based type, or termed back-propagation (BP) type, and (ii) gradient-free type. Note that the BP-type algorithms are effective only when the neuronet structure is selected appropriately since the structure is important to the performance [269]. However, to select an appropriate structure for a feed-forward neuronet is always a painful job because it is a long, difficult process. Therefore, how to develop an efficient and effective algorithm for feed-forward neuronet is challenging and valuable.

CKD has become a public health problem which threatens seriously people's health and life not only in China, but also in the rest of the world. As GFR is a commonly used index for early detection of CKD, an effective, efficient and accurate GFR-estimation method is significant for clinical applications. Nevertheless, due to some uncertain distinctions between Chinese people and Western people or people in/from other countries, traditional GFR-estimation equations are usually less effective for Chinese people [273,274]. Thus, GFR-estimation methods for clinical applications in China are highly desirable at the present stage [269].

Based on the WDD subalgorithm and LM method, this chapter develops and investigates an algorithm called WASD for the feed-forward neuronet aiming at solving the problems existing in traditional algorithms. Moreover, in order to address the problem of CKD for clinical applications in China and also to verify the efficacy of the WASD algorithm, numerical studies about estimating GFR by the WASD neuronet and traditional GFR-estimation equations are conducted and compared.

## 25.2   Neuronet Model and WASD Algorithm

In this section, we develop and investigate a three-layer feed-forward neuronet termed WASD neuronet with multiple inputs and one output.

### 25.2.1   Neuronet model

From a practical point of view, Villiers and Barnard [275] have shown through extensive studies that, with the same level of complexity, three-layer feed-forward neuronets are better than neuronets with multiple hidden layers. It is mainly because feed-forward neuronets with multiple hidden layers are more likely to trap into local minima. In this chapter, the WASD neuronet focuses on the three-layer feed-forward neuronet model with multiple inputs and one output which is shown in Fig. 25.1.

Specifically, suppose that there are $M$ sample pairs $(\mathbf{x}_k, \gamma_k)$ with $k = 1, \cdots, M$, where sample input $\mathbf{x}_k = [x_{1k}, x_{2k}, \cdots, x_{mk}]^{\mathrm{T}} \in \mathbb{R}^m$ and sample output $\gamma_k \in \mathbb{R}$. Then the neuronet shown in Fig. 25.1 can be expressed by the following equation:

$$y_k = \sum_{i=1}^{N} w_i \varphi_i \left( \sum_{j=1}^{m} x_{jk} \omega_{ij} + \beta_i \right), \tag{25.1}$$

where $m$ and $N$ denote the numbers of input- and hidden-layer neurons, respectively; $\omega_{ij}$, $\beta_i$ and $w_i$ are the input weight (linking the $j$th input-layer neuron to the $i$th hidden-layer neuron), the bias (of the $i$th hidden-layer neuron) and the output weight (linking the $i$th hidden-layer neuron to the output-layer neuron), respectively. The $i$th hidden-layer neuron activation function $\varphi(\cdot) : \mathbb{R} \to \mathbb{R}$;

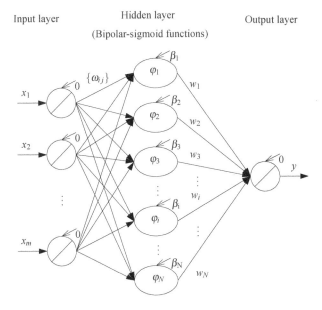

**FIGURE 25.1**: Model structure of multi-input WASD neuronet for GFR estimation.

and $y_k$ is the neuronet output. As shown in Fig. 25.1, the activation functions for input and output layers are identity functions, while those for the hidden layers are all bipolar-sigmoid functions (i.e., tan-sigmoid functions). Generally, if a neuronet structure is given in advance, the input weight $\omega_{ij}$, bias $\beta_i$ and output weight $w_i$ can be tuned through a training algorithm like BP algorithm to minimize a cost function, such as the following mean squared error (MSE) between the neuronet output $y_k$ and the sample output (i.e., reference output, target output, or desired output) $\gamma_k$:

$$e = \frac{1}{M} \sum_{k=1}^{M} (\gamma_k - y_k)^2.$$

### 25.2.2 WDD subalgorithm

To overcome the inherent weaknesses of BP-type algorithms, based on the polynomial interpolation and approximation theory, the authors have recently constructed some types of feed-forward neuronets and presented a WDD subalgorithm which calculates the output weights directly [17,99]. It is worth mentioning that such neuronets are different from the general feed-forward neuronets (see Fig. 25.1) in the following aspects. First, the input weights are fixed to be 1. Second, the activation functions for hidden layer are polynomials (instead of sigmoid functions). Last, the hidden-layer biases are zero. Then, with a given structure, the output weights can be calculated by the WDD subalgorithm in a short time (much faster than BP-type algorithms) and the trained neuronet shows a satisfactory performance of generalization. In addition, we present the following WDD subalgorithm [17,99,276] for the neuronet shown in Fig. 25.1.

Define output-weight vector $\mathbf{w}$, target-output vector $\gamma$ and input-activation matrix $\Psi$, respectively as

$$\mathbf{w} = \begin{bmatrix} w_1 \\ w_2 \\ \vdots \\ w_N \end{bmatrix} \in \mathbb{R}^N,\ \gamma = \begin{bmatrix} \gamma_1 \\ \gamma_2 \\ \vdots \\ \gamma_M \end{bmatrix} \in \mathbb{R}^M,\ \Psi = \begin{bmatrix} \varphi_{11} & \varphi_{21} & \cdots & \varphi_{N1} \\ \varphi_{12} & \varphi_{22} & \cdots & \varphi_{N2} \\ \vdots & \vdots & \ddots & \vdots \\ \varphi_{1M} & \varphi_{2M} & \cdots & \varphi_{NM} \end{bmatrix} \in \mathbb{R}^{M \times N}.$$

Then, the steady-state output-weight vector of the three-layer feed-forward neuronet (as shown in Fig. 25.1) can be determined directly as

$$\mathbf{w} = (\Psi^{\mathrm{T}}\Psi)^{-1}\Psi^{\mathrm{T}}\gamma. \tag{25.2}$$

In addition, formula (25.2) can be rewritten as $\mathbf{w} = \mathrm{pinv}(\Psi)\gamma$, where $\mathrm{pinv}(\Psi)$ denotes the pseudoinverse of input-activation matrix $\Psi$, which equals $(\Psi^{\mathrm{T}}\Psi)^{-1}\Psi^{\mathrm{T}}$.

### 25.2.3    WASD algorithm

To get a desired performance, incorporating the WDD subalgorithm, the authors have recently presented the training algorithm called WASD. The WASD algorithm can determine the optimal output weights and structures of neuronets automatically, and the determined neuronets have shown excellent performances especially in terms of function approximation and generalization [51, 65, 125]. Furthermore, according to [277], WASD is attempted to train the general feed-forward neuronets (with unipolar sigmoid activation functions for hidden layer) and an acceptable outcome is obtained.

Note that the trained neuronet generally requires more hidden-layer neurons in many cases and it is most likely because the input weights and biases are not well utilized (or, say, without tuning). In [278], the LM method, which is a variation of quasi-Newton algorithm, has been shown as one of the most efficient methods for neuronet training. With the purpose of fully utilizing the input weights and biases of neuronets, the LM method (referred to [269, 279] for details) is employed in this chapter for the neuronet shown in Fig. 25.1.

To achieve an efficient and effective neuronet with a simple and economical structure, by combining the WDD subalgorithm and LM method, a training algorithm called WASD for the neuronet (shown in Fig. 25.1) is thus used in this chapter.

**Remark 4**    Note that the WASD algorithm used in this chapter consists of 3 main stages: pruning-while-growing (PWG), twice-pruning (TP), and Levenberg-Marquardt (LM) tuning. Through the PWG technique, a neuronet with a fundamental structure is obtained. By this technique, the trained neuronet has shown satisfactory effectiveness in function approximation. However, whether the neuronet is redundant in this case is a problem that deserves further investigation. Therefore, the TP is developed to attempt to simplify the neuronet which is obtained through the PWG technique. Finally, the LM method is exploited to tune the input weights and biases for the full use of all parameters of the neuronet. Reasonably speaking, all parameters of the neuronet including input weights, biases, output weights and the number of hidden-layer neurons have been considered thoroughly in this fast training algorithm. For convenience, a neuronet trained through the WASD algorithm is called WASD neuronet in this chapter.

### 25.3    GFR Estimation

Along with the development of society and the changes of environment, CKD has become a public health problem which threatens people's health and life seriously. With the consideration that

GFR is a commonly used index for early detection of CKD, an effective, efficient and accurate GFR-estimation method is significant for clinical applications. In this section, numerical studies about estimating GFR by the WASD neuronet and traditional GFR-estimation equations are conducted and compared.

### 25.3.1 Traditional GFR-estimation equations

From the medical perspective [274, 280], GFR can be estimated from some clinical measurements including serum creatinine (i.e., scr) and demographic and clinical variables such as age, sex, ethnicity, and body size. Some GFR-estimation equations have recently been proposed as follows. Chinese equation [281]:

$$\text{C-GFR} = \begin{aligned} &1.227 \times 186 \times \text{scr}^{-1.154} \times \text{age}^{-0.203} \\ &(\times \, 0.742 \ \text{if female}). \end{aligned} \tag{25.3}$$

Reexpressed 4-variable MDRD equation [280, 282]:

$$\text{R-GFR} = \begin{aligned} &175 \times \text{scr}^{-1.154} \times \text{age}^{-0.203} \\ &(\times \, 0.742 \ \text{if female}; \ \times 1.212 \ \text{if black}). \end{aligned} \tag{25.4}$$

Previous Japanese equation [282]:

$$\text{J1-GFR} = \begin{aligned} &0.741 \times 175 \times \text{scr}^{-1.154} \times \text{age}^{-0.203} \\ &(\times \, 0.742 \ \text{if female}). \end{aligned} \tag{25.5}$$

New Japanese equation [283]:

$$\text{J2-GFR} = \begin{aligned} &0.808 \times 175 \times \text{scr}^{-1.154} \times \text{age}^{-0.203} \\ &(\times \, 0.742 \ \text{if female}). \end{aligned} \tag{25.6}$$

Note that all these equations are derived from traditional regression methods of statistics, with a significant disadvantage that the regression models cannot reflect the true situation. Apparently, artificial neuronets are suitable alternatives due to their special properties such as parallel distributed processing, learning and generalization.

### 25.3.2 Numerical studies

In this chapter, we use the data of Chinese patients with CKD from the Division of Nephrology, Department of Internal Medicine, the Third Affiliated Hospital of Sun Yat-sen University, Guangzhou, China from January 2005 to December 2010. The total data contain 1180 individuals with 8 characteristics which consist of 7 inputs (i.e., sex, age, height, weight, albumin, serum creatinine, and urea) and 1 output (i.e., GFR). The data-sets with detailed characteristics can be referred to in Zhang et al. [269]. Without loss of generality, the 7 inputs/attributes and 1 output have been normalized to the range [-1,1] before using the WASD algorithm in numerical studies.

To verify the WASD algorithm's effectiveness and efficiency, 50 trials have been conducted in numerical studies and verifications. WASD algorithm characteristics such as training time, the number of hidden-layer neurons $N$ and the pruning rate (i.e., the ratio of the number of hidden-layer neurons pruned via TP to that before TP) can be seen from Table 25.1 and Fig. 25.2. Note that the mean training time of WASD algorithm is 1.40 seconds, which means that WASD algorithm owns a fast learning speed. This is mainly because it has combined the WDD subalgorithm and LM method. The number of hidden-layer neurons, as we know, is quite important to the neuronet performance. Therefore, it is relatively reasonable that the mean number of hidden-layer neurons obtained via WASD algorithm is 11.68 since the number is neither too large (e.g., $> 100$) nor too small (e.g., 1).

**TABLE 25.1:**    Training results of WASD neuronet for 50 trials.

| Training result | Min | Max | Mean |
|---|---|---|---|
| Training time $t_{tra}$ (s) | 0.71 | 2.90 | 1.40 |
| Number $N$ of hidden-layer neurons | 5 | 26 | 11.68 |

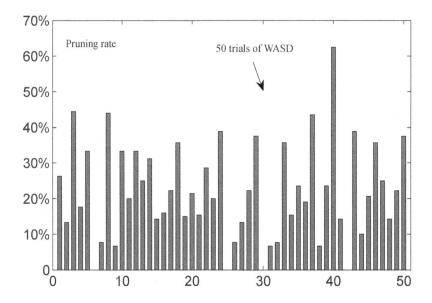

**FIGURE 25.2**: Pruning rates of WASD neuronet via TP technique.

As observed from Fig. 25.2, the TP technique can prune the hidden-layer neurons almost in every trail successfully (i.e., 46 out of 50) with the maximum pruning rate 63% indicating that more than half of the neurons can be pruned sometimes.

Although the characteristics (e.g., training time and structure) of the WASD are important issues that should be considered, we always pay more attention to the generalization of neuronets. Accuracy [percentage of estimated GFR within a 30% (or 15% or 50%) deviation from the reference GFR] is one of the most important parameters to evaluate the performances of models in clinical applications [274, 280]. Thus, the corresponding estimating results via WASD are shown in Fig. 25.3 and Table 25.2. From Fig. 25.3, we can see that the GFR-estimation results via 50 trials are effective and stable. As observed further from Table 25.2, in the 50 trials, the mean accuracy within 15%, 30% and 50% deviations are 42.7%, 73% and 88%, respectively. These indicate that WASD is a feasible, stable and excellent algorithm for neuronet training.

### 25.3.3    Comparisons with GFR-estimation equations

For comparative and illustrative purposes, the popularly used GFR-estimation equations (i.e., C-GFR, R-GFR, J1-GFR and J2-GFR) in clinical applications are studied in this chapter. Table 25.3 shows the corresponding estimation results of Equations (25.3) through (25.6) and the WASD neuronet. As seen from the table, the estimation results via Equations (25.3) through (25.6) are not so satisfactory as expected. For example, the accuracy within a 30% derivation via the J2-GFR equation is 50.4% which is far lower than 70%, though it is the highest one among such

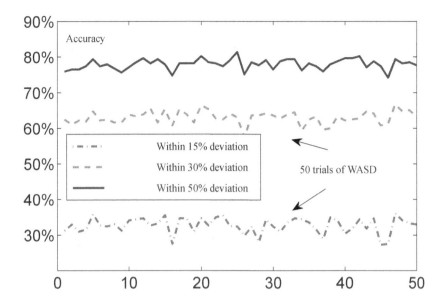

**FIGURE 25.3**: Numerical results of GFR estimation within 15%, 30% and 50% deviations via WASD neuronet for 50 trials.

**TABLE 25.2:** Numerical results of GFR estimation within different deviations of testing set via WASD neuronet for 50 trials.

| Within 15% deviation | | | Within 30% deviation | | | Within 50% deviation | | |
|---|---|---|---|---|---|---|---|---|
| Min | Max | Mean | Min | Max | Mean | Min | Max | Mean |
| 37.2% | 46.1% | 42.7% | 67.3% | 76.8% | 73.0% | 84.2% | 91.4 % | 88.0% |

4 equations. It is probably because some uncertain distinctions exist among people from different areas/countries. Thus the traditional GFR-estimation equations are usually less effective for Chinese people. In contrast, by comparing the mean estimation results via WASD algorithm with those of traditional equations, we can see that the WASD neuronet shows a better estimation performance than Equations (25.3) through (25.6). Specifically, for the accuracy within a 15% (or 30% or 50%) derivation, the result obtained through WASD algorithm is around 20% higher than those through Equations (25.3) through (25.6). These results substantiate that WASD algorithm is really effective and efficient for the application of estimating GFR. As a matter of fact, WASD algorithm, being a training algorithm, can also be exploited for solving plenty of problems involved in estimation, multiclass classification, function approximation, and so on, which will be investigated in the future.

The above results of numerical studies have substantiated the efficiency, effectiveness and superiority of the proposed WASD neuronet which incorporates the WDD subalgorithm and LM method with two techniques (i.e., PWG and TP). More importantly, the WASD neuronet has a significant value in GFR estimation of CKD for clinical applications because of its high GFR-estimation accuracy which is around 20% higher than those of traditional GFR-estimation equations.

**TABLE 25.3:**    Numerical results of GFR estimation within different deviations of testing set via traditional equations in comparison with WASD neuronet for 50 trials.

| Accuracy | C-GFR | R-GFR | J1-GFR | J2-GFR | WASD (Mean) | WASD (Max) |
|---|---|---|---|---|---|---|
| 15% deviation | 16.6% | 27.5% | 22.6% | 24.3% | 42.7% | 46.1% |
| 30% deviation | 35.2% | 48.1% | 47.2% | 50.4% | 73.0% | 76.8% |
| 50% deviation | 59.6% | 71.1% | 69.6% | 71.3% | 88.0% | 91.4% |

## 25.4    Chapter Summary

In this chapter, for three-layer feed-forward neuronet training, we have presented a WASD algorithm, which has combined the WDD subalgorithm and the LM method. In addition, the PWG and TP techniques have been developed in the WASD algorithm to achieve a neuronet with a simple and economical structure. Furthermore, the WASD neuronet has been applied to estimating GFR so as to address the problem of CKD for clinical applications in China. The efficacy of the WASD neuronet has been further substantiated through numerical studies about estimating GFR.

At the end of the chapter and also the end of the book, it is worth mentioning again that this book has systematically solved the inherent weaknesses of the BP-type neural network (simply, neuronet) while improving its performance, by means of using various kinds of linearly independent or even orthogonal activation functions. Note that this book mainly focuses on solving tough problems of conventional AN with single hidden layer, which is the basis of and also work toward deep neural networks. In the past years, deep neural networks have served as powerful computational tools and have attracted widespread interests from both researchers and engineers in developing fields of computer mathematics, computer science, and artificial intelligence [284–286]. On the basis of the comprehensive and systematic research of conventional AN, this book also aims to open a new door toward further research and applications of deep neural networks with multiple hidden layers, as the difficult problem of WASD has now been solved truly, systematically and methodologically. The in-depth research of the deep neural networks based on the WASD algorithm would be an interesting and open topic for readers, researchers and engineers in the future.

# Bibliography

[1] Y. Zhang, D. Jiang, and J. Wang. A recurrent neural network for solving Sylvester equation with time-varying coefficients. *IEEE Transactions on Neural Networks*, 13:1053–1063(5), 2002.

[2] Y. Zhang and S.S. Ge. Design and analysis of a general recurrent neural network model for time-varying matrix inversion. *IEEE Transactions on Neural Networks*, 16:1477–1490(6), 2005.

[3] Y. Zhang and J. Wang. Recurrent neural networks for nonlinear output regulation. *Automatica*, 37:1161–1173(8), 2001.

[4] Y. Zhang and J. Wang. Global exponential stability of recurrent neural networks for synthesizing linear feedback control systems via pole assignment. *IEEE Transactions on Neural Networks*, 13:633–644(3), 2002.

[5] J. Schmidhuber. Deep learning in neural networks: an overview. *Neural Networks*, 61:85–117, 2015.

[6] G.E. Dahl, D. Yu, L. Deng, and A. Acero. Context-dependent pre-trained deep neural networks for large-vocabulary speech recognition. *IEEE Transactions on Audio, Speech, and Language Processing*, 20:30–42(1), 2012.

[7] Y. Xu, J. Du, L.R. Dai, and C.H. Lee. An experimental study on speech enhancement based on deep neural networks. *IEEE Signal Processing Letters*, 21:65–68(1), 2014.

[8] Y. Xu, J. Du, L.R. Dai, and C.H. Lee. A regression approach to speech enhancement based on deep neural networks. *IEEE/ACM Transactions on Audio, Speech and Language Processing*, 23:7–19(1), 2015.

[9] L. Deng, G. Hinton, and B. Kingsbury. New types of deep neural network learning for speech recognition and related applications: an overview. In *Proceedings of International Conference on Acoustics, Speech and Signal Processing*, pages 8599–8603, 2013.

[10] B. Boutsinas and M.N. Vrahatis. Artificial nonmonotonic neural networks. *Artificial Intelligence*, 132:1–38(1), 2001.

[11] A.S. d'Avila Garcez, K. Broda, and D.M. Grabbay. Symbolic knowledge extraction from trained neural networks: a sound approach. *Artificial Intelligence*, 125:155–207(1–2), 2001.

[12] Y. Zhang, S.S. Ge, and T.H. Lee. A unified quadratic-programming-based dynamical system approach to joint torque optimization of physically constrained redundant manipulators. *IEEE Transactions on Systems, Man, and Cybernetics*, 34:2126–2132(5), 2004.

[13] B.H.M. Sadeghi. A BP-neural network predictor model for plastic injection molding process. *Journal of Materials Processing Technology*, 103:411–416(3), 2000.

[14] W.M. Jenkins. Neural network weight training by mutation. *Computers and Structures*, 84:2107–2112(31–32), 2006.

[15] X. Xu, Y. Zhang, and Z. Mao. A method of dynamic growing and pruning the hidden layer nodes in a feedforward neural network. *Journal of Zhongkai Agrotechnical College*, 11:20–23(4), 1998.

[16] Y. Zhang, X. Xu, and Z. Mao. Java programming-language with application in ANN. *Journal of Jinan University (Natural Science Edition)*, 19:108–112(1), 1998.

[17] Y. Zhang, L. Li, Y. Yang, and G. Ruan. Euler neural network with its weights-direct-determination and structure-automatic-determination algorithms. In *Proceedings of International Conference on Hybrid Intelligent Systems*, pages 319–324, 2009.

[18] J.M. Mathews and K.D. Fink. *Numerical Methods Using MATLAB*. Pearson Education Inc., Beijing, China, 2004.

[19] G. Mo and K. Liu. *Function Approximation Method*. Science Press, Beijing, China, 2003.

[20] Y. Zhang, T. Zhong, W. Li, X. Xiao, and C. Yi. Growing algorithm of Laguerre orthogonal basis neural network with weights directly determined. In *Proceedings of Intelligent Computing: Advanced Intelligent Computing Theories and Applications-with Aspects of Artificial Intelligence, Lecture Notes In Artificial Intelligence*, pages 60–67, 2008.

[21] Y. Zhang, W. Li, C. Yi, and K. Chen. A weights-directly-determined simple neural network for nonlinear system identification. In *Proceedings of International Conference Fuzzy Systems*, pages 455–460, 2008.

[22] H. Demuth, M. Beale, and M. Hegan. *Neural Network Toolbox 5 User's Guide*. MathWorks Inc., Natick, Massachusetts, USA, 2007.

[23] Y. Zhang. *Object-Oriented Software Implementation of Artificial Neural Networks*. M.E. Thesis, South China University of Technology, China, 1999.

[24] M.X. He and P.E. Ricci. Differential equation of Appell polynomials via the factorization method. *Journal of Computational and Applied Mathematics*, 139:231–237(2), 2002.

[25] C.S. Lin. *Numerical Analysis*. Science Press, Beijing, China, 2003.

[26] F.A. Costabile and F. Dell'Accio. Expansion over a rectangle of real functions in Bernoulli polynomials and application. *BIT Numerical Mathematics*, 41:451–464(3), 2001.

[27] F.A. Costabile, F. Dell'Accio, and M.I. Gualtieri. A new approach to Bernoulli polynomials. *Rendiconti di Matematica*, 26:1–12(7), 2006.

[28] Y. Zhang and G. Ruan. Bernoulli neural network with weights directly determined and with the number of hidden-layer neurons automatically determined. In *Proceedings of International Symposium on Neural Networks*, pages 36–45, 2009.

[29] D. Kincaid and W. Cheney. *Numerical Analysis: Mathematics of Scientific Computing*. China Machine Press, Beijing, China, 2003.

[30] P. Guo and M.R. Lyu. Pseudoinverse learning algorithm for feedforward neural networks. In *Advances in Neural Networks and Applications*. WSES Press, Athens, Greece, 2001.

[31] P. Guo and M.R. Lyu. A pseudoinverse learning algorithm for feedforward neural networks with stacked generalization application to software reliability growth data. *Neurocomputing*, 56:101–121, 2004.

[32] D. Zhang. *New Theories and Methods of Neural Networks*. Tsinghua University Press, Beijing, China, 2006.

[33] J.F. Shepanski. Fast learning in artificial neural systems: multilayer perceptron training using optimal estimation. In *Proceedings of International Conference on Neural Networks*, pages 465–472, 1988.

[34] Y. Zhu. Iterative solutions of the linear least squares subject to linear constraints. In *Proceedings of International Symposium on Speech, Image Processing and Neural Networks*, pages 749–752, 1994.

[35] M. Brucoli, L. Carnimeo, and G. Grassi. Associative memory design using discrete-time second-order neural networks with local interconnections. *IEEE Transactions on Circuits and Systems I: Fundamental Theory and Applications*, 44:153–158(2), 1997.

[36] K. Zhang, G. Ganis, and M.I. Sereno. Anti-Hebbian synapses as a linear equation solver. In *Proceedings of International Conference on Neural Networks*, pages 387–389, 1997.

[37] A. Ciaramella, R. Tagliaferri, and W. Pedrycz. Fuzzy relations neural network: some preliminary results. In *Proceedings of International Conference on Fuzzy Systems*, pages 469–472, 2001.

[38] W.E. Leithead and Y. Zhang. $O(N^2)$-operation approximation of covariance matrix inverse in Gaussian process regression based on Quasi-Newton BFGS methods. *Communications in Statistics – Simulation and Computation*, 36:367–380(2), 2007.

[39] R.P. Lippmann. An introduction to computing with neural nets. *IEEE ASSP Magazine*, 4:4–22(2), 1987.

[40] G.L. Carl. Advances in feedforward neural networks: demystifying knowledge acquiring black boxes. *IEEE Transactions on Knowledge and Data Engineering*, 8:211–226(2), 1996.

[41] S.Y. Daniel and X.Q. Zeng. Hidden neuron pruning for multilayer perceptrons using a sensitivity measure. In *Proceedings of International Conference on Machine Learning and Cybernetics*, pages 1751–1757, 2002.

[42] B. Niu, Y.L. Zhu, K.Y. Hu, S.F. Li, and X.X. He. A cooperative evolutionary system for designing neural networks. In *Proceedings of International Conference on Intelligent Computing*, pages 12–21, 2006.

[43] D.R. Wilson and T.R. Martinez. The need for small learning rates on large problems. In *Proceedings of International Joint Conference on Neural Networks*, pages 115–119, 2001.

[44] X.H. Yu and G.A. Chen. On the local minima free condition of backpropagation learning. *IEEE Transactions on Neural Networks*, 6:1300–1303(5), 1995.

[45] G.-B. Huang, Q. Zhu, and C.-K. Siew. Extreme learning machine: theory and applications. *Neurocomputing*, 70:489–501(1), 2006.

[46] G.-B. Huang. What are extreme learning machines? Filling the gap between Frank Rosenblatt's dream and John von Neumann's puzzle. *Cognitive Computation*, 7:263–278(3), 2015.

[47] W. Zhao, D.-S. Huang, and G. Yunjian. The structure optimization of radial basis probabilistic neural networks based on genetic algorithms. In *Proceedings of International Joint Conference on Neural Networks*, pages 1086–1091, 2002.

[48] F. Melgani and S.B. Serpico. A Markov random field approach to spatio-temporal contextual image classification. *IEEE Transactions on Geoscience and Remote Sensing*, 41:2478–2487(11), 2003.

[49] G.-B. Huang and C.-K. Siew. Extreme learning machine: RBF network case. In *Proceedings of International Conference on Control, Automation, Robotics and Vision*, pages 1029–1036, 2004.

[50] J. Tian, M.-Q. Li, and F.-Z. Chen. A three-phase RBFNN learning algorithm for complex classification. In *Proceedings of International Conference on Machine Learning and Cybernetics*, pages 4134–4139, 2005.

[51] Y. Zhang, J. Chen, D. Guo, Y. Yin, and W. Lao. Growing-type weights and structure determination of 2-input Legendre orthogonal polynomial neuronet. In *Proceedings of International Symposium on Industrial Electronics*, pages 852–857, 2012.

[52] Y. Zhang. Dual neural networks: design, analysis, and application to redundant robotics (Chapter 2). In *Progress in Neurocomputing Research*. Nova Science, New York, USA, 2007.

[53] Y. Zhang and S.S. Ge. A primal neural network for solving nonlinear equations and inequalities. In *Proceedings of IEEE Conference on Cybernetics and Intelligent Systems*, pages 1232–1237, 2004.

[54] Y. Zhang, J. Wang, and Y. Xia. A dual neural network for redundancy resolution of kinematically redundant manipulators subject to joint limits and joint velocity limits. *IEEE Transations on Neural Networks*, 14:658–667(3), 2003.

[55] Y. Zhang, X. Dong, H. Bai, S. Shen, and S. Guo. The research and realization of English characters recognition technology based on artificial neural network. *Journal of Xinyang Agricultural College*, 14:23–26, 2004.

[56] D.E. Rumelhart and J.L. McClelland. *Parallel Distributed Processing*. The MIT Press, Cambridge, UK, 1986.

[57] W. Guo, Y. Qiao, and H. Hou. BP neural network optimized with PSO algorithm and its application in forecasting. In *Proceedings of IEEE International Conference on Information Acquisition*, pages 617–621, 2006.

[58] Y. Zhang, W. Liu, C. Yi, and W. Li. Weights immediate determination for feed-forward neural network with Legendre orthogonal basis function. *Journal of Dalian Maritime University*, 34:32–36(1), 2008.

[59] X. Xiao, X. Jiang, and Y. Zhang. General polynomial neural network and its structure adaptive determination. *Journal of Chongqing Institute of Technology (Natural Science)*, 23:97–99(7), 2009.

[60] K. Narendra and S. Mukhopadhyay. Adaptive control of nonlinear multivariable systems using neural networks. In *Proceedings of IEEE Conference on Decision and Control*, pages 3066–3097, 1994.

[61] X. Liang and Q. Li. *Multivariate Approximation*. National Defence Industry Press, Beijing, China, 2005.

[62] L. Xu and J. Yang. A survey of recent development of multivariate approximation. *Advances in Mathematics*, 16:241–249(3), 1987.

[63] Y. Zhang, W. Liu, B. Cai, and X. Xiao. Number determination of hidden-layer neurons in weights-directly-determined Legendre neural network. *Journal of Chinese Computer Systems*, 30:1298–1301(7), 2009.

[64] C.F. Dunkl and Y. Xu. *Orthogonal Polynomials of Several Variables*, Cambridge University Press, Cambridge, UK, 2001.

[65] Y. Zhang, Y. Yin, X. Yu, D. Guo, and L. Xiao. Pruning-included weights and structure determination of 2-input neuronet using Chebyshev polynomials of class 1. In *Proceedings of World Congress on International Intelligent Control and Automation*, pages 700–705, 2012.

[66] Y. Zhang, Y. Chen, X. Jiang, Q. Zeng, and A. Zou. Weights-directly-determined and structure-adaptively-tuned neural network based on Chebyshev basis functions. *Computer Science*, 36:210–213(6), 2009.

[67] Y. Fu and T. Chai. Nonlinear multivariable adaptive control using multiple models and neural networks. *Automatica*, 43:1101–1110(6), 2007.

[68] Z. Sheng, S. Xie, and C. Pan. *Probability and Statistics*. Higher Education Press, Beijing, China, 2005.

[69] Y. Zhang, Z. Kuang, X. Xiao, and B. Chen. A direct-weight-determination method for trigonometrically-activated Fourier neural networks. *Computer Engineering and Science*, 31:112–115, 2009.

[70] J. Su and S. Ruan. *MATLAB Practical Guide*. Publishing House of Electronics Industry, Beijing, China, 2008.

[71] Y. Zhang. *Analysis and Design of Recurrent Neural Networks and Their Applications to Control and Robotic Systems*. Ph.D. Dissertation, Chinese University of HongKong, China, 2002.

[72] Y. Zhang, X. Yu, D. Guo, J. Li, and Z. Fan. Weights and structure determination of feed-forward two-input neural network activated by Chebyshev polynomials of class 2. In *Proceedings of Chinese Control and Decision Conference*, pages 1100–1105, 2012.

[73] X. Xiao, Y. Zhang, X. Jiang, and A. Zou. Weights-direct-determination and structure-adaptive-determination of feed-forward neural network activated with the 2nd-class Chebyshev orthogonal polynomials. *Journal of Dalian Maritime University*, 35:80–84(1), 2009.

[74] X. Zhang and Q. Li. *Multivariable Approximation*. Defense Industry Press, Beijing, China, 2005.

[75] Y. Zhang, W. Li, X. Yu, L. Xiao, and J. Chen. The 3-input Euler polynomial neuronet (3IEPN) with weights-and-structure-determination (WASD) algorithm. In *Proceedings of International Conference on Modelling, Identification and Control*, pages 1222–1227, 2012.

[76] L. Wang and T. Sui. Application of data mining technology based on neural network in the engineering. In *Proceedings of International Conference on Wireless Communications, Networking and Mobile Computing*, pages 5544–5547, 2007.

[77] Y. Ma, K. Liu, Z. Zhang, J. Yu, and X. Gong. Modeling the colored background noise of power line communication channel based on artificial neural network. In *Proceedings of Wireless and Optical Communications Conference*, pages 1–4, 2010.

[78] Y. Zhang, K. Li, and N. Tan. An RBF neural network classifier with centers, variances and weights directly determined. *Computing Technology and Automation*, 28:5–9, 2009.

[79] S. Ding, C. Su, and J. Yu. An optimizing BP neural network algorithm based on genetic algorithm. *Artificial Intelligence Review*, 36:153–162(2), 2011.

[80] L. Liu, C. Li, and Z. Wu. Weierstrass approximation theorem in the promotion of multifunction. *Journal of Nanyang Institute of Technology*, 1:85–87(6), 2009.

[81] P. Peng and Z. Li. Extension and application on Weierstrass approximation theorem. *Journal of Henan Institute of Education*, 18:1–2(1), 2009.

[82] Y. Niu. On the generalization of Weierstrass approximation theorem. *Journal of Inner Mongolia University for Nationalities*, 25:614–616(5), 2010.

[83] H. Lu and F. Qi. Function approximation by multidimensional discrete Fourier transform based neural networks. *Journal of Shanghai Jiaotong University*, 34:955–959(7), 2000.

[84] G. Bretti and P.E. Ricci. Euler polynomial and the related quadrature rule. *Georgian Mathematical Journal*, 8:447–453(3), 2001.

[85] Q. Luo and F. Qi. Generalizations of Euler numbers and Euler numbers of higher order. *Chinese Quarterly Journal of Mathematics*, 20:54–58(1), 2005.

[86] R. Wang and X. Liang. *Multivariate Function Approximation*. Science Press, Beijing, China, 1988.

[87] S.J. Chapman. *MATLAB Programming for Engineers*. Science Press, Beijing, China, 2003.

[88] S.S. Ge and C. Wang. Adaptive neural control of uncertain MIMO nonlinear systems. *IEEE Transactions on Neural Networks*, 15:674–692(3), 2004.

[89] G.P. Zhang. Neural networks for classification: a survey. *IEEE Transactions on Systems, Man, and Cybernetics, Part C: Applications and Reviews*, 30:451–462(4), 2000.

[90] K. Nose-Filho, A.D.P. Lotufo, and C.R. Minussi. Short-term multinodal load forecasting using a modified general regression neural network. *IEEE Transactions on Power Delivery*, 26:2862–2869(4), 2011.

[91] G.A. Rovithakis, I. Chalkiadakis, and M.E. Zervakis. High-order neural network structure selection for function approximation applications using genetic algorithms. *IEEE Transactions on Systems, Man, and Cybernetics, Part B: Cybernetics*, 34:150–158(1), 2004.

[92] S. Kollias and D. Anastassiou. An adaptive least squares algorithm for the efficient training of artificial neural networks. *IEEE Transactions on Circuits and Systems*, 36:1092–1101(8), 1989.

[93] N.E. Cotter. The Stone-Weierstrass theorem and its application to neural networks. *IEEE Transactions on Neural Networks*, 1:290–295(4), 1990.

[94] L.K. Jones. Constructive approximations for neural networks by sigmoidal functions. *Proceedings of the IEEE*, 78:1586–1589(10), 1990.

[95] A.R. Barron. Universal approximation bounds for superpositions of a sigmoidal function. *IEEE Transactions on Information Theory*, 39:930–945(3), 1993.

[96] Y. Zhang, W. Lao, Y. Yin, L. Xiao, and J. Chen. Weights and structure determination of pruning-while-growing type for 3-input power-activation feed-forward neuronet. In *Proceedings of International Conference on Automation and Logistics*, pages 212–217, 2012.

[97] S. Yang and C.S. Tseng. An orthogonal neural network for function approximation. *IEEE Transactions on Systems, Man, and Cybernetics, Part B: Cybernetics*, 26:779–785(5), 1996.

[98] F.H.F. Leung, H.K. Lam, S.H. Ling, and P.K.S. Tam. Tuning of the structure and parameters of a neural network using an improved genetic algorithm. *IEEE Transactions on Neural Networks*, 14:79–88(1), 2003.

[99] Y. Zhang, Y. Yang, and W. Li. *Weights Direct Determination of Neural Networks*. Sun Yat-sen University Press, Guangzhou, China, 2010.

[100] M. Zhang, H. Han, and J. Qiao. Research on dynamic feed-forward neural network structure based on growing and pruning methods. *CAAI Transactions on Intelligent Systems*, 6:101–106(2), 2011.

[101] C. Gao. On power series of functions in several variables. *College Mathematics*, 23:125–129(3), 2007.

[102] K. Kodaira. *An Introduction to Calculus*. Posts and Telecom Press, Beijing, China, 2008.

[103] D.F. Charles and X. Yuan. *Orthogonal Polynomials of Several Variables*. Cambridge University Press, Cambridge, UK, 2001.

[104] Y. Zhang, Y. Wang, W. Li, Y. Chou, and Z. Zhang. WASD algorithm with pruning-while-growing and twice-pruning techniques for multi-input Euler polynomial neural network. *International Journal on Artificial Intelligence Tools*, 25:1650007(02), 2016.

[105] Y. Sun, S. Zhang, C. Miao, and J. Li. Improved BP neural network for transformer fault diagnosis. *International Journal of Mining Science and Technology*, 17:138–142(1), 2007.

[106] C. Lu, B. Shi, and L. Chen. Hardware implementation of an on-chip BP learning neural network with programmable neuron characteristics and learning rate adaptation. In *Proceedings of International Joint Conference on Neural Networks*, pages 212–215, 2001.

[107] A. Lallouet and A. Legtchenko. Building consistencies for partially defined constraints with decision trees and neural networks. *International Journal on Artificial Intelligence Tools*, 16:683–706(4), 2007.

[108] C.-C. Peng and G.D. Magoulas. Advanced adaptive nonmonotone conjugate gradient training algorithm for recurrent neural networks. *International Journal on Artificial Intelligence Tools*, 17:963–984(5), 2008.

[109] M. Mangal and M.P. Singh. Analysis of multidimensional XOR classification problem with evolutionary feedforward neural networks. *International Journal on Artificial Intelligence Tools*, 16:111–120(1), 2007.

[110] C. Tao and T. Zhang. Speaker-independent speech recognition based on fast neural network. *International Journal on Artificial Intelligence Tools*, 12:481–487(4), 2003.

[111] X. Yao. Evolving artificial neural networks. *Proceedings of the IEEE*, 87:1423–1447(9), 1999.

[112] X. Yao and Y. Liu. A new evolutionary system for evolving artificial neural networks. *IEEE Transactions on Neural Networks*, 8:694–713(3), 1997.

[113] G.K. Smyth. *Polynomial Approximation*. Encyclopedia of Biostatistics Second Edition, Wiley, London, 2004.

[114] L. D'Ambrosio. Extension of Bernstein polynomials to infinite dimensional case. *Journal of Approximation Theory*, 140:191–202(2), 2006.

[115] P.N. Tan, M. Steinbach, and V. Komar. *Introduction to Data Mining*. China Machine Press, Beijing, China, 2010.

[116] C.D. Meyer. *Matrix Analysis and Applied Linear Algebra*. Society for Industrial and Applied Mathematics, Philadelphia, USA, 2001.

[117] M.T. Heath. *Scientific Computing: An Introductory Survey*. McGraw-Hill, New York, USA, 2002.

[118] S. Wu. Discuss on the same solution theorem of linear equations again. *Journal of Southern Institute of Metallurgy*, 18:165–168, 1997.

[119] R. Hecht-Nielsen. Theory of backpropagation neural network. In *Proceedings of International Conference on Neural Networks*, pages 593–605, 1989.

[120] W. Baxt. Application of artificial neural networks to clinical medicine. *Lancet*, 346:1135–1138(8983), 1995.

[121] R. Lacher, P. Coats, S. Sharma, and L. Fant. A neural network for classifying the financial health of a firm. *European Journal of Operational Research*, 85:53–65(1), 1995.

[122] S. Knerr, L. Personnaz, and G. Dreyfus. Handwritten digit recognition by neural networks with single-layer training. *IEEE Transactions on Neural Networks*, 3:962–968(962), 1992.

[123] Y. Zhang, F. Luo, J. Chen, and W. Li. Weights and structure determination of 3-input Bernoulli polynomial neural net. *Computer Engineering and Science*, 35:142–148(221), 2013.

[124] C. Yang, R. Duraiswami, N. Gumerov, and L. Davis. Improved fast Gauss transform and efficient kernel density estimation. In *Proceedings of IEEE International Conference on Computer Vision*, pages 664–671, 2003.

[125] Y. Zhang, J. Chen, S. Fu, L. Xiao, and X. Yu. Weights and structure determination (WASD) of multiple-input Hermit orthogonal polynomials neural network (MIHOPNN). In *Proceedings of Control and Decision Conference*, pages 1106–1111, 2012.

[126] X. Zhang and H. Liu. Pattern recognition of shape signal by variable structure neural network. *Journal of Iron and Steel Research*, 13:62–66, 2001.

[127] H. Chen, X. Du, and W. Gu. Neural network and genetic algorithm based dynamic obstacle avoidance and path planning for a robot. *Journal of Transcluction Technology*, 17:667–671(4), 2004.

[128] X. Gao and S. Cong. Comparative study on fast learning algorithms of BP networks. *Control and Decision*, 16:167–171(2), 2001.

[129] Y. Zhang and N. Tan. Weights direct determination of feedforward neural networks without iterative BP-training (Chapter 10). In *Intelligent Soft Computation and Evolving Data Mining: Integrating Advanced Technologies*. IGI Global, Pennsylvania, USA, 2010.

[130] Y. Zhang and D. Guo. Optimal-structure determination of power-activation feed-forward neural network. *Computer Engineering and Applications*, 47:29–31(2), 2011.

[131] Y. Zhang, L. Qu, J. Liu, D. Guo, and M. Li. Sine neural network (SNN) with double-stage weights and structure determination (DS-WASD). *Soft Computing*, 20:211–221(1), 2016.

[132] J.H. Friedman. Greedy function approximation: a gradient boosting machine. *Annals of Statistics*, 29:1189–1232(5), 2001.

[133] Y. Lu, N. Sundararajan, and P. Saratchandran. A sequential learning scheme for function approximation using minimal radial basis function neural networks. *Neural Computation*, 9:461–478(2), 1997.

[134] V. Kadirkamanathan and M. Niranjan. A function estimation approach to sequential learning with neural networks. *Neural Computation*, 5:954–975(6), 1993.

[135] E. Romero and R. Alquezar. A new incremental method for function approximation using feed-forward neural networks. In *Proceedings of International Joint Conference on Neural Networks*, pages 1968–1973, 2002.

[136] K. Deimling. *Nonlinear Functional Analysis*. Springer-Verlag, Berlin, Germany, 1985.

[137] J.G. Taylor. *Mathematical Approaches to Neural Networks*. Elsevier Science Publishers, The Netherlands, 1993.

[138] F. Perez-Cruz, G. Camps-Valls, E. Soria-Olivas, J.J. Perez-Ruixo, A.R. Figueiras-Vidal, and A. Artes-Rodriguez. Multi-dimensional function approximation and regression estimation. *Artificial Neural Networks*, 2415:757–762, 2002.

[139] J.J. Wang and Z.B. Xu. Approximation method of multivariate polynomials by feedforward neural networks. *Chinese Journal of Computers*, 32:2482–2488(12), 2009.

[140] H. Hornik. Approximation capabilities of multilayer feedforward networks. *Neural Networks*, 4:251–257(2), 1991.

[141] B. Llanas and F.J. Sainz. Constructive approximate interpolation by neural networks. *Journal of Computational and Applied Mathematics*, 188:283–308(2), 2006.

[142] F.M. Ham and I. Kostanic. *Principles of Neurocomputing for Science and Engineering*, McGraw-Hill Higher Education, New York, USA, 2000.

[143] G. Cybenko. Approximation by superpositions of a sigmoidal function. *Mathematics of Control, Signals, and Systems*, 2:303–314(4), 1989.

[144] K.I. Funahashi. On the approximate realization of continuous mappings by neural networks. *Neural Networks*, 2:183–192(3), 1989.

[145] K. Halawa. A method to improve the performance of multilayer perceptron by utilizing various activation functions in the last hidden layer and the least squares method. *Neural Processing Letters*, 34:293–303(2), 2011.

[146] G.T. Wang, P. Li, and J.T. Cao. Variable activation function extreme learning machine based on residual prediction compensation. *Soft Computing*, 16:1477–1484(9), 2012.

[147] G.-B. Huang, L. Chen, and C.-K. Siew. Universal approximation using incremental constructive feedforward networks with random hidden nodes. *IEEE Transactions on Neural Networks*, 17:879–892(4), 2006.

[148] P.L. Bartlett. The sample complexity of pattern classification with neural networks: the size of the weights is more important than the size of the network. *IEEE Transactions on Information Theory*, 44:525–536(2), 1998.

[149] K.G. Sheela and S.N. Deepa. Performance analysis of modeling framework for prediction in wind farms employing artificial neural networks. *Soft Computing*, 18:607–615(3), 2014.

[150] J. Mahil and T.S.R. Raja. An intelligent biological inspired evolutionary algorithm for the suppression of incubator interference in premature infants ECG. *Soft Computing*, 18:571–578(3), 2014.

[151] J.J. More. The Levenberg-Marquardt algorithm: implementation and theory. *Numerical Analysis*, 630:105–116, 1978.

[152] J.L. Steven. *Linear Algebra with Applications*. Prentice Hall/Pearson, New Jersey, USA, 1999.

[153] E.W. Cheney and W.A. Light. *A Course in Approximation Theory*. American Mathematical Society, Washington, USA, 2000.

[154] Y. Zhang, D. Guo, Z. Luo, K. Zhai, and H. Tan. CP-activated WASD neuronet approach to Asian population prediction with abundant experimental verification. *Neurocomputing*, 198:48–57, 2016.

[155] J. Lassila, T. Valkonen, and J. M. Alho. Demographic forecasts and fiscal policy rules. *International Journal of Forecasting*, 30:1098–1109, 2014.

[156] H. Booth. Demographic forecasting: 1980 to 2005 in review. *International Journal of Forecasting*, 22:547–581, 2006.

[157] J.M. Alho. Forecasting demographic forecasts. *International Journal of Forecasting*, 30:1128–1135, 2014.

[158] P.K. Whelpton. An empirical method for calculating future population. *Journal of the American Statistical Association*, 31:457–473, 1936.

[159] A.E. Raftery, N. Li, H. Sevcikova, P. Gerland, and G.K. Heilig. Bayesian probabilistic population projections for all countries. *Proceedings of the National Academy of Sciences*, 109:13915–13921(35), 2012.

[160] P. Gerland, A. E. Raftery, H. Sevcikova, N. Li, D. Gu, T. Spoorenberg, L. Alkema, B.K. Fosdick, J. Chunn, N. Lalic, G. Bay, T. Buettner, G.K. Heilig, and J. Wilmoth. World population stabilization unlikely this century. *Science*, 346:234–237(6206), 2014.

[161] D. Guo, Y. Zhang, L. He, K. Zhai, and H. Tan. Chebyshev-polynomial neuronet, WASD algorithm and world population prediction from past 10000-year rough data. In *Proceedings of Chinese Control and Decision Conference*, pages 1708–1713, 2015.

[162] United Nations. *World Population Prospects: The 2012 Revision, Highlights and Advance Tables*. United Nations, New York, USA, 2013.

[163] C. McEvedy and R. Jones. *Atlas of World Population History*. Penguin Books Ltd., Middlesex, England, 1978.

[164] Y. Zhang, J. Chen, W. Lao, Z. Zhang, and Y. Chou. Comparison on prediction abilities of single-input neuronets activated by different polynomials. *Journal of System Simulation*, 26:90–96(1), 2014.

[165] M. Cui, H. Liu, Z. Li, Y. Tang, and X. Guan. Identification of Hammerstein model using functional link artificial neural network. *Neurocomputing*, 142:419–428, 2014.

[166] Y. Zhang, Y. Yin, D. Guo, X. Yu, and L. Xiao. Cross-validation based weights and structure determination of Chebyshev-polynomial neural networks for pattern classification. *Pattern Recognition*, 47:3414–3428(10), 2014.

[167] United Nations. *World Population Prospects: The 2017 Revision, Key Findings and Advance Tables*. United Nations, New York, USA, 2017.

[168] Y. Zhang, D. Chen, L. Jin, Y. Wang, and F. Luo. Twice-pruning aided WASD neuronet of Bernoulli-polynomial type with extension to robust classification. In *Proceedings of International Conference on Dependable, Autonomic and Secure Computing*, pages 334–339, 2013.

[169] T. McKeown, R.G. Brown, and R.G. Record. An interpretation of the modern rise of population in Europe. *Population Studies*, 26:345–382(3), 1972.

[170] D. Bloom, D. Canning, and J. Sevilla. *The Demographic Dividend: A New Perspective on the Economic Consequences of Population Change*. Rand Corporation, Santa Monica, California, USA, 2003.

[171] P. Demeny. Population policy dilemmas in Europe at the dawn of the twenty-first century. *Population and Development Review*, 29:1–28(1), 2003.

[172] D. Kirk. *Europe's Population in the Interwar Years*. Taylor & Francis, Oxfordshire, UK, 1969.

[173] W.F. Willcox. The expansion of Europe in population. *The American Economic Review*, 5:737–752(4), 1915.

[174] L.A. Kosinski. *The Population of Europe: A Geographical Perspective*. Longmans, London, England, 1970.

[175] J.E. Cohen. Human population: the next half century. *Science*, 302:1172–1175(5648), 2003.

[176] Y. Zhang, X. Yu, L. Xiao, W. Li, and Z. Fan. Weights and structure determination of artificial neuronets (Chapter 5). In *Self-Organization: Theories and Methods*. Nova Science Publishers, New York, USA, 2013.

[177] Y. Hirose, K. Yamashita, and S. Hijiya. Back-propagation algorithm which varies the number of hidden units. *Neural Networks*, 4:61–66(1), 1991.

[178] F. Rosenblatt. The perceptron: a probabilistic model for information storage and organization in the brain. *Psychological Review*, 65:386–408(6), 1958.

[179] M. Minski and S. Papert. *Perceptrons: An Introduction to Computational Geometry*. The MIT Press, Cambridge, Massachusetts, USA, 1969.

[180] Y. Zhang, J. Wang, Q. Zeng, H. Qiu, and H. Tan. Near future prediction of European population through Chebyshev-activation WASD neuronet. In *Proceedings of International Conference on Intelligent Control and Information Processing*, pages 134–139, 2015.

[181] P. Mellars and J.C. French. Tenfold population increase in Western Europe at the neanderthal-to-modern human transition. *Science*, 333:623–627(6042), 2011.

[182] J. Goldstein, W. Lutz, and S. Scherbov. Long-term population decline in Europe: the relative importance of tempo effects and generational length. *Population and Development Review*, 29:699–707(4), 2003.

[183] E. Grundy. Ageing and vulnerable elderly people: European perspectives. *Ageing and Society*, 26:105–134(01), 2006.

[184] J.B. Schechtman. *Postwar Population Transfers in Europe 1945-1955*. University of Pennsylvania Press, Philadelphia, Pennsylvania, USA, 1963.

[185] J.W. Vaupel and E. Loichinger. Redistributing work in aging Europe. *Science*, 312:1911–1913(5782), 2006.

[186] T.M. Smeeding. Adjusting to the fertility bust. *Science*, 346:163–164(6206), 2014.

[187] Y. Zhang, Y. Ding, J. Ren, X. Li, and H. Tan. Use of WASD neuronet in projecting the population of Oceania based on 1000-year historical data. In *Proceedings of Chinese Automation Congress*, pages 23–28, 2015.

[188] X. Peng. China's demographic history and future challenges. *Science*, 333:581–587(6042), 2011.

[189] P. Dasgupta. The population problem: theory and evidence. *Journal of Economic Literature*, 33:1879–1902(4), 1995.

[190] X. Peng. China's demographic challenge requires an integrated coping strategy. *Journal of Policy Analysis and Management*, 32:399–406(2), 2013.

[191] N. Keilman, D.Q. Pham, and A. Hetland. Why population forecasts should be probabilistic-illustrated by the case of Norway. *Demographic Research*, 6:409–454(15), 2002.

[192] J.J. Hopfield and D.W. Tank. Computing with neural circuits: a model. *Science*, 233:625–633(4764), 1986.

[193] G.E. Hinton and R.R. Salakhutdinov. Reducing the dimensionality of data with neural networks. *Science*, 313:504–507(5786), 2006.

[194] D. Marchiori and M. Warglien. Predicting human behavior by regret driven neural networks. *Science*, 319:1111–1113(5866), 2008.

[195] Y. Zhang, C. Yi, D. Guo, and J. Zheng. Comparison on Zhang neural dynamics and gradient-based neural dynamics for online solution of nonlinear time-varying equation. *Neural Computing and Applications*, 20:1–7(1), 2011.

[196] Y. Zhang, D. Guo, and Z. Li. Common nature of learning between back-propagation and Hopfield-type neural networks for generalized matrix inversion with simplified models. *IEEE Transactions on Neural Networks and Learning Systems*, 24:579–592(4), 2013.

[197] P.J. Werbos. *Beyond Regression: New Tools for Prediction and Analysis in the Behavioral Sciences*. Ph.D. Dissertation, Harvard University, USA, 1974.

[198] C. John, M. Bruce, and M. Jeff. *The Population of Oceania in the Second Millennium*. Australian National University, Canberra, Australia, 2001.

[199] Y. Zhang, W. Li, B. Qiu, J. Qiu, and H. Tan. Northern American population data recovery from 1500AD to 1950AD as well as prediction using WASD neuronet with 513-year data. In *Proceedings of Chinese Automation Congress*, pages 41–46, 2015.

[200] M.R. Haines and R.H. Steckel. *A Population History of North America*. Cambridge University Press, Cambridge, UK, 2000.

[201] P.K. Whelpton. *An Empirical Method for Calculating Future Population*. Springer, Berlin, Germany, 1977.

[202] J.E. Cohen, M. Roig, D.C. Reuman, and C. GoGwilt. International migration beyond gravity: a statistical model for use in population projections. *Proceedings of the National Academy of Sciences*, 105:15269–15274(40), 2008.

[203] Y. Zhang and C. Yi. *Zhang Neural Networks and Neural-Dynamic Method*. Nova Science Publishers, New York, USA, 2011.

[204] S.M. Phelps, M.J. Ryan, and A.S. Rand. Vestigial preference functions in neural networks and tungara frogs. *Proceedings of the National Academy of Sciences*, 98:13161–13166(23), 2001.

[205] Y. Zhang, H. Wu, Z. Zhang, L. Xiao, and D. Guo. Acceleration-level repetitive motion planning of redundant planar robots solved by a simplified LVI-based primal-dual neural network. *Robotics and Computer-Integrated Manufacturing*, 29:328–343(2), 2013.

[206] C.G. Calloway. Why did the Anasazi all live in national parks? Indian histories, hemispheric contexts, and America's beginnings. *William and Mary Quarterly*, 58:703–711(3), 2001.

[207] S.B. Desai, A.B. Dubey, L. Joshi, M. Sen, A. Shariff, and R. Vanneman. *Human Development in India*. Oxford University Press, New York, USA, 2010.

[208] C.M. Lakshmana. Population, development, and environment in India. *Chinese Journal Population Resource Environment*, 11:367-374(4), 2013.

[209] A. Sharma, B.K. Sahoo, P. Saha, C. Kumar, and A. Gandhi. *India Human Development Report 2011: Towards Social Inclusion*. Oxford University Press, New York, USA, 2011.

[210] Y. Zhang, W. Li, L. He, J. Qiu, and H. Tan. Population projection of the Indian subcontinent using TP-aided WASD neuronet. In *Proceedings of Fuzzy Systems and Knowledge Discovery*, pages 23–28, 2016.

[211] P.K. Whelpton. *Mathematical Demography*. Springer, Heidelberg, Germany, 1977.

[212] Z. Wu and N. Li. Immigration and the dependency ratio of a host population. *Mathematical Population Study*, 10:21–39(1), 2010.

[213] A. Beger, C.L. Dorff, and M.D. Ward. Irregular leadership changes in 2014: forecasts using ensemble, split-population duration models. *International Journal Forecasting*, 32:98–111(1), 2014.

[214] N. Li and S. Tuljapurkar. The solution of time-dependent population models. *Mathematical Population Study*, 7:311-329(4), 1999.

[215] L. Kuznetsov and P. Domashnev. Product quality control on the basis of stochastic neuronet model of through technology. *Systems Science*, 31:111–119(3), 2005.

[216] R.J. Sclabassi, D. Krieger, R. Simon, R. Lofink, G. Gross, and D.M. DeLauder. NeuroNet: collaborative intraoperative guidance and control. *IEEE Computer Graphics and Applications*, 16:39–45(1), 1996.

[217] S.H. Hong, L. Wang, T.K. Truong, T.C. Lin, and L.J. Wang. Novel approaches to the parametric cubic-spline interpolation. *Image Processing*, 22:1233–1241(3), 2013.

[218] D. Guo, Y. Zhang, L. He, K. Zhai, and H. Tan. Chebyshev-polynomial neuronet, WASD algorithm and world population prediction from past 10000-year rough data. In *Proceedings of Chinese Control and Decision Conference*, pages 1702–1707, 2015.

[219] W. Lutz, W. Sanderson, and S. Scherbov. The end of world population growth. *Nature*, 412:543–545(6846), 2001.

[220] W. Lutz and K.C. Samir. What do we know about future population trends and structures? *Philosophical Transactions of the Royal Society B: Biological Sciences*, 365:2779–2791(1554), 2010.

[221] Y. Zhang, J. Liu, D. Guo, S. Ding, and H. Tan. Power-activated WASD neuronet based Russian population estimation, correction, and prediction. In *Proceedings of International Conference on Computational Science and Engineering*, pages 1232–1236, 2014.

[222] L. Lei. Population problem in Russia. *Population Journal*, 3:27–31, 2001.

[223] R. Sil. Which of the BRICs will wield the most influence in twenty-five years? Russia reconsidered. *International Studies Review*, 16:456–460(3), 2014.

[224] W. Lutz, W. Sanderson, and S. Scherbov. The coming acceleration of global population ageing. *Nature*, 451:716–719(7179), 2008.

[225] J. Sola and J. Sevilla. Importance of input data normalization for the application of neural networks to complex industrial problems. *IEEE Transactions on Nuclear Science*, 44:1464–1468(3), 1997.

[226] W. Ma. Development and current situation of Russian population. *Russian Central Asian & East European Market*, 2:7–12, 2008.

[227] D. Ediev. Application of the demographic potential concept to understanding the Russian population history and prospects: 1897–2100. *Demographic Research*, 4:289–336(9), 2001.

[228] M. Ellman. Soviet repression statistics: some comments. *Europe-Asia Studies*, 54:1151–1172(7), 2002.

[229] J. Liu, Y. Zhang, Z. Xiao, T. Qiao, and H. Tan. Fast, finite, accurate and optimal WASD neuronet versus slow, infinite, inaccurate and rough BP neuronet illustrated via Russia population prediction. In *Proceedings of International Conference on Intelligent Control and Information Processing*, pages 140–145, 2015.

[230] D. Guo and Y. Zhang. Novel recurrent neural network for time-varying problems solving. *IEEE Computational Intelligence Magazine*, 7:61–65(4), 2012.

[231] M. Felice and X. Yao. Short-term load forecasting with neural network ensembles: a comparative study. *IEEE Computational Intelligence Magazine*, 6:47–56(3), 2011.

[232] D. Coyle. Neural network based auto association and time-series prediction for biosignal processing in brain-computer interfaces. *IEEE Computational Intelligence Magazine*, 4:47–59(4), 2009.

[233] Y. Zhang, J. Liu, X. Yan, B. Qiu, and T. Qiao. WASD neuronet prediction for China's population. In *Proceedings of IEEE International Conference on Information and Automation*, pages 797–802, 2015.

[234] United Nations. *World Population Prospects: The 2012 Revision, Methodology of the United Nations Population Estimates and Projections*. United Nations, New York, USA, 2014.

[235] J. Sola and J. Sevilla. Importance of input data normalization for the application of neural networks to complex industrial problems. *IEEE Transactions on Nuclear Science*, 44:1464–1468(3), 1997.

[236] M. Hvistendahl. China's population growing slowly, changing fast. *Science*, 332:650–651(6030), 2011.

[237] J. Rubio, P. Angelov, and J. Pacheco. Uniformly stable backpropagation algorithm to train a feedforward neural network. *IEEE Transactions on Neural Networks*, 22:356–366(3), 2011.

[238] J. Durand. The population statistics of China. *Population Studies*, 13:209–256(3), 1960.

[239] Y. Zhang, P. He, J. Wen, L. He, and H. Tan. China population prediction with the aid of fast, optimal and accurate WASD neuronet compared with BP neuronet. In *Proceedings of Chinese Control Conference*, pages 3673–3678, 2016.

[240] B. O'Neill, D. Balk, M. Brickman, and M. Ezra. A guide to global population projections. *Demographic Research*, 4:203–288(8), 2001.

[241] United Nations. *World Population Prospects: The 2015 Revision, Total Population*. United Nations, New York, USA, 2015.

[242] D. Rumelhart, G. Hinton, and R. Williams. Learning representations by back-propagating errors. *Nature*, 323: 533–536, 1986.

[243] L. Yann, Y. Bengio, and G. Hinton. Deep learning. *Nature*, 521:436–444(7553), 2015.

[244] X. Xiao, Y. Zhang, X. Jiang, and X. Peng. Approximation-performance and global-convergence analysis of basis-function feedforward neural network. *Modern Computer*, 301:4–8, 2009.

[245] Y. Zhang, Z. Xiao, D. Guo, M. Mao, and H. Tan. USPD doubling or declining in next decade estimated by WASD neuronet using data as of October 2013. In *Proceedings of International Symposium on Intelligence Computation and Applications*, pages 712–723, 2015.

[246] B.M. Friedman. *Debt and Economic Activity in the United States*. University of Chicago Press, Chicago, United States, 1982.

[247] M.E. Chernew, K. Baicker, and J. Hsu. The specter of financial Armageddon–health care and federal debt in the United States. *The New England Journal of Medicine*, 362:1166–1168(13), 2010.

[248] J.A. Young. Technology and competitiveness: a key to the economic future of the United States. *Science*, 241:313–316(4863), 1998.

[249] V.D. Ooms. Budget priorities of the nation. *Science*, 258:1742–1747(5089), 1992.

[250] L. Sarno. The behavior of US public debt: a nonlinear perspective. *Economics Letters*, 74:119–125(1), 2001.

[251] A. Greiner and G. Kauermann. Sustainability of US public debt: estimating smoothing spline regressions. *Economic Modelling*, 24:350–364(2), 2007.

[252] J. Aizenman and N. Marion. Using inflation to erode the US public debt. *Journal of Macroeconomics*, 33:524–541(4), 2011.

[253] H. Bohn. The behavior of U.S. public debt and deficits. *The Quarterly Journal of Economics*, 113:949–963(3), 1998.

[254] A. Ferone and L. Maddalena. Neural background subtraction for pan-tilt-zoom cameras. *IEEE Transactions on Systems, Man, and Cybernetics: Systems*, 44:571–579(5), 2014.

[255] P. Henriquez, J.B. Alonso, M.A. Ferrer, and C.M. Travieso. Review of automatic fault diagnosis systems using audio and vibration signals. *IEEE Transactions on Systems, Man, and Cybernetics: Systems*, 44:642–652(5), 2014.

[256] S.S. Ge, C. Yang, and T.H. Lee. Adaptive predictive control using neural network for a class of pure-feedback systems in discrete time. *IEEE Transactions on Neural Networks*, 19:1599–1614(9), 2008.

[257] Z. Wang, Y. Liu, M. Li, and X. Liu. Stability analysis for stochastic Cohen-Grossberg neural networks with mixed time delays. *IEEE Transactions on Neural Networks*, 17:814–820(3), 2006.

[258] H. Kabir, Y. Wang, M. Yu, and Q. Zhang. High-dimensional neural-network technique and applications to microwave filter modeling. *IEEE Transactions on Microwave Theory and Techniques*, 58:145–156(1), 2010.

[259] X. Liang and J. Wang. A recurrent neural network for nonlinear optimization with a continuously differentiable objective function and bound constraints. *IEEE Transactions on Neural Networks*, 11:1251–1262(6), 2000.

[260] Y. Zhang, W. Lao, L. Jin, J. Chen, and J. Liu. Growing-type WASD for power-activation neuronet to model and forecast monthly time series. In *Proceedings of International Conference on Control and Automation*, pages 1312–1317, 2013.

[261] M. Krejnik and A. Tyutin. Reproducing kernel hilbert spaces with odd kernels in price prediction. *IEEE Transactions on Neural Networks and Learning Systems*, 23:1564–1573(10), 2012.

[262] Q. Pang, X. Liu, and M. Zhang. Traffic flow forecasting based on rough set and neural network. In *Proceedings of International Conference on Natural Computation*, pages 1920–1924, 2010.

[263] A.F. Atiya, S.M. El-Shoura, S.I. Shaheen, and M.S. El-Sherif. A comparison between neural-network forecasting techniques–case study: river flow forecasting. *IEEE Transactions on Neural Networks*, 10:402–409(2), 1999.

[264] N.L.D. Khoa, K. Sakakibara, and I. Nishikawa. Stock price forecasting using back propagation neural networks with time and profit based adjusted weight factors. In *Proceedings of International Joint Conference SICE-ICASE*, pages 5484–5488, 2006.

[265] G. Zhang, B.E. Patuwo, and M.Y. Hu. Forecasting with artificial neural networks: the state of the art. *International Journal of Forecasting*, 14:35–62(1), 1998.

[266] W. Yan. Toward automatic time-series forecasting using neural networks. *IEEE Transactions on Neural Networks and Learning Systems*, 23:1028–1039(7), 2012.

[267] G.P. Zhang and M. Qi. Neural network forecasting for seasonal and trend time series. *European Journal of Operational Research*, 160:501–514(2), 2005.

[268] G.P. Zhang and D.M. Kline. Quarterly time-series forecasting with neural networks. *IEEE Transactions on Neural Networks*, 18:1800–1814(6), 2007.

[269] Y. Zhang, S. Ding, X. Liu, J. Liu, and M. Mao. WASP neuronet activated by bipolar-sigmoid functions and applied to glomerular-filtration-rate estimation. In *Proceedings of Chinese Control and Decision Conference*, pages 172–177, 2014.

[270] X. Liu, X. Pei, N. Li, Y. Zhang, X. Zhang, J. Chen, L. Lv, H. Ma, X. Wu, W. Zhao, and T. Lou. Improved glomerular filtration rate estimation by an artificial neural network. *PLOS ONE*, 8:1–9(3), 2013.

[271] K. Hornik. Multilayer feedforward networks are universal approximators. *Neural Networks*, 2:359–366(5), 1989.

[272] T. Chen and H. Chen. Universal approximation to nonlinear operators by neural networks with arbitrary activation functions and its application to dynamical systems. *IEEE Transactions on Neural Networks*, 6:911–917(4), 1995.

[273] X. Liu, C. Wang, H. Tang, Y. Tang, Z. Chen, Z. Ye, and T. Lou. The application of glomerular filtration rate estimation equations in chronic kidney disease. *Chinese Journal of Practical Internal Medicine*, 29:532–535(6), 2009.

[274] X. Liu, C. Wang, H. Tang, Y. Tang, Z. Chen, Z. Ye, and T. Lou. Assessing glomerular filtration rate (GFR) in elderly Chinese patients with chronic kidney disease (CKD): a comparison of various predictive equations. *Archives of Gerontology & Geriatrics*, 51:13–20(1), 2010.

[275] J.D. Villiers and E. Barnard. Backpropagation neural nets with one and two hidden layers. *IEEE Transactions on Neural Networks*, 4:136–141(1), 1992.

[276] Y. Zhang and W. Li. Gegenbauer orthogonal basis neural network and its weights-direct-determination method. *Electronics Letters*, 45:1184–1185(23), 2009.

[277] Y. Zhang, L. Qu, J. Chen, J. Liu, and D. Guo. Weights and structure determination method of multiple-input sigmoid activation function neural network. *Application Research of Computers*, 29:4113–4116(11), 2012.

[278] L. Hamm, B.W. Brorsen, and M.T. Hagan. Comparison of stochastic global optimization methods to estimate neural network weights. *Neural Processing Letters*, 26:145–158(3), 2007.

[279] M.T. Hagan, H.B. Demuth, and M.H. Beale. *Neural Network Design*. China Machine Press, Beijing, China, 2002.

[280] A.S. Levery, J. Coresh, T. Greene, L.A. Stevens, and Y. Zhang. Using standardized serum creatine values in the modification of diet in renal disease study equation for estimating glomerular filtration rate. *Annals of Internal Medicine*, 145:247–254(4), 2006.

[281] Y. Ma, L. Zuo, J. Chen, Q. Luo, and X. Yu. Modified glomerular filtration rate estimating equation for Chinese patients with chronic kidney disease. *Journal of the American Society of Nephrology*, 17:2937–2944(10), 2006.

[282] E. Imai, M. Horio, K. Nitta, K. Yamagata, and K. Iseki. Modification of the modification of diet in renal disease (MDRD) study equation for Japan. *American Journal of Kidney Diseases*, 50:927–937(6), 2007.

[283] S. Matsuo, E. Imai, M. Horio, Y. Yasuda, and K. Tomita. Revised equations for estimated GFR from serum creatinine in Japan. *American Journal of Kidney Diseases*, 53:982–992(6), 2009.

[284] D. Graupe. *Deep Learning Neural Networks: Design and Case Studies*. World Scientific Publishing Company, Singapore City, Singapore, 2016.

[285] C. Perez. *Deep Learning and Dynamic Neural Networks with Matlab*. CreateSpace Independent Publishing, Washington, D.C., United States, 2017.

[286] A.L. Caterini and D.E. Chang. *Deep Neural Networks in a Mathematical Framework*. Springer, Berlin, Germany, 2018.

# *Glossary*

**AI:** Artificial intelligence

**AN:** Artificial neuronets

**BP:** Back-propagation

**BPE:** Batch-processing error

**CBO:** Congressional budget office

**CKD:** Chronic kidney disease

**EU:** European Union

**FIBPN:** Four-input Bernoulli-polynomial neuronet

**FIEPN:** Four-input Euler-polynomial neuronet

**GDP:** Gross domestic product

**GFR:** Glomerular filtration rate

**GT:** Growing-type

**HASE:** Half average square error

**HP:** Hermite polynomials

**LM:** Levenberg-Marquardt

**MIBPN:** Multi-input Bernoulli-polynomial neuronet

**MIEPN:** Multi-input Euler-polynomial neuronet

**MIHPN:** Multi-input Hermite-polynomial neuronet

**MIMOBPN:** Multiple-input-multiple-output Bernoulli-polynomial neuronet

**MISAN:** Multi-input sine-activation neuronet

**MLP:** Multi-layer perceptron

**MSE:** Mean square error

**PAG:** Pruning-after-grown

**PG:** Pure-growing

**PWG:** Pruning-while-growing

**RBFN:** Radial-basis-function neuronet

**RE:** Relative error

**RMSE:** Root-mean-square error

**SAD:** Structure-automatic-determination

**SISO:** Single-input-single-output

**SMAPE:** Symmetric mean absolute percentage error

**SU:** Scalar update

**SVD:** Singular value decomposition

**TP:** Twice-pruning

**TPDO:** Total public debt outstanding

**TS-WASD:** Two-stage weights-and-structure-determination

**UN:** United Nations

**USPD:** United States public debt

**VU:** Vector update

**WASD:** Weights-and-structure-determination

**WDD:** Weights-direct-determination

**WPP:** World Population Prospects

# *Index*